BALLET: BIAS AND BELIEF

Three Pamphlets Collected
and Other Dance Writings of
Lincoln Kirstein

Ballet:
Bias and Belief

Three Pamphlets Collected
and Other Dance Writings of
Lincoln Kirstein

With an Introduction and Comments by
Nancy Reynolds

DANCE HORIZONS · NEW YORK

We wish to thank the following publishers who have granted permission to reprint material from their copyrighted works: *Dance Magazine;* The Nation Associates, Inc.; *The New Republic;* New York State Theater Edition of *Playbill* ®, published by American Theatre Press, Inc.; Prentice-Hall, Inc.; Theatre Arts Books; Condé Nast Publications, Inc. (*Vogue*).

ISBN 0-87127-133-8

Library of Congress Catalog Card Number 82-083628

Printed in the United States of America

Dance Horizons, 1801 East 26th Street, Brooklyn, N.Y. 11229

Contents

Sour Gripes: A Gracious Postscript
             by Lincoln Kirstein   *ix*

Lincoln Kirstein: Apologist for the Dance
             by Nancy Reynolds   *xiii*

PART I: SEVENTEEN ARTICLES (1930-1978)
   WITH INTRODUCTORY COMMENTS
        BY NANCY REYNOLDS

The Diaghilev Period (1930),   *3*
Homage to Michel Fokine (1933),   *27*
Working with Stravinsky (1937),   *31*
Prejudice Purely (1934),   *37*
Stardom: Slav and Native (1938),   *43*
Martha Graham (1937),   *47*
Our Ballet and Our Audience (1938),   *53*
Transcontinental Caravan (1939),   *59*
Martha Graham at Bennington (1938),   *69*
About *Billy the Kid* (1938),   *73*
The American Ballet in Brazil, Argentina,
   Chile, and the West Coast (1941),   *77*

Alec: Or the Future of Choreography (1953), *97*
Foreword to *Gagaku* (1959), *107*
Balanchine's Fourth Dimension (1972), *111*
The Policy of a Ballet Company (1975), *121*
Classic Ballet: Aria of the Aerial (1976), *127*
The Performing Arts and Our Egregious Elite
(1978), *133*

PART II: *THREE PAMPHLETS COLLECTED
WITH A NEW FOREWORD (1967)*

Blast at Ballet (1937), *157*
Ballet Alphabet (1939), *285*
What Ballet Is About (1959), *365*

INDEX, *437*

BALLET: BIAS AND BELIEF

Three Pamphlets Collected
and Other Dance Writings of
Lincoln Kirstein

Sour Gripes:
A Gracious Postscript

PROSE FOLLOWING IS POLEMICAL, MOST OF IT WRITTEN FOR POLITICAL ENDS, TO PROMOTE ITS AUTHOR AS AN AUTHORITY. This enterprise started as an amateur operation and remained one. At first, I had neither experience nor command. Journalism was by way of obtaining a passport granting entry into an area which seemed forbidden and unassailable. Naturally, nothing would have worked without gusto for the target in view; enthusiasm is the sole ingredient which sustains a readership of accounts of days dead and gone. Critics observe, more or less attentively, trying to make sense of subjects and objects at hand, particularly concerning events which are unfamiliar or even unknown. Such is a fair launching pad, but the aim of the amateur, and particularly of the amateur impresario, is less pure.

Early on I knew what I wanted to do, but had no notion of how to do it. I did not touch the big world; the court of Diaghilev was more remote than Peter the Great or Louis XIV. A college education, particularly one vaunting the hollow prestige of Harvard, and an apprenticeship in the use of a good library promoted something approaching a reputation for erudition. By extension this could be pushed into a simulacra of knowledge. But any genuine comprehension comes from the immediacy of the witnessed event, and in the late 'twenties and early 'thirties, chances to see a rich balance of dance weren't easy to come by. A great number of the performances which nostalgia later sanctified were poor by current standards and gave false values. Correction of such initial impressions is often received as treachery, churlishness or poor taste. But there is a gang of "critics" who live on moribund criteria and rosy memoirs.

Rather than attempting to lodge the essence of a performance or the quality of performers, most of my writing added up to rungs in a ladder by which I tried to assimilate through rumor and gossip enough small talk to hold my own in the company of elders and betters. An opuscule on Michel Fokine, with whom I briefly studied, was published in England through Arnold Haskell, who was, after Cyril Beaumont, the dean of Britain's founding fathers of balletomania. I was then befriended also by A.R. Orage of *The New English Weekly*, whom Eliot and others considered the best editor of his generation. He slapped me with some home truths; I learned I was no lily-white champion of the good and beautiful, but rather a young man, ignorant and ill-mannered, in however a hurry.

My writing about Martha Graham illustrates a general strategy. The first piece I wrote, appearing in *The New Republic*, was inked in vitriol. It's what I believed at the time; time has done little to dilute its venom. However, subsequent pieces had the tone of religious conversion, indited on a game-plan of "If you can't beat her, join her." I came to realize her huge theatrical attraction and longed to partake of it. At the same time I was convinced that everything emanating from her particular genius was pernicious heresy, rooting in self-limiting solipsis, idiosyncrasy and a mindless affront to apostolic legitimacy of traditional method. From my infantile instinctive opposition I have not wavered. My intellectual or moral dishonesty served theatrical purpose, and gained brownie points for liberal, or even a catholic, interest in the entire spectrum of theatrical dancing. Theater is built of honest lies and immoral impersonations, so for work which Graham and Balanchine managed on the same program I've no apology.

When Nancy Reynolds gave me sheets of my collected journalism, I was surprised at the number of words and persistence of their appearance from around 1930 to 1970, how repetitious the tone, how lacking in renewed gusto or perception. Scholars years hence, at their feckless dissertations on dance criticism from *Soho Weekly News* or *The Village Voice*, *Hudson* and *Bennington* quarterlies, will not have derived much information from back numbers of *The Nation*, or various dance organs which let me go on. What might be gathered would be the progress of a career—mine. Compared to the relentless, microscopic and betimes pulverizing lens of Edwin Denby or Arlene Croce, there is not an article here bears competition with any of their quotidian duties. I hurled a lot of loose historical information, with a veneer of academic research, in the face of a small but growing public, at first profoundly unaware and uninterested in the claims of ballet as an autonomous art and craft.

There were a lot of nasty paragraphs about minor figures and events, particularly those solicited by Klaus Mann, the unfortunate editor of *Decision,* a brother-in-law of Wystan Auden. Auden scolded me. "Why, if these dancers are so lousy, do you trouble to write about them?" I was a naughty show-off with *arriviste* bad manners. Such childishness should be spanked. My tone, thereafter, may have been sweetened, but it was then I lost much ambition to be a serious commentator on dancing which did not, essentially, grab me. In truth, I had one narrow and deep preoccupation: Balanchine. The preponderance of my "criticism" was mere excuse in several forms and styles—shrewd, stupid, stubborn or silly—to promulgate his work, method and morality. I wrote a dozen "essays" defending him for the liberal academic press, mostly repeating a few convictions. These aren't much fun to re-read.

Pieces chosen are by way of documental history, and may throw light on the day-to-day behavior of Balanchine's labors, with his dancers' response. They are reasonably honest as far as they go, which is not far. They were indited as notes toward some eventual full record. When time came to write it, they reduced themselves to captions for photographs. I no longer had patience, energy or interest; I was too involved with process, descriptions of which tended to fall into repetitive categories. Individual repertory ballets hold interest, but descriptions of their invention and first performance merge into a bland memorial fog.

I try about as hard to forgive trespassers as the next fellow, but the amount of appalling coverage of dance "events" in weekly Manhattan drives me toward sin. I no longer count myself among the sinners. For the last dozen years I've neither read nor written about particular dancers, except as mandated or dictated by or to the *New York Times* or elucidated in *The New Yorker.* I don't know what happens outside the State Theater. When people ask me what I think about the Dutch, Stuttgart or Paris, I sincerely answer: I don't think about them. Gossip and small talk once served well enough, but now the shades of night are falling fast. I think great dancing and great dancers are not worth being stenciled on bruised wood-pulp.

The ideal critic is by way of being a teacher, whatever the increment of literary pretensions may frame description. Most listeners have tin ears; dance observers, tin eyes. They hear and sketch surface tension and relaxation without curiosity as to the structure of the languages of sight or sonority. Gut reactions are good enough. They save valued time for TV "educational" treatment. News readers seek comfort and quittance from daily notices as warning, corroboration or lax advice: "Well—it got a very good *review.*" Sometimes agreement with a critic's tone saves money from the box office, while general laziness is further salvaged, but this has nothing to do with explicit, considered or imaginative reception from a clean eye. But, as with theater, film critics, book reviewers and political pundits, their games are so corrupt, inefficient and ignorant that one is thrown upon one's own devices whatever their acumen or energy.

Edwin Denby taught how to look at bodies in motion. He was guided by the best music critic of our epoch. Virgil Thomson's delicate domestic surgery and international omniscience, his true-lover's hatred of the shoddy, shopworn and dilute, gave Edwin his head. His manner was more decorous and sweetly kind, but just as hygienic. I disagree infrequently with Arlene Croce about some of our dancers, but rarely about dancing, and even then I am forced to wonder whether or not . . . Maybe . . . Oh, dear. The didactic function is the only useful one. Individual sensibility from most writers about dance is nowhere as professional, comprehensive, knowing or funny as the run of sports writing, or that which attaches itself to the science of ballgames or stock cars. Few dance journalists know even the basics of their subject, although they are facile in borrowing French nomenclature of discrete steps, just the same way amateur chefs appropriate the cant of lean cuisine. I did the same when I started, and the pieces eliminated from this collection have an identical virtue.

July 4, 1982   L.K.

Lincoln Kirstein:
Apologist for the Dance

LINCOLN KIRSTEIN IS A RARE, PERHAPS QUINTESSENTIALLY AMERICAN, COMBINATION: A MAN OF ACTION AND A MAN OF THOUGHT. Born into a family of influence and affluence, his several autobiographical works—including the novel *Flesh Is Heir* and his remarkable "Entries from an Early Diary"—chronicle an early life of privilege. As a young man, he had the intellect, the money, and the connections to penetrate the artistic (and social) circles of London and Paris with ease. It was an orbit in which he undoubtedly could have remained—a passionate, questing, persuasive, but undisciplined dilettante, with no measurable artistic ability of his own.

But as everyone with an interest in the dance already knows, Kirstein chose something else. He chose action, and he chose America. Moreover, despite his own verbal precociousness, he chose primarily to champion non-verbal arts: in the performing area, the ballet; in the visual, painting, sculpture, and photography.

Kirstein's most important activities, of course, were to import and employ George Balanchine and to effect for him an ambiance for creation, then to set in motion mechanisms that would eventually result in the formation of the New York City Ballet. In relation to the dance world, however, he has also held high official positions or played major or founding roles in, among others, the New York City

Ballet's predecessor companies—American Ballet, American Ballet Caravan, Ballet Caravan, and Ballet Society—City Center of Music and Drama, Inc., Lincoln Center, the Dance Archives—first at the Museum of Modern Art, later at the New York Public Library (Dance Collection)—and the periodical *Dance Index;* in theater, American National Theater and Academy (ANTA), American Shakespeare Festival Theater Academy; in art, Harvard Society for Contemporary Art, Pippin Press, and, as consultant, exhibition organizer, and cataloguer, the Museum of Modern Art and other museums; in music, Pro Musica Antiqua; in literature, the quarterly *The Hound & Horn.* He has also sponsored artists, underwritten courses, and funded concerts—as well as entire performance seasons. In addition, there have been over 300 writings from his pen.

By his own admission, Kirstein is an advocate of "creative conservatism"—that is, the conservation (or preservation) of ideals and structures that have lasted for centuries. In 1934, he wrote: "Tradition, or the sum of classic and romantic reactions, or orthodoxy or the large history of any art form, is patient and inevitable. It eats what is digestible in its progress and rejects the smaller heresies of individual personalities. . . . The experimental reaction against the academies, and the academies are only the right hand of tradition, is valuable and negative. But it is inevitably followed by reaction against tradition, and two negatives are positive." More than forty years later, he was quoted: "The first principle is that Creation is a unique act. It happened once, and everything else is invention and discovery. I never had the feeling that the 'permanent revolution' of modernism meant anything." Kirstein's idea that tradition provides the framework for the new in art found its complement in Balanchine's neoclassicism.

Kirstein is an admirer of virtuosity ("digital dexterity"), distance, and impersonality in art, qualities to be found in the work of Balanchine and the painter Pavel Tchelitchew. He is against self-expression and naturalism; in favor of discipline and structure ("legibility"); drawn to the static, airless (and figurative) world of the "Symbolic Realists"—George Tooker and Paul Cadmus, with their studied worlds in tempera—and to the frozen clarity in the photographs of George Platt Lynes and Walker Evans. Kirstein's art is an "artificial" one: elaborate conceits are its substructure; hard-gained technical mastery is everywhere in evidence. Clearly, he likes the artifice: spectators should be aware not only of the struggle to achieve but of the burning brain behind the creation. He professes to hate "modernism," although he is eminently a man of the twentieth century (and, in sponsoring Balanchine, has been involved in some of the most progressive art of our time).

In some ways, while causing the pot to boil, Kirstein has been the man on the outside—he is the catalyst, not the creator—an American Diaghilev, active in art and the lyric theater, who recalls a day when an individual, not a corporation or board of directors, made a difference. In pursuit of his ideals, he has been driven by a zeal and devotion as hot-blooded as his tastes are "cold." He has also understood that, as catalyst or servant of the arts, he is, paradoxically, also a leader, a bully, and an autocrat; as a young man, he envisaged a "plan for the seizure of power over artists of this country."

In his own writing, Kirstein has been something of a pioneer, as well as a passionate advocate and an enviable stylist; in his twenties, he wrote a history of theatrical dance that is still in use for introductory university courses; with the founding and editing of *Dance Index*, he assisted in formulating a new discipline, dance history; in art, he resurrected numerous reputations, including those of Nadelman, Lachaise, and Rimmer; and mounted one of the earliest cases for photography as an art form. In all of his writing, wide-ranging scholarship, erudition, baroque and informed use of language, and opinions flow freely.

In 1946, Merle Armitage observed that "the most articulate and penetrating spokesman for a steadily emerging dance consciousness to be found on either side of the Atlantic [is] Lincoln Kirstein. . . . [He is] ballet's most courageous and perspicacious writer." Few dance lovers then, or today, would argue.

For some time, it has been suggested that a selection of Kirstein's non-book dance writings be issued; there are over one hundred from which to choose. His first published dance article, "The Diaghilev Period," appeared in 1930, when its author was only 23; the last, presumably, has not yet been seen.

Kirstein has always written about dance, first contributing to his own magazine, *The Hound & Horn*, then as columnist and dance critic for *The Nation, The New English Weekly, Dance Magazine,* and *The Dance Observer*, among others. Through the early 'forties, his articles also appeared in *Theatre Arts, Modern Music,* and such disparate forums as *Town and Country, Harper's Bazaar,* and various newspapers.

In the early days, sometimes in weekly columns, he defended the classical ballet against two demons: American modern dance and a "Russian" brand of ballet, ostensibly based on Diaghilev but diluted by a partial generation's remove. At the same time, he was reviewing some of the great performers of the day: Graham, Wigman, Chabukiani, Buddy Ebsen. He also wrote—endlessly—of the time when America would have ballet companies the way it had symphony orchestras. He did this when the idea seemed preposterous, when most of the ballet seen in this country was either "Slav" or naive. He argued that, with the establishment of proper schools, there was no reason American bodies could not dance. Of course, the vessel through which the "Americanization" of ballet was to occur was George Balanchine.

During the 'forties he wrote less, probably because he had turned his attention to the editing of *Dance Index,* and later, to organizing Ballet Society. He also went to war.

With the 'fifties, Kirstein concentrated in his writing on Balanchine and the problems of running a company—repertory selection, the creation of new ballets, and so forth—reflecting both his concern with the nascent New York City Ballet and the fact that he must have been too busy directing things to argue for them in print. As the years have passed, responsibilities increased, and his visions have begun to come true; he has written fewer articles and fewer commentaries on the current scene, but more books. In the 'sixties, Kirstein spoke mostly as the established director of a major company; by the 'seventies, he had withdrawn his attention almost completely from the performance arena and concentrated his efforts on elaborate and learned reviews of other people's books. Early in 1982, coincidental with his 75th birthday, it was announced that he was at work on memoirs.

"Prejudice Purely" is the title of a Kirstein diatribe against Martha Graham, and there are those who would argue that this would be a proper title for a great deal of his opinionated early work. Kirstein has always been committed and has never been afraid to say so. Indeed, he has many times "said so" at such length and with such conviction that his reasoning has been carried away in the process. Observers might be amazed (and amused) that he once predicted Balanchine's chief interest would be "choreodramma," that he has argued for audience participation and the elimination of the proscenium arch! What is more remarkable, however (despite momentary aberrations), is that this hot-headed, dogmatic, and irascible young man knew his mind at an early age; his goals and ideals have remained consistent over the years, even in the face of a natural mellowing with age—the lifting of his siege mentality—and, of equal significance, despite the achievement of much that he sought. For it will be seen that Kirstein was not in love with the idea of argument, but with the ideas he was arguing for. Once these were attained, he did not escape to others, merely for the sake of activity. In this regard, he has survived success. Intimations of the future will be found in his very first article, "The Diaghilev Period," in which he wrote of "the classical dance . . . its cold multiplication of a thousand embroideries . . . divested of the personal." This was some years before he met Balanchine and perhaps before he had even formulated his ideas about bringing ballet, through Balanchine, to America, but their ideals are seen to have had a rare accord from the beginning. His interest in a school, a company, and an eminence for America in ballet—all of which have been achieved—were all voiced early and hotly pursued. And he *never* has become reconciled to modern dance. (In 1971, he would still write: "The Modern Dance, like *Modern Art* and *Modern Music*, are all victims of what Baudelaire called 100 years ago the decrepitude of art: the insistence of personalism, expressionism, idiosyncracy against the service of the deselfed Self.")

Even more than the principles of Balanchine, Kirstein's unwavering bedrock has always been an intense commitment to the classical ballet. He has argued its "absolutism," its "aristocracy," its "abstract perfection" at length. Kirstein once wrote an essay entitled "In Defense of the Ballet." This would seem to have been his life's work. He wrote another essay called "The Persistence of Ballet." This would seem to be his credo.

In selecting the seventeen articles that form Part One of this collection, the author decided that many of his pieces had been superseded by later writings and so did not need to be seen again. This is particularly true of the polemics of the 'thirties, many of which found their way, in one form or another, into "Blast at Ballet," which, with "Ballet Alphabet" and "What Ballet is About," also contains the essence of Kirstein's numerous definitions of classical ballet and a generous sampling of his scholarship: Kirstein's erudition is fully in evidence, however forbidding his prejudices. (It might be remembered that his historical research was carried out by consulting a wide variety of sources, many of them devoted to other subjects. There was no field of inquiry called "dance history," and in many areas, Kirstein was the first to synthesize entirely disparate materials into a "history" serving the dance.)

Because of fuller representation elsewhere, emphasis is directed away from extended historical articles in the present selection. Kirstein as historian is eminently on view in his books—*Dance: A Short History of Classic Theatrical Dancing; Fokine; Movement and Metaphor;* and *Nijinsky Dancing*—as well as anonymously in Romola Nijinsky's biography of her husband, in the introduction to *The Classic Ballet* by

Muriel Stuart, in numerous encyclopedias, and in his editing of *Dance Index*.

Other pieces were found to be ephemeral or inferior. What is left in the following pages refers to Lincoln Kirstein at every stage of his career, from admiring student to elder statesman commenting on the affluent performance scene that began in the mid-sixties. In between will be found Kirstein's analysis of two of the three he considers the most influential choreographers of the twentieth century—Fokine and Balanchine (Nijinsky is the third); several polemics on Martha Graham and the Russian Ballet; references to Kirstein's involvement with the American Ballet, Ballet Caravan, American Ballet Caravan; ruminations on the future of choreography and choice of repertory from the General Director of the New York City Ballet; a late article on the nature of the classical ballet; and a meditation on the Gagaku and the nature of Eastern aesthetics. It is a range touching on Kirstein as critic, commentator, analyst, preacher, explorer, polemicist, director, advocate, and scholar.

The writings are arranged in rough chronological order, within loose subject groupings. As compiler, I would like to acknowledge as indispensable reference *Lincoln Kirstein The Published Writings 1927-1977: A First Bibliography* (New Haven: Yale University Library, 1978) and the assistance of Barbara Naomi Cohen-Stratyner.

N.R.

Part One

Seventeen Articles
(1930–1978)

The Diaghilev Period

Kirstein first saw the Diaghilev Ballets Russes at the age of 15 in 1922; by the time the following article was written, he had seen them several times more: "I was addicted, as in a love affair," he wrote of his visits in 1926. In fact, he had been infected with the "red and gold disease" since childhood. He saw Pavlova at 13, but missed his only chance to see Nijinsky: his mother would not take him when the Diaghilev company performed in Boston in 1916.

This youthful article, a tour de force of research and an early vehicle for Kirstein's interpretive abilities, touches many bases. Much more is revealed than Kirstein's feelings of awe and appreciation for Diaghilev, particularly his thoughts about the nature of dance and his inborn affinity for the work of Balanchine.

In 1927, while still an undergraduate at Harvard, Kirstein had founded The Hound & Horn, *"a magazine of arts and letters," with Varian Fry. Other editors would include R.P. Blackmur, Bernard Bandler, A. Hyatt Mayor, Allen Tate, and Yvor Winters. Although* The Hound & Horn *had the dubious distinction of rejecting a submission from Hart Crane ("The Tunnel," an excerpt from "The Bridge"), it had the very real distinction of publishing original work by Ezra Pound, T.S. Eliot, Katherine Anne Porter, James Agee, Michael Gold, Granville Hicks, Glenway Wescott, Harry Crosby, Irving Babbitt, Edmund Wilson, and e.e. cummings. The magazine's policy (not always observed) was to publish only American writers. Its penultimate issue was a highly praised monograph on Henry James.*

◊ Reprinted from *The Hound & Horn* 3:4 (July/Sept. 1930), 468-501.

Kirstein wrote only two articles of substance on dance for The Hound & Horn. *He also published his own poetry and contributed pieces on art, film, theater, and literature. By 1934, he had diverted his money to dance—George Balanchine and the School of American Ballet—and the magazine ceased to exist.*

N.R.

I

AN AMERICAN TOURIST was hunting the back alleys of Venice, one hot morning in the middle of last August, for a church in which Domenico Theotocopulos must have worshipped. He saw its tower from afar, on the edge of a small canal, and passing under an arch, found a barge of black and gold moored to the church steps. Beadles in cocked hats, holding brass rods, bore wreaths into the church and he followed into the cool noon dusk. When his eyes were accustomed to the gloom, he saw opposite him a great Byzantine ikonostasis. The Baptism, the Last Supper, their gesso and gilding turned bronze, glowed above a bier, blanketed with heaped-up flowers. Suddenly he became aware of mourners, and the fact that this was, indeed, a funeral. Faces, somehow familiar, ignored him as he passed out into the sunlight, and leaving, he heard the first words of the Greek Orthodox service for the dead. Not until three days later, reading the *London Times*, did he learn that he had unwittingly attended, in San Giorgio dei Greci, the obsequies of a great Russian:

> Serge Diaghilev was born in the district of Novgorod on March 19, 1872. His early career was varied, and he studied, if he did not practice, all the arts. While reading law in St. Petersburg, he turned his attention to music but took to journalism in 1897, and more especially to the criticism of art. He organized the first great exhibition of Russian art in Western Europe, founded an important journal of art (Mir Iskousstva) which lasted from 1899 to 1905, and in 1903 he was in Paris and producing *Boris Godunov* with a company that included Chaliapin. Thus be began his services to Russian art which he was later to extend to that of most European countries.

Serge Diaghilev, more than any other single person, was responsible for the growth and maintenance of a tradition in contemporary painting, music and dancing. Picasso is not the gold mine of 57th Street and the rue de la Boëtie wholly because he invented cubism, but in a great measure because Diaghilev commissioned him to decorate Satie's *Parade* and de Falla's *Three Cornered Hat,* and in a succession of ballets furnished this great decorator with the chance to display himself on a grand scale. Stravinsky Diaghilev found in a class in harmony, and, irritated because his old master Liadov was slow in scoring some Russian fairy tales, ordered *The Fire-*

bird. Then followed *The Rite of Spring, Petrouchka, Pulcinella, Les Noces, Renard, King Oedipus* and *Apollo, Leader of the Muses:* the works by which the composer is known. Without Diaghilev the great tradition of classical ballet dancing might have died of dry rot, or disuse. Instead, first with Fokine, Nijinsky, Pavlova, later with Massine, Dolin and Lifar he made it greater and more popular than ever before. Diaghilev was a synthesizer, a catalyst, who could image in three dimensions the perfect combination of the right dances, for the right music, in the right decor; and by right we must read inevitable.

II

The skeletal structure of classical ballet dancing was developed in France and Italy throughout the seventeenth and eighteenth century. Stretching back to the dances before the ark, the tradition of folk dancing became stylized with usage, finally achieving a mechanical technique which allowed exact repetition. Toe dancing was codified into a rigid system of five positions, in which the arms, accented by hieratic arrangements of hands and fingers, the legs by linear conformities of feet and toes, were made capable of weaving countless ingenious variations upon a strong formal foundation. During the nineteenth century the technique was intensified into a sterile formula. Dancing masters who had gone from Marseilles and Milan to St. Petersburg were impressed by what they saw of indigenous folk dancing and incorporated parts of its attractive gaucherie into their curriculum. The technical excellence displayed was phenomenal. Girls were kept exercising at the bar, pointing, bending, taking their attitudes and little else for a year or two, until the master saw a hundred legs tap the same line on the floor at the same instant with an accuracy which was as sterile as it was precise. But when this amazing control of muscular perfection was put to a worthy use, in a setting which had not been stylized out of any common emotional reference, it served as a rigid framework for the ingenious variations and surprising floutings of itself, which depended on its initial strictness and strength.

Twenty-two years ago Serge Diaghilev started as the impresario of the Russian Ballet. His previous technical training in law, in esthetics, in music, his inherent gifts of taste, his consciousness of the chic, his appreciation of social snobbery and his passion for the beauty of surprise and of youth—these in a combination of brilliant energies and practical qualifications made him the isolated genius that he was. The ballet in St. Petersburg had almost petrified between the onslaughts of Italian opera and the strictures of such great classical choreographers as Petipa and Cecchetti. With Fokine as producer and Nijinsky as choreographer and premier danseur, Diaghilev instituted a Romantic revolution culminating in the first

5

night of the *Rite of Spring*, no less full of implications than the debut of *Hernani*—one of those revolutions which seem to save art from its crippling ideas of perfection once in a hundred years.[1] The dances now invented were based partly upon the old tradition and partly on an archeological interest in Russian folk dancing, as echoed in the music not of Tchaikovsky, but of Rimsky, Moussorgsky and Borodine. The ballets were *Prince Igor*, *Schéhérazade*, *Thamar*, *Firebird* and the *Rite of Spring*. Leon Bakst, with his brush strokes of Oriental illusion, turned everything behind the proscenium into a conflagration of impressionistic palettes, a riot of the sensualism of stuffs and smouldering colors which must still signify to many Americans the spirit of the Russian Ballet. To us, wrapped purely in the eclectic classicism of the 1930s, the dances of fifteen years ago seem, perhaps, inflated, boisterous, and, in spirit, as creased and dusty as the old scenery in front of which they were, until last year, still danced. It is true that they were very much in their own epoch. Their effectiveness was based not wholly on the inherent beauty of a perfect synthesis, but on the physical attraction, the almost animal appetite of their audience for color—tomato reds, sunflower yellows, grass greens, and not the monochromatic, neatly indicated decors of the years before and after. Their attraction was also partly due to the amazing physical violence of the dancers as people, in orgiastic simulacra.[2] Nijinsky leaped into the air like a sword flashed from its scabbard. The brass and clangor of Tartar emperors, arming from Kazan, bronze thighs through slashed silver pantaloons, in a

---

1. In Carl Van Vechten's *Music After the Great War*, there is an adequate description of the première of the *Sacre du Printemps*, more valuable as suggesting the atmosphere of aggressive experiment which Diaghilev always managed to stir up than as a factual description. "A certain part of the audience, thrilled by what it considered a blasphemous attempt to destroy music as an art, and swept away with wrath, began very soon after the rise of the curtain to whistle, to make catcalls, and to offer audible suggestions as to how the performers should proceed. Others of us, who liked the music and felt that the principles of free speech were at stake, bellowed defiance. . . . The figures on the stage danced in time to music they had to imagine they heard and beautifully out of rhythm with the uproar in the auditorium. The intense excitement of a young man behind me, under which he was laboring, thanks to the potent force of the music, betrayed itself presently when he began to beat rhythmically on the top of my head with his fists. My emotion was so great that I did not feel the blows for some time. They were perfectly synchronized with the beat of the music. When I did, I turned around. His apology was sincere. We had both been carried beyond ourselves."

2. In A. E. Johnson's book on the ballet [*The Russian Ballet*, 1913] there is a detailed narrative of *Schérérazade*, the most generally successful of the first ballets. His powers in prose capture at least something of the essential feeling of the piece: "The fires of passion smouldering in the heart of Zobeide leap forth on the instant. A woman scorned or a woman denied—her fury is a thing few men, and least of

tempestuous rout across the stage, evoked a fairyland which was a thousand times more satisfactory than thin puppets of heretofore, for these heroes sweated from their labors, their blood pouring out upon the white breasts of prostrate princesses in a palpable, tangible vision, separated from an audience only by music and lights.

The great star of Diaghilev's first nights was Nijinsky. Those who saw him retain an imperishable memory of sinewy vitality, a fountainous energy and a quality of physical presence, a mysterious personal charm which has never been approximated. Whether he raped a veil as in *The Afternoon of a Faun* ("elusive being, midway between the human and the animal, he has consciousness of nothing beyond his figs, his grapes and his flute," said Cocteau. "As he smoothes with his tongue his jaw, piebald like a horse-chestnut, his quaintly fascinating face seems to resent the weight of the horns upon his head. Could we hear him, one imagines he would laugh and bleat almost in the same breath and all the while his wrinkled brow attests his yearning to cross the border that separates instinct from intelligence") or bounded through an open window, so high that it took six strong pairs of hands with a mattress to break his fall[3] or threaded the almost inextricable maze of the original partition of the *Rite of Spring,* he was an unforgettable artist, and it is useless for one who never saw him to attempt a further evocation of his image. His febrile brilliance spent itself like a rocket and in the tragedy of his insanity; and in the great insanity of the war, Diaghilev's ballet rounded out its first chapter.[4]

---

all an emasculate poltroon, can face. A frightful paroxysm shakes the panting queen. Like a tigress baulked of her prey, etc., etc. . . .

"Palpitating with the vehemence of her expectant desires, Zobeide stands before the open portal, clutching her breasts with eyes glued to the dim recesses beyond. There is a pause, which adds a new delicious torture to her thirsty cravings; then with agile bound, light footed, there comes leaping toward her a young Negro [Nijinsky]."

3. From Jean Cocteau's *Igor Stravinsky and the Russian Ballet.* "It was in 1910. Nijinsky was dancing the *Spectre de la Rose.* Instead of going to see the piece, I went to wait for him in the wings. *There it was really very good.* After embracing the young girl the spectre of the rose hurls himself out of the window. . . . and comes to earth amongst the stage-hands who throw water in his face and rub him down like a boxer. What a combination of grace and brutality! I shall always hear that thunder of applause, I shall always see that young man, smeared with grease-paint, gasping and sweating, pressing his heart with one hand and holding on with the other to the scenery, or else fainting in a chair. Afterwards, having been smacked and douched and shaken he would return to the stage, and smile his acknowledgments."

4. In *Transition,* Volume I, No. 3, there is a story called "The Silent House" by Philippe Soupault in which there is developed a tragic description of Nijinsky

III

The saga of the ballet is really fit subject for an epic. Only with a poet's license may we obtain even the palest echo of the spirit and essence of the ballet as a company. An heroic adventure, its protagonists were tragedians of the first rank. As W. A. Propert says in his valuable book, *The Russian Ballet in Western Europe:*

> That Diaghilev's enterprise should have survived the war is astonishing, and the record of his journeys between 1914 and 1918 is a convincing proof of his courage and determination. The thunderbolt fell within a week of the termination of that memorable Drury Lane season, and many of the more important members of his company hurried back to Russia. He carried his company over to America, fulfilled his engagements there and was back in Europe by the autumn of 1915. There was a wonderful little season in Paris in December, when he produced *The Midnight Sun,* and earned no less than £4000 for the Red Cross. Then away again to America in January, 1916, for three months, and after a summer spent in Spain another long season opened at New York in the autumn. Between the 16th of October and the end of February, 1917, the company danced in over fifty towns through the length and breadth of the United States. Then again back in Europe, April was spent in Italy, May in Paris and June in Spain. Between July and September they were in South America and returned finally to Europe in November, 1917, spending their time in Spain until they could get through to England, where they landed in August, 1918.
>
> It was a tremendous Odyssey, carried through under conditions that might have daunted the old Greek himself, and it involved no less than eight Atlantic crossings through all the perilous times of the submarine warfare.

After the war Diaghilev turned his back on Russia and on its legacy. The empire of the Romanovs was his chief link with the east; the Renascent proletariat, replacing the romance he had made so much of, banished him to an indefinite exile. For of course the ballet's is an aristocratic realm. It depends on autocracy, absolutism, the projection of individuals against an anonymous mass. Logically enough when Diaghilev and Prokofiev produced their ballet inspired by the U.S.S.R., *The Beat of Steel [Le Pas d'Acier],* it was rather an empty gesture; the superficial patterns of

---

"dressed in a long, dark-grey coat, a light straw hat with a black band, and thick yellow boots, very pale like those worn by hunters or chronic invalids," walking in a closed garden, guarded by his intern, or else in the room above pacing the floor to the cracked gramophone record of "Invitation to the Waltz" (the music of the *Spectre de la Rose*).

human pistons and dynamos were surprising only on first sight—and besides, Diaghilev had well exhausted any possible exploitation of the near Orient. Those who at first regretted the passing of *Sadko, Prince Igor* and *Schéhérazade* came to realize they were, after all, mainly necessary for their epoch and that the epoch had fulfilled itself.[5]

The impresario ranged about him for such attendant talents as fitted his hands. He went from the east to the heart and brain of the west, and with his unerring chemistry, dissolved Derain into Rossini: behold *La Boutique Fantasque;* Matisse in Stravinsky: *The Nightingale;* Picasso in Manuel de Falla's *The Three Cornered Hat.* I must rely again on W. A. Propert, whose words, so much fairer than mine, may hint at the essential qualities of the first mentioned, which was typical of Diaghilev's important change in the direction of his second period:

> . . . Derain's *La Boutique Fantasque* (1919), and a gayer more exhilarating entertainment it would be difficult to imagine. His company had certainly de-Russianized themselves, and *Paris 1870* was glitteringly stamped over the whole production. . . . Here was to be the first example of the far reaching change that had come over the ballet—the work of a man who, with the zeal of a primitive, combined the science and sensibility of the twentieth century; who had come fresh to his work unspoilt by any acquaintance with stage conventions. . . . It was like the work of a ten-year-old schoolgirl, and yet the simplicity of its design was so transparently sincere, there was such a feeling of air and space everywhere—the color of the background was so clear and cool as seen through the brown screen, and above all there were such enchanting arrangements of fruits and flowers painted on the wings, that one forgave all those yards of ugly colour and the impossible furniture.

The curtain rises on Derain's toy shop, with a huge clerk's desk; the blue shades are drawn to discover a stiff painted paddle-wheel steamer on the back drop. The fat storekeeper has his assistant, a bounding imp of a

---

5. At the time of Bakst's death Paul Morand reviewed his achievement in the light of the later non-Bakstian ballets. "It is true that his art is too often vulgar, barbaric, effective only as a blow between the eyes; but such as it is, it has now become an historical phenomenon with its fifteen years of influence upon manners, the theatre, the city, books, and music. . . . It has been said that it was a Jewish art, with its emphasis upon raw tones, its passion for gold and precious metals, its dearth of line, its nomadic origins, its Oriental sensuality, its contempt for architectural construction. Bakst was, in fact, a Jew; and it was the great Israelite audiences that established the success of the Russian Ballet, that first great international success, marked by the boldness of the audience's dress, its immodesties, extravagant coiffures, depilated bodies, cosmetics; by that mixture of all modes to the point where one could not always distinguish between the house and the stage."

black-haired boy, with eyes like shoe buttons, hair like a mop and a moustache à la Charlot, and they dust up the shop. Ladies and gentlemen of 1870 with their fantastic children come in to buy. Demonstration of performing poodles, Russian toys, tin soldiers and a pair of can-can dancers. These last unfortunates are each bought by different families and are wrapped up to be taken away in the morning. During the night, the animals and toys come to life, assist the lovers to escape; in the morning the irate families return to discover they have been tricked, attack the storekeeper with bottle green parapluies and are routed by the resurrected denizens of the shop—exultation of the shock-headed assistant—grands jeux; ronde; coda; rideau—and while the large outline of the plotted action comes first to the mind there are those unforgettable details; the horrified gestures of spoilt American children, the kick of the ladies to get their bustles right, the pitiful smirking swagger of the can-can dancer, the distracted tossing abandon of the storekeeper's assistant, all engendered a deliciously conscious overtone that this is all very ridiculous, but here, in its frame, very true.

The milieu, the setting of 1870, the introduction of the can-can dancers—each has its own significance in the development of the Diaghilev ballet. Part of its charm was its constant sense of the recreation of a mood, as exemplified by an historical epoch, with an ultimate preoccupation with the present. For it was not 1870 that one saw through the enamelled lorgnons of the *Boutique Fantasque,* but a Lanvin lady of 1920 rustling her grandmother's ball dresses. Up to this time the ballet had used a subject matter that was overtly aristocratic: king, slaves and emperors, all the panoplies of princes, or at least the illuminated fairy books of princelings. Now it assumed a higher aristocracy, the remote and special aristocracy of the chic, the familiar texts of the commonplace, seized out of their context, transported to the plane of selection in recreation, and thus rehabilitated.

IV

The development of the ballet is the development of choreography, however much painting and music may contribute to its atmospheric presentation, and by a summary reconsideration of the principal choreographers of the Diaghilev dynasty one can gain an approximate idea of their ultimate achievement. Michel Fokine directly inherited the classical dance. Says André Levinson, that invaluable well of information on such matters: "The classical dance can be succinctly characterized by the use of beats on the points and beats of *elevation.* It contains the traditional symmetrical forms of the *pas de deux,* a choreographical poem in three verses, in a rigid framework: the *adagio,* which is a chain of movements and pirouettes by the ballerina supported by the dancer; the two *variations,* that of the ballerina and that of the dancer, whose more restricted art is confined to leaps, the entrechat and series of pirouettes; lastly the *coda*, in which the dancer alternates with the ballerina a succession of accelerated measures that mount up to the *presto* and end in a whirlwind of movements and dizzy complicated turns, crossing the stage diagonally." This of course may have the background of the corps de ballet, whose evolutions are foil and background for the principal dancers. Fokine invented *Les Sylphides (Romantic Reverie in one act),* one of the most beautiful of classic ballets in this formal idiom. One remembers swans swimming in late twilight—only the thunder of their wings is muted to swishings of long *tutus,* as paired ladies revolve in an inexpressible gravity of consecutive action in the midst of a shadowy park. But Fokine, with the customary violence of one who so well appreciates the tiresome tradition of his education, became a most passionate revolté against it. He embraced the gospel of Isadora with all his body and mind and did his best to inculcate this freedom into the Royal [Imperial] Ballet School. Propert again: "The *Ballet d'Action* in Russia up to 1900 still retained its old form, the story being told by gesture and the dances being treated as interludes, more or less illustrative. By judiciously complicating the plot and multiplying the auxiliary characters, by adding a procession here and there, and, if possible, an apotheosis, it was not difficult to spin it out to the regulation four or five acts." Came the Duncan: "She told of the ecstasy of the opening flower and of spirits attuned to the music of the spheres, and in the end her Greek draperies acquired all the significance of a prophet's mantle. . . . While Fokine disapproved of her indifference to technique, he equally disapproved of the others for the misuse they made of it. So he set about to create his own ideals. He imagined a ballet whose romance should go hand in hand with high accomplishment and where the unity of aim of the single dancer should inform the movements of the whole company." Fokine as a reformer was invaluable. As an artist he gave us *Petrouchka* and *Les Sylphides,* but it rested with his followers to rid the ballet of its ingenious tedium, its lack of integration between acted episodes and those danced, and the overemphasis on an elaboration of purely decorative action.

To Vaslav Nijinsky is really due the credit for that specialized quality of dancing which was the eventual contribution of Diaghilev's Ballet. First in his own dances in *Petrouchka* and *Jeux,* later in the *Afternoon of a Faun* and the *Sacre du Printemps* he created an intensity of abstracted intellectual physicality[6] which the rest have developed, modified into something less than its

---

6. From Cocteau's "Notes on the Ballets" in the *Decorative Art of Léon Bakst* by Arsène Alexandre, London, 1913: "[Nijinsky in *Carnaval*] half Hermes, half harlequin, cat and acrobat by turns, now frankly lascivious, now slyly indifferent, and

11

original purity. In addition to the contribution of a great individual technician and the gift of his quality as a person, Nijinsky incorporated Fokine's knowledge of the classical ballet, with his subsequent revolt from it and in addition something of Jaques-Dalcroze's eurhythmic dancing. If I seem to lean too heavily on Mr. Propert's admirable book, I can only say that it is better to quote him frankly than to do him the injustice of a restatement. "In the *Sacre*[7] we see for the first time the polyrhythmic dancing that Dalcroze had suggested. Nijinsky illustrated it by his setting one group of dancers to beat out softly the contrapuntal accompaniment of a theme which was being directly and more forcibly danced by another set.

"Technically the ballet was of extreme interest. It required great courage on the part of Nijinsky to discard every traditional grace that we had learned to expect. . . . Instead of arms moving in rippling curves we saw them strained rigidly downwards or as rigidly bent at the elbow, and instead of the silence of feet that had seemed scarcely to touch the ground they flew over, we heard the stamping and shuffling of insistent shoes."

Nijinsky lived to originate the idea of the ballet as an organism broken up into interacting members, dancing in relation each to itself and to each other, keeping the time of its unit in relation to the great pulse of the whole. Contrary to what might be expected this does not present the effect of confusion, disordered patches of irrelevant and over-active limbs, but rather a subtle shifting of an ever-changing pattern which weaves triply a rhythm, movement, and color into a human tapestry of ordered and profound complexity. His feverish activity in the invention of three ballets in a year and a half at the age of twenty-three besides his insistent appearances on the stage finally cracked him, but it provided Massine, Balanchine and Lifar with a contribution of combinations and an idiom no less important than the original five positions.

---

all the time the school boy up to every trick the turned-down collar of his dress suggests, as emancipated from the control of the laws of gravity as he is mathematically exact in the elaboration of his antic graces. The embodiment of mischief and desire, arrogance and self-satisfaction and a hundred things besides, with the drollest little nods of his head and strange side-long glances from the shelter of his lids, one shoulder held higher than the other and the cheek bent to meet it, his left hand on his hip, his right palm outstretched. Nijinsky danced his way through *Carnaval* to a din of uninterrupted applause."

7. From Muriel Draper's *Music at Midnight,* description of the first London performance: "The sight of human beings moving in an abstract geometric design that became a symbol of eternal emotions, beyond-human in its effect, increased the force with which the music invaded you. When it ceased, people broke and ran, sat motionless and unapproachable, cried with rage and assaulted sensibilities. (You call that *art* do you? You call it *music?* 'My God' rushed to the bar for a drink or tried to laugh it away.)"

Fokine freed the ballet from the chains of a sterile academism; Nijinsky gave it the language of an intellectual complexity; it was left to Leonide Massine then at the age of eighteen to integrate the gifts of his predecessors. Massine's first great contribution was in *Parade*, a ballet in one act by Jean Cocteau; music by Erik Satie; scenery and costumes by Pablo Picasso; produced in 1917. The literary and philosophical background of the ballet is sufficiently complicated to justify a quotation from Cocteau's own description of it.[8] For *Parade* was the *Sacre* of the middle Diaghilev period— the period of the Parisian *dadas,* the heirs of Guillaume Apollinaire— which resulted eventually in such more pretentious ballets as Nabokov's *Ode.* Cocteau is perennially occupied with the alchemy of the familiar, the rehabilitation of the commonplace. The consciousness of one's own epoch, so amazingly acute in the twentieth century, reaches its apogee in him. With Satie and Picasso he wished to present to us a poem of ordinaries, of such usual types that only by their isolation and caricature are they surprised out of banality, and in their escape lies our interest. The mood of *Parade* is that of the exterior of a provincial fair; the platform outside side-show booths before the exhibition starts. It is the mood of the commencement of all harangues, specious, but tacitly specious, and the audience as well as the actors are painfully conscious of the deception.

"For Reality Alone, even when well concealed, has power to arouse emotion.

"The Chinaman pulls out an egg from his pigtail, eats and digests it, finds it again in the toe of his shoe, spits fire, burns himself, stamps to put out the sparks, etc. . . .

"The little girl mounts a race-horse, rides a bicycle, quivers like pictures on the screen, imitates Charlie Chaplin, chases a thief with a revolver, boxes, dances a rag-time, goes to sleep, is shipwrecked, rolls on the grass on an April morning, buys a kodak, etc.

"As for the acrobats, . . . the poor stupid agile acrobats—we tried to invest them with the melancholy of a Sunday evening after the circus when the sounding of *Lights Out* obliges the children to put on their overcoats again, while casting a last glance at the 'ring.'

"Erik Satie's orchestra abjures the vague and the indistinct. It yields all their grace, without pedals. It is like an inspired village band.

"I composed, said Satie modestly, a background for certain noises which Cocteau considers indispensable in order to fix the atmosphere of his characters."

Here indeed was something else again. Suggestive and atmospheric,

---

8. "The Collaboration of 'Parade' " from *Cock and Harlequin,* by Jean Cocteau.

Parade had perhaps more to do with poetry and philosophy than dancing but it was the seed from which the full-blown flower of the ballet would at last blossom and die. Here was no quaintness of such a work as the *Boutique Fantasque*. The quality of the strangeness here, its peculiar "quaintness," was a provincial nostalgia, a love and a loathing for the contemporary moment, the epoch of the daily paper and the telegraph, in itself sufficiently diffuse as to be generally incomprehensible—but in its effect extremely powerful. Much of the dancing here was allowed to disintegrate into ponderous shufflings, the painting into chaos and the music into a series of negligible noises; but in its exquisite snobbery, in its ecstasy of precious eclectism, it presupposed the culmination of whole traditions of all the arts, to give point and pathos to their perversion here. And about this time, in spite of its *succès d'estime*, its comparative financial success, and its crowded houses, the professional wise-acres started prophesying the ultimate downfall of the ballet or announcing its death as a fait accompli. But Diaghilev was usually cleverer than his critics. His excursions into the eccentric were guided by a prescience of style that was uncanny. Perhaps he created the ensuing style. It surely followed his wake with extraordinary alacrity. Diaghilev still kept *Igor* and *Sylphides* in his repertory, he still had his troupe dance *Carnaval* and *Petrouchka*, *The Afternoon of a Faun* and the *Sacre*. But the public, to make up for their original antagonisms, clutched their hard earned preferences all the tighter to their habitual taste and were reluctant to accept any further innovation. The lesson of the past in relation to experiment seems never to be learned. Perhaps the initial antagonism provides the spring of release for the new work. At any rate Diaghilev followed *Parade* with such ballets as *Romeo and Juliet*, the rehearsal of a ballet in itself; with *Pastorale*, the filming of a moving picture, in which the premier danseur entered on a clever bicycle as a telegraph messenger. His excursions into native iconography in England were perhaps less fortunate but surely as elaborate. In *The Triumph of Neptune*, Diaghilev, the Sitwells and the scenery of Pollock's passementerie theatres of the early Victoria, evolved a ballet lacking the distinction of similar French creations. Perhaps the English legend itself wanted the kind of raciness to which Diaghilev was accustomed. This, only to show that he was by no means unerring or always successful. His England is the usual decorative England of the continental—stuffy, suggestive of wet tweeds and foggy afternoons, bound volumes of *Punch*, Dickens; later of du Maurier. *"Le Romantisme puéril d'un peuple des grands enfants rieurs, querelleurs et crédules est admirablement rendu,"* says M. André Levinson, *"par les décors, coloriages ombrés à la plume, imagerie naive agrandie a l'échelle de la scène."* But in passing it is only fair to say that it was England and not France which supported the ballet in the last days of its existence, and it was England and not France that had talked of a national home for the ballet had Diaghilev lived.

14

Massine was also responsible for two ballets which combined a felicity of dramatic action with a grace of choreography that had not been seen before. The *Good Humored Ladies* retained the wit of Goldoni but never resorted to the archeology of a mere commedia dell'arte, and the *Three Cornered Hat* more than recalls Alcaron, but it is a dramatic dance rather than a mimed play. For many these combinations of continuous coherent action marked the height of invention in the ballet. It was surely a comprehensible, beautiful and intelligent expression in itself, and these ballets never tired in repetition, but the quality of invention they expounded was shown so exhaustively and inevitably in these two ballets that it was immediately obvious that the development of choreography lay in other directions.

Massine's most fortunate invention was, perhaps, *Les Matelots,* music by Auric, decor by Pruna; as originally danced with Lopokova, Danilova, Slavinsky and Woizikowsky [it] is—with *Apollo, The House Party, The Cat* and *Sylphides*—in the top hierarchy of the later Diaghilev repertoire. The stage had simple curtains of dull red, brown, blue, and side-strips of white. A large cube like an enormous toy block had its four sides painted with cupids, lovers, a ship, a lonesome lass, which, turning, accentuated the incident, giving the narrative key as the action progressed. It was danced by six people alone. The young girl, her girl-friend, sailors and a musician who lead the final triumphant dancing-march with a tin fork and spoon. The Matelots are Parisian blue-jackets; blue and white barred shirts, blue cap with the red pom-pom and tight, revealing trousers. The girl is a Catholic maiden of passive charm and haughty receptivity; her confidante an eager wench, a matter-of-fact shop-front lass. Its simple plot—of betrothal, farewell, reappearance in disguise (three attachable beads and a pipe)—the test of devotion and the triumph of love, is the basis for the action. All the otherwise inexpressible, romantic charm attendant on seafaring men from Ulysses and Sinbad to Ishmael and any common seamen on Riverside Drive of a Sunday afternoon, their loose leggedness, bravado, their talent for gaming, the breadth and gesture of their leer, thumb back, low grin, legs out, find a frame, a defining stylization here. The movements are abrupt, surprising, yet always bear some implication or reference to natural gestures, whether the sailors dance with real chairs, or slap imaginary cards on the ground, or hitch their pants or support their girls with that ghostly echo of a posture which betrays the rigidity of the classic regimen beneath it all. Massine had taken the greatest pains in the episodic transitions, the hint of comedy, the suspicion of sadness, the nostalgia of expectancy, so that the dramatic unit is a symphony of the poetry in human situation.

Massine at present designs the dances for Roxy's ballet in New York. In this position of considerable importance, it is a pity he has not more power to exercise his amazing ingenuity and his splendid talents as a great original dancer. At least he has been given the chance to arrange the dances for the League of Composers' production of the *Rite of Spring* this April. Massine was the first of the "clever" choreographers.[9] A perfect classical dancer, he took an almost pedantic delight in perverting or satirizing the old formal steps. He introduced a kind of stylish rigidity, a conscious gaucherie, which his followers were often to transmit into an ingenious pattern of meaningless surprises as empty as the original academic formula on which it was based.

VI

And then there was Diaghilev himself, a personality of the utmost distinction, combining in his fantastic character elements of practical facility, capacity for action and an exuberant invention which made the ballet possible. M. Henri Prunières described him thus in his memorial written at the time of his death: "Those who did not know him cannot imagine the extraordinary attraction of this big, snub-nosed man, with the enormous head, the black hair parted with a large white lock, heavy jaws, sensual lips, fine eyes of velvet darkness. He wore a monocle and had a slouching walk like the Monsieur de Charlus portrayed by Marcel Proust." It was inevitable that legend should have grown up about him in his life, and of necessity it was on a grand scale parallel to his creations. He was reputed to be at once the wickedest and kindest man in Europe, both the stupidest, the most vulgar, the shrewdest and the most smart. Perhaps by quoting Lydia Lopokova who knew him better than most, one can realize some segment of his mercurial temperament. "Then there was his cunning with which he knew how to combine the excellent with the fashionable, the beautiful with the *chic*, and revolutionary art with the atmo-

---

9. A typical example of the more outrageous Massine, the Massine at whose door some laid the decadence of the ballet, was the production of *Mercure* at Beaumont's Soirée de Paris described in the *Criterion* by W. H. Shaw. "*Mercure* left one uncertain. The effect produced on the first night audience was indicative. The younger generation led by Louis Aragon became so excited that they leapt from their seats, running through the theatre to the loge of the Comte de Beaumont, screaming in menacing tones, 'Vive Picasso! Vive Picasso,' as if uncertain whether to thank or damn him for presenting anything so thrilling. . . . The curtain rose on a tableau representing night in a manner entirely new to Picasso, an abstract composition made of canvas and wire. The three graces were done by three mechanical figures which were many times as large as the dancers who carried them across the stage. The dance of Chaos was executed by a group of dancers entirely covered by different colored tights, reaching even over their faces, crawling across the stage, supporting other dancers on their heads and backs."

sphere of the old regime. Perhaps this corresponded to something in his own nature. In spite of his love for the *dernier cri* and the emancipation of his taste, no one could ever have called Diaghilev a 'highbrow.' He was an orthodox believer and devoted slave of Emperors and Kings. Indeed, he was a convinced snob, and it was not only thoughts of the box office which made him so spry and contented when the King of Spain, the Duke of Connaught or even the Aga Khan was in the theatre! He was superstitious; charms, potions, love-philtres were not entirely outside his mentality." He indulged himself equally in his passion for puppies, for Machiavellian intrigue, and for four-handed arrangements of Glinka and Cimarosa. In trying to recollect those qualities which made his success possible Lopokova first cites his extraordinary authority, as ruthless as the traditional Romanov, whose blood was supposed to flow in his veins. As she says, it was no easy task to get such a three ring circus as Rimsky, Stravinsky, Prokofiev, Debussy, Ravel, Poulenc, Auric, Milhaud, De Falla, Respighi, Strauss and Matisse, Braque, Derain, Laurencin, Utrillo, Gris, Rouault, Picasso, Bakst, Chirico, and Pavlova, Karsavina, Bolm, Nijinsky, Mordkin, Dolin and Lifar to work together. The difficulties in the way of savage professional jealousies, procrastination from both musical and artistic supports, and recurrent and insistent bankruptcy which Diaghilev surmounted are heroic chapters in his saga, which, so vital to his success, will of necessity be forgotten. Naturally he made enemies. His increasing power had become dictatorial. He could make the reputation of a painter, a musician or a dancer in a single night. "And lastly," wrote Lopokova, "as the force without which I think, the rest could not have been enough, there was the personal motive of his successive attachments to Nijinsky, Massine, and Lifar. It was his unceasing preoccupation to educate, inspire, and develop the natural talents of these dancers and choreographers to the utmost limit of their possibilities. It would be half true to say that all this energy was exercised, the great Opera Houses of the world rented, and the most famous musicians and artists commissioned in order that a splendid *ensemble* might be created for their setting off, that glory should surround their triumphs and the most perfect opportunities be offered for their self-expression." Muriel Draper in regretting the passing of the ballet gives an unforgettable picture of Diaghilev at a rehearsal. "Abortive democratic principles, the socialization of the arts for the standardized benefit of the prolific 'brotherhood' of man, the lack of one great figure to dominate so many interrelated parts of the world as have been thrown pell-mell together, all these currents have accelerated the temporary eclipse of the grand scale. . . . They are losing the code, and with a universal increase of intelligence and technical virtuosity that is in almost exact inverse ratio to standards of value, there is little left that can be presented on the grand scale. What there is of it

17

Diaghilev captured and salvaged. I have sat with him in almost empty theatres during rehearsal and heard him say to the chef d'orchestre very politely—

" *'Non, non, non maître. Pas tout à fait ca. . . . Pas tout à fait ça. Est-ce que je me trompe, ou est-ce que ce n'est pas un tout petit trop. . . . trop lent? En tout cas, essayons-le un to-o-out petit peu plus vite. C'est bien possible que j'ai tort.'* Or to a dancing figure on the stage, *'Non, Non, Non ma chère petite. Non. L'estomac n'est pas fait de bois—attendez, attendez, écoutez-moi—ni de caoutchouc. Non, chère, non. L'estomac est fait de la chair, après tout, de la bonne chair.'* And so on and so on until by a series of almost chemical emanations rather than actual directions, he had changed the atomic structure of bodies, scenes and sounds.''

"I once asked him if he could express in words the exact thing of which he was possessed that brought about this subtle synthesis of flesh and light and tone vibration.

" *'Je ne sais pas, je ne sais pas, ma chère Muriel, je ne sais pas. Un toouout petit peu de la connaissance, peut-être, et beaucoup de l'amour. . . . Je ne sais pas.'* ''

Diaghilev had his court and for twenty years at least he was king of the European arts. A beneficent despot, the power of his unified and isolated authority, with the exception of the Bavarian King's Wagnerian interlude, has parallels only in the eighteenth century and before, when Boucher and LeBrun created an academy and a taste. It is something to have recreated the art of dancing, to have given painting practically its only escape from easel-painting, to have provided music with the proper channels to exploit its polyphonic dissonances and return to melodic line. Diaghilev did more. He created a taste in and of his own period, he set up the only referable standards of aesthetic excellence in the first quarter of the twentieth century, and provided the only great market for a unified creative endeavor. Two things he loved to idolatry: the physical aura of youth in action; the intellectual brilliance of surprise. He was a king who created not empires, but a world, who defined with a synthesis of men and their arts, with the transitions of movement in mass, color and music a nobility that had no other way of being demonstrated. Diaghilev's style was more than a modish fashion, an ephemeral chic. Unique in itself, it expressed the same aristocracy of perception and intensity, usually with tragic overtones, that all great artists have known and erected. While watching a ballet one could say simply, "There lies nobility, grace, perfection." With words this style is definable, but the very symbols that read abstractions traduce its essence. In the grave sobriety, the untiring effortless fountain of Mozart, in the ironic and passionate delicacy of Greco; in such gay and heroic characterizations as Mercutio's and Hotspur's; in the cadences of Racine and Congreve, and in the elegance of Wren and Bernini, there is that living, tremendous exuberance of human divinity which so often the Diaghilev ballet tangibly and triumphantly expressed. In recreating the past, whether in Russia or Versailles, in seizing from the present its most precious seconds whether at a house party,[10] a tennis game (Nijinsky and Debussy's *Jeux*), or a factory, Diaghilev chose the best of life's stream, presented it to those living who could best receive it, in the most fitting of all possible forms.

VII

If the choreography of the first Russian ballets was characterized by its massive emphasis on colorful loose dancing, chaotic gesture, a narrative sequence in action and a romantic reaction from the strictures of the five classical positions, the last Russian ballets were distinguished by the reverse. Its development had run the logical gamut from the intense and reactionary romanticism of Michel Fokine to the intense and reactionary classicism of Georges Balanchine (Balanchivadze). For it was he and not Massine who determined the indicative line of the last ballets, although he depended on Massine as much as Massine originally on Fokine. In its first years the by-words of ballet were "grace," "beauty of movement," "line," meaning roughly, smooth transitions from one balanced position to another. Under Massine, with his incorporations of various extraneous influences, such as music-hall[11] and musical comedy dancing, this grace was replaced by a certain abruptness, clipped gestures, strained final positions, so awkward in themselves that they immediately and satirically recalled the smooth attitudes which they burlesqued. Generally taken to be awkward and gauche, they seemed to many, rather, stylish, pointed, accentuating, accenting those gestures which in their customary slippery sequence had lost any isolated meaning. Massine was accused of design-

---

10. *Les Biches*, choreography by Nijinska (sister of the dancer), music by Poulenc, décor by Marie Laurencin, was surely one of the happiest of all ballets, the perfect definition of the charm of contemporaneity in relation to tradition. The music, with its lovely parody of César Franck, the boys in sashed blue bathing suits, the ladies in pink, grey and black garden party dresses; the entrance also of Nemtchinova so well described by Cocteau—the type of the perfect entrance. "*L'entrée de Nemtchinova est proprement sublime. Lorsque cette petite dame sort de la coulisse, sur ses pointes, avec de longues jambes, un justaucorps trop court, la main droite, gantée en blanc, mise près de la joue comme pour un salut militaire, mon coeur bat plus vite on s'arrête de battre. Ensuite, un grout sans flechissement combine les pas classiques et les gestes neufs.*"

11. In Cocteau's *Boeuf sur le Toit*, the three Fratellinis, star clowns of the Cirque d'Hiver, were taken over to mime the leading roles. How admirable an American ballet would be, music by Cole Porter, with the addition of Clayton, Jackson and Durante, whose precision, tempo and irony approximate the later Russian ballets in essence more than anything else in America.

19

ing ballets with an excess of movement, in so much as the eye never was at leisure. His introduction of acrobatics as in *Mercure* was generally deplored. Such vulgarisms were not only displeasing to the smoothly trained eye, but they *ruined the dancers* for such delicate work as in the classical *Sylphides,* which is to say that Schönberg or Satie ruins one's fingers for Chopin or Tchaikovsky. But Massine's real forte was in his comic scenes, the Italian and Spanish deceptions, the barbed wit, and brilliant personal deceit of Goldoni and Alcaron.

Balanchine's triumphs were the *Cat,* the *Prodigal Son,* the *Ball* and *Apollo, Leader of the Muses.* The ballet disintegrated after Diaghilev's death, and perhaps circumstances will not allow the full development of this brilliant choreographer, who must certainly have developed into one of the ablest of all Diaghilev's designers, for not only was his energy and invention prodigious, but he well understood the dangers attendant on the unintelligent if entertaining implications of the "clever," acrobatic Massine dance, and in the *Cat* and *Apollo* he produced two of the finest of all the ballets since their inception. His dances had the spareness, the lack of decoration which is by no means a lack of refinement, the splendid capacity to display individual gesture against a background of unrhythmical massed gesture. Sometimes his ingenuity ran away with him, as in the *Prodigal Son,* when four lines of dancers are ranged as on a grandstand, and their hands shoot out like the struck letters of a typewriter in a sequence which is distinguished only as a surprise. Or as in the same ballet, when the shaven men pair off back to back, then slide down until they are sitting against each other on air, and scuttle off sideways like a battalion of crabs. These of course were intended as semi-satirical accents, but they had the same undesirable effect as an over-elaborate image in a poem, which throws off the continuous emphasis of the piece as a whole. It is true he engaged in acrobatics and influences from the music hall as well. But he had an excellent precedent for such borrowings. Did not Nijinsky and Fokine borrow from Dalcroze and Isadora, and Massine from Spanish folk dances, and the can-can of the Moulin de la Galette, and the Valser of the Prater? The ballet of Balanchine was more difficult to follow, perhaps, required more of an effort, in so much as the human eye accepts more readily easy variations, just as the human ear accustoms itself more readily to tones in transitions bounded by the more obvious tonal intervals. Extremely apropos of Balanchine are the words of M. Valerian Svetloff: "I have always maintained that an art fixed immovably in its forms is doomed. I have said that Fokine, by his great talent, has stirred the classicism of Petipa out of its inertia, has given it new life, for classicism is the source of the art of the ballet." The last period of the ballet was and must be considered a period of transition, not of decadence. Balanchine in the *Cat* and in *Apollo* was leading out of mere ingenuity into a revivified, purer, cleaner classicism. He had drawn on his predecessors, and with the utilization of his own peculiar invention, had created a classical ballet as pure as *Sylphides* or the *Swan Lake*, but with more depth of emotional intensity. Who having seen it will ever forget the *Cat?* When the curtain rose on Gabo and Pevsner's construction in mica, steel and black oil cloth, a group of young men arranged in tandems of four, bore on their collective backs their leader, Lifar, the new Nijinsky. The music of Henri Sauguet— *Je ne suis pas de mon époque,* he said—it is indeed rather that of a more acrid Offenbach—crashed out the chords of a prancing entrance and the human chariot deposited its load in the centre of the stage. The young man prays Aphrodite, an implacable divinity of isinglass and white, to suffer his beloved, a cat, to come to life. His prayer is granted and thence, Nikitina, her *tutu* covered with a layer of isinglass, floats on to the scene in an entrance of exquisite and indescribable delicacy, gravity and precision. The dances are of the older sort, combinations of attitude, entrechat, rond de jambe, pas de basque, etc., of the strict regime. But with what tragic overtones is this rigid idiom invested, when Aphrodite to test the love of the cat-girl sends a mouse across the stage. She reverts to type, following it off the floor to assume her white mittens and mask of cat. How desperately the young man is caught by his overwhelming grief, how he shivers his life away, until he falls on his side, head painfully unrelaxed off the ground in rigor mortis. Then his companions file in, bearing skeletons of great shields, whose shifting outlines, more than their own bodies, describe his funeral march, and he is borne off, over their heads, music, setting, dancing, maintaining an atmosphere of pure tragedy, an exaltation of loss which can only be described as Attic.

Apollo, Leader of the Muses was even sparer, more remote. The god with hair of gilt enamel, chitoned in crimson silk, danced with Terpsichore, Polyhymnia and Calliope, each dressed by Chanel in the most touching of divine chiffons, cinctured by striped Charvet cravats, as perennially fashionable in the Faubourg St. Germain as on the uplands of Olympus. Here were the old pas d'action, variations and combinations ending in the customary apotheosis, when the sun god's harnessed chariot comes out of the sky for him.

There is no plot. The inspiring of the Muses is a sufficient subject for dances in the old style, with all the emphasis on easy formal transition, a delicacy in the extended line of the body that is by no means a reversion to nineteenth-century choreography, for just as Stravinsky's music transcended Delibes and Tchaikovsky, through the *Sacre* or no matter what, so Balanchine has transcended Petipa, by way of *Prince Igor, Les Matelots* and the *Boutique Fantasque.* Always in the last analysis the classical dance is the most satisfactory; its cold multiplication of a thousand embroideries—divested of the personal, if more romantic charm of pantomime—never become cloying. One may love a ballet of surprise just as much, perhaps, after the first astonishment at decor or invention wears off, but in ballets like *Apollo*, the slight crassness that accompanies elaborate conceit never detracts from the nobility of the unerring linear architecture. This ballet more than any other indicated the direction of Balanchine's ultimate attack. Lifar, the premier danseur, famous for his acrobatics, had proclaimed his decided attraction not to the ingenious complications of the *Ball* and the *Prodigal Son* but to the classical choreography of the masters Petipa, Legat and Cecchetti. This winter he arranged and danced Beethoven's *Prometheus* at the Opera in Paris, which gives some glimmer to the future of the dance.

For to many the future of the dance is very black indeed. To be sure there is an enormous interest in dancing today; witness the extravagant success of the Denishawns, Kreutzberg, Argentina and the score of Sunday evening entertainers foreign and indigenous. The Denishawns have some interest in their reproduction of Eastern dances, but purely the interest of a good copy; Kreutzberg has only the subjective fascination of postwar German painting, of Pierrot Lunaire. Argentina defines the limits of a perfection, which is by nature of itself limited. The rest, such dancers as attempt "reforms" in the classical ballet—Wigman, Bodenwieser, Laban, and their American parallels—lack the two chief necessities of fine dancing—a formal training and a sense of the aristocracy of style. Solo dancers are never as effective as with the background of a ballet, and the aimless emotional vacuity, the appalling facility of loose gesture under the guise of free dancing that we find in most Americans are far less interesting than the precision of Albertina Rasch or a Tiller corps.

As M. Valerian Svetloff says: "Talent is an all-embracing spirit, it is contented with seven notes, seven primary colors and five positions in dancing; with these it will perform marvels in art, such marvels as will remain young when the present generation, and those that follow it, are in their graves." The classical ballet, once its idiom is incorporated in the mind of the dancer, transcends the heavy self-consciousness of naturalistic dancing, which is always intent on translating the postures of "natural" walking and running into the language of the dance. But in walking and running, for example, the feet and hands are blunt ends, to arrest the flow of lines; by a stylized lengthening of them as in ballet, the eye carries the linear transition easily. For classical ballet dancing is at once the most rigid and elastic of bodily expression. It is the Catholic absolute dogma of the dance. To be sure there are the Calvinists, the Christian Scientists, and lesser creeds without the law; messengers of beauty in batik draperies, bearing paper hydrangeas in a cardboard urn. They lack the hardness, the muscular accuracy, the coordinated precision of those dancers trained at the barre. Their repertoire is always looser, less coherent, less integrated.

The world needs a new Diaghilev to reintegrate the arts, but to save dancing in particular from a facile oblivion.

It is, of course, somewhat pointless to attempt the description of the ballet to one who has never seen it, whose only connection with formal dancing is the "prologue" to a moving picture or the interlude of a musical comedy. It is hard to convey the feeling of loss one has, having seen it, fearing never to see it again. But it is exactly the same as if one were deprived of a literature, a whole language of expression; for instance to wake up one morning and know one could never read Tolstoi or Proust or Shakespeare again, never to see Poussin, Greco, or Cézanne, never again Gabriel's *garde-meuble* on the Place de la Concorde, or Chartres, or San Marco, never hear again the B Minor Mass or *Don Giovanni*.

VIII

And the social reverberations of the ballet were not wholly negligible; in the minds of some at least there were serious moral implications. If at the first great nights at the Châtelet the audience included Geraldine Farrar, M. Briand, Isadora Duncan, Gabriel Fauré, Grand Duke Pavel, Caillaux, Saint-Saëns, Octave Mirabeau, the last nights in London were beheld by an equivalent aristocracy of art, letters, and politics. During the intermissions, Miss Sitwell held her court on Covent Garden stairs, to block the upward passage of the Poet Laureate. Prince George sits in a corner with an unknown lady elaborately unobserved. The latest meteors down from Oxford and Cambridge swell the large and androgynous cohorts of intelligent enthusiasts, and these have startled the jeremiads of that nervous Savonarola, Mr. Wyndam Lewis. He fulminated against the ballet as the ultimate snobbish and vapid bagatelle of high-Bohemia, the vile afterbirth of the purple nineties. But what Mr. Lewis really objected to was the sight of a great many more or less wicked young people enjoying themselves, contrasting (favorably, no doubt) the formal perfection of the ballet with the formal corruption of their own lives. The gossip that buzzed around its corridors was as lively, as professional, as malicious as at Trianon. One can only hope that there were St. Simons on both sides of the channel during the last twenty years. For, S. (a delightful dancer of some seasons ago) disappeared with a Finnish lady and contracted leprosy—rewards of the narrow path. There is being kept in abeyance a dancer greater than Nijinsky to replace the present favorite. He was found on the top of a steppe and has been educated at Diaghilev's expense for fifteen years. Stravinsky's orthodox Mass has been refused. Markevitch, the sixteen-year-old musician, will definitely emerge from his obscurity to replace Stravinsky. The composer in a dudgeon has withdrawn the rights on all his ballets. Diaghilev is bankrupt, only the generosity of Lord

Beaverbrook keeps him at Covent Garden; Stravinsky's Mass will be produced in Monte Carlo in the spring. In spite of the antagonistic critical silence in all the Beaverbrook press, the present season is, bless God, a financial success; now X, Y, Z, and so on can be paid. But the extraordinary thing about this gossip was the high degree of technical and personal information it presupposed. The audiences of the ballet had been reared in it. They were as willing to talk about an entrance, a new invention or elision in the choreography, as to scandalize about the dancers. There was no necessity of explanatory lectures, program notes. And the intelligence, the quickness to perceive, the willingness to follow wherever adventures of the mind, the ear, the eye led, made possible amazing voyages in invention, and all the explorations of Diaghilev and his ballet. Equally on the stage, the insistence on a hierarchy of social values accomplished marvels. There was the implicitly accepted favorite of Diaghilev. There may or may not have been accompanying rancor behind the scenes, the feeling that not merit alone had accomplished a meteoric rise. But on the stage, when good dancing was to be done, there was an intentness of purpose, a passionate intensity at impersonalized abstract perfection, unalloyed by the intrusion of emotional competition. There was no attempt at outdancing one's partner, as so often on our stage actors outplay their supporting company. All the dancers had an exquisite realization of their place in the time, the dress, the atmosphere of the ballet, and of their place, their tempo, their spiritual attitude in dancing. Merely because when lined up at the time of curtain calls the premiers danseurs were so frequently smothered with bouquets of carnations, the ladies were no less gracious or adorable for accepting the young men's flowers, torn from their more tangible tributes. The recognition of the proud filling each, in their way, of their proper place, in every relation personal and artistic was that religion, which was the style of the ballet.

The style the Russian ballet embodied was to be sure a peculiar and restricted kind of style, a style of manners, an aristocracy of charm, a selection of all the noblest and most desirable qualities to despite life's darkness, in an eternal living definition of the qualities which we find great in painting, sculpture, music and letters. Words fail at every turn, and one can only rely on such inscribed and immediate beacons to parallel the qualities here to be inferred. The style, the aristocracy of charm the ballet knew so well was known by Poussin in his *Inspiration of the Poet;* Manet in his *Olympia* and Seurat in the *Grande Jatte* felt the style of contemporaneity which had links with all greatness in the past, and the power of such great projection into the future. The graciousness, the swing, the delicacy of such a style was realized by the unknown Attic sculptor of the Berlin goddess bearing a pomegranate; most fittingly in Carpeaux's *Danse.* The grandeur of its kinetic and noble sobriety Monteverdi inscribed in *Orfeo;*

its playfulness, its geniality Mozart interlined within *Les Petits Riens*. But describing the ballet is more fatuous than even attempting to paint pictures with words. How can one ever suggest the delicacy of pause, the void in action that gives dance its accent; the vision of arms and legs in exquisite interplay from symmetry to asymmetry, from rest to violence, or to feel the ineffable charm, warming one like friendship—to see men and women moving together in a sympathy of gesture, a prescience of progressive action that is at once complete coordination, ease; the poetry of life. And Cocteau's first impression of the ballet is true of a last look and every look: "Their thrilling dances then gave me a sharp pang of yearning to get a closer view of things immeasurable and unattainable, such as no poem of Heine's, no prose of Poe's, no fever dream has ever given me, and, since, I have invariably had the same sensation, at once sub-conscious and acute, which I attribute to the silent and nebulous precision of all they do."

Homage to Michel Fokine

Aside from Duncan-style classes as a child, Kirstein had never danced. But as a young man of impassioned nature who already had visions of establishing an "American" ballet, it was important for him to temper the intoxication of his addiction by physically experiencing the effort, the challenge, and the pain of actually dancing. So in 1932, at the age of 25, he chose Fokine, then the most famous teacher in New York, for his first ballet lessons.

Kirstein being Kirstein, it was not enough merely to take class; he interviewed his teacher at length, and these conversations provided the basis for the following piece as well as the monograph he published in 1934. Kirstein also wrote from personal experience: as a Diaghilev enthusiast, he had seen the Fokine repertory alive.

For a while, Kirstein wrote in 1973, he had considered forming his "American" ballet around Fokine.

He also wrote that, at the time Fokine was his teacher, he was embittered and difficult, having been denied access to the world's major stages for years. But this aspect of Fokine's temperament is not reflected in the writings of the 'thirties; rather, it is Kirstein's own despair at the state of ballet in America that is projected—he sees no native tradition worthy of his attention and a humiliating American failure to provide a dignified arena for the talents of the master he considered to have "created the [modern] Russian Ballet." (Although most of Fokine's work in America was for music halls and Broadway—and included a stillborn flirtation on the part of Hollywood—soon after Kirstein's pieces were

◊ Reprinted from *The New English Weekly* 3:15 (July 27, 1933), 350-351.

written, he again found appropriate scope for his abilities with René Blum's Les Ballets de Monte Carlo, then with de Basil, and finally with Ballet Theatre.)

Kirstein's early advocacy of Fokine was passionate, but it is apparent both from his writings of the 'thirties and from later works that for him the far greater heroes of twentieth-century dance were Diaghilev, Nijinsky (as choreographer), and, eventually, Balanchine.

N.R.

OF ALL THE ARTS, dancing most depends for its continuance upon memory. Photographs only recall segments of action, and up to the present no one has been occupied in recording ballets by cinema. And so, while forgetting may be so fatal, it is tragic to forget, while there is yet time to remember, the work and genius of a living force, however isolated he may be, by an ocean and twenty years, from the present seat of activity in ballet. Michel Fokine is still very much alive. He trains the best dancers that exist in the United States, a country which abounds in technical excellence and poverty of ideas. Fokine is not an impresario or an entrepreneur. He has been a great dancer and is still a great choreographer.

It is painful to enumerate the reasons for his lack of creation in America, but it is necessary to explain away suspicions that he lacks work because he no longer can compose. The ballet of the Metropolitan Opera House, where he should have been master for the last fifteen years, is governed by as narrow a policy of Italian prejudice against Russian music and dancing as exists in the world, and not even sentimental associations in New York City can save the institution from the oblivion it so richly deserves. Ever since Diaghilev was seen as a threat to the Italian autocracy in 1916, the Metropolitan had to put a crippling embargo on any creative effort, guarding themselves from attack by producing a few works by Stravinsky after they had become favourites over the radio. Yet when they finally staged *Petrouchka* in a Chauve Souris background, not Fokine but another dancer was asked to stage his masterpiece; what they lost through his faulty memory they gained by eliminating any possibility of Fokine's use of their stage.

In the meantime, denied the one possible position in America fitting his talents, he has danced in recitals and has produced his ballets in the Scandinavian countries and in South America. Recently, writers in England, who, after Russia, love dancing more than any country in the West, have suggested that Fokine be asked to London. First M. Dandré, in his touching life of his wife, then Mr. Adrian Stokes in the *Week End Review*, and finally Mr. Mark Perugini in the *Dancing Times*.

During the recent season in Paris, now being shown in London, the influence of Fokine, although separated from his name, was powerfully felt. Never had the Polovetsky seemed so brilliant, never *Sylphides* such a masterpiece of the architecture of classical dancing. At the Opera the first dancers produced *Spectre de la Rose,* and in the roster of the other programs were at least four new creations which owed their ideas almost directly to him.

From his first work with the students of the Imperial School in St. Petersburg with *The Vine* and *Eunice* to his first work for Diaghilev in *Pavillon d'Armide,* Fokine created with breathless activity in little more than four years' time *Carnaval, Sylphides, Narcisse, Cléopâtre, Schéhérazade, Prince Igor, Festin, Spectre, Daphnis and Chloe, Dieu Bleu, Thamar, Oiseau de Feu, Coq d'Or* and *Petrouchka,* besides the work he did on the side for Pavlova and the Maryinsky Theatre. There are at least seven ballets in the list which hold their own with anything that has been created in the interim, and exceed in imagination and solid construction perhaps everything since, save Nijinsky's *Faun* and *Sacre du Printemps.*

Would Fokine seem vieux-jeu now? Could he adapt himself to "modern" choreography? One hopes not. Fokine's style—at times Dionysiac, arriving independently at similar conclusions to Duncan, yet supported by a technique that could stand them; at times drawing from the rich sources of Russian national dances, always conscious of the eighteenth century of Noverre, and of Petipa in the nineteenth—was a continuous, melodic, consecutive line, giving fullest play to the dancer's extended silhouette, as against the post-War "style"—abrupt, broken, abdominal, reactionary in its static revolt. It is the psychological moment for a return to Fokine as a structural departure for the future. We can stand a little integration after the dilution of the late Diaghilev exercises and from the spasmic hypnosis of Central European gestures. We often forget that ballet is primarily not decor nor music, but dancing, not an edition-de-luxe by a member of the École de Paris but a design by a choreographer. Fokine is a fine teacher, not only transmitting the inheritance of the strictest purity of classical gesture but also re-creating the finest of national dances, tempering the five positions with movement from the soil.

In times when any steady will can shortly be canonized as revolutionary, it is important to realize the primary importance of Fokine as a real cleanser and invigorator of movement. In his famous letter to the directors of the Imperial School he did more to change dancing than any man since Noverre. It is hard to imagine into what a petrification choreography had fallen at the end of the nineteenth century, until Fokine said that no longer should there be any presupposed, merely formal gestures. Mimetic action must follow the subject matter at hand. The hands, arms, the whole body must be liberated for dancing, not merely twinkling feet. Groups of the corps de ballet no longer should stand idly as a background for the soloists, but form an integral part of the action. Finally, the mise en scène, costumes, scenery and music must be coherently conceived with the danced action.

Whatever threatens the world in the way of economic disaster, we need what Michel Fokine alone can give us in the science of dancing. He was once the victim of an historical accident. He was once, and is becoming again, an historical necessity.

Working with Stravinsky

The first company formed by Balanchine and Kirstein, the American Ballet, made its professional debut in the spring of 1935. After a projected cross-country tour was canceled, the young company thought it had been saved from extinction by an invitation from the Metropolitan Opera to become the resident ballet troupe.

This alliance, although uneasy from the start, provided three years of salary for Balanchine's dancers, but, perhaps to the relief of all, a contract for the 1938-39 season was not offered.

During the ballet's years in residence, Balanchine had not enjoyed the restrictions inherent in choreographing for opera, and he and Kirstein found the Met's attitude toward independent ballet inhospitable. (Scattered performances of Serenade, Reminiscence, *and* The Bat, *on programs with short operas, were about all that was allowed.)*

The chief creative efforts of Balanchine during his tenure were his mounting of Gluck's Orpheus *in 1936 (with decors by Pavel Tchelitchew), and the Stravinsky Festival in 1937—two evenings of* Apollon Musagète, Le Baiser de la Fée, *and* The Card Party—*with the composer conducting. The music for* The Card Party *was commissioned by Edward Warburg in 1936 on behalf of the American Ballet (the first Stravinsky commission from a Kirstein-Balanchine company); the two other scores had already been written.*

The Stravinsky-Balanchine collaboration had been and would continue to be both

◊ Reprinted from *Modern Music* 14:3 (March/April 1937), 143-146.

profound and productive. Balanchine has created more than thirty works to Stravinsky's music, including the acknowledged masterpieces Apollo, Orpheus, Agon, Movements for Piano and Orchestra, Violin Concerto, Symphony in Three Movements, Divertimento from "Le Baiser de la Fée," *and* Duo Concertant.

In 1972, the New York City Ballet produced a second Stravinsky Festival, somewhat more elaborate than the first (twenty-two new works by various choreographers in eight days), and in 1982, the Company mounted a Stravinsky Centennial Celebration (ten new works in nine days).

Recent publication of Stravinsky correspondence reveals that, for the New York City Ballet, Stravinsky was something more than Balanchine's most congenial living collaborator; in 1951, on the subject of a ballet to complement Apollo *and* Orpheus *(which eventually turned out to be* Agon*), Kirstein wrote: "Balanchine, Robbins and myself consider you our father and our future."*

The letters also provide a rare documentation of a specific contribution by Kirstein to the creation of a ballet (his work is mostly behind the scenes and remains unknown to the general public, sometimes even to the participants). It appears that the references to seventeenth-century court dances in the score of Agon *derive from a suggestion of his. (The title of the ballet came from Stravinsky.)*

N.R.

WHEN WE DECIDED to ask Stravinsky to write for the American Ballet* there was no question of providing the composer with even the suggestion of a subject. And, as a matter of fact, we were ignorant of his choice for six months after the contract was signed.

He had, some time before, already commenced work upon an idea of his own. Since Ida Rubinstein's commissions for *Le Baiser de la Fée* in 1928 and *Perséphone* in 1933 he had written no ballets. Another company had more recently made offers for a new work; his *Firebird, Petrouchka* and *Les Noces* were already in their repertory. But Stravinsky objected to the meagre orchestral presentation that a traveling company could afford him, and he wanted more favorable treatment for the new work.

The orchestration and piano score of *Jeu de Cartes* (The Card Party, Ballet in Three Deals) were finished simultaneously in November, 1936, and we received the score on December second. The title page also credits M. Malaieff, a friend of Stravinsky's painter son, Theodore, with aid in contriving the action. The scene is a card table at a gaming house, and the dancers are members of the pack. The choreography must closely follow

---

*In June 1936 Stravinsky received a commission from Edward Warburg, director and co-founder with Mr. Kirstein of the American Ballet.

indications of composer and librettist because the action, in numbered paragraphs, refers to equivalents in the score itself.

Three deals of straight poker are demonstrated, played literally according to Hoyle. Sudden apparitions of the Joker, to whom these rules do not apply, destroy the logical suits of the three hands. At the end of each deal giant fingers of otherwise invisible croupiers remove the rejected cards.

The musical opening of each deal is a short processional (march, polonaise or valse) which introduces the shuffling of the pack. For the card play—deals, passes, bets—there are group dances, solo variations, and finales according to the familiar usage of classic ballet.

The music is dry, brilliant, melodic and extremely complex in its rhythmic pattern, a synthesis of purely creative yet evocative passages, balanced by fragments definitely reminiscent of Rossini, Delibes, Johann Strauss, Pugni, Ravel, Stravinsky's *Capriccio,* and jazz in general. The score is so compact, so various, and so willful that either the choreography must be its exact parallel in quality or else it had better be presented as a concert piece, in which form it will of course, like all Stravinsky's music, be heard sooner or later.

Stravinsky, it seems, expended his utmost care on the skeletal choreographic plan and on his music. George Balanchine brought all his theatrical information and the resources of his knowledge of the classic dance into designing the dances, which were about half done when Stravinsky first saw them. (Stravinsky and Balanchine had worked together on previous occasions. In 1924 Balanchine, fresh from Russia, presented *Le Rossignol* as a ballet, and in 1928 he created the Diaghilev premiere of *Apollon Musagète.*)

When Stravinsky saw the first two deals of *Jeu de Cartes,* he expressed an enthusiasm, an interest and a criticism which was as courtly as it was terrifying. The ballet, as with so many Russians, is deep in his blood. It is not only a question of childhood memories of interminable performances at the Maryinsky Theatre, or of the famous works he has himself composed or seen. Stravinsky completely understands the vocabulary of classic dancing. He has more than the capacity to criticize individual choreographic fragments, doubled *fouettés* here, a series of *brisés* accelerated or retarded, or points of style as in the elimination of pirouettes from a ballet which is primarily non-plastic but one-dimensional and card-like. His is the profound stage instinct of an "amateur" of the dance, the "amateur" whose attitude is so professional that it seems merely an accident that he is himself not a dancer.

The creation of *Jeu de Cartes* was a complete collaboration. Stravinsky would appear punctually at rehearsals and stay on for six hours. In the evenings he would take the pianist home with him and work further on the tempi. He always came meticulously apparelled in suede shoes, marvelous checked suits, beautiful ties—the small but perfect dandy, an elegant Parisian version of London tailoring. During successive run-throughs of the ballet he would slap his knee like a metronome for the dancers, then suddenly interrupt everything, rise and, gesticulating rapidly to emphasize his points, suggest a change. This was never offered tentatively but with the considered authority of complete information.

Thus at the end of the first deal, where Balanchine had worked out a display of the dancers in a fan-like pattern to simulate cards held in the hand, Stravinsky decided there was too great a prodigality of choreographic invention. Instead of so much variety in the pictures he preferred a repetition of the most effective groupings.

It is not that he is tyrannical or capricious. But when he writes dance music he literally sees its ultimate visual realization, and when his score is to be achieved in action he is in a position to instruct the choreographer not by suggesting a general atmosphere but with a detailed and exactly plotted plan. For all questions of interpretation within his indicated limits of personal style or private preference, he has a respectful generosity. He is helpful in a wholly practical sense. For example, realizing that when he conducts the performances he may have a tendency to accelerate the indicated metronomic tempi, he ordered the accompanist to play faster than heretofore for rehearsal, to take up a possible slack when the ballet is danced on the stage itself. On another occasion he composed some additional music to allow for a further development in the choreography.

As with the music and dancing, so with the costumes and scenery. Before his arrival we had been attracted by the idea of using a set of medieval playing cards and adapting them in all their subtle color and odd fancy to the stage. Forty costumes and the complete scenery were designed before he arrived in America. Upon seeing the sketches Stravinsky insisted they would place the work in a definite period and evoke a decorative quality not present in his music. He called for the banal colors of a deck of ordinary cards, forms and details so simple as to be immediately recognizable. Stravinsky's precise delimitation gave Irene Sharaff, the designer, a new orientation, and strangely enough a new freedom for clarity and originality.

Stravinsky has about him the slightly disconcerting concentration of a research professor or a newspaper editor, the serious preoccupation of a man who has so many inter-related activities to keep str ₃ht and in smooth running order that he finds it necessary to employ a laconic, if fatherly and final politeness. The effect is all the more odd coming from a man who is at once so small in stature, and who, at least from his photographs, appears not to have changed a bit in twenty-five years. When he speaks it seems to be the paternal mouthpiece of a permanent organization or institution rather than a creative individual.

We had difficulties of course in choosing from all his repertory two other ballets to complete the evening on which *Jeu de Cartes* will receive its premiere. A possible re-studying of *Petrouchka*, *Firebird* or the *Sacre* was rejected because of present or imminent productions by other companies. *Pulcinella* was obviously too close in spirit to the *Card Party.* But at length *Apollon* was selected, because both Balanchine and Stravinsky wished to present it in the choreography of its Paris presentation. In his *Chroniques de Ma Vie*, Stravinsky wrote that Balanchine "had arranged the dances exactly as I had wished—that is to say, in accordance with the classical school. From that point of view it was a complete success, and it was the first attempt to revive academic dancing in a work actually composed for the purpose."

The third ballet, *Le Baiser de la Fée,* first produced in 1928 for Ida Rubinstein by Nijinska, has never been seen in North America. At a single hearing in concert or on a piano it may seem thin and unrewarding. But as music for the traditional theatrical dance it is both graceful and original. It is less a salad of Tchaikovsky quotations, as is frequently assumed, than a projection of the method which Tchaikovsky created, of framing the classic dance as ritual drama. It is less a recapturing of the epoch of *Giselle* than it is another facet of the creative attitude of Stravinsky.

Stravinsky is a composer who meets each problem within the tradition of the theatre, a tradition which he has helped to create, in which he resides, and onto which he continually builds.

Prejudice Purely

Although at times it seemed he hated everybody, Kirstein's two especial "bête-noires"
during the 'thirties and early 'forties were "Russian Ballet"—embodied in the Ballet
Russe de Monte Carlo (and later, in the Original Ballet Russe)—and American modern
dance—in particular, the work of Martha Graham. One was too theatrical, the other not
theatrical enough; one represented a dreamland, the other a gritty reality; one was swathed
in the glamour of another era, now tawdry; the other considered it a virtue to have no
glamour at all. Both, he found, in their separate ways, glorified the performer over the
dance itself.

    Kirstein's many excoriations of the "Russian Ballet" were perhaps understandable.
In addition to their promoting (and prolonging) a retardataire aesthetic that he honestly
opposed, he must have been jealous in the face of their expensive Hurok management,
which included resounding P.R. campaigns that attracted society and money. Kirstein
was struggling to keep his own company (later, companies) alive; when the "Russians"
(most of whom were not Russian at all) came to town, they appeared at the best theaters
and got all the reviews. And, beginning in 1940, the Ballet Russe performed some of the
*same repertory—*Le Baiser de la Fée, Poker Game [The Card Party], *and*
Serenade—*to excellent notices as had Kirstein's American Ballet some years earlier to*
very little notice at all. The American Ballet's unpleasant experiences at the Met, which
left the company without employment, did not help.

    In any event, by the 'sixties, "Russian Ballet" had died a slow death of natural

◇ Reprinted from *The New Republic* 78 (No. 1010, April 11, 1934), 243-244.

causes, its over-dressed, nostalgic, and simple-minded spectacles having fallen out of favor with audiences, its escapism and exaggerated showmanship no longer valid theatrical attributes.

Kirstein's feelings about Graham were more complex. Although he may never have acquired a taste for her personal brand of expression, he surely must have realized that he, as director of the American Ballet, and, more particularly, of Ballet Caravan, his touring chamber company with a repertory of vernacular subjects, was fighting the same battle as Graham, in a different way: against the elaborate and outmoded conceits of the Russians, in favor of a new manner of dance expression, rooted in America. Ballet Caravan and Martha Graham shared the same manager, the peppery Frances Hawkins; Ballet Caravan made its debut at the citadel of modern dance, Bennington College (Graham was a member of the opening-night audience). Kirstein was clearly fascinated by her, although he does not say so: he encouraged Muriel Stuart, one of the instructors at his school, to study with Graham to see what she was up to; one School of American ballet bulletin even announces that Graham will teach there, although it is doubtful that she did so (Stuart gave modern classes there, however).

Clearly impressed with her integrity, if not with her idiom, Kirstein tried hard to appreciate Graham in such articles as "Martha Graham at Bennington" and the chapter he wrote for Merle Armitage's monograph of 1937. But he never really made peace with her. As for the rest of modern dance, for Kirstein it was almost unworthy of discussion in print.

N.R.

CRITICISM OF DANCING IN AMERICA is in that fortunate young condition when there are as yet few dance critics, and no formulated standards of praise or blame but personal preference. Hence, without risking any abstract definitions between the difference in dance, gesture or motion, the following remarks on Miss Martha Graham as an artist are governed by purest of personal prejudice.

When one pays for a ticket to a theatre in order to see performed in front of footlights, framed in a proscenium, a recital of dancing, it seems fair to assume that one expects to see theatrical dancing. There are many other kinds of dancing, to be sure: folk-dancing, for example, which is not to be seen but to be done; or ritual or religious dancing, which is to be experienced in a more than spectacular sense. Theatrical dancing involves certain limits that give rise to necessary conventionalities or artificialities. The audience must be thought of, sitting with their eyes uptilted to the line which, in high-relief, is the dancer's plane or sphere of action. When such a dancer as Shankar dances adaptations of East Indian ritual or folk dances, in the West, he theatricalizes them in order to save their impact across the footlights. Escudero's second and equivocally successful season was caused by his excessive purity of genre, his monotony of spectacle.

The elements of theatrical dancing are surprise, glamor, brilliance and consistency within its chosen medium.

Every so often there comes on to the dancer's scene a personality sufficiently arresting to dispense with the ordinary canons of theatricalism, who can hold audiences by the specific weight of her inherent magnetism. These persons need no tradition. They are usually messianic and original. As usual, their "school" or "system" cannot survive the mortality of its creator. Such a dancer was Isadora Duncan, and such another is Martha Graham.

Miss Graham is not a theatrical dancer. Her admirers proudly assert she is more than merely that. If so, what is she? Or more blankly, what does she wish to convey? Is it movement, abstractly considered as being sufficiently beautiful in her own variety and ingenious composition? Miss Graham realizes that motion is not enough alone. Is it movement and gesture? Gesture must relate to a succession of basic ideas, of indications. What, to be short, is Miss Graham's subject matter? Her subject matter, as is the case with all originals, who are neither innovators nor traditionalists, is herself. It is by association also perhaps vaguely, herself as a particular sort of woman. It is the Pioneer Woman which an Oklahoma millionaire vainly tried to formulate in a competition of American sculptors. It is the wood-cut woman of a Lynd Ward vignette for Whitman. It is stark, earth-riven, gaunt, inward-eyed woman. It is not feminine, since it has neither amplitude nor richness. Although she has used a few men in her performances, it is impossible to imagine many doing her dances. Her girls, cleanly trained, are disguised, as nearly as possible, to look like Martha Graham, same grave mask, long hair, eyes focused inside their heads. She dances; one searches in vain for a better word, and they follow, in an invented vocabulary of gesture, abrupt, monotonous, repetitious as her music, which is of linear simplicity, an amelodic continuum of cumulative hypnosis. Her jumps are jolts; her walk, limps and staggers; her runs, heavy, blind impulsive gallops; her bends, sways. Her idiom of motion has little of the aerial in it, but there's a lot of rolling on the floor. In her group dances there is achieved a rudimentary polyphony, a see-saw of asymmetrical counterpoint.

Miss Graham scorns make-up. One is never for a second allowed to forget this is Martha Graham. Those girls are Martha Graham's group. Her long pale mask, her deep eyes, her expression half between pain and foetal blindness, has the ambiguous, frightened humor of an idiot's games. This ambiguity is chronic. In her last concert, for example, she so failed theatrically that an ironic dance was seen to be humorous only after it was over. Then the audience, not to be caught off their guard a second time, laughed all through the rest of the program, regardless. Yet when during her number, and it is nearly always the same number no matter what the program calls it, in which a boy's unsteady voice spelled out *bee are ee ay dee,* no one laughed, nor was this curious lapse of awareness even mentioned in the criticisms of her recital. It was as if a priestess had belched. The congregation more than forgave her: they did not hear.

Miss Graham's fanatic audience is always cited as the chief bulwark of her popularity. It is surely fervent and vocally loyal. Mr. John Martin has made excellent use of a word, *metakinesis,* which has an emphatic connection. Thus, one can become sympathetically exhausted after watching Miss Graham work. However, there are other considerations to be made about a *metakinetic* audience, too problematical for good manners. Even a dancer cannot be held responsible for her admirers. This audience is solid and limited, sufficient to fill a theatre the three or four times a year she appears. Does this constitute a following? This audience is static. Miss Graham's position does not shift from year to year. She neither influences the traditional forms of theatrical dancing, nor does she affect fashion in women's clothes, nor does she represent any older civilization to America, or America to Europe, as did another semi-priestess, Isadora Duncan.

Of Miss Graham's sincerity there can be no doubt. Of her personal modesty and hard work there is not one gain-saying voice. Yet where is the faith of which she is a prophet? Till now, there is none obvious except in herself, neither an expression nor an interpretation except of her own subjective limits, and a demonstration of the limits of those girls who have submitted themselves to her.

What issue is there from Graham? Has she affected the history of gesture, even as little as Dalcroze, Laban or Wigman? Can it be utilized to make masses of people enjoy dancing again themselves? One doubts if such a visceral, deliberate, subhuman and spasmic grammar can have any future except in its own silence. For, whence springs its impulse: What is its reason? In Isadora ebullience was its own reward. There was a difference when she came on the stage. She was not a mimic, but her characterizations of qualities and tensions were greater than the body she inhabited. Even with the Tri-color around her, it was more Rude's Amazon than a California girl singing the "Marseillaise." Miss Graham has been in Mexico, though it is not surprising that the Indians had little enough to offer. She is credited with knowing enough of the regimen of ballet to have consigned it to the hell of the orthodox. Yet when will she ever be as impressive as in the Chosen Maiden's dance in Massine's partition of *The Rite of Spring,* where he remembered what he could of Nijinsky, and how Nijinsky, instead of abandoning ballet, literally threw it over? It tossed like a coin, with the other face up, as sterling on one side as on the other.

Ultimately speaking, Martha Graham is another American "group dancer." Her superior concentration allows her to command a larger "group audience." Has it grown? Will it grow? Can her dancing be applied to others who are impervious to her personal appeal? Has any mode of dancing attached to a single name lasted longer than its inventor's theatrical life?

Stardom: Slav and Native

THE IMMINENCE OF WAR in the world has exerted its inevitable and universal effect already, even on the dance. More than one prognosticator pointed out that the Big Apple of 1938 is just a streamlined parallel of the tango of 1914.

In 1914 the Russian Ballet, again in London, on July 25 celebrated the one-hundredth performance in a gala at Drury Lane. *Le Coq d'Or* received its debut and Leonide Massine appeared for the first time in western Europe as Joseph in *Josephslegende,* the music by Richard Strauss, the book by Count Kessler and von Hoffmansthal. Bakst's high-heeled pattens for Madame Potiphar à la Veronese are now on sale again all along upper Fifth Avenue.

Now in 1938, Massine is in Monte Carlo for his twentieth spring season, rehearsing the *Seventh Symphony* of Beethoven and preparing *Tristan Fou,* idea and decor by Salvador Dali and Harpo Marx, music by Richard Wagner and Cole Porter.

Massine, with great indignant fanfare, split from de Basil, for whom he had been ballet-master for the last five years, and with heavy American backing founded a troupe of his own. The wily Colonel, however, very much a dictator of our epoch, has effected a combination of the secession forces after Massine's departure, and next October we will see them together again, producing very much the same as over the last five years.

The reunion was enforced by backers of both sides for excellent reasons

◊ Reprinted from *Dance Magazine* 4:3 (June 1938), 14-15.

of economy, centralized control and fear of competition. Thus the channels of traditional theatrical dance arrange themselves in their blind dynastic functioning, as they always have in the past.

What is the next step? There are three.

1938-39: The Slavo-International company headed by its already well-publicized stars will make another tour in America, including a corps de ballet, partly recruited from the Paris White-Russian schools, partly from America and England.

1939-40: The year after this, when the closing of international frontiers or the general disaster will have made free travel impossible, the Slavo-International company will still return to America, but with a difference. Only the stars will come back. The corps de ballet can be entirely recruited from the United States at far less cost. It will be a far better corps de ballet than previously.

1940 et seq.: The Slavo-International ballet will change its name to the all-American Ballet to coincide with the rising tide of nationalist sentiment which will then be sweeping us towards our age-old defense of our common-cultural heritage with England. Five of the Russian stars will be there, and all the rest of the personnel will be Americans, with a trifling exception. The impresario, director-general, ballet-masters, stage director, treasurer, and the control of the governing corporation will be, naturally, White Russian.

Colonel de Basil, at the debut of the choreographic-symphonic version of the *Star Spangled Banner* will accept an honorary Colonelcy in the United States Army. As we will be allies of Soviet Russia at that time, there will be a momentary embarrassment at the reception following the grand gala. The embarrassment, however, will be only momentary.

Why is it that any amount of American money can still be raised for two Russian companies and none for American ones? Because the chronological situation for an American ballet is not yet ripe. Mass audiences, while prepared for the dance by the tours of de Basil, are still under the blackmail of the Diaghilev formula: they still think that Russian Ballet is one word, and everything that can possibly be done by high-powered publicity enforces this blackmail.

They say there has not been enough time to develop the Americans. Maybe that is true. It took the French, Italians and Scandinavians about fifty years to do their job on the Russians some hundred years ago. Things happen quicker today and the Russians have been at us for about twenty now.

More seriously, they will tell you that while the Americans, or rather "you Americans" make excellent corps de ballet, what with your athletic figures and marvelous discipline (ah, the Rockettes), you have, alas, no stars, no artists with *the* (our) temperament.

44

The question of stars is a ticklish one. A star is a performing artist with possibilities for exploitation. They must have some basic talent which will be recognizable to the public as the personally embodied reason why they are getting their money's worth.

There are many kinds of stardom, but the Russians have enforced a stereotype of ballerina and first dancer which must be replaced before the Americans can believe in themselves. The Slav stereotype is suave, youthful yet wisely unreal, tinged with courtly nostalgia which somehow sets the dancers apart from their audience, like royalty. Their sex appeal is dark and anomalous. They are people from another time and place, and that they are here before us is in itself exotic.

It produces mystery, glamour and is theatrically sound. But it is by no means the only kind of stardom.

Take, for example, the American film stardom, not Garbo or Dietrich, but the home product like Carole Lombard or Gary Cooper.

The stereotype of Garbo is the parallel of the Slav pattern for ballet, the alien, unreal and wondrous angle. But the movies have also developed an American plan for theatrical frankness, freshness, vitality, roughness edged with tenderness, and a competence which does not mask, but which presents as effectively as possible, the careful naivete of the second-generation pioneer or frontier girl.

All our dance stars have something of this.

Fred Astaire is the apotheosis of the gallant amateur. He's not really a dancer at all, one might think. Just a nice young man, but where did he learn all those tricks? Ginger Rogers is a riot when she gets near a piano. Paul Draper just dropped in to do a little routine he tapped out after the last Toscanini broadcast. Patricia Bowman can only be thought of as "Patsy" and the kid sure can dance. Somebody found Buddy Ebsen and Hal Le Roy at a co-ed prom and they've been nice enough to come over and show us their stuff. Eleanor Powell does that number she did for the Campfire Girl's Jamboree—except the movie people have been "wonderful" about it. Ray Bolger, to be sure, *was* in vaudeville, but he's sort of crazy and he makes you feel it's like a party. Paul Haakon is so cheerful, so endlessly bouncing, manly and nice-looking that he seems like someone everyone already knows, or at least wish they knew.

The quality of the distinguished amateur become a finished professional is also a very theatrical asset, and the Americans can't be beat at it.

Why are the Americans all so frank and free, no side, no nonsense?

Because their training was not in the Imperial academies or in the Parisian imitations of them, but at dance school recitals, night clubs, vaudeville, musical shows and films.

Their dance floor was always nearer their audience than abroad. Gymnasium floors, normal school auditoriums, small polished hardwood hot-spot surfaces are different from the grandeur of proscenium frames, the big orchestras, flowers over the footlights and the security of prestige born of a long social and theatrical tradition.

The Russians and their American backers will accept those of our artists into their future troupe who most closely resemble themselves. Their repertory is pastiche and pastiches of good dancers will serve them well. They will be allowed to keep their names for the sake of the new all-American angle, but the style and attitude of their imitative dancers can be easily absorbed into the Slav formula.

As for the others, they will be told they have no possibilities for stardom. But that will be all right. By that time a generation of Americans, well-trained and interested, will have arisen.

These will not have seen the *original* Russian Ballet, the golden age of Nijinsky, Karsavina and Pavlova. They will have seen only the dilution, the vulgarization of it, and it will attract them less than it does us.

The Russian Ballet will seem to them like the "artistic" numbers in the old *Follies,* or in spectacles like *Mecca, Aphrodite* or *The Miracle.*

We always retain an affection for our glamorous vulgar enthusiasms of our salad days, and they are useful in showing us how not to do likewise.

Martha Graham

PERHAPS A SKILLFUL DRAUGHTSMAN could do it, or a painter. Someone with an evocative connection between their memory, their present eye, and a sharp hand that could put it down for someone else to see. Otherwise it is impossible to give another person any idea of the difference between what Martha Graham looked like to me when I first began to see her and what she seems to me now. I cannot assume that the change is entirely with me or entirely with her. But there is a very great change and I submit my analysis of it because I think it is not an uncommon experience for some of the people who have watched her for the last seven years.

Even then she seemed strong, so strong in fact that I could only with the greatest difficulty look at her at all. I saw her as a sort of rigid embodiment of a principle I did not wish to understand. I felt her as an arrogant and blind assertion of gesture and movement which were both repellent in themselves, and based on some substructure as capricious as it was sterile. What I considered to be her brand of stark hysteria antagonized my sympathy, and her exhaustingly arbitrary invention angered my eyes. I left her concerts, to which I could not but continue to go, irritated to the point of exasperation and physically worn out. I told this to one of her earliest and most powerful admirers. He nodded his head like a diagnostician, and said "Exactly," as if it was sure proof of some toxin working. I was suspicious of it just as I would be suspicious of some active and inexplica-

◊ Reprinted from *Martha Graham,* edited by Merle Armitage. Los Angeles: [the editor], 1937, pp. 23-33.

47

ble energy which was not an immediate personal threat but which might be the demonstration of some power I had best beware of since I could not be sure how it would next affect me. It worried me like a headache. Her wiry concentration, her awkward, jarring idiosyncrasies and stammering activity repelled me so strongly that I was continually drawn back to see her almost to exorcise myself of curiosity, or to lay the ghost of all the irritating questions which raised themselves when I watched her.

Why was all this so violent? I was very accustomed to dancing, and it had long been my first interest. Perhaps that was just the reason. I was brought up on the Russian Ballet, and I had an exclusive and obsessive passion for it. I had not seen enough dancing to know that not only were there other kinds of dancing, but that the Russian Ballet at that time was a dilute replica of an original intention, and that its later developments were decorative survivals depending on shocks from many extraneous sources other than dancing, to keep it alive. I had not seen the original Russian Ballet of 1909 to 1919. My first experience of it was the post-war period of 1923 when the School of Paris had displaced the original Russian collaborators, and when Diaghilev was in the full throes of the cubist revolution. It was all extremely theatrical, physically stimulating and violently opposed to the accepted exotic complacencies of *Schéhérazade, Cléopâtra,* or *Prince Igor.* It made no difference that the dancing was only a little less important than the music, and that the painters' portion—the dresses and the decor, were the real excuse for the whole show, which was, in essence, anti-theatrical and anti-choreographic.

So, when I first saw Graham, I mistook her attitude, confused her approach, and decided it was all very old-fashioned, provincial, unresourceful and ultimately uninteresting in comparison to the urbane sights and sounds, the perverse, acid disharmonies and nervous excitement then active in the disintegration of the classic tradition of the ballet. I went to Graham expecting to be shocked further than by the collaborations of Picasso, Cocteau and Massine. I was unequipped for her simplicity and self-blinded to her genuinely primitive expression. For me the primitive was the primitivistic, the Stravinsky of *Sacre* and *Noces,* with all their attendant resources of complex colour, historic reference and elaborate orchestration. The archaic was the archaistic of the *Afternoon of a Faun;* the contemporary was the chic of *Parade* or *Les Biches.* This solitary dancer, not even a girl, with her Spartan band of girls seeming to me to press themselves into replicas of the steel woman she was, appeared either naive or pretentious, which, I could never fully decide. But the force of the personality of the woman magnetized me continually.

It is the theatrical aspect of dancing that attracts me most, and it was her specifically conceived work for the theatre that first overcame my blanket resistance to her. After seeing the dances in Katherine Cornell's *Romeo and Juliet,* and after watching rehearsals for the living choral frieze in John Houseman's production of MacLeish's *Panic,* I felt I had a nucleus of comprehension, or at least satisfaction in her work which might, in time, absolve me from further hate. By that time my long love affair with the Russian Ballet had resolved itself in something less than an affectionate friendship, and my dissatisfaction with the heirs of Diaghilev opened my mind, of necessity, to other possibilities for dancing. Seeing Wigman as a soloist, and later as a composer, however, further momentarily confused me. Somehow I expected a corroboration of my original opinion of Graham in watching Wigman. What I actually felt was her enormous difference from the American, and chiefly that assertion of blind, vague, quasi-mystical self-expressionism which is the unfortunate universal heritage of the descent from Wagner. Yet my own acumen was insufficiently skilled to reconcile the difference between Graham and Wigman. Certain superficial similarities, such as the use of percussion, furthered a confusion already aggravated by an instinctive concept of their genuine opposition.

The rest of the history of my larger comprehension of Graham is too subjective to be of much interest and would involve autobiographical rationalization, half-truth and accident which is interesting only to the writer. To admit the element of a gradual revelation by unfrightened eyes would be nearer the truth and just as logical. Yet I cannot pretend that where once I thought was all blackness has become in a flash, all light. I believe that in Graham's work of five and six years ago there were still elements of her own unachieved revolt, unassimilated and inorganic, which coincided with those insecure and immature philosophies of Spenglerian decay and European snobbery with which I was then equipped and which colored my opinion of her art. The lack of necessity for a continuation of that particular energy imperative in an artist's first personal revolt brings a breadth and freedom impossible and even undesirable in earlier stages. The concentration demanded to cleanse inertia from any tradition or form is seldom attractive and often as repulsive as the dead growth for which it is the specific antidote. But this concentration remains nervous, and after it has won its fight can exert itself into a calmer and more expansive activity.

To write descriptions of dancing is even more aimless than to paint pictures of music. One can at least quote musical phrases or point to a handy phonograph. Most photographs are intrinsically as subjective and unsatisfactory as dance criticism, and the so-called "candid" camera is the greatest trickster of all. So far the films have given us no hint of the record for which we hope with some confidence. So to write about Martha Graham's dances would be only interesting if the writer was the equivalent of his subject. It is a pity that the public is so prone to take what they are given from the daily unequipped and undigested press, yet one cannot flatly decide there is no valid place for writing about dancing. One is much struck by reading William Butler Yeats' vindication of his drastic editing of Wilde's *Ballad of Reading Gaol:* He simply said his own position as a poet permitted it. This proud statement is irrefutable. We are interested in seeing Dunoyer de Segonzac's or even Bourdelle's drawings of Isadora Duncan, but who takes the trouble to read the "Appreciation" of even such genial critics as Huneker or H. T. Parker? They seem like the quaint testimonials of lovers. Even a great poet's opinion, like Gauthier's rhapsodies to Fanny Elssler or Taglioni only serve to cause a lifetime's vain work for scholars. What were they *really* like? The most one can do about Graham is to see her. The seeing is at once the supreme satisfaction and the principal praise. The quality so powerful in the visionary realm of space is dilute in speech and faint in print. When Ruth St. Denis or Shankar or Kreutzberg speak of Graham, one can listen with respect. What Isadora would think of her would be fascinating. That Toumanova admires her is interesting, and yet . . .

And yet one must say something, not exactly for the record, not even for one's children who are doomed to the same questions we share about the last generation, but rather as one leaves the theatre saying to people we don't even know—"Wasn't it wonderful?"

The dance and the dramatic stage are pre-eminently the fields of creative art in which women have equalled and can surpass men on their own terms. Three American women have meant more to contemporary dancing than any other three women of any nation, and one can almost say as much as any three other men. Ruth St. Denis showed a new conglomerate nation the dance idioms of all its component peoples in a form which they could credit with intensity and dignity, and she laid the foundation for an interest in the possibility of theatrical dancing on a continent which had suffered from the blasts of puritan hatred for a frank and fluent physicality. Isadora, by the large assertion of her personal vision, gave the idea, if not the form, of dance as an unassailable position for serious endeavor, in terms of an immediate necessity. Martha Graham, in developing a usable technique and a powerful presence, has employed not merely the exotic cultures of the world, nor the vision of a past perfection, but she has, on their foundation, erected a personal classicism and a contemporary expression suitable and equal to her place and time.

Graham's whole achievement is forcefully apparent over the last year. Her technical usages seem as well forged as the group of dancers who have been trained to demonstrate them. The story of her heroic struggle against all sorts of resentments and inertia is very fragmentarily echoed in such opposition as my own. As proof of her arrival, of that arrival free of the necessity to attack further the immediate sources from which she has sprung, and free to create works in the scope of a serene maturity, are two large facts, increasingly obvious. The first is the least important, but it has its interest. Graham is considered almost an academy by certain dancers and dance enthusiasts who, appreciating her present work, have forgotten the fifteen years of varied experiment, rejection and influence which have gone into smelting her ore into its present ingot. They forget the years of theatrical experience, the time with Denishawn, the investigation of Greece, Mexico, and our own Southwest, the French Gothic, the Far East, and every technical device or innovation available to a dancer. And so when Graham emerges with a new direction or even an accentuation, an extension of an old one, they sometimes accuse her of a change which seems to them a betrayal. They have decided what kind of movement they will expect from her, and if this tendency is not demonstrated as orthodox, she is declared her own first heretic. It was not the most comforting of cynics who said that he loved his friends but he adored his enemies. Every strong artist can resist the head-on attack of their convinced opponents, but the impatient solicitude and insinuating pressure of admirers is even harder to take, particularly when they personally identify one aspect only in the admired artist with the entirety of their admiration.

The other and far more important testimonial of Graham's immediate situation is the work she has presented in the last two years. The pieces for her group are longer, more varied and grow more as dramas danced than as fragmentary dramatic dances. She is the protagonist against a background of her group that is sometimes choral, and sometimes a group that collectively complements her as a balancing soloist. Her use of decor even when it is not completely successful, as with the "Mobiles" of Calder, or Noguchi's forms, shows her intention of presenting a synthesis refusing none of the responsibilities that the theatre offers. The two straight lines that point herself against the segment of the fence-rails in *Frontier* are at once cleanly suggestive and helpful to her dance, enlarging the perspective and at the same time centering her on the stage which is broad plains and a sector of the globe.

It is distressing and confusing to invoke nationalistic qualities as a preeminent value in an artist's essence today, particularly when every praise of nationalism seems an affront and a threat to a wider understanding of the peoples of the earth who are fighting to keep their integrity as human beings against the pressure of Fascism. But Martha Graham has a specifically American quality which cannot be ignored and which must be apparent to everyone. It is not a red, white and blue patriotic exuberance, nor even the naive free-blown boundlessly hopeful openness of the young continent which Europeans always professed to see in Isadora. America has become middle-aged, if not mature in the last twenty years. Graham's connection with our continent is less racial than essential and geographical. She has in *Frontier* much of the courage of Whitman's unachieved dream, but she has also a more realistic and present spirit. By now she has presupposed the ferocious, bland, hysterical puritanism of "Act of Piety" and "Act of Judgment" which Hawthorne would have so completely recognized. She has created a kind of candid, sweeping and wind-worn liberty for her individual expression at once beautiful and useful, like a piece of exquisitely realized Shaker furniture or homespun clothing.

Artists working today are not ignorant of the scope of times through which they live. There have been few occasions in modern history when, due to recent advances in communications and the scientific interpretation of history, artists have been so conscious of their position in relation to the large events smashing around them. But there are very few of these artists, however sincere, who either from lack of skill, talent or concentration, have been equal to the material with which their times provide them. When Martha Graham presented *Immediate Tragedy* she made a keystone masterpiece of the same powerful wave-length as the concatenation of energies operating throughout the world today. The news from Spain in daily cables alternately frightens and thrills us. The battle of Spain is *the* immediate tragedy of our lives, far more so than the Great War. In her dance we do not think of Graham as an exponent of the "modern" dance, or even of dancing at all. But only by the dance can such an intense, clear and sweeping vision be inscribed. In it she is an artist who can presuppose not only a technical mastery which is now as triumphantly universal as it was once aggressively personal, but she is also a conscious creator who has resolved the atmosphere of Spanish history from the Inquisition to Guernica, the temperature of violence and pride, that staggering human pride in which she has erased the means of her art to give us a positive declaration, a revelation of catastrophe and ultimate control.

Our Ballet and Our Audience

In 1936, to give his dancers summer employment—and to test a thesis about "American" ballet—Kirstein formed Ballet Caravan, a company of twelve. The idea was that a group of American dancers would perform new repertory based on American subject matter, with choreography, scores, and decors commissioned from American artists. Although not all of the repertory contained all of these elements (there were ballets to Mozart and Bach, for example), during the course of its existence the company produced several completely American ballets, notably Filling Station, Billy the Kid, and Yankee Clipper. (Kirstein wrote the librettos for these three works, and others.)

Ballet Caravan grew and made several transcontinental tours, becoming far more than a summer-circuit endeavor. But it was not an artistic success. The company was well intentioned but lacked theatrical glamour: after four years, it remained "small time." So Kirstein admitted defeat and abandoned the enterprise in 1940.

Despite the unblinking optimism expressed in such articles as "Our Ballet and Our Audience" and "Transcontinental Caravan," in which he pleaded for and defended the unadorned validity of American artists and subjects, in 1940 Kirstein wrote differently—of disappointment, failure, and blind belief: "It was the era of instruction rather than construction. . . . I cannot pretend there was a single invention comparable in finesse, sophistication or performance to the most slipshod and reworked 'novelty' in the popular Russian repertory. . . . I was depressed by the continual subservience of the sprouting American choreographers to European imaginative standards, and in my impatience tried

◊ Reprinted from *The American Dancer* 11:9 (July 1938), 22-23.

to shortcut the unforgiving slow spiral of growth. I had seen the late Diaghilev repertory in situ. Combining a certain forgivable chauvinism with an amateur's taste, . . . knowing all the questions, I thought I had all the answers. . . . I was so absorbed in the details that I overlooked any doubts as to the quality of the collaborations. While I could not soberly have believed it, I behaved as if to be native was enough. . . .

"At the end, even before the money gave out, I knew what was wrong, and even the dancers themselves scarcely believed in the venture. The general run of my company had a much more surgical eye than I had. They were more professional. They knew our company had only its own self-constructed repertory, without the prestige of a Spectre *or* Sylphides. *And to be just, one must admit that in their dancing school they had been taught their idiom via* Spectre, Sylphides *and* Lac des Cygnes. *. . . They knew the taste of the American public much better than I did in my naive, reckless and expensively hopeful testing. The experiments which didn't even partly succeed I carefully analyzed, to forgive all the mistakes involved. But the audience did not. It heard our toe shoes squeak over all the music our two excellent pianists could muster. It realized that twenty on stage is half a crowd. The audience had seen the Russian Ballet and had paid no more for it than for us. There was no question about the money's worth."*

While Ballet Caravan may have been an abortive effort in Kirstein's personal goal of forming a permanent and progressive company, Anatole Chujoy credits its tours across the country with stimulating the regional ballet movement.

N. R.

EVERY SO OFTEN somebody still asks whether or not the ballet is a genuinely popular form of the dance, whether or not American audiences are "ready" for it, whether or not it is an alien thing with only a snob appeal. As for the popularity of ballet as theatrical amusement, one has only to point to the five transcontinental tours of the de Basil troupe, and the existence of at least six resident American companies. America has always been "ready" for ballet. In a recent article in the *Musical Quarterly* on American theatrical dancing from 1750 to 1800, by M. H. Winter, we find a wealth of material indicating our early native interest in traditional dancing. This culminated in the tour of Elssler and other continental stars toward the middle of the nineteenth century, the ballets in *The Black Crook,* down to Pavlova; St. Denis, Duncan and our own day. It is difficult to see how ballet has merely a snob appeal. Certain critics habitually erect an imaginary audience of gray-haired dowagers in diamond dog-collars, who are escorted into the precincts of decadent ballet by witless, rich and senile dotards. It's rather a quaint picture and it is calculated to demonstrate the class appeal and moribund spirit of ballet today. The only place where one any longer finds diamond dog-collars is in the columns of Mr. John Martin of the *New York Times,* and his colleague, Mr. Lucius Beebe of the *Herald Tribune.*

In the last two years I [Ballet Caravan] have played some one hundred theatres along the Atlantic seaboard, from Maine to Florida, and only as far west as Pittsburgh. When one calls some of the houses theatres perhaps it is flattery. Our small company has danced on gymnasium floors with rosin partly obliterating the basket ball markings, in reconverted barns, in high-school and normal-school auditoriums, in big and little colleges, and in many large theatres. I cannot pretend that our receptions were unanimously favorable, or our performances a hundred per cent standard of perfection. In fact, the only reason this is of any interest is that in both cases they were about average, or a little better than average. This is important: There was nowhere in all those varying conditions and places that the audiences were not really interested. There was one hostile audience in a college in New Hampshire. The stage was so bad we sat the audience on it and performed on the floor. Theatrical glamor was reduced to a minimum, and the boys who'd just come in from football practice could almost have untied the girls' toe shoes. They came with that charming friendliness of bad children who pay their dime so they can hiss the villain. The atmosphere to say the least, was ominous, and yet, after a little while, as soon as they decided nothing was being put over on them, they were agreeable.

In many places we have played two and three times. Provincial audiences have an absolutely open mind. Indeed they come to the theatre wanting to like whatever they pay to see. They are more than half won before the curtain rises, assuming they can be got into the hall at all, and when they take to something, they have an affection for it which overlaps from season to season. Different ballets obviously please different localities, and as much as possible we try to arrange our repertory with this in mind. As time goes on, one senses a formula that will please an American audience. This has not been easy to do, as the issues are frequently clouded by the dominant presence of the Russian repertory. We Americans have, as yet, no native ballets as popular as *Sylphides* or *Petrouchka*. Due to the fact that the de Basil repertory was largely associated with Diaghilev and that Nijinsky or Karsavina or other renowned dancers created or danced in many of the roles, the audience sees a kind of double-exposure—the actual dancers, and their famous shadows. Even if the performances are not brilliant, they are backed up by the prestige of the last twenty years. Sooner or later our audiences will see the ballet without this false aura. It is useless and inefficient for an American company to try to imitate that Russian repertory which is already an imitation, or to attempt to compete with Russian dancers on their own ground. The best we can do is to find our own formula and plug it with our own dancers.

American audiences, as I have found them, like ballets with a given subject and a definite plot. Atmospheric ballets such as *Sylphides* or *Cimaro-*

siana, works with a purely musical theme, or an abstract suite of dances are interesting only when performed by a huge company or with the enlivening presence of some spectacular artist. Style or even technical prowess for its own sake is less attractive when it is not connected in some way with a literary meaning, however slight. People like to see not only what is happening, but they also like to recognize the characters of the action. They like to have the style of their movement corroborated from their own experience. Our two greatest successes have been Eugene Loring's *Yankee Clipper* and Lew Christensen's *Filling Station,* both story-ballets with native subjects.

Yankee Clipper was conceived at Ogunquit, Maine, in the early fall of 1936, with the rollers of the Atlantic dashing in all along the miles of beach. Loring worked hard for nearly a year gathering material from every conceivable source for the style of his gesture, from such widely dissimilar corners as newsreels, the movie of *Captains Courageous,* whaling museums, postcards and records of African native chants. All of the sources were available and comprehensible to our audiences long before they were welded into a ballet. Loring's success lay in his constant consciousness of his audience. It was not so much a matter of giving the public what they wanted, since frequently they don't know what they want. The problem was to give them something they would like when they saw it, and this Loring did.

It was a little different with *Filling Station.* We had been searching for a contemporary American theme for two years. Somehow the present doesn't seem to lend itself to the lyric form of ballet as easily as the past, partly because we're still under the moral blackmail of the nostalgia in Russian Ballet, although Diaghilev himself, particularly at the end of his life, frequently made works with contemporary social and satirical themes. Lew Christensen and Virgil Thomson, together with Paul Cadmus the painter, after considerable thought and observation, hit on an American theme of today and everyday, with a style set in the manner of the comic-sections of Sunday papers. This pervading atmospheric frame was already familiar to everyone as were the characters who came to inhabit it. The Filling-Station Assistant, the Truck Drivers, the Motorist's Family, the Country Club couple, the Gangster and the State Trooper were known from real life and from the realistic symbolism of the films. The addition of the idiom of classic dance gives the ground structure of daily experience a new excitement and a new grandeur.

There is no possibility at the present moment to make comparisons odious or otherwise between the big Russian troupes and the little American ones. But there are several curious sidelights which can be mentioned. The success of the Russians is logical, deserved and to be expected. But many audiences are starting to have an almost proprietary interest in our

American companies. They feel they have some real connection with American born and bred dancers who are creating a medium which, though developed abroad, as did the ancestry of all our arts, has, nevertheless, come to have more and more meaning for everyone who was raised on this continent. Audiences cannot look at the American companies at the present, expecting to find them replicas of the Russians. They must realize our own solution will resemble the Ballet Russe even less than the Russians resembled the French and Italians from whom they sprung. The creation of a really American ballet depends in a great part on our audiences who must have fresh eyes and open minds. They must look at American dancing the way they look at American films, not as an imitation of Soviet, French or English films, but as something in themselves. With the cooperation of our audiences we will be able to give our dancers an impetus and a security which will create the native stars we so much need.

Transcontinental Caravan

THIS IS A COMPILATION of some notes taken on a few performances of the first transcontinental tour of the Ballet Caravan which started in early October, 1938.

In previous years the Caravan had made tours along the Atlantic seaboard from Skowhegan, Maine, to Havana, Cuba, but only as far west as Pittsburgh. The present tour covers the entire United States. These notes are mostly restricted to the general subject of theatrical dancing, which, remembering the wonderful people and the marvelous places we saw, were perhaps the least interesting and instructive to us, although perhaps informative to others who intend similar trips. It started in:

Detroit, at 11 o'clock on a nice fall morning when everyone that could have been should have been outside in the country. However, the theatre designed as a huge Aztec temple in a skyscraper was full of ladies whose husbands, it was explained to us, refused to leave home in the evenings and hence would not go to the theatre. Hence the 11 A.M. curtain. It's no cinch to dance three ballets just after breakfast. The first performance of any tour is very hard sledding. Breughel's wonderful picture of a Flemish wedding dance at the Museum.

Fort Wayne. I talked about dancing in America over the radio. The man

◊ Reprinted from *Dance Magazine* 5:5; 6 (Feb.; March 1939), 14–15; 8, 38.

that questioned me (there was no script) was very clever in finding questions that were in themselves related to what his listeners already knew, so that it made my answers less odd to the many people who have not seen much dancing. As a professional person, he had respect for dancing as a profession. He inquired of its problems as if it were real estate or radio. Hence the conversation was really informative.

Chicago. The company enjoyed the hospitality of Berenice Holmes' studio where a lot of last-minute rehearsing made ready the world premiere of Aaron Copland's and Eugene Loring's *Billy the Kid.* We drove Miss Holmes out of her own dancing rooms, but I found her quite content in the back of the studio, modeling a clever small figure of a classic dancer. It had the essential accuracy only a good dancer could know how to render and it reminded me of Helen Wills Moody's tennis sketches. Ann Barzel chaperoned us all over and robbed her own splendid collection by giving me a very curious early parody libretto of *La Sylphide.*

Milwaukee. This is Eugene Loring's home town. I had wanted to do his two ballets, *Yankee Clipper* and *Billy the Kid* here. But the sponsors refused to permit *Billy;* they said it was not a fit subject for a ballet. I increasingly realize that what most American sponsoring committees think they want is a moderate-sized Russian ballet. If it's American it isn't ballet. After the performance, our success was indicated by the fact that we were requested to perform *Billy the Kid* next year. Ruth Page and her company, in from a tour, attended the performance. She complained about the use of Lew Christensen's hands in the Bach *Air and Variations.*

I bridled somewhat, considering him perfect, but Gisella Caccialanza silenced me.

She said, "You are quite right, Miss Page . . . Lew, watch out for your fingers."

She is Cecchetti's god-daughter.

Ripon. The students at the college here are all studying dietetics and decided in advance that dancers must be on some special regimen. They were horrified at the haphazard, if colossal, way in which we eat. Raymond Weamer, a pupil of Laurent Novikoff's, joined our company, which relaxes the pressure a little bit. Now, we try to have soloists only dance two ballets in an evening, and three in all.

Cheney. A two-day train trip across Dakota and Montana to Washington state. Marjorie Moore, with her usual wild ambition, tried to do barre work between the beds in the sleeper. Then she tried to get more space in the baggage car. This was not a success.

The Cheney performance had been worried over for months in advance. We arrived at 5:30, performed at 7:15 and had to catch the Seattle train at 9:30. They refused to hold the train, but the arrangements went like clockwork and we had time for a sandwich. Few people in an audience ever realize (why should they?) what happens before and after the curtain rises. But rushes such as this unquestionably affect a performance.

Seattle. If I had my way I would own Mrs. Cecilia Schultz's Moore Theatre. It is a perfect size for dancing, with a nice house and huge stage. Mrs. Schultz has wonderful ideas for the Northwest, and is an extremely courageous and independent woman. Mary Ann Wells gave a party for the company after the performance in a handsome studio overlooking the harbor.

Portland. This is the home of the brothers Christensen and Ruby Asquith. Harold Christensen and Ruby were interviewed on a street-corner over a radio hook-up.

The Christensen seniors are of Danish-Mormon stock and have been dance teachers and musicians in Utah and Oregon for generations. In them and in their pupils, Lew, Harold, Ruby and Natalie Lauterstein (an excellent teacher and dancer in their school), is combined the best traditions of the school of Auguste Bournonville and the lost days of big time American vaudeville. It is somehow suitable that the Danish-Americans should work up here in the North West. Like the Spaniards in California, there's something in the American weather which attracts its European apposites.

Martinez. We drove out from San Francisco to this very handsome auditorium across the big new bridge lit in the fog with golden sodium flares. I spent the morning in the de Young Museum with my college friend, Tom House, who works there. A marvelous collection of California civil dress and wedding clothes, wonderfully shown with excellent period rooms, so theatrical that they could be transported to the stage with scarcely a change.

San Jose. I spoke at the State Teachers' College and later Lew Christensen, Marie-Jeanne and Gisella Caccialanza gave a demonstration of classic ballet technique. The preponderance of lay training here is, of course, in the modern dance. But the questions were all very intelligent and sympathetic. Fred Danieli for the first time danced the chief role in William Dollar's Bach ballet. It is difficult and he looked well in the vast hall of the Civic Auditorium here.

Visalia. This place was not easy to get to. The performance was a Sunday matinee and due to the presence of the clergy and competition with their services, we were not allowed to do either *Filling Station* or *Billy the Kid.* Nevertheless, it was almost the smoothest and best-received performance so far.

San Francisco. I attended the dress rehearsal of Willam Christensen's ballets before they go on tour with their own company and with the San Francisco Opera, of which he is ballet master.

Bill is Lew's and Harold's brother, and toured with us for a while in the first year of the Caravan. He has some very strong dancers whom he brought down from Portland, notably a charming red-haired girl, Janet Reed, and a very tall boy, Chetwood, who has the basis for a fine classic technique. He will be the answer to all the good too-tall girl dancers who are so much trouble to find partners for.

I liked their *Romeo and Juliet,* which was compact. The duelling was much better worked out than in Lichine's *Francesca da Rimini.*

I saw a good class given by Nina Verchinina, and a charming academic number she had arranged for her small pupils. Our own performance was held in the big Opera House, the finest theatrical plant in which I have ever worked. Only on such a stage can perfect performances ever be expected. Tonight was as perfect as I ever hope to see, and for the first time I had a real sense of the security of a strong working organism capable of producing a spectacular success.

Fresno. Mrs. Dorothy Stetson, our combined manager, governess and confidante, was on hand as usual. In fact, she was needed because there was a certain inevitable let-down after the San Francisco effort. Todd Bolender hurt his leg quite badly in *Yankee Clipper,* but cheerfully continued dancing while I was alarmed to see tears of pain continually plow through his make-up.

Santa Ana. The pianos were on the stage here as there was no place for them in the pit, and for me this took the whole edge off the performance. Architects continually design large, handsome auditoriums without the slightest interest in the stage floor, the off-stage room, the pit, or any of the conveniences which make good performing possible.

San Diego. The company promptly disappeared to Tijuana. I spoke on the radio and at the college. Two very well-trained young boys came on the stage after the performance. We said they could join us the next time we came through. The Southern California material, as far as the bodies of their girls and boys go, is (like their divers and tennis players) the best possible.

Long Beach. We performed in a huge hall at the end of a pier. The roaring Pacific banged its breezes into the stage every time anyone opened a door.

Two students of Arnold Schönberg came to play a ballet intended for the Russian Ballet. It sounded like a Brasiliana, starting with *Sylphides* and ending with *Igor.* I asked them if they had never heard of jazz. They were crushed. They protested that even we used Ravel and Bach. I tried to explain indeed we did, but only if Bach and Ravel wrote it. Loring changed the death of *Billy the Kid.* Now Lew Christensen's revolver shot is a ricocheting series of double tours ending in a real shock.

Pasadena. Marie-Jeanne danced the Bach particularly well, which was fortunate, as Adolph Bolm, Stowitts and Oukrainsky were all in the audience. I lunched with Mr. Bolm. He protested that I had done less than justice to him in my *Blast at Ballet,* that he had always urged American dancers to keep their own names. He was extremely interesting about the difficult politics of ballets at the Hollywood Bowl and on the coast in general.

We also played El Centro and Occidental College at Eagle Rock, but I stayed in and around Los Angeles. I discussed with Merle Armitage, America's most intelligent impresario, the idea for an homage to Diaghilev, to be published next fall on the tenth anniversary of his death. Armitage was all through the 1916–17 American tour. His previous fine books show what he could do with such an anthology.

Los Angeles. (The Auditorium). This was of course our biggest excitement as far as audience went, so far. Isabel Morse Jones of the *Times* had been particularly kind in stimulating interest, as indeed had all the papers and radio stations. No one does publicity like they do here. Consequently the responsibility was considerable.

Then a lot of Hollywood people were here: Jesse Lasky, Jr., and his wife, who used to be at our school; Frank Tuttle, who sent us Nana Gollner, etc. I was too nervous to look at *Clipper,* the first ballet, partly because Armitage insisted on doing an all-American program, instead of opening as usual with a classic ballet. There was so much noise in the house that I walked from the stage into the front. I had never hoped for such a demonstration. I knew we couldn't be that good—but on the other hand, it was reassuring that so many people thought so. Lew Christensen's turns in *Filling Station* burned holes in the floor. Gisella was given an ovation in her role of the Rich Girl in *Filling Station* (she comes from here), and Marie-Jeanne and Loring in *Billy* were applauded past any decent pauses in the music. Much too excited to sleep, we took the bus at 12:30 A.M. for Phoenix, Arizona.

Phoenix. The floor here would have been a good surface for a skating rink. Mrs. Linde, our sympathetic manager, solemnly winked as some four cans of lye disappeared into buckets of hot water. We did not think of what the janitor would say tomorrow. As it was, Fred Danieli took a brilliant tailspin in *Filling Station,* but he covered it so well that we thought it might be a good addition.

When the curtain rose on our cactus desert for *Billy the Kid,* there was delighted applause. Michael Kidd's dashing riding on his imaginary horse also was yipped to the echo. A nice boy about fifteen years old came on the stage for an audition. He was so badly trained that it was heartbreaking, yet he had no other choice.

Miami (Arizona). A thrilling ride over the mountains in a bus whose driver handled it, as he said, like a kitten. Miami is a remote mining town, and we were the first ballet they had ever seen. I'd rather dance for a completely unprejudiced, even if ignorant, audience, than for the kind who feels outraged if there are no white tarlatans in sight.

Tucson. More cowboy country. The men seem to be disguised as dancers. We saw two ranch hands argue solemnly for five minutes before going in to see Gary Cooper in *The Cowboy and the Lady.* In the movie theatre the ushers were disguised as Gary Cooper who looked like the ranch hands and the whole thing took on the aspect of double exposure.

Las Cruces. This is the real *Billy the Kid* country. At Old Mesilla, Loring had his picture taken with the original Billy's manacles, rifle and pistols. Sheriff Pat Garrett (danced by Lew Christensen) often stayed with his prisoners at the Amador Hotel (where we also slept), on whose walls still hang a vigilante notice warning the real Billy to leave town or prepare for a "grand necktie" party.

El Paso. The company poured across the Mexican border into Juarez to see a bullfight. It was like Walt Disney's *Ferdinand.* Except the bulls were dry cows and the fighters were two middle-aged American ladies who twisted the poor beasts' tails till they rolled over.

We had one marvelous evening with the champion square-dance team of Texas, who showed us all they could make us learn—*Varsovienne,* military schottische, fancy galops, etc. Square dancing is enormously popular here and indeed never seems to have gone out of fashion. The men's clothes, cow boots, hats and neckerchiefs went very well with the girls, who wore either adaptations of old dresses, or else very chic modern ball dresses. They had a great deal of natural elegance and a peculiar charm of style enhanced by the monotonous drawling rhymed chant of the calls which directed the figures.

PART TWO

BY THE TIME the Ballet Caravan had reached Dallas, Texas, the performances had noticeably increased both in smoothness and intensity.

Even after a trying train ride I had almost ceased to worry about possible slip-ups. I knew that mishaps will happen, but probably out of an instinct for self-preservation I had stopped being nervous, and hence the nervousness of the company had decreased. I no longer feared to look at a performance. With a rather surgical eye I would watch ballet after ballet and make a more or less dispassionate diagnosis.

Dallas. As soon as I got to the hotel I found Mr. John Henry Rogers, an excellent theatrical critic and playwright, waiting to interview me. Mr. Rogers had perhaps justifiably been nettled by my continual insistence on 100% Americanism in the ballet.

I tried to show him that my program was not one of nationalist prejudice or blind chauvinism, but merely was a personal attitude I was attempting to demonstrate in the work of my own company.

Mr. Rogers told me much about the regional painters and showed me a delightful mural by Jerry Bywaters in his own house, which would make excellent dance decor.

I also lectured, or rather permitted myself to be subjugated to John Rosenfield's caustic questioning at the Hockaday School. Mr. Rosenfield, the well known Dallas music and dance critic, has done a great deal to stimulate interest in dance in Texas.

I had very much wanted to present *Billy the Kid* in Dallas, but due to the two recent big state celebrations in the vicinity, the sponsors felt they had had enough of Wild West pageantry. However, the next night at Denton, the Dallas newspapers sent over their critics to cover it and indeed many of the previous audience came again.

San Angelo. I had come here to lecture to a conference of women's club leaders before the Caravan arrived. There is a great deal of interest in dance here, and there are several schools. The girls all take ballet, but the boys limit themselves to tap and acrobatic, submitting to the usual prejudice that ballet is artistic and hence effeminate.

All the ranchers were particularly pleased with *Billy the Kid.* I had fears that they might have considered it pretentious of us, easterners, to show them bronco-busting and gun-play, but as a matter of fact they were quite pleased that we thought the Wild West a fitting subject for the classic dance.

Austin. The University of Texas has the biggest gymnasium I have ever seen. Two basketball games could be played on *the stage* alone, at the same time.

Some seven thousand students watched our performances and the applause rolled around in the rafters like detonating dynamite. I had a very interesting talk with Mr. Ransom of the Department of English about Texas folklore and the researches of Dr. Frank Dobie. A great wealth of source material can be found in the various published collections of play-party songs.

Fayetteville, Arkansas. A very long bus jump. The audience, west of the Ozarks, was very rowdy.

The football team streamed in around the middle of the Ravel *Promenade* (Dollar) and whistled cheerfully whenever a girl on the stage was touched by a boy. During the romantic waltz of Ruby Asquith and Erick Hawkins, they carried on so that it sounded like a Flash Gordon serial was being run instead of a ballet.

After the performance our patient but much harassed pianist, Pablo

Miguel, said, quoting Sarah Bernhardt's epitaph on one of her American tours:

"They still have Indians."

Tulsa, Oklahoma. I happened to run into Maurice de Vinna in the street. He roomed next to me in college and I had not seen him for nine years. He is, oddly enough, the dance critic here. He described Gisella Caccialanza's tipsy rumba in *Filling Station* as having a certain sodden grace which pleased him very much.

He took me to see a number of paintings by young men of the Osage nation who are responsible for a renaissance of American Indian pictorial art.

Edmond. An extremely friendly public. I have become a barometer of audience reaction. I can scent friendliness or apathy the first thirty seconds I am in the auditorium and from that I can usually determine what quality the evening's performance will have.

It's almost impossible to warm up a cold house, but on the other hand, the dancers take fire from a sympathetic opening burst of applause.

Emporia, Kansas. It seems like a long way from home. The performances themselves are a pleasure. But the intervening waiting around and traveling become increasingly irksome as Christmas draws near.

The company goes to the movies like they were taking to drugs to blot out boredom. Except that we seem to be on the same circuit as *Angels with Dirty Faces* and it has followed us around for two weeks.

Charleston, Illinois. A very handsome WPA-built state gymnasium with an excellent stage and equipment.

The performance was scheduled to start at 8:30 but at 6:30 there was a whole big family calmly sitting down with a picnic supper. They watched our barre work, limbering up and class, and explained that at the last concert (U. S. Government Marine Band) they had come too late to get in. Now they were taking no chances.

Yellow Springs, Ohio. Antioch College holds its attractions in an old opera house. The building looked as if it were about to go up in smoke.

The audience, however, was very fashionable and seemed delighted.

We had to get back to Dayton by a late bus to catch our train.

The green and red warning flares all along the great fields of the twin airports gave me an idea of what one day could be done with electricity on the stage, not for illumination, but to take the place of paint.

Kansas City. Here is the handsomest auditorium in America. Modern, beautifully designed, with superb equipment, everything seemed to be set for a perfect engagement. However, the floor of the stage had been soaked in creosote to preserve it against dry-rot and the oil continually oozed out to make a slick surface.

It took the edge off the Bach ballet, as everyone was afraid of falling.

There were no accidents, but we all felt let down in so much as they could not perform with the abandon that the rest of the theatre seemed to evoke.

Toronto. A very official audience with the Lieutenant Governor-General, etc. We felt the Canadians would have preferred some white tarlatans and Russian music.

Everyone was as polite and cold as the weather.

Rochester, New York. I was born here and had not been back in a long time. I had two fascinating evenings with the pianist Leopold Mannes, who temporarily interrupted his musical career to discover and perfect (with Leopold Godowsky, his fellow pianist) the Kodachrome process of color photography.

His work has gone so well that he goes back now to the concert stage. He has made some demonstration films of the Thelma Biracree Dancers for the Kodak exhibit at the two World's Fairs.

Dr. Howard Hanson, the director of the Eastman School, extravagantly complimented our pianists, Miguel and Miss Rittman, for their spectacular accompaniment and asked us to come back and dance to their symphony orchestra.

With which invitation the first half of the season's tour ended.

IT WAS a remarkable adventure for me. I learned not only that New York is not America but that Americans genuinely love good dancing if they are allowed to see it.

I realized that we were best received in places where either they had seen no dancing at all, or where they had seen everything. In those places, for example, where they had seen a little and where, as one manager told me, "we want to be transplanted into realms of fairyland," the reaction was occasionally cold and frequently negative.

Maybe we should have done a ballet with swans and Viennese waltzes. But I still doubt it. It only takes a little more time for all of America to recognize and love the quality of indigenous dancing to which it has given birth.

Martha Graham at Bennington

The most popular and durable ballet produced by Ballet Caravan was Eugene Loring's Billy the Kid, *with music by Aaron Copland, decor and costumes by Jared French, and libretto by Kirstein. The ballet was first seen on October 16, 1938, and is still in the repertories of American Ballet Theatre and several regional companies.*

In addition to such sources as The Life and Times of William Bonney, *illustrations of Frederic Remington, and such folk tunes as "Git Along, Little Dogie," "Old Chisholm Trail," and "Bury Me Not on the Lone Prairie," Kirstein has said that Graham's* American Document, *which he reviewed in "Martha Graham at Bennington," was influential in the creation of* Billy the Kid.

N.R.

ISADORA DUNCAN, Ruth St. Denis, and Martha Graham seem part of the same continuous line. Each of them by the dominance of a unique personality created an epoch in theatrical dancing apart from the classic academic tradition of the rest of the Western world. The work of each has used for a basic impulse, a structure of philosophic or moral concepts, which has served them better than collaboration with great musicians, painters, or poets. Isadora's Greece was a native expression of Californian pantheism at the expansive end of the last century. Ruth St. Denis's discovery of

◇ Reprinted from *The Nation* 147:10 (Sept. 3, 1938), 230–231.

the East reflected a search for absolute ideas of Oriental truth which Emerson shared and which Fenellosa furthered. Martha Graham finds the expression of her deeply American attitude in her own America. The subject matter of her *American Document,* as it immediately proclaims, is our time, our place, our dangers, and our chances of survival. It is the most important extended dance creation by a living American, and if there has been another in any other time more important, there is no record of it.

Bennington, Vermont, is a native American town in the sense that it fulfills perhaps a foreigner's idea of provincial America better than a Southern or Western city of its size would do. It has a New England meagerness, the constraint of sturdy independence, lacks any desire to imitate or presume to the estate of a larger city. The State Armory, which the Bennington School of the Dance has been permitted to appropriate for its fourth annual festival, is not a theater with a stage, and its own peculiar floor plan unquestionably gave a definite character to Miss Graham's choreography. In the excitement of the occasion, with interest divided among the programs of the various teachers and students, it may have been difficult to obtain a proper perspective of the importance of Graham's work as a theatrical fact. When it is presented in New York in the fall, it will be seen as an isolated achievement, as well as a vitally rich vein of dance form and material for future development.

American Document is conceived on the basic skeletal structure of a minstrel show. It opens and closes with a parade of participants, using gestures borrowed from minstrel strut and cake-walk. Its episodes are linked by drum rolls and fanfares of acrobatic movement. Its solo numbers are projected against a choral background. It utilized Ray Green's coherent musical score of a spare consistency. It employed a male voice as oracle, comment, and interlocutor declaiming statements from classic American papers. Its episodes commenced with an introductory duet, a preamble for a grave circus, a kind of annunciatory dominant chord of motion from which the rest of the symphony was to be amplified. There followed an Indians' lament for the spirit of the land they had lost, then a statement of Puritan fury and tenderness, an elegy of the emancipated Negro slaves, and a finale of contemporary self-accusation, a praise of our rights, and a challenge to our own powers to persist as democracy.

The whole piece was so nobly framed, so flawlessly executed, that every other work, new or old, offered at the Bennington Festival seemed by comparison puerile, unprofessional, or academic. Graham's work had the sober, frank sincerity of a Thanksgiving hymn heard in the open air. Its surface finish resembled some useful Shaker wood-turning. Its exalted plasticity of formal movement was as proud and objective as a New Bedford whaler's figurehead. The Puritan duet, with Graham in severe white, her partner naked except for white shorts and a dark coat of tan, had as antiphonal Jonathan Edwards's terrible words on fornication and damnation spoken against parallels from the Song of Songs. The tenseness of its emotion, the extreme projection of restrained physicality, rendered the adolescent elements in the audience uncomfortable. Its solemn purity was hard for the shy-eyed of all ages to take. It is so serious that it can only touch those who have the courage to look at it. Happily, most of the audience were too occupied in experiencing it to be frightened of its feeling.

In a short notice there is no space for the complete analysis this work demands. The use of the voice, the dominance of the ideas back of its creation, the quality of Graham's idiosyncratic gesture formulating just what she meant to say, were all miraculous. Graham in her Indian solo was a monument for which the vanishing American has waited three centuries, built from native folk gesture and ritual movement. In the end, in a plain bright red dress, with her dancing a balance of suavity and abruptness, her somber levity and steady stops, she seemed an incarnate question of everything we fear and hope for in our daily lives.

Her own dance group, clothed in simply cut clothes of clean transparent colors, made their first entrance like a troupe of erect peacocks driving a chariot. They were ably augmented by the group of lay and professional students from the Bennington School of the Dance. Miss Graham's partner was Erick Hawkins. His strong, solid, angry human dancing provided a splendid support, a positive male presence. Since he had ballet training, he was unacceptable to some of the "modern" dance purists, who were too prejudiced to look at him with clean eyes. Graham's use of a dancer trained in another classicism showed that elasticity which makes her unique in an experimental field. Hawkins, in the questions voiced at the end of the piece, stood and walked like a workman's best idea of himself as a dancer. Nor shall I forget for a long time the presence of the interlocutor, Housley Stevens, Jr., or his beautiful manly voice and arresting appearance, so open and yet so decently serious. He also moved like a dancer, and he spoke grave and alarming words with splendor, because he understood and meant them. Arch Lauterer's distinguished setting was memorably used. At the words "Declaration 1776," four doors at the back suddenly were flung wide open and four blue-clad dancers appeared like visual trumpets.

American Document should be presented in New York not as an ordinary Sunday-night "modern" dance concert but as a legitimate theatrical creation. It is dance-drama of the first importance, and is in itself ample justification for everything else the Bennington School may or may not have done in the last five years.

About *Billy the Kid*

IT IS NOT EASY to find efficient subjects from American sources which are suitable for presentation in the idiom of the classic traditional theatrical dance. It is made harder by the production of such popular ballets on American themes as Massine's *Union Pacific,* in which the building of a railroad was treated as if it were interior decoration for a Russian tearoom. It was rich, full of colorful characters, employed a large company on a big stage, and *represented* an "American" ballet. It *was,* as we know, just another Russian ballet, but it confused lots of people.

No American company can compete with the Russians on their own ground, and none wants to. But when the Russians shift their ground and dance on ours, we can lick them every time. Witness Catherine Littlefield's *Terminal,* Ruth Page's *Frankie and Johnnie,* and the Ballet Caravan's *Filling Station.* To me, in spite of the magnetism and pressure of the great White Russian supremacy, ours is the definite direction of ballet on this continent, and I feel, except for activity in the Soviet Union which is still an enigma for us, any creative activity the ballet may have in these inflammable years must continue to be on this continent.

Since the Russian Ballet is, in most people's minds, the standard of theatrical dancing, it might be illuminating to imagine how the Russians would have handled *Billy the Kid.* This is Eugene Loring's new character-ballet to Aaron Copland's score. It is about an American desperado

◊ Reprinted from *The Dance Observer* 5:8 (Oct. 1938), 116.

named William Bonney. Born in New York at the end of our Civil War, he went west with his mother, killed twenty-one men "not counting niggers and Mexicans" before he had lived twenty-one years, and was shot by his best friend, turned sheriff.

I bet the Russians would have seen Billy as a lonely, romantic, tragic little character framed in dances based on Spanish sources, as in *Le Tricorne*. The Mexicans, it is true, called him "El Chivato," and he is remembered as a fine dancer at ranch parties. The Russians would fill the stage with roaring gun-play, stage the pantomime in the false-naive hurry-up rhythms of a "Western" serial film. Billy's death would be the final curtain and one can imagine an ironic reprise of "Bury Me Not on the Lone Prairie," with Stravinskyian cadences.

Our approach was different. Billy the Kid is not the hero of this ballet, but rather are the times in which he lived. He was an heroic type, yet he was not unique. He was typical in so much as he reflected many others like him. He could not have existed except for his particular historical epoch. This was the peak of our expanding frontier, before the law came, and when your only security was in your trigger-finger. Billy represented the basic anarchy inherent in individualism in its most rampant form. The grandfather of the city gangster, he had certain talents which might have, at another time or place, made him a poet or a painter. As it was, this talent had only one outlet, murder. In this he was skillful as a surgeon, and as he became more accomplished in killing, his destiny was rendered the more inevitable, isolated and irrelevant.

Loring starts his ballet, not with Billy, but rather with the empty prairie, set with the bare silhouette of cactus columns. To a swelling march, the people who came across our plains move across our stage. Cowboys, a gold-prospector, women in work clothes, indicate a persistent, blocked recoiling yet forward movement. Billy as a child led by his mother makes his appearance in a street-scene. Pioneer women, girls from a dance hall, Mexicans, a sergeant from a U. S. army-post become involved in a knifing. By accident Billy's mother is killed and the boy stabs her murderer, starting his chain of slayings. This is all as an introduction.

The technical question of the killings in pantomime bothered us a lot. Gunshots, even the presence of property guns we ruled out. Billy's victims could not litter up the floor. Loring found a device which solved his problem. In the actual story, Billy had met a shady character known only as "Alias." We took Alias as a chameleon figure, a changeable snaky villain who although shot or stabbed, again and again always turned up like a bad penny to be killed again. Sheriff, false guide, card-sharp or jail-keeper, he represented the multiple victim of Billy's hair-springed anger, which in the end was only the death of him. Alias is always recognizable by his face, and his green reptile's coloration, though his costumes change with his character.

I doubt if the Russians would have thought of it in just this way. Maybe so, but even then they would not have conceived of the curious movements Loring invented for his action—movements which, while they are no replicas of *jarabe,* Virginia Reel or polka, use a grain of gesture which only someone who has been brought up here could have felt. The gunfight is not literal pantomime with guns pointed to blaze, but rather a conflict with separate bodies. The variation of the sheriff who changes from Billy's best friend to John Law is a pocket rodeo compacted into terms of classic technique. The lamentation over Billy dead, and the rejoicing over Billy buried recalls Remington's sober, accurate studies, not realistically but lyrically, and yet with an essential, local, specific accuracy.

The ballet ends not with Billy's personal finish, but with a new start across the continent, this time the march taken up a little more solidly by benefit of one more step achieved in the necessary ordering of the whole generation's procession. It's a flag-raising more than a funeral. Billy's lonely wild-fire energy is replaced by the group force of the many marchers.

No American could have composed a *Petrouchka.* Maybe *Billy the Kid* could never have existed except for *Petrouchka,* but we rather not think of it as an "American *Petrouchka.*" The comparison is unnecessary, as the older work is a great spectacle, as well as a drama, and the scale of *Billy* is, of necessity, small. The idea is big, however, and I feel the whole execution has been largely maintained. Aaron Copland's score uses real cowboys' songs as melodic material, but with an extraordinary finesse and tenderness. It is in no sense an *arrangement* of "Goodbye Old Paint" harmonized in counterpoint to "Red River Valley." His lonely, spare, sweet harmonies suggest the weather, the earth and space of western territory very actively. Jared French's clothes are realistic. There is not much exaggeration, as there is little exaggeration in Loring's gesture. But the clean blue and dusty red, the sage green and rocky browns show clothes cut for wearing in the saddle. They were clothes for use, and their splendor is in a dramatization of their utility, not in their incidental picturesqueness.

Anybody is convinced of the importance of a work with which he has been intimately associated. Maybe I overrationalize *Billy.* Yet I don't think so. It is a familiar story, but it becomes fabulous in the degree that Loring's dances are intense and evocative. To me it's not a decorative revival, a pastiche of the Wild West in stylized dumb-show. To me it is as bare and haunting as one of the ballads themselves, "The Streets of Laredo," for example, heard without any forced throatiness, not over the radio, perhaps even thinly sung, but in the open air. This melody is very sharp and it still touches us because it is a part of everything which we recognize as something that is responsible for us and to which we're always responsible.

The American Ballet in Brazil, Argentina, Chile, and the West Coast

In 1941, under the auspices of the State Department, and through the particular offices of Kirstein's friend Nelson Rockefeller, Co-Ordinator of Inter-American Affairs—who was criticized for spending money "on ballets, not bullets"—the American Ballet Caravan, a company combining the forces of Ballet Caravan and the American Ballet, embarked on a five-month "good-will" tour of South America. (Later, as Governor, Rockefeller would be extremely helpful in bringing the New York State Theater into being.) For the trip, Balanchine created two of his enduring masterpieces, Ballet Imperial and Concerto Barocco; Serenade, Errante, Apollo, The Bat, and Divertimento were among his other works seen by the South Americans. The choreography of Lew Christensen, William Dollar, Antony Tudor, and Eugene Loring was also represented. (Many of the works composed especially for presentation in South America were never seen elsewhere.)

In addition to his role as manager, Kirstein was to investigate and report on promising local artists; new decors for Apollo and Serenade were commissioned on the spot, as was the score for Fantasia Brasileira by Francisco Mignone, for which Balanchine provided choreography.

◊ Reprinted from The American Dancer 14:11; 12; 15:1; 2 (Sept.–Dec. 1941), 8–9, 19, 23; 12–13, 25, 29; 10–11, 31; 16–17, 30.

According to Kirstein and other participants, the tour was difficult (but exciting): wartime conditions caused shortages and particularly affected transportation. More than a month of the trip had to be cancelled for financial reasons.

Within a year, Kirstein would be back in South America, this time in the role of consultant on Latin-American art to the Museum of Modern Art (with which several of the Rockefellers were involved). Balanchine also returned to South America in 1942—to Buenos Aires—where he choreographed Concierto de Mozart, *created dances for the opera* Marouf, *and staged* Apollo. *With new decor by Pavel Tchelitchew, this* Apollo *is said to have been the most beautifully designed version in the long history of that ballet.*

Although no Balanchine-Kirstein company has been back to South America, the New York City Ballet has undertaken several tours sponsored by the State Department—to Europe (including Russia), Japan, and the Philippines.

N.R.

THE AMERICAN BALLET IN BRAZIL

PART I OF A TRAVEL DIARY

I FLEW DOWN to Rio. Three months afterwards it blurs into a vague memory of incessant buzzing, and increasing pressure of small needles attacking your eardrums. I recall a choir of ten very small black orphans singing spirituals for the benefit of their orphanage at the airport near Charleston, South Carolina. At Trinidad the windows of the Clipper were shuttered to prevent anyone observing military objectives. At San Juan, Puerto Rico, there was a big dance of very young society people. As I rose to catch the plane at four-thirty A.M., the dance was just concluding and the tired Latin American chaperones, one to every pair, in wilted evening dress were piling into sleepy taxis. The pilots were all extremely young and without a word of reassurance inspired us with a complete sense of confidence although we crossed hundreds of miles of only sea and jungle where landing was out of the question.

We first landed in the far north of Brazil at a town called Belem (Bethlehem), formerly known as Para. It has wonderfully faded plaster facades, soft pink and yellow, with a park full of band stands like gondolas dropped off eighteenth century balloons. The dining-room of the hotel was formerly the auditorium of a theatre. A marble plaque memorialized the fact that Anna Pavlova danced here on her last Brazilian tour in 1923.

Rio de Janeiro: I arrived a week ahead of our company and proceeded to try to educate myself not only in the difficult tongue of Latin-American official and professional behavior, but also of Portuguese. Portuguese is probably not in itself any harder than Russian, but since it seems to resemble other Latin tongues, one's confusion is all the greater on finding it is pronounced nothing at all as written, and the writing looks odd enough to us. Then, as all over South America, the question of bureaucracy is paramount. It is hard for an ordinary North American to realize the importance of official rank, of the connection between, for example, a Municipal function (The Theatre) and a Federal function (Customs). In one case, in order to bring in a box of blank discs for recording folk-music for dances, which, to be sure, was neither personal luggage, nor theatrical luggage, nor commercial property, as the Chief of Customs stubbornly but logically insisted, an order had to be procured via our helpful, long-suffering Embassy directed to the Brazilian Bureau for Press and Propaganda, though actually to the President of the Republic, who with a flourish of the pen released our small box of blank records. Otherwise we simply would never have received it.

The American Ballet travels, exclusive of 135 pieces of personal baggage, with 68 large trunks of theatrical effects. Filtering this through customs officials onto a fleet of trucks into a theatre is no cinch. I met our company on a tender put at my disposal by the Police Department of Rio, which maintains mysterious connections with the Teatro Municipal. On the boat I collided with Paul Draper who was down to welcome Heidi Vosseller, his bride-to-be. If I had not been on the police tender I doubt if we would be off the deck now. The police pushed us through.

We had almost a week of rehearsals in Rio. The dancing class maintained by the Prefect of the District of Rio who controls the Municipal Theatre is run by Mme. Maria Olneva, formerly with Anna Pavlova. She graciously suspended all her own classes, which were preparing for the opera season, and allowed Mr. Balanchine, our choreographic director, the use of her handsome studios. We also made great friends with Constantin Welchek, the able ballet-master of Saô Paolo's Municipal Opera, who sent magnificent flowers to all four premieres of our subscription series.

His Excellency T. Jefferson Caffery, the Ambassador of the United States of America to the United States of Brazil, asked us all to the Embassy for a party in honor of the sculptor Jo Davidson who had completed his bust of Getulio Vargas, the President of Brazil. Naturally, the Embassy, a beautiful open pavilion with marble floors at the end of a garden, was swarming with local Americans. Eddy Duchin and his orchestra, who had only flown down the day before to open at the Copacabana's Golden Room, had the local dance situation expertly in hand. Our own dancers justified for the first time all the overweight of their personal baggage by appearing in the latest New York summer magnificence, the smartest people at the party. One of the young secretaries of the Embassy, making polite conversation to my wife while trying to keep an eye out for important new arrivals, said he was sorry that none of our girls had been able to come. A dozen dancers were indicated to him. He had no idea they ever appeared out of tutus, off point, or spoke in a voice below a scream.

Our opening at the Municipal Theatre was the occasion also of the first real collaboration of the American Ballet with a South American artist. I had known the painter Candido Portinari from the New York World's Fair, where his big decorations at the Brazilian Pavilion had led to his one-man show at the Museum of Modern Art. Mr. Balanchine had given the original Lurçat costumes and scenery of his *Serenade* to the Monte Carlo Ballet. This was the first ballet composed for our company, the original American Ballet in 1934, while in it our first dancer, Marie-Jeanne, made her successful debut with the Monte Carlo in the fall of 1940 as guest artist.

Portinari was a great admirer of Balanchine's and made a number of sketches for the decor from which we selected a free interpretation of the sky over the Southern Hemisphere with the stars of the Southern Cross intertwined with two meteors. The drop, although simple, was extremely effective. The costumes were made in less than a week in the studios of the Teatro Municipal.

I still think I was right about the choice of our opening program, although using the music of Tchaikovsky for two ballets in one evening might easily seem monotonous. However, the Russian Ballet frequently gives *Swan Lake* and *Aurora's Wedding* in one evening. We opened with *Serenade* to the music of the *Serenade for Strings*. I cannot pretend our dancers were not nervous. Rio de Janeiro prides itself on its ancient musical culture. The Monte Carlo was here last season with its world-famous dancers. Nor can I say that the Portinari collaboration was a triumph. The public was not prepared for his quiet and, to our way of thinking, perfect solution of a rather simple problem. They would have preferred something violent and "modern"; upsetting. It was merely from their point of view, suitable, in "good taste."

Filling Station came in the middle. Virgil Thomson's music has been heard all over America, but in Rio, lacking a hot jazz trumpet and having only a timid percussion player, I was afraid for Lew Christensen's opening variation, brilliant as it was in the dancing. But the movies had already paved our way. The Motorist and his Wife, the State Trooper, the Rich Couple from the Country Club, and the Gangster were familiar as a comic strip. The public commenced to warm up. But it was still no triumph.

As I walked through the corridors of the theatre after the intermission, and *Filling Station* actually had gone over well enough, with its excellent new trick ending which Balanchine had suggested to Christensen, I had a sudden attack of fright. I kept away from our Ambassador's Box. I avoided the compliments of Madame Lourival Fontes, the beautiful wife of the Chief of Press and Propaganda. I felt our whole venture was a dismal flop. The six months of preparations, all the nerves, the worry were useless. Our company was simply not insistent enough to overcome the deep-rooted prejudice against them held, as far as artistic prestige goes, consciously or unconsciously by almost every educated South American.

Balanchine has composed in his short life I suppose at least fifty ballets for Diaghilev, for the Monte Carlo, for Copenhagen, for the Paris Opera, for his own company. He is a quick worker, but I think *Ballet Imperial* was done in less than a week. Set to the brilliant score of Tchaikovsky's almost unknown *Second Piano Concerto,* and amazingly performed by our young staff pianist, Simon Sadoff of Jersey City, this is Balanchine's tribute to the Maryinsky Theatre, to the indestructible tradition of Russian lyric art, which he himself saw survive one world war and revolution. *Ballet Imperial* is composed in the idiom of Petipa and Ivanov. There is no deformation of "modernism" in it. It is straight classical dancing for forty-five minutes. It employs a large corps de ballet and numerous soloists. It is set in Doboujinsky's splendid reconstruction of the epoch of Alexander the First. In the background, through the columns of the Admiralty is to be seen the spire of the fortress of Peter and Paul, in a cold winter dusk. The costumes are the court dress of Russia in 1825.

Ballet Imperial is not an American ballet. It is a Russian ballet danced by an American company. And yet it was perfect to cap the evening on our initial appearance in South America. For, first of all, it proved to a packed house of skeptics that Americans born and bred all over the Northern Continent from Boston to Los Angeles, and trained in New York in our own school, could really dance. This needed proving.

Then again its sumptuousness not only of color in costume and decor but of music, of choreographic invention and of personal execution was a satisfactory conclusion to what might have otherwise been a dubious debut. After Balanchine, to whom the success of our whole venture is due more than to any other one man, I felt grateful to Emanuel Balaban, our brilliant conductor, who tore the house down with Tchaikovsky's pyrotechnics.

Marie-Jeanne, our ballerina, danced incredibly well. Her nervousness had completely disappeared. She was wonderfully dressed with her hair very high, wearing a beautiful tiny imperial coronet of diamonds that Balanchine designed for her. She wore two large aquamarines given by a Brazilian admirer, and she really looked and danced like a princess. She received a heavy tribute of flowers, some in yellow and green, the Brazilian colors, and at the end a big red, white and blue bouquet from our own people.

The company deserved its eighteen curtain calls. The impresario of the theatre, who has a son in the Italian army and who does not love the democratic Americans, embraced me and said such success had not been known in his theatre since Caruso, or no, he corrected himself, smiling, since Pavlova. Anyway, it was what I had hoped for and I was glad to be able to cable home that we had been lucky so far. Why one consciously chooses to live through evenings of such agony will always remain a mystery, particularly to the people who suffer most from them. And our Ambassador was pleased. *Ballet Imperial* was his idea of a ballet.

The rest of the season had its ups and downs. I had gotten to know every critic in Rio and found them, although with two exceptions, music critics, exceptionally well informed. They all knew the books of John Martin, Haskell, André Levinson, and Henri Prunières. They knew much more about American music than I did about Brazilian, although they soon educated me. Reuben Navarra of *O Jornal* and Antonio Garcia de Miranda of *Los Diarios Associados* are two of the best dance critics I ever read. Together with Nicanor Miranda of *O Estado do Sao Paolo* they constitute an enviable and formidable critical battery.

We had two surprising successes in Rio. William Dollar's *Juke Box,* to the very hot swing-music of Alex Wilder *(It's so Peaceful in the Country)*, was not liked by anyone at our dress rehearsals in New York. In spite of the fact that we reiterated it was a dress rehearsal, the public we had invited judged it as a finished work, which was understandable but scarcely fair. To make matters worse, Lew Christensen, as the Football Hero, sprained his ankle on the morning of that dreadful dress rehearsal.

But in Rio, *Juke Box* was a triumph. The combination of jazz with classic ballet, although previously exploited by Balanchine in *I Married an Angel*, etc., and by Bill Dollar himself in his dances for Dwight Wiman's *Great Lady,* and in our show for the Ford Ballet in the 1940 World's Fair, was a complete novelty. The music, real jazz but scored for large symphonic band, sounded surprisingly well, and Tom Lee's sets and costumes were widely admired. (*Juke Box* was also extremely successful in Saô Paolo).

The other unforseen success was Balanchine's *Apollon Musagète.* This, one of Igor Stravinsky's most perfect scores, was originally commissioned by Mrs. Elizabeth Coolidge for the Library of Congress and there performed in 1927 with choreography by Adolph Bolm. Balanchine in the same year created it for Diaghilev, with Serge Lifar, and thereby achieved that ungrateful artist's reputation. In 1937, Balanchine set it anew for the American Ballet, Stravinsky conducting, at the Metropolitan Opera House in New York.

In Brazil we reset this ballet, as much as possible according to Stravinsky's wishes. He had, in his autobiography, expressed himself displeased with the original decor by Bauchant. We employed a young Brazilian stage decorator, Santa Rosa, who also made the superb chariot for us with four horses to carry Apollo off to heaven, but these were so heavy that after carting them all over South America we had to abandon them at the foot of the Andes due to their excess weight. Their wings wouldn't carry them even in a Pan-American plane.

Apollon Musagète is I think Balanchine's greatest contribution to the history of traditional choreography. Out of it a whole school of gesture has subsequently been developed, with hardly a nod of thanks to him. It was not successful in New York due to the nature of an occasion which regrettably emphasized the non-dance elements of the evening.

In Rio the success of *Apollon* was in direct proportion to all of our surprise at it. Maybe the name of Stravinsky had something to do with it. Certainly Lew Christensen's inspired rendition of a cruelly difficult technical role had a great deal. He was very nervous the first night. He could even barely let his newly acquired wife, our other ballerina Gisella Caccialanza, sew on his gilt leggings. But his turns exploded and his beats fairly crackled. The ovation at the end was something to live for. And the little pupils of the local dancing academy presented Balanchine with a wreath of bays, which he gave to Lew who didn't know what to do with it, while everyone took pictures.

We did a lot of things in Rio besides climb Corcovado, the Pao de Asucar, and watch Paul Draper dance his great farewell samba at the Golden Room of the Copacabana Casino. I called on Maestro Heitor Villa-Lobos, the monument of Brazilian music, to pay our respects. Balanchine, our conductor Balaban, and myself spent some time with the composer Francisco Mingone, from whom we ordered a ballet *Fantasia Brasileira*. (This was produced in Santiago de Chile, August 27, 1941.) We went to a secret meeting of an Escuela do Samba, a samba school, which the police had previously closed since there had been an outbreak of the *Macumba* ritual. We were given a magnificent party by Señor Costa do Ribiera and his enchanting wife on the feast of Saô Jôao, in the manner of Pernambuco, with a great log fire and Bahia cooking, a terrific samba band and everyone in Brazil whom we had expressed a desire to meet, including His Imperial Highness Dom Pedro, pretender to the Braganza throne of Brazil (see Bertita Harding's *Amazon Throne*). Dom Pedro, as far as I know, is the only pretender encouraged by the country to whose throne he pretends. He may not expect to be Emperor of Brazil, and he is a fervent Brazilian patriot, but he certainly takes himself engagingly seriously as the living personification of the Imperial Tradition. He reminded all of us of Charles Boyer in *Mayerling*. He looks like a Hapsburg, with the big chin, the soft blonde moustache, and the benevolent despotic eye.

Brazil is incredibly rich in folk sources of poetry and music, which are only beginning to be realized in North America. James Doyle and Preston

Corsa, our singers for Lew Christensen's Mexican Ballet *Pastorela* had been lent a recording apparatus by the Music Division of the Library of Congress. They recorded folk-songs and dances non-stop, only scratching the surface.

Our season in Rio was all too brief. But we had to get on to Saô Paolo for our scheduled performances there, and Louis Jouvet and his great troupe of French comedians were hard on our heels at the Teatro Municipal. Our last night in Rio was spent in a wonderful evening with Jouvet and Madeleine Ozeray, talking about Pavel Tchelitchew who had designed *Errante* for us and who had done *Ondine* for them. We were to see Jouvet and Madeleine weeks later in Buenos Aires in their perfect performance of Molière's *Ecole des Femmes*.

Saô Paolo was like Seattle, a bristling North American city as unlike Rio as one could imagine. The orchestra there was pretty confused by *Billy the Kid* to say nothing of *Juke Box,* or our Stravinsky.

In Saô Paolo, the American Vice Consul, John Hubner III proved himself to be a combination of Aladdin's lamp, Florence Nightingale, Thomas Cook and the ideal foreign office servant. I wanted to meet all the artists and composers in Saô Paolo in one day. Hubner gave lunch, cocktails, dinner and after-dinner for me, each with a different set of people. One of our girls was ill. He provided a diagnostician and three specialists. Worst of all we had no way to get to Buenos Aires; due to the war all ordinary boat schedules were disrupted. Hubner got hold of one friend, head of the State Railways, another friend had a private yacht, and a third would have chartered a flight of planes. Fortunately a boat suddenly appeared, but Hubner would have gotten us there if there had been nothing but pack mules.

We saw little of the real Brazil, the Brazil of the Amazon, of the big farms, of the North. But we did see enough to know how rich it is for any artist. We were invited by the municipalities of Saô Paolo and Rio to return in 1943 with the same dancers and a new repertory. We all of us wished we could have accepted with any degree of assurance we'd ever be back.

THE AMERICAN BALLET IN ARGENTINA

PART II OF A TRAVEL DIARY

WHEN WE THINK of South America in North America, we frequently just say Southamerica without much realizing that Brazil and Argentina, Peru and Ecuador are separate republics, not different states in the same country, each with a special climate and a particular accent. When the Ballet left Brazil after almost a month, we could pretty well decipher our notices in Portuguese. We could ask for the few necessary things to eat, and we could thank everybody very much.

In Buenos Aires we started to know the language that would serve us all the rest of the trip. We learned the technical Spanish terms for footlights, spots and floods, surprise-pinks and midnight-blues. Just about when we left we could carry on a conversation about something more absorbing than the weather. But many more people prefer to speak English rather than endure our Spanish and it was often hard to get much practice.

After our premiere in Rio, I tried to find out as much as possible about the Argentine audience. It's not much help to ask a Brazilian what the Buenos Aires public is like. Brazilians consider Rio a kind of superior Paris and Buenos Aires little better than an inferior Barcelona. However, it didn't take me overnight to discover that Buenos Aires is scarcely a city of barbarians.

We arrived at the airport on the night of their national holiday. The city seemed bigger than Chicago. The drive in from the field covered more built-up space than any other place I'd ever been. In the heart of the city, hundreds of public buildings were lavishly outlined with electric lights. The huge bulk of the Colon Theatre seemed on fire. The streets were wide and newly faced and all the traffic was going in the "wrong" direction.

I managed to meet as many people as quickly as I possibly could. I had been given letters by our Embassy in Rio, to Sr. Ignacio Pirovano who is both dictator of local café society and director of the important Museum of Decorative Art. His mother-in-law heads the Amigos del Arte, a gallery very much like our own Museum of Modern Art. I asked Pirovano how he thought we should arrange the repertory for our opening programs. His taste, like most of his friends, was predominately French; he had seen only a little North American art, and that little he didn't much like.

I had the pleasure of seeing Madame Victoria Ocampo who is perhaps the most distinguished literary figure in all South America. It is she who publishes the brilliant review *Sur,* has translated Virginia Woolf and André Gide, and who had just issued the first number of a new Free French magazine. She was particularly interested in the fact that we were performing Stravinsky's *Apollon Musagète.* Stravinsky was a great friend of hers. She had arranged the first performance of his *Perséphone* in South America, declaiming the poetry herself in her wonderful classic French diction. She showed me the manuscript score that Stravinsky had written out for her.

And I became good friends with Maria Rosa Oliver, who is certainly the best neighbor North American arts and letters have in South America. She was the first to translate O'Neill's plays into Spanish, and to see they were produced. She appropriates every one of our artists or writers as soon as they appear and sees that each one of us gets to know not only the great port of Buenos Aires but the Argentina of the plains and provinces which she loves so well. Maria Rosa had herself just published a splendid children's *Geographia* with fine colored illustrations by the painter, Horacio Butler. She started us off at once on our new Argentine ballet, with Butler and the gifted young composer, Alberto Ginastera, whose choral ballet *Panambi* is in the repertory of the Colon.

Maria Rosa Oliver told me that I was to listen to no one in Buenos Aires for advice on our repertory. We should feature our American ballets; she knew enough of what we had done to be certain these would be our biggest success. She said our classic ballets would carry themselves. She insisted we must feature our *difference* from any other ballet repertory.

She was entirely right, down to the last detail. In Buenos Aires we gave nineteen performances in twelve days. The biggest hits were Eugene Loring's *Billy the Kid*, William Dollar's *Juke Box*, and Lew Christensen's Mexican ballet, *Pastorela*. I had been rather worried about showing *Pastorela* in South America. It employs a religious subject, uses Spanish to be sung in a special setting, and perhaps Latin Americans would resent it, in the way we resented the Russian Ballet's "American" numbers, like *The New Yorker* or *Union Pacific*.

But *Pastorela* had the advantage of the collaboration not only of Lew Christensen, our designer Alvin Colt, the composer Paul Bowles, but also of José Martinez who conceived the idea and found the old words, Blas Galindo who arranged the orchestration, and José Fernandez who helped with the authentic dance steps. It was a Mexican ballet in fact, not only in the program credits.

Pastorela delighted the Argentines because they saw in it a reverent use of folk-material, not in an exotic or purely decorative style, but simply and with a definite connection to a living primitive tradition. All through Chile and Peru, composers and painters kept coming backstage to suggest local legends which could be transformed as we had done in *Pastorela*.

We were extremely busy with continual rehearsals and performances. However, we managed to visit quite a few local dancers. The ballet at the Teatro Colon came every night to our theatre and acted as our guides around town. One of them had been in the same beginners' class years ago at the Scala in Milan with our young ballerina, Gisella Caccialanza, when they were both studying under Gisella's godfather, Enrico Cecchetti. I was delighted to find the English artist and dancer, David Grey, also working at the Colon. The last time I had seen him was with Igor Schwezoff in Holland, in the summer of 1933, where I had gone to help Madame Nijinsky complete the biography of her husband.

David introduced me to Esmé Bulnes, the accomplished *maestra* of the Colon ballet, and Balanchine, Christensen, Dollar and myself got up very early one morning to watch their class, held in a vast circular room with removable barres, under the huge stage of that colossal house.

The Colon is a vast establishment. The performances I saw there of *Carmen* and *Otello* were staged with infinitely more care and splendor than those at our Metropolitan. Margarete Wallman's dances for the gypsy scene were freshly conceived and well performed. I was interested and touched by talking to Madame Wallman, learning from her that it was not so easy working for any opera company, not even for the Colon. She was working herself into a collapse, preparing at the same time a new version of de Falla's *Three Cornered Hat,* a revival of *La Boutique Fantasque,* a new ballet based on Oscar Wilde's "Birthday of the Infanta," and a "complete" version of *La Belle au Bois Dormant,* to be danced non-stop in forty-five minutes.

We also had the good fortune to meet Mercedes Quintana de Conord in her beautiful modern studio, constructed for her by her husband, an architect and film designer. She is a splendid classic dancer, serving as ballet mistress and teacher for the Teatro Cervantes, which is a national theatre, while the Colon is the theatre of the Municipality of Buenos Aires. Quintana is tiny, blonde, with a strong, clean classic technique reminding us very much of Catherine and Dorothie Littlefield. She showed us a number of Argentine folk dances including *La Pericon Nacional,* the *gato,* and the two types of tango which she had devised for a native film.

Quintana explained that the tango has never been a gaucho or country dance, that it was a development of the *maxixe* of about 1905, that it came from the cabarets of the Port, in a real apache form, and only later invaded the salons. We wanted very much to have Quintana perform with us in a suite of folk-dances of her own design at a special Allied benefit performance, but it became impossible, due to the pressure of our performance schedule. One can hardly mount a new ballet on tour, particularly with a choreographer who is unfamiliar with a given company.

So many absorbing things happened to us in Argentina that it is impossible to record half of them here. We particularly remember with delight a visit to El Rincon, the beautiful farm or *estancia,* of Madame Julia Bulrich de Saint, who is devoted to all dancers and who entertained Eglevsky, Danilova, and many other dancers from the Ballet Russe at her house last year. At El Rincon we met some real gauchos in their work clothes, who spoke *criollo,* the mixed language of the plains, and who showed us the movements used for throwing their types of lasso, and for branding cattle.

On returning from Uruguay, our ballet toured the Argentine provinces, giving a series of some twelve performances in the towns of Rosario, Cordoba and Mendoza. In Cordoba, Balanchine had a long interview with Manuel de Falla, the great Spanish composer of the *Three Cornered Hat,* who is finishing his most important work *Atalantida,* in a small village nearby. De Falla promised us the score of *Atalantida* as soon as it would be completed. But since he has been working on it for over ten years already, we could not hope for it soon.

And then there happened the most exciting thing that could possibly have hit any ballet company. When we arrived at the small town of Mendoza at the base of the highest portion of the Andes, only half a day away from Santiago de Chile beyond the cordillera, we were struck. The worst winter storms in years had smashed the railroads, obliterated the mountain village of Caracolles with twenty-two people in its railroad station, and shut the highway for six months.

We had the choice of going back by train to Buenos Aires, then down far south through the innumerable small lakes in motor launches which only carried a dozen people at a time, and then up to Santiago, a distance of two thousand miles—or traveling north via Tucuman and La Quiaca through Southern Bolivia, over to the coast town of Antofagasta, and down to Santiago, perhaps even longer. In the meantime, our orchestra was waiting for us in Santiago, as well as the impatient subscribers to our season. So, after nine days of exasperated hanging around a good hotel, with its gambling casino and movie house, in an atmosphere of the Lunt-Fontanne *Idiot's Delight,* the entire American Ballet, complete with scenery, costumes, lights, and personnel of fifty one people climbed into four Pan-Air Boeing transport planes and majestically flew the cordillera, between the two highest peaks in the Western Hemisphere. There had been so many delays no one believed we were actually going to fly on that Sunday morning when we all had driven down to the airport at 6 A.M. for the third consecutive day. But the weather was magnificent.

Fred Danieli was a little nervous. He had never flown before, and the Andes were quite a start. Dunia Mironowa, our wardrobe mistress, who had been all over the world for fifteen years with Pavlova, hated the oxygen. I was considerably disturbed as to what would happen to all our trunks and personal baggage which had been sent by rail north through Bolivia. But there was nothing to fear. We crossed, flat as on a stage floor, at about 19,000 feet. We could have taken it at 22. In the United States they consider 8,000 pretty high flying. Our pilot dipped to show we were just above the statue of the Christ of the Andes. The colossal walls of snow and coppery sun-lit ice were grander than the Hollywood set for *Lost Horizon.* None of us felt the altitude; no one was sick, and once over the snow-fields no one even felt dizzy. One hour and seven minutes after we had left Mendoza airport, we were being photographed in Santiago de Chile, surrounded by a cheering crowd of wholly incredulous spectators. It must have been the first time in history that bombers had flown a ballet.

THE AMERICAN BALLET IN CHILE

PART III OF A TRAVEL DIARY

THE CULTURAL LIFE of Chile, at least those branches devoted to the fine arts, is under the benevolent dictatorship of Domingo Santa Cruz, one of the most able composers, as well as one of the most brilliant administrators in both the Americas. Santa Cruz has spent twenty years of his life battling for the artistic autonomy of his country. He has managed to have a tax placed on all moving-picture performances and other shows of a commercial nature, and from this revenue he supports a superb symphony orchestra, schools of music and the plastic arts, and only this year, a school of ballet. He is also a subtle politician and has achieved a formula whereby all these agencies are manipulated through the great national university, which is permanent, and not through the Government administration, which is transient. However, the present regime in Chile is extremely enlightened, socially minded, anti-fascist, and one senses in Chile a spirit of energy and possibility, found scarcely anywhere else in South America.

I knew at once upon meeting Santa Cruz just as I had felt with the Mexican Carlos Chavez and our own Aaron Copland, that we must work together. He invited me to his house where I saw the work of his son Dominguito, who, although only seventeen years old, does remarkable pictographic novels in a very personal style, reminding me of Milton Caniff's "Terry and the Pirates." Santa Cruz played on his small pipe organ five short pieces scored for strings. I was impressed with their strength, freedom and nobility. Without using any folklore whatever for thematic material, he has suggested the stern atmosphere of the Colonial domination of Latin America by the Spanish governors. Our ballet to this music is to be called *The Noble Dances of the Viceroy*. The music is not exactly affected by Hindemith, yet Santa Cruz has used a base of mediaeval Spanish polyphony the way the author of *Saint Francis* employed mediaeval German.

The musical life of Chile is very rich. I was introduced to Don Carlos Isamit, another interesting composer, who has spent years among the Araucanian indians in the South. These tribes were the only ones never conquered by the Spaniards, and their culture is perhaps the purest from outside influence on the continent. Joseph Robinson, Second Secretary of the British Embassy, wrote me a note reminding me I had known him at Harvard fifteen years ago. He has organized "The Ambassador's Choir," an admirable chorus of young local British boys who sing at neighboring churches. Robinson swung all the aid of the influential English colony to our ballet, and helped make it a very great success.

Balanchine now started to create *Fantasia Brasileira,* the music for which had been commissioned from the Brazilian composer, Francisco Mignone, in Rio de Janeiro. The costumes and scenery by Errico Bianco of Saô Paolo had been executed in Buenos Aires, and Balanchine created the choreography in less than a week in Santiago de Chile. *Brasileira* is a brilliant and gay evocation of the spirit of Rio in Carnival time, not the urban downtown Rio, but rather the city of the great beaches and sub-tropical outlying districts. Our Latin-American ballerina, Olga Suarez, in a fiercely red taffeta ruffled samba skirt, created a sensation in the leading role. *Brasileira,* if the truth were told, is about as Brazilian as *Prince Igor* is early Russian. Actually, it is a character ballet based on authentic rhythms, admirably useful to close a program. The orchestra employed all sorts of strange native instruments dispatched to us from Rio by airmail. Our young pianist, Simon Sadoff, played the very difficult piano part (the ballet is conceived in the form of a piano concerto) with amazing virtuosity, and Emanuel Balaban, our conductor from Rochester, New York, interpreted the complicated manuscript score as if he'd been born in Brazil. Balaban's patience and victory over each new orchestra, over every new local situation was miraculous.

Brasileira was a real triumph, not only in Chile, but also in Peru and Colombia. I know there is a great future for a Latin American ballet repertory, but the creators of it cannot invent by remote control. They must immerse themselves in local atmosphere as Balanchine, Christensen and Dollar did, digging out from the seaport cantinas of Valparaiso, Rio and Guayaquil, cheap dance halls, farm parties and café concerts, the essential folk quality of each country.

I never failed to be amazed by Balanchine. He has always had a remarkable disposition for work, quiet, patient, undemanding, yet perfectly firm. But on this fantastic tour, the difficulties of which can never be appreciated by anybody but the dancers themselves, and which will never be admitted even by them, Balanchine repeatedly accepted less good accommodations than anyone else, was always the last to be paid, the first to come into a theatre, the last to leave. He loved every inch of the journey and his own personal prestige became enormous. Long after we left Buenos Aires came insistent offers to return to the Colon.

In Santiago we had the fun of seeing a lot of Rudolph Pescht and Ernst Uthoff, two of the best dancers of the original Jooss Company who were just about to open the Chilean Government's Ballet School, under a two-year contract to Domingo Santa Cruz. They have obtained large airy studios and a phenomenal registration. William Garret, of our company, and a graduate of The School of American Ballet in New York, was requested to stay on and teach here as well as to dance in the Opera.

We had also a considerable amount of social life. Federico Sanchez de

Loria Errazuriz, whom we soon knew as Federico, who claims ninety-one first cousins of the great Errazuriz family, and is a Knight of Malta, took us out to the beautiful suburb of Los Leones where his immediate family has built five houses in one large park. His court dress of the Maltese order looked like a Bérard ballet dress, with its white plume and Spanish ruff. He had found an old portrait of George Washington which must have been sent down to Chile on a Yankee clipper-ship a century ago. He insisted we take it, also other pictures, furniture, practically his whole house. My wife admired a beautiful small iron enamelled tree which sprouted bohemian glass scent-flagons. He put it in her hands. She said she couldn't possibly accept it. It was too lovely. He looked at her solemnly. "I shall smash it if you don't." She has the tree but we managed to leave Washington behind.

Lieutenant John R. Guenard of the United States Cavalry, stationed with the crack Chilean cavalry regiment just outside of the city of Santiago, invited our whole company to the barracks to watch the military jumping. Under the leadership of Lieutenant Nijil, Chile has repeatedly won the big recent prizes at Madison Square Garden in New York City. Guenard proudly presented the ballet to Major Garcia, in command of the regiment, to Nijil and all their comrades. The jumping was really beautiful. The men were preparing for a big contest the following week and spared neither themselves nor their horses. After the jumping, we were given a collection in the Salle d'Honneur of the Club des Officiales with excellent pisco sours, a drink smoother than honey with the punch of a cannon. The Japanese cherries were blossoming outside and June Graham, formerly of the Littlefield Ballet, who had married Joe Johnson in Montevideo, said how pretty they looked. Major Garcia gave a command and the next thing we knew, two orderlies stripped a tree and covered our dancers with pink blossoms. Marjorie Moore, who had created a sensation in Santiago in Tchelitchew's *Errante*, admired an officer's medal. He took it off and pinned it on her sweater. I had a hard time packing the kids off to rehearsal before the officers had anything left but their shirts.

The regiment attended the ballet as our guests and gave a banquet for us at the Military Club. I decided not to go as I felt my presence might cramp their style. I know little of the further adventures of the cavalry except from rumors. I can swear ten of them hired a car and followed the ballet, not only to Viña del Mar, the resort town where we were the guests of the Municipality, but also up the coast practically to the Peruvian border.

It was necessary for me to return to New York after the Chilean season. Our company embarked on an excellent small Chilean boat with two hundred head of cattle. Aside from this, the boat was practically their private yacht. It took nine days for them to sail from Valparaiso to Lima, Peru, while I was back in Washington after flying only two and one half days from Santiago.

THE AMERICAN BALLET ON THE WEST COAST

PART IV OF A TRAVEL DIARY

To MOST NORTH AMERICANS, South America means Rio and Buenos Aires. Vaguely we know that Lima and Bogota exist, but we rarely think of them as having theatrical seasons. Peru, Colombia and Venezuela, however, have long traditions of operatic performances, although ballet companies hardly ever make the long and difficult trip up the West Coast. The American Ballet Company includes a personnel of forty-eight persons besides the complete equipment of scenery, costumes, lights and incidentals. It was remarkable that throughout our entire five-month journey the only sickness suffered was the common cold, toothaches and one lone case of jaundice. Our medical precautions had been extensive. Every one of us had received injections against typhoid, paratyphoid, yellow fever, malaria and smallpox. But there were no snake or spider bites, no violent reactions from extreme changes of altitude, and what was really miraculous, no dysentery.

The company arrived at Callao, the port of Lima, on September 8, 1941, after a nine-day voyage from Valparaiso on the S.S. *Maipocho.* In reality, it was the yacht of the American Ballet, for besides the hundreds of head of cattle in the hold, the members of the Ballet had the boat to themselves.

Everyone had warned us how difficult Lima would be. The taste of the public is conservative, and ballet as such is not very well known. We had learned quite a lot, however, by successive baptisms by fire in the other capitals, and in Lima at least, due in great part to the labors of Mr. Philip Barbour, our official mentor, no stone was left unturned to make our debut a really extraordinary event.

The auspices were extraordinarily brilliant. The premiere was attended by the President of the Republic and his wife, Sra. Enriqueta de Prado, their children Manuel and Rosita, the Chief of the Army, the English and American Ambassadors, and representatives of all Embassies and Legations in Lima, with the exception of the German, the Italian and the Japanese. To make everything perfect, Aaron Copland, the composer of *Billy the Kid,* happened to be in Lima, and conducted a superb performance of his own score. We received the greatest ovation of our tour after that performance, more prolonged applause than in Rio or Buenos Aires or Santiago.

A number of the dancers took a plane to visit the Inca remains at Cuzco and Balanchine took a number of excellent photographs of the colossal rock foundations. They were forced to return to Lima sooner than expected, because, with the help of our Embassy a number of extra performances were scheduled. There was a week of uncertainty due to the tense political situation between Ecuador and Peru. Because of the war between the two countries, it was decided to omit Quito from our regular itinerary, but a group of our first dancers, headed by Mr. Barbour who lectured in Spanish, flew to Quito and gave a series of very successful demonstrations on the classic dance.

The company left Lima on the 25th of September on the excellent Grace Line steamer, *Santa Elena,* which had a fine pool and first rate food. Using the deck-rail as a *barre,* morning classes were not suspended even in the five-day voyage to Buenaventura. Beatrice Tompkins, one of our ablest soloists, wrote me the following. I was by that time back in Washington, making a report on the first half of our tour.

"We arrived at the port of Buenaventura on September 30th, where we spent the night, and next morning left for Cali. There we gave three performances, under very interesting conditions. For one thing, we were there in the dry season when water pressure is very low, and consequently the electric light very weak. Trying to put on a good stage make-up in semi-darkness was a real problem. However, the stage lights were also affected, and I imagine our audience couldn't see whether the make-up was good or bad!

"We were a little worried about our reception in Cali, because there had been no ballet company there for sixteen years. Much to our delighted surprise, the audience evidenced great enthusiasm, and expressed the hope that we would return 'ere long.

"We left for Manizales October 3rd, riding all day on a not too comfortable train. However, the scenery was so magnificent—right in the midst of the awe-inspiring Andes—that hot, cold, tired and dirty as we were, there was very little complaining.

"We gave two performances in Manizales, a small town, which at first glance seemed not at all the sort of place for any ballet company. But we had large and very enthusiastic audiences. We danced in a very big and very old movie house. The dressing rooms were little square boxes made of tin, and the floor of the stage was full of holes and very slippery. But there were no casualties, and the audience loved us, although they had never seen a ballet before. Sunday was election day and that meant practically a civil war! Bombs were thrown, and there were riots on every street corner. We were afraid that our performance that night would be interrupted in some way, if by nothing more than the election returns. But the audience's enthusiasm for the ballet made them forget the riots of the day, and all was peace.

"We left the next morning at nine o'clock for Medellin, in a fleet of ten automobiles. The only way to get to Medellin was by motor, through the Occidental branch of the Andes. It was a magnificent, though hair-raising, drive, over precipitous dirt roads. At one point, we almost had to turn back. A bridge we were to cross had partially collapsed, and as we came to it, natives were starting to repair it, in very leisurely fashion. We were told it would take two hours, so some of us took advantage of that time by bathing in the river, trying to remove some of the dust and grime acquired on the drive. Most of the company walked across the bridge after it had been repaired, afraid that the bridge would collapse when the cars went over it. But it stood the test, and cars and all reached the other side safely.

"At long last, we reached Medellin, and opened there October 7th, to a very unpleasantly noisy audience. The only paper in town had written us up as an extremely immoral company! We went through the program accompanied by cries of *"Malo"* and *"Feo"* and expected a vegetable or two at any moment. But we got very good notices, and our next performances were beautifully received.

"On the 10th of October, three planes took us to Bogota, where we opened at the new Teatro Municipal, which is the pride and joy of Bogota, and is rather like a smaller Radio City Music Hall. The altitude of 8,500 feet bothered us quite a lot, but we managed somehow although I'm sure the audiences could hear us heaving our way through the various ballets."

After the season in Bogota, the company departed in twelve motor cars for Caracas. "To get there meant crossing three branches of the Andes, along dirt roads, really just narrow ledges hewn out of the sides of the mountains. Twisting and turning, up and down, for three days. Our drivers were amazing. We stopped for a few minutes' rest at various little towns, but the food was not edible for us from the effete U. S. A. So we lived on what we had bought in Cucuta in case of such an emergency.

"When we stopped at these villages we'd take our various baskets and bundles to the village square, sit under the trees, and pool our store of cheese, crackers, etc. In every village we were encircled by dozens of natives."

After a successful season in Caracas the company embarked from La Guaira on November 6th for New York. Every country in South America had been visited except the two interior Republics of Paraguay and Bolivia. Three times the company had been flown by plane, back and forth across the Andes, over one hundred performances had been given. For the first time South American audiences had seen North American dancers in combination with our decor by U. S. artists, and our symphonic scores played by their orchestras. We had added three ballets to our repertory by Brazilian, Argentine and Chilean composers and painters. We had received marvelous notices and invitations to return to every country. We had made many close personal friends, and there was not one of us, who, on coming back, did not want to return. If we could have been sure of peace time conditions, we might have wandered on through the Caribbean Islands, Cuba and Mexico. But we had been working for nearly eight months and a rest would do no harm.

Some day I will write a detailed account of the tour with all its difficulties and curious accidents. But for the present, I feel it was a genuine success from every point of view.

Alec: Or the Future of
Choreography

Although he cast his lot decisively with Balanchine, it seems clear that Kirstein envisioned the development of other choreographers as well. The new bodies he planned to train would need a lot to dance.

There is no question but that Kirstein saw the New York City Ballet (which came into existence in 1948) and its forerunner, Ballet Society (1946-48), as functioning along Diaghilevian lines. Consider the original announcement for Ballet Society: "Each [new work] will have the planned collaboration of independent easel painters and progressive choreographers and musicians, employing the full use of avant-garde ideas, methods and materials." The production that led to the creation of the New York City Ballet was just such a many-sided collaboration: Orpheus, *with choreography by George Balanchine, a commissioned score by Igor Stravinsky (worked out nightly, as the choreography progressed by day), commissioned decor by Isamu Noguchi. The programs of Ballet Society, while featuring Balanchine's choreography, also gave opportunities for creating ballets to John Taras, Todd Bolender, William Dollar, Merce Cunningham, Lew Christensen, and Fred Danieli; new music for dance was written by Elliott Carter, Rudi Revil, Stanley Bate, John Cage, Carter Harmon, Richard Arnell, and Vittorio Rieti, as well as by Stravinsky; decors were commissioned from Aline Bernstein, Kurt Seligmann,*

◊ Reprinted from *Dance News Annual [1]:1953,* edited by Winthrop Palmer and Anatole Chujoy. New York: Alfred A. Knopf, 1953, pp 41-53.

Esteban Francés, Joan Junyer, David Ffolkes, Robert Drew, Horace Armistead, and Corrado Cagli, as well as from Noguchi.

In keeping with this concept, in the young days of the New York City Ballet, Kirstein made an effort to secure the choreographic services of established figures such as Sir Frederick Ashton and Antony Tudor, and to develop younger talent, of which the most exciting by far was Jerome Robbins. But commissioned scores and decors were fewer from the beginning.

One of the things at which Diaghilev excelled was the discovery of new talent. At the time Alec *was written (1953), the New York City Ballet was harboring a youthful and ambitious Robbins; Kirstein, perhaps thinking this was only the start, was already speculating on the difficulties of nurturing promising choreographers.*

But this was not to be: more than thirty years after the founding of the Company, Balanchine dominates the repertory (there is a strong Robbins component), usually with distinguished musical support, but, since Stravinsky's death, without musical collaboration, and the decorative element in most presentations is either missing completely or produced by "house" designers.

Although the New York City Ballet has thus far failed to develop any major choreographers (Robbins was already partially formed when he joined the Company), it has produced a number of directors (some of whom also function as the type of "useful" choreographer that "Alec" became). They include Robert Barnett, Lew Christensen, John Clifford, Kent Stowell and Francia Russell, Robert Weiss, Patricia Wilde, Maria Tallchief, John Taras, Todd Bolender, Fred Danieli, and Patricia Neary.

N.R.

JUST AS a preponderance of great dancers in the past has been female, most of the choreographers have been male. The male principle, by instruction and design, has determined the executive prowess of girls and women. A few famous male dancers have been grateful for dances designed by ladies. There are familiar parallels in other fields; lady painters have been far between, though if few, yet frequently exquisite. Lady composers of music are more of a rarity, but cantatrices are legion and actresses are numerous. Female architects are scarce; choreography is the fluid architecture of human mass in space and time.

At the present (1953), we are suffering from a paucity of choreographers. From this we have suffered for four hundred years. The combination of gift and authority which saves time at rehearsal—for the dancer must know what he wants to have done, and can at once teach other dancers to do it, determining that a new work gets itself on a given stage at a given night—is rare. It is rare today as it always has been. It might be curious to consider exactly how it might be rare tomorrow.

While almost anyone with three years of training in the classic academic theatrical discipline (ballet) can be expected to string together steps that may be read as some sort of dance, few students develop into dance designers. The nature of the strength used in performing, in absorbing the patterns of others in order to appear clearly in a large design with other dancers, takes an energy that at its most effective is seldom inventive. The assimilation of a chain of tricky steps, the need to perform well and project personally, exhausts other potentials in the pattern-making, which many good performers otherwise may well have had. Few ballet-masters have not been at one time efficient performers; their knowledge of performance, the fact that they too have been actually successful in pleasing the public, gives them the necessary confidence to demand intense performance in others, and permits the given troupe of performers to submit to their highly personal schemes and patterns.

Boys are not lucky with dancing; their parents too often feel it is fine for their sisters, but sissy for themselves. It is a little better off now than it was ten years or twenty-five years ago, but it still is not very good. It is now decent for a male child to practice the piano, but to move his whole body in time to music is still considered questionable. A boy may paint with impunity, sing for the radio, and almost act (for films), but there is little cash connected with dancing; our practical Puritan inheritance has franchised the uses of the male body for professional sport, not for dancing. However, some boys still dance, and some very young ones are now dancing. From this less than a handful will come the one or two choreographers of the nineteen-sixties and seventies. They are in schools today. Maybe they are presently so young that they don't even mind being in classes where almost everyone else is a girl. Maybe their pride can survive the atmosphere of the awkward minority. Maybe they can stick long enough to graduate into a more advanced group, where there are more boys, on the verge of appearing on the stage. Then the moment will come when they must face being sucked into Broadway or television, even though on a part-time basis at first, eventually being lost to their serious and trying craft.

Should they survive up to the age of seventeen, they face the military draft. At the moment when, after long years of tiresome training, they are getting to feel a trace of confidence, they must have known for quite a while that time must be taken out for the wars. Some will feel it as an End. Others must have so strong a direction that they will realize that even two years out, backed up by honest previous training is by no means an irreparable discouragement. But let those draft-boards who take this setback lightly compare a similar truncation in training in the education of any young ballerina; for two years—a girl of seventeen stops dancing. Who can expect her ever to be a first dancer?

So, with all these unfavorable and unhappy conditions in mind, let us project the career of some young choreographer, who, in 1953, at the age of seventeen-plus, can't wait for the draft, nervously volunteers for the Navy, is accepted, and even after many months, each of which seems like ten years, still hopes that he can dance. Let us call him Alec Lasagna. His mother was of Swedish descent, his father Italian. She was a dietician; he was a contractor. She believed in manual and physical training; he loved the opera. Their only son hated boxing, but was good on the parallel bars. He had no voice, but played the piano. He was entered in the High School of Performing Arts in New York City. This caused some domestic difficulties. His father's concrete-mixing plant was on Long Island, but Alec showed such promise and such passion for his work that he was permitted to live with an aunt in Manhattan. His classes with Lillian Moore and the keyhole sight he caught at once from her of the grand styles of the past gave him enough corroboration of his own instinct to determine his subsequent career.

Alec will have been born too late to have seen much of the bona fide Russian ballets of the 'thirties and 'forties. At the age of eight he caught a performance of Alexandra Danilova in *Le Beau Danube*. This proved the same sort of vocational revelation that Anna Pavlova combusted over the provinces of the world forty years before. Watching her waxen limbs, feeling that fierce concentration of freshness, delight and power, he knew he was Called. He saw Youskevitch in *Giselle;* he knew he would never have cheekbones as high as that, nor a profile so nobly, sadly elegant. He despaired. Later, he saw Margot Fonteyn as the Sleeping Princess; he knew he could never support so weighty a spirit of such impalpable graciousness. He was humbled. In 1950 he saw Maria Tallchief as the Firebird. He was dazzled and excited as if her turns had set turning in him something that would never stop until he could actually pirouette the obsession out of his system. He knew what he wanted: perfect power in perfect repose, hidden mastery, dominion, without apparent domination—the strength of the silent waters building up steadily purring dynamos in a dam whose walls were music and whose electricity was muscle. He wanted to become a Choreographer.

The Navy was no nightmare, he found sheepishly that he thoroughly enjoyed it. He passed a few terrible moments, but after Boot Camp at Great Lakes, where he spent most of the time playing the piano for the massed choir practice, he found himself at the Boston Navy Yard, attached as yeoman to a ship in drydock. He had a sympathetic Chief who collected L.P. recordings. And later he would have had just enough sea duty to make him feel almost like a sailor. More weekends than he could ever imagine would have been spent in New York. Then he will have discovered Balanchine.

He will still have clung to the idea that he is a dancer; yet he had hardly danced except in school. There, he had been strongly attracted by the modern dance; it seemed completely digestible; the idiom he could grasp at once, and composition with the few elements at hand seemed easy and satisfying. There was no endless road to virtuosity. Quite broad effects were not impossible to project with happy speed. And at this epoch he would have been a bit of an intellectual. His young girlfriends did not approve of Balanchine; there was no Soul there; all his ballets were the same; Balanchine did not care about dancers much, and never thought about boys. Balanchine had no psychological overtones, and never seemed to have been influenced by Joyce, Yeats or Kafka. All the Balanchine ballets were only about dancing. It took the perspective afforded by the Navy to show Alec that the ballet was indeed chiefly about dancing, and that probably he would never be much of a dancer.

Alec was discharged early in 1954. Veterans of the Korean campaigns who wanted to dance as a career, unlike those of the war before, had no rights under the G.I. Bill, which reformed itself to eliminate beauty schools and dancing schools. Alec had little money. But his father had been successful, building ranchhouses near Syosset. Alec's mother felt the boy deserved a chance at his own aims, after two years out. He entered the School of American Ballet. His first interview was unsatisfactory; by now quite tall, he looked much older than twenty. His previous training seemed to count for little; practically, he might just as well start all over again. He was placed in a class with small children; his first real friend was a boy of ten, grimly serious, in whom Alec saw himself, ten years before. But somehow, he was able to make a private game of this starting-all-over. He tried to wipe his mind into a blank. He became, for the purposes of his boring classes, a child again. Doggedly he pursued the conquest of Correctness, but there was little release in action. Must it all be *this* tiresome? Could he stand it? Doubts that he had never permitted to arise before now started to betray him.

But there is little of any directed energy lost, and that gift or power which made him want to dance in the first instance, yet robbed him of early chances to perfect his prime instrument—his body—soon enough to insure its virtuosity compensated him with a rare capacity for analysis. Alec found he enjoyed the pleasures of his mind. He started to think. He began to make first steps towards thinking with his body. He came to comprehend that choreography was not a projection of the personal designs of the choreographer as performer, but rather of a pattern-maker for quite other performers whose physiques and personalities bore slight resemblance to his own. Because he would never appear as first-dancer, because he had long known he was no Youskevitch, the normal incipient narcissism remained vestigial in him. He would never have to please the public in his own person. He heated up his pride for others. He attempted to analyze for himself what was the essence of the choreographic secret.

Was dance design to be pretext for performers, or some pattern superior to performance? He inspected the ballets in the current repertory; he tried to find out why other ballets had been dropped. This was his homework. He reduced the structure of each ballet to formulas. He dissected them as if they had been anesthetized on a table before him. He read books. In the memoirs of the Diaghilev era he discovered how much accident, hazard, expedience, opportunism, and irrelevance went into the collaborations that created ballets which, in spite of their dubious provenance, nevertheless remained in the repertory for years. He pondered the fact that many works, famous at their debut, evaporated when robbed of their original casting, and that other works, stronger than their stars, were continually reproduced for two or three decades, in three or four companies in five or six revivals.

Alec will have to have outside help, having little money. At first he will have taken a job, part-time, as an usher in the Radio City Music Hall. He had, it is true, been offered the position as a dancing master for a small class of more-than-well-to-do children whose mothers wished to spare them the dangers of working with other children of their own age who might become professional. Alec will have correctly estimated that labor so parallel to his own interest, yet in which he was not genuinely interested, would tend to exhaust him emotionally even more than physically. Ushering at the Music Hall was more fun than controlling spoiled children. But, God knows, it will have been absolutely tiring too.

Robbed of his chances under the G.I. Bill, he naively addressed himself to the great educational foundations, of whose inspired benevolence and liberal policy he was increasingly to hear. He set himself to apply for some category of fellowship or scholarship to enable him to study, not as a dancer, but as a choreographer. He could not seem to arrange appointments to see anyone in authority at the James Foundation. The Ford Foundation was clearly too big to bother with. The gentlemen at the Rockefeller Foundation would have been surprisingly kind and encouraging had he wanted to write a survey of the state of choreography in the Eastern Atlantic States (and the Maritime Provinces of Canada) between 1911 and 1951. For this he could have received a thumping grant-in-aid. But he merely wanted to become a practicing choreographer, alas, and there was no precedent or existent formula whereby the Foundation could risk half-a-dozen thousand dollars on so precarious a project.

Anyway and every way, he will have persevered. After analyzing the peripheral needs of the ballet school and the ballet company, he made himself increasingly useful in a growing number of small ways. He answered the telephone for dancers in rehearsal. He checked toe shoes and learned the secrets of individual feet. By bringing coffee to dressing-rooms, he got to know dancers. He became indispensable. He was promoted to presenting on stage the flowers sent by the dancers' admirers. He had never admired the delivery of flowers by the stage-servants at the Metropolitan Opera House. He asked Maria Tallchief how she wanted her flowers to be handed to her. She rehearsed him. He analyzed the size and weight of each bunch; he had a firm step and a charming bow. He groomed himself carefully; he made his face up in a healthy non-professional tan. Soon the company gave him a tuxedo. Nowhere, before or since on the American stage, will bouquets have been offered with such confident elegance.

As the seasons passed, he approached a modest academic correctness in his own dancing. He felt the muscles in his legs harden. He even began to watch the position of his arms. He found that girls' arms are not boys' arms. He started to note the difference between the style of his instructors: the older graduates of the Imperial Russian schools of the pre-First War, and the dominant manner of the later Balanchine ballets. He tried to find where the Fokine influence left off, and the new, dryer style began; he found that the new style was even older than Fokine, and yet could not have come into existence without the smoother freedom of the romantic philosophy. Alec thought all the time. He thought with his mind as a working mechanism, just as his body was a working machine. He developed his machinery by listening and by seeing. There was always an L.P. recording being played somewhere: he started to analyze the choreography of instrumentation. He haunted the opera. He tried to figure the placement of breath in dramatic singing and the phrasing of breath in dramatic dancing. He considered of what music was made, and which music was most made for dancing. His were no discoveries to change the history of criticism; they were simply the start of preferences to project a style. He looked at sculpture and small objects. He tried to penetrate the secrets of static plasticity, and the sense in three-dimensional torsion and balance. Human and animal anatomy began to absorb him; he saw how frontal design could capitalize on the meaning of masses of muscle, how muscle described form, and how the proper presentation of forms intensified the sense in the rapid shifts of design which the interlacing bodies made in the frieze and braids of dancing. He looked at sculpture and small objects, in the Egyptian wing at the Metropolitan Museum and at the Cloisters: an ivory whip-handle of a leaping horse; a portable altar of the whole story of the Journey of the Magi in twenty-four miniature tableaux. He found that static plastic is a facet of the diamond sphere of motion. He slowly came to realize that choreography is an echoing of order, that all order is a reflection of a superior order, that all important art is religious art, and that he would never be merely a decorative artist. This was a tremendous decision, because he began also to see that in our time order has been all but overwhelmed by obsessive idiosyncrasy, personal mannerism, and the egomaniacal vogues that atrophy the mind and deform the ego by self-indulgent improvisation and ignorant accidental choice.

Alec would be a bright boy; he was also a good boy, and this goodness would be apparent. At first he would claim only the amused tolerance of the other students and dancers; then, their affection; finally, their respect. At the beginning, he will have asked their advice about the execution of small steps and their combination; this was both flattering to the artists and useful to the apprentice. He will have found out quickly that combination is the commencement of invention, that certain sequences cannot combine harmoniously, and that certain suites have a magnetic inevitability. He would discover whether or not his limited palette, or small chords of steps, jumps, kicks, twists, and turns were grateful in execution, as well as feasible. Other dancers would try them for him. And this was all pursued according to his deliberate plan. From elementary advice requested, within two years, he would find himself prescribing little variations, so that when he would have his first chance to compose a *pas de deux* for actual performance (for a benefit for the Endowment Fund for a library at the High School of Performing Arts, where he had started his own training), he would find that even professional dancers were quite willing to submit to his patterns. He did not, in the first place, waste their time. He knew what he wanted. And if this *pas de deux* (to music by Mendelssohn) will not ever have replaced any of the grand duets of Petipa or Balanchine, nevertheless the number was neatly designed, made its own sense, and—what was even more promising—had its own ironic commentary on the style of Balanchine and Petipa.

For Alec was not an original. In him nothing emerged that had not been seen before. Everything he thought and did came from some attributable source that he frankly traced and acknowledged. Without much natural brilliance, he knew he was working not in a loosely original, but rather in a tightly traditional, field, and that he was slowly (but surely) pushing into a part of that tradition. His first little *pas de deux* amounted at once to a graduation exercise (for himself as apprentice ballet-master), a thesis on developed dance-design in the mid-twentieth-century style, and a tasteful comment on the wry dryness and elegant intimate domesticated formality of the later Balanchine. It was a triple-exposure, but a bit more than a snapshot, for it made a clear and sensitive composition. There would be no doubt about it. Alec would have artistic and theatrical authority, for he had developed his body in training, and he would have schooled his mind past most of the demands one would have ordinarily expected of it.

So let us leave this luckless boy on the verge of a promising career. Luckless, but well-trained, with the gifts of head, hands, and heart, who would be absorbed into the New York City Ballet Company, as assistant to its Administrative Director. Lew Christensen, who had been a skillful performer himself, realized in Alec a variant of himself at half his age. It was Christensen indeed who proposed to Alec the music for his first full-length ballet. This was a suite of six pieces drawn from Handel's *Royal Fireworks* music. Christensen assigned him a few dancers and a few rehearsal hours from the company's working time. Alec knew his dancers of old, and he wasted no words or minutes. His ballet was accomplished within three weeks, though the company was even then performing. He took his soloists and worked the group numbers around them, fitting it all together as he could, but it was sufficiently clear in his own mind before he started so that his joinery was cleanly achieved. Balanchine would have been busy; he would have seen Alec around backstage, but would certainly not know his name. But Christensen asked him to look at the finished *Fireworks,* which involved three first dancers and a corps of eight. Alec conducted his rehearsal as if he were a cabinetmaker offering a commissioned dining-room table. Balanchine would not be slow to see that the piece was nicely turned and well-finished and would stand up under the weight of an ordinary meal. He would give orders to Madame Karinska for the eleven dresses to be created forthwith. Jean Rosenthal invented a modestly ingenious device whereby, in Alec's finale, a pyrotechnical display showered the dancers, whose pirouettes seemed to combust into Fourth-of-July sparklers.

In *The New York Times* of the following morning, John Martin will have written:

> Young Mr. Lasagna is definitely worth watching. The miniature fireworks display of last evening may well prove more than an explosion of a packet of penny-crackers. Underneath the apparent informality, there is strong structure, wit and some delicacy. It would be surprising if in his debut, Alec Lasagna has not created that rarest of theatrical properties, a valid repertory piece.

And Walter Terry, in the *New York Herald Tribune,* would be even more enthusiastic:

> Make no mistake about it, Alec Lasagna is a young ballet-*master.* His *Fireworks* is a youthful ballet master's-piece. To be sure, there were more than a few moments when *his* master, Balanchine, was fleetingly evoked, but the overwhelming impression was of a luxurious kinesthetic security.

And so, a new choreographer will have been born. It must be recalled here that Alec knew he would never be a star dancer, that he was too tall to dance, that he started very late, and that he joined the Navy. And after his first success, there will have been offers from television, the films and Broadway, and all the attendant demons that beset each brilliant career.

But possibly his authority, which was growing unshakeable, the pleasure he will have been able to take in his mind, and above all his sense of anti-decoration, of superior orderings, will have made him a ballet-master of use to the profession.

Foreword to *Gagaku*

The New York City Ballet toured Japan, Australia, and the Philippines in 1958. Kirstein apparently was quite intrigued by Japan, and the following year, as the Company celebrated its tenth anniversary, he arranged for the importation of the Gagaku dancers and musicians of the Japanese Imperial Household. Gagaku literally means noble or elegant music; the all-male troupe of twenty-two performers was direct descendants of the court group founded in the eighth century. New York critics praised the Gagaku for "stately flow of movement," "elaborate ritual and pageantry," and "visual sumptuousness," recalling ancient myths. The subjects of the dances included praying for good wine; polo; "Dance for the Festival of the Household God of the Oven"; and flowers in a spring garden.

A dance performance of Gagaku is called "Bugaku," a word that later surfaced as the title of a Japanese-flavored Balanchine ballet. The set for that ballet—a carpeted platform set off by Chinese-red railings—owed its inspiration to the Gagaku.

Appearing on some of the same programs as these ancient dances was Balanchine's brand-new Episodes, *widely regarded at the time as a telescopic view into the twenty-first century.* Episodes *also marked the final stage in Kirstein's sparring match with Martha Graham, who was invited to produce half the program and did so without controversy.*

N.R.

◊ Reprinted from *Gagaku*, text by Robert Garfias, calligraphy by Yasuhide Kobashi. New York: Theatre Arts Books, 1959, unpaged.

WE PRAY FOR One World, not one world of monolithic unity but of the rich vitality and variety of the many worlds that may, one day, be one in independent diversity. Our two great Worlds of East and West have never before been so interdependent, so linked by tension and by mutual attraction. The fascination of East for West and West for East is the key of our time. The visit of Gagaku, the musicians and dancers of the Imperial Japanese Household, is a symbol of extraordinary depth and importance, of the possibility of bridging culture, time and place.

Gagaku, founded in 703 A.D., is the oldest institution performing music and dance in the world. Its tradition of imperial support, hereditary personnel and artistic repertory is uninterrupted. It has had, until recently, an almost secret, almost a sacred life. It is possible that more people will see Gagaku in the United States on its epoch-making tour than have ever beheld it in the Imperial Music Pavilion in Tokyo or at one of the great shrines at Ise or Nara.

However, we must school our ears to hear, our eyes to see Gagaku. We are accustomed to sounds and sights arranged quite differently by measures of time and space. In the West, time nervously passes; in the East, man passes through imperturbable time. In America, space is unlimited; our prairies stretch from sea to shining sea. In Japan, the islands are strictly circumscribed; mountains are terraced, foot by foot. Music and dances in their rich accumulation from all South East and Central Asia, already a thousand years old in some cases when Gagaku was founded, found a haven and a home in Japan, for there was nowhere else to move on to, save into the Pacific.

So there survived elements from Persia, Mongolia, Thailand, Korea, Japan itself, of an almost unimaginable antiquity. Think for a moment what was happening in Western Europe in 703 A.D.; in Nara there was a great court. But what is more, a pre-Buddhist culture that we are only beginning to prize today, along with Etruscan and Cycladic art, had long preceded the Chinese priests and architects who had made Nara a shrine city of unsurpassed splendor. Kyoto itself was not founded until almost a century later. Gagaku performs sacred and secular dances; the ceremonial movement derives sometimes from folk-sources, Persian polo, Korean barge-poling, Chinese military discipline, but it has been refined, essentialized, formalized, in the atmosphere of the Imperial Court, a precinct, at least, of symbolic serenity; only the all-powerful can be truly serene; calm not rage is the sole sign of authority; one of the most beautiful Gagaku dances is of military origin but it is known as a dance of peace, for authority has been established and maintained by noble soldiers.

This music, these dances are, to Westerners, slow. That is, they seem so to those eyes which are habituated to divisions of time which are accelerative, unlimited, and often, undifferentiated. Gagaku dances have a limited vocabulary of movement; we are accustomed to a frenetic brilliance in physical virtuosity. But when the West sees dancing, it is for theaters; Gagaku is not theatrical dancing for a great audience. It is movement designed to be done at court or shrine, for a philosophic, moral or religious purpose: for the inthronization of emperors, for the marriage of crown princes, for the completion of shrines, for the in-gathering of the first rice. The dancers wear no make-up; sometimes they are masked; they are clad as priests or accoutered as warriors; their arms and armor are not stage-properties; they are the consecrated and personal property of an imperial household.

It is not so much what these dancers and musicians *do*, although what they do is beautiful, hypnotic, absorbing, even after the immediate strangeness has worn away. What is important is what these musicians and dancers *are*. In the West, all is the doing; in the East all is the being. In Japan, Gagaku, the ceremonial and sacred dance; Noh, the religious drama and the art of the Geisha, the secular craft of refined relaxation, spell Accomplishment; Gagaku, Noh, and the wholly separated skill of private entertainment are institutions of the accomplished.

Our Western dictionary defines accomplishment, first of all, as completion; there is argument among musicologists and historians exactly as to when Gagaku was frozen; few think there has been much change since 1150 A.D. Accomplishment is also "that which completes or equips thoroughly." The visual splendor of Gagaku dress, the perfection of detail in arms and armor, the immaculate presentation of individual performers is unparalleled in the West. Finally, accomplishment is "an element in excellence of mind, or elegance of manners, acquired by education and training." The Western world has long known of the symbolic disciplines of tea-ceremony and flower-arrangement. Many tourists have testified to the fascination of Kabuki, the popular 17th century classical theater. Today, more and more Americans are falling under the fascination of Zen philosophy in its multiple aspects; many American soldiers have been conquered by the powerful attraction of ritual wrestling, ritual fencing and ritual archery.

Gagaku is not a dead art; it is a completed art that is performed within its own limits of perfection; it has meanings for the West, on many levels. It is not easy to grasp completely at first viewing or hearing. Perhaps some Westerners will credit it with as much subtlety, mastery and depth as the glaze on a pot, or the individual character of calligraphic stroke. New dances are made today for contemporary occasions. The first dance that will be seen at the General Assembly of the United Nations has only just been composed in honor of the recent marriage of Prince Akahito, the Imperial heir. Igor Stravinsky, the greatest western composer and musicmaster for our ballet dancers first heard Gagaku by an amateur group in

Los Angeles, of which the author of the monograph that follows was a leading member. In his *Conversations,* Stravinsky writes: ". . . a new demand for greater in-depth listening changes time perspective. Perhaps also the operation of memory in a nontonally developed work (tonal, but not eighteenth-century-tonal system) is different." Stravinsky, conducting this year in Japan for the first time, expressed his deep interest in Gagaku, as many American composers will.

Gagaku is a precious possession of the Japanese Imperial Household, whose symbols are the jewel, the mirror and the sword. Perfection, the face of self, civil authority, have survived their dim origins in Shinto credence, and are living repositories of powerful ideas. It was the great privilege of this writer to witness Ninjo-mai, perhaps the most sacred as well as the oldest of all the dances, performed only in the Imperial Palace, and at the Grand Shrine of Ise, at Ise, itself. The dance was done under very modern circumstances. The first team of Shrine dancers and musicians was gone for the day, on duty at a ceremony of importance some distance away. But the Chief Priest responsible, in order not to disappoint honored guests, arranged for this most moving of dances to be danced to an excellent electronic tape-recorder. The dancer was a young man, neither attached to the Imperial Household nor in any way a hereditary shrine-servant. He was only the Captain of the local judo team; he was also a magnificent dancer. It was not his expressiveness that moved us, or his personality, or his virtuosity. It was his gravity, the fulfilled correctness of his immaculate presence, the elevation, not alone of his spirit, but of the spirit of what he danced. His being as well as his doing was the praise of God.

American dancers and lovers of dancing will welcome Gagaku, not alone as a magnificent gift from a splendid culture, but as an exemplar of the sources of our theater, our one world-theater, which was, first of all, ordered movement to honor the changing seasons, the survival of life, love and creation. Gagaku is a wonderful show, but something more. It is an embodiment of truth framed in every splendor human hands and minds have contrived to praise the principle that may, if we can manage to realize it, help us in our own struggle towards perfection.

Balanchine's Fourth Dimension

There seems little one can add at this point to the Kirstein-Balanchine story, one of the remarkable cross-fertilizations in the culture of the twentieth century. Kirstein has been quoted as saying, "My pleasure is to make it possible for him to do what he wants." Sharing the same convictions before they met—that tradition was at the base of the new— the two men together forged what has come to be known as an "American" style of dancing.

At Kirstein's invitation, Balanchine came to America in 1933, established the essential school, formed a series of companies, and eventually achieved stability with the creation of the New York City Ballet in 1948. Balanchine became arguably the greatest choreographer of the twentieth century (with competition, at most, from Ashton, Graham, Cunningham, and perhaps Tudor), enlarging the technical possibilities of dance as he sought new artistic ends.

As might be expected, Kirstein has provided numerous analyses of the Balanchine aesthetic as well as of the individual ballets. In "Balanchine's Fourth Dimension" and, at further remove, in "The Policy of a Ballet Company," he addresses the "physical" Balanchine, discussing matters of technique, teaching, and the Balanchine "instrument." Kirstein's images are generated by notions of bodies in space. He is concerned with Balanchine's velocity of motion—that kinetic energy charging the "material of dancing" that is the subject of many of his ballets.

N.R.

◇ Reprinted from *Vogue* 160:10 (Dec. 1972), 118–129, 203, 205–206.

TO START, let us assume certain facts which appear to be, at least statistically, verifiable. There is no important dance company in the West today that does not desire to have included in its season one or more of George Balanchine's ballets. The Royal Ballet alone this winter is presenting three of his works new to the British repertory. There is no state or civic company in Europe east of the Iron Curtain, in Canada, Australia, or South America that ceases to make urgent requests for more of the same. Of what other living choreographer is this true?

Music is partner to dancing. Balanchine was the self-chosen colleague of Stravinsky for half a century, the most important and fertile collaboration of its kind since Petipa's with Tchaikovsky. Furthermore, Balanchine has been credited with (or, often as not, accused of) choosing and establishing a contemporary archetype, journalistically labeled "the Balanchine dancer": a tall, slim girl with a small head, long legs, cool temperament, and athletic virtuosity. No other choreographer, past or present, has had attributed to him or her so severely idiosyncratic a choice. Also, in proficiency, prolificity, musical capacity, and personal style, Balanchine occupies a contemporary position that is isolated, prominent, and, to a degree, popular.

This says little of the quality or variety of his accomplishment, of his work's wit, elitism, arrogance, passion, or playfulness. These vibrate as subjective judgments. If "beauty is in the eye of the beholder," so then is elitism, arrogance, and the rest. These abstractions do not refer specifically to Balanchine's choreography, his maps of movement, but rather to an overall attitude governing the nature of dancing itself. Balanchine's means for composition—measured first by a sonorous metric: music—are at once highly personal and radically academic. They subsume his notion of the training of performers, which precedes a choice of dancers with whom he feels he can work. This depends not only on a preference for a certain type of physique as raw material but also on the acceptance of a discipline by aspirants from the first stages of instruction. As he told an anxious mother thirty-five years ago when she was worried about whether or not her greatly gifted if headstrong daughter would ever become a Ballerina (with a capital "B"), "La danse, madame, c'est une question morale." (P.S. She did; and it was not a question of morals, which were local and lax, but of morale and morality, which were solid.)

The platonic ideal of "a Balanchine dancer" is not necessarily an androgynous nymphet who might as easily be an Olympic champion fencer, skater, diver, or equestrienne. In popular terms, however, mastery at peak levels in these sister disciplines roughly illustrates his requirements. It may be noted that in such display, one element is lacking: self-expression, personality; what used to be called "soul." The aims of sport are not those of art. The chief competition a dancer faces is in a mirror; it is the image of a self whose imperfections must be conquered, whose perfectibility must be exercised if any perfection is ever to be won. There are no statistical records to be broken nor championships to be won. The supreme judges are teachers and ballet masters to whom an aspirant commits herself or himself. When applause is won, it is for victory over no opponent but for victory against the pull of gravity, coincidental with homage to music. It also depends on moral or metaphysical factors that many find convenient to ignore or distasteful to admit. Such hinge on opinions of the artist's identity or sense of self; a relationship to, or consideration of, one's proper position in a repertory company.

A committed Balanchine dancer (with a small "d") comes to realize that Personality (with an enormous "P") is a bundle of haphazard characteristics frozen in a pleasing mask for immediate identification and negotiable prestige. No matter what is danced—and it makes little difference—stardom dims the dancing. What is danced is perforce secondary. There are two types of ballet companies: those interested in selling stars and those occupied in demonstrating and extending the dance, as such.

In order to propose any impartial opinion regarding ballet, one must take into account several sectors of opinion-makers or -possessors. These are, in varying levels of influence, teachers and students of dancing, journalists and/or critics, and audiences, of various persuasions. There is a further and largely irrelevant judgment, set down long after the fact of performance, emanating from historians.

Teachers and their students are influential framers of opinion at a basic technical level; they know about dancing in the same way the ball-game public appreciates baseball and football from having played these games from the age of nine. Local studios in far-flung communities provide raw material that later comprises focal companies. These studios are not, in a strict sense, schools comparable to civic or state academies, since instead of a specializing faculty the instruction is from single teachers. It is often by chance alone whether very young students are helped or hurt by such study. In a few cases, there are, to a limited degree, excellent teachers whose natural good taste and (uncommon) common sense manage to endow them with analytical methods that, at the most, do no harm. But at best, such training is useful only for the first few years, for soon bright students will surpass their teachers in technique alone.

When Balanchine first came to the United States in 1933, he brought with him principal teachers responsible for his own training in the Russian Imperial and State schools. Such training was exceptional, a vital factor in the development of companies and repertories. The French and Italians dominated nineteenth-century classic dance. In our time, leadership and mastery in education have been Russian, with important Scandinavian additives. Teaching methods were developed on a basis of contact with constant performance. Academies provided dancers for opera houses; small children were continually dancing on the same stage as their teachers. Dominant performer-instructors passed from stage to classroom and back. What was designed as spectacle was later analyzed and repeated as training exercise.

From 1914, Balanchine had the benefit of two generations of such teaching, which bridged repertories that were the inheritance of the "Romantic" era of the 1830's and '40's through the revolutions of Fokine and Nijinsky under Diaghilev from 1909 through 1919. A major advantage of the Russian schools has been strong male teachers, not alone for boys but as builders of strength in girls.

A disadvantage in many of our provincial studios is the lack of encouragement (on their parents' part) of male aspirants, although excellent material is widely available. Balanchine has been responsible for a philosophy that has treated girls as if they were as athletic as their brothers. He has proved they can be fiery hummingbirds rather than dying swans, with the capacity of channel swimmers. The present virtuosic power of American *corps de ballet* dancers is, in large part, due to his insistence on, or imitation of, his demanding requirements. His idea of what is stylish and suitable for American dancers is a marriage between the court manners (consideration or formal courtesy) of Saint Petersburg when he was a boy and the improvisational energy and spark of Manhattan's musical comedy, which, as a young man, he staged influentially for Rodgers and Hart musicals and Goldwyn films in the decade of 1935–45.

Some teachers, and consequently their students, consider Balanchine's orientation a physical and/or mental tyranny. A common complaint is that certain bodies (but more importantly, temperaments) don't "feel comfortable" under his system. These may transfer a vague discomfort into more precise antipathy. Their very natures (or "souls") resist Balanchine's requirements. Their muscular structures are consequently justified in revolt. A few tell themselves that, in his rigorous classes, they can be "crippled." It is naïve of pretenders to any discipline to consider "comfort" as a criterion. When students train, as often as not, their normal adaptability channels what energy they've been granted into habits that can be repeated with the least thought or effort. Only a comparatively few candidates enjoy extending their own presences to extremities of possibility.

The majority of dance instruction, not only in America but all over the Western world, is far more primitive, for example, than similar teaching of piano, violin, or woodwind. If a student does not have unusual energy, perspicacity, or the luck to realize lacks in a local teacher, preferences and habits transmitted early tend to take over. Young dancers, when they join a company, discover to their amazement (and their mothers' dismay) that their training to date has not only been incomplete but damaging. Balanchine takes no dancers who have not survived (or have not been subjected to) such training or who will not submit to what his notion of what body-and-mind should realize. His system is not "comfortable" but, finally, it can be comforting.

Superior professionals with considerable Parisian or Scandinavian reputations have come to him comparatively late. What led them to quit security, place themselves at his rude disposal? A sense that he, before anyone else in their time, had extended the parlance of spectacular human movement through a methodology based on workable traditions which he had absorbed, upon which he built and is still building. At the start of such a connection, there can be a real crisis of accommodation. Balanchine's severity, strict analysis, and rationale of certain arcane technical considerations go counter to what is diversely and widely taught.

"Comfortable" in a new and unfamiliar structuring some dancers are not and never will be. Within a short time, however, if a generosity or openness of temperament is granted, many are comforted by a fresh enlargement of capacity and outlook which, if at first only to themselves, seems miraculous.

First, but less important than Balanchine's more innovative contributions, are some purely mechanical extensions or modifications that have increased both idiom and practice, which are more apparent in classroom than onstage. He has emphasized an extension of three-dimensional plasticity not alone in *épaulement*—the expressive carriage of head-and-neck-on-shoulders, where due to the vivid magnetism of the face it is focused to show first—but to the entire body. He has accentuated a spiral dominance in asymmetry as against frontal symmetry in an attack on static positioning, which tends to interrupt a flow of movement for the sake of stability. Three-dimensional plasticity, the difference between a bas-relief and a freestanding figure released in air and action, has its most legible artistic definition in the *contrapposto* or opposition of bodily members in baroque sculpture.

In one sense, Balanchine is a mannerist sculptor, following the *maniera* or grand manner of posturing derived from Michelangelo's exaggeration and re-creation of possibilities in the nude. Balanchine has accentuated a reappraisal of the *plié,* the bending and rising on the soles and heels, in a manner that runs counter to much foreign practice. Balanchine's classes accentuate an apparent "off-balance," a dominant kinetic follow through, the reverse of a head-on, four-square "correctness."

Among purely mechanical factors Balanchine has accentuated acceleration of movement. The driving, processive insistent quality in Stravinsky's rhythmic progress has been translated by Balanchine into a metric. Before 1909, important soloists danced their assignments with staccato or fast sections while the *corps de ballet* was reserved for quick passages chiefly in the *ballabile* that would end a scene or act.

To a great extent, Balanchine has de-soloized the classic dance, demoting the *prima ballerina assoluta*, a heretofore sacred monster, by promoting the corps to work in ways that previously would have been the property only of soloists. This process of democratization has caused vocative journalism and professional antagonism to his methods. He is rumored to be uninterested in strong "personalities"; therefore his attitude results in a dehumanization of individuals, a restriction of "emotion" and, alas, "soul."

There is truth here, but such criticism must be read in context. A local teacher in a small town needs the advertisement of a potential star-personality upon which to pin reputation and livelihood. Local teachers may latch onto an energetic child (and as often the child's overambitious mother), equipping both with great nonsense about what will succeed for their dual ends. Often this has been assiduous imitation of some notability, preferably stolen from films or television.

Shirley Temple can be accused of having inadvertently deformed a generation of American dancers; prior to that, Anna Pavlova provided similar service; and contemporary parallels are not hard to hunt. But whether or not a young dancer from Seattle or San Diego, Miami or Minneapolis eventually gets to Balanchine is no prank of fate.

Through a decade's support by The Ford Foundation, local studios that have, for one reason or another, been magnetized by the meaning of Balanchine's repertory, sent their best students to be subjected to his tender mercies. Many, if not most, of these have joined his company and have done much credit to their earlier instruction. For those who have not been so magnetized and whose capacities have not fulfilled his demands, it is easy to see how his regimen appears tyrannical. And, as for the dehumanization of dancers, it must be understood that he considers them not as "personalities" but as embodied spirits—in fact, as angels, messengers sent with certain glad tidings incarnate in their persons which are capable of being taught—not as a collection of accidental tastes, preferences, or prejudices come by through ignorance of a wide world or its plentiful and difficult history.

An advanced student, as the most recent full-fledged member of a company, becomes merely primary material for manipulation. It may be that an entirely new start must be made, and one hard to face. Bright hopes are dashed: "Where am I?" "When was I supposed to be so good?" "Where is this?" "What am I doing here?"

Conversely, other young dancers who showed hardly as much promise before they joined the company find themselves promptly precipitated into important service. This abrupt procedure is inherent in Balanchine's

116

practice. In the older official troupes, promotion and position was by tenure, almost irrespective of talent, since the *prima ballerina assoluta* was guaranteed her perquisites. Balanchine's attitude is not more "democratic," since it depends on a self-proclaimed, obvious, and legible aristocracy of talent. It is not so much a question of how long a dancer has worked in a school or a company but the given capacity for the given moment.

A crisis comes in some dancers' lives when they cannot stomach a system that seems to reduce *their* notion of themselves to another's. Why should anyone know better than oneself how one should be best deployed? If a performing artist has inner confidence and a sense of service, a collective situation is comfortable; and realization of it acceptable. Some come to recognize that Balanchine is not stupid; he does not waste his human resources.

Dancers devoted to and comfortable with Balanchine consider finally that his interest in them is not personal; that they are to be judged as jewels and are to be handled as a skilled craftsman sets stones. They have been faceted and polished to a high shine; but they cannot by themselves set themselves into a ring, necklace, or tiara. Some believe he can make them glow, not as stars but as gems.

A decade ago, a male dancer on the verge of a world career thought to please Balanchine by offering himself—on his own terms—as a Star. He was told that when he tired of playing the Prince in *Giselle,* he could come around again. *Giselle*-itis is an incurable malady and battens on itself. There have been numerous tentative approaches on the part of renowned performers who, for one reason or another, imagine that contact with Balanchine's repertory somehow insulated from Balanchine's self might grace their careers. Balanchine is uncomfortable with them, for essentially they wish to surrender nothing of their characteristic personalism. They may wish to enhance it by a spin-off from his brand of magic.

Similarly, some of Balanchine's own dancers decide that he is not "attracted" by their "personalities." Usually, this has meant they want to dance *Giselle.* Students are brainwashed early by being told that *Giselle* and *Hamlet* are two peaks of performance possibility.

Journalism and criticism are supposedly two disjunct services; as practiced, neither adds much to analytical understanding of what actually goes on when dancers perform. These exercises are usually displays of personal sensibility unsupported by technical information, which would be the mandatory equipment of any reporter of a piano or violin recital, to say nothing of the symphonic repertory, chess, or basketball.

Few critics who cover or smother ballet have spent time in a classroom or can compare the several styles of teaching methods. Both the idiom and design of ballet are considered to be self-evident from observation of performers' personalities. The daily or weekly story commands little space and small time to fill it. *How* she or he danced is saluted; but the essence of *what* has occurred eludes formulation in hurried words.

As for the general public: it is an odd beast. Its appetites and curiosities are hydra-headed. It has thousands of eyes, ears, and is in fact no single creature but composed of multiple members and bands of partisans who express their pleasure, participation, or lack of it, in as many manners. The most gross is thrilled and soothed by *les monstres sacrés* of theater and sport, whose professional deformation has arrived at incandescent narcissism. A sort of sexual satisfaction is released in mutually self-congratulatory howlings and hurlings: *bravo, brava, bravi,* 'mid cascades of bouquets. From this beast, claques are recruited which rev up factitious enthusiasm that is as evident in the hysteria of opera buffs and rock singers as balletomanes.

Then there is a middle public that is amused by all sorts of spectacle from Shakespeare to the circus, and that, on occasion, is not averse to good dancing if it is bright, cheerful, and brief, for the attention span is short.

Finally, there is an informed or specialist public which brings to the theater experience in comparative judgment strengthened by interest in other arts and crafts, sciences and ideas, sharing the culture of museums and libraries and familiarity with musical literature. It inclines towards a dominantly visual imagination. It looks and listens in a combined operation. It has a somewhat clinical consideration of what its eyes reflect. It absorbs spectacle in depth, dispassionately passionate. It is not blinded by prejudgment. This public comes to look with an openness that is responsive to the quality of the pageant's whole deployment, beyond personalism or personality. It comprises the ideal normal subscription audience, which Balanchine has relied on for support for the last thirty-five years and which has seconded other enlightened support from the principal foundations.

The celebration of the achievement of Stravinsky as a composer for dancing, held in New York last June, proved, among a bouquet of felicitously staged works, that Balanchine's most recent choreographic invention was the culmination of a historic progress. In three works (out of a dozen)—two of which were presented on the opening night *(Symphony in Three Movements; Violin Concerto)* and in a third smaller but possibly more perfect entity *(Duo Concertant)*—he displayed an inventiveness that here was as far ahead of *Agon* (1957) as *Agon* was of *Apollo* (1928). In three constructions of complex subtlety, Balanchine's unique additions to the skill and science of composed body movement were revealed as never before.

When Balanchine was composing his full-evening's version of *A Midsummer Night's Dream* (which he always insisted was, in this case, not Shakespeare's but Mendelssohn's), he was continually puzzled by the problem of how to demonstrate by physical movement the verbal fireworks of Bottom's account of his dream-journey. Nick Bottom, the weaver, has been enchanted by Oberon the Fairy King, transformed into a donkey, loved by Queen Titania, and then restored to his original lowly estate. Awakening, Bottom feels his head for those long hairy ears that are no longer his and tries to make sense of what-all he has (possibly) dreamed:

"Methought I was—there is no man can tell what. . . . Methought I had . . . but man is but a patched fool, if he will offer to say what methought I had. The eye of man hath not heard, the ear of man hath not seen, man's hand is not able to taste, his tongue to conceive, nor his heart to report what my dream was."

Here Shakespeare was parodying a famous New Testament passage:

". . . Eye hath not seen, nor ear heard, neither have entered into the heart of man. . . ." *(I Corinthians: ii, 9)*

What Balanchine has been able to do with his kind of dancer is to conceive a dimension of spectacle in which music is seen and dancing is heard, but to which no words apply. In this he has imposed and employed a metaphysic that has to do with the nature of order and with persons or selves in that ordering. In his peculiar fusion of music with movement, errant or arrant personalities have no place. The structure of the music is invested by the bodies of girls and boys in driving motion. They recline on a visual and aural counterpoint and harmony that is both rhythmic floor and expressive cushion and springboard. They are not costumed but uniformed; not starred but ignited. They are not machines but provocatively stripped musculatures. Their specific anatomies are not mechanized but objectively motivated in a self-governing frame, dictated by the flow, balance, harmonics, speed, and exuberance of sound. Physicality in the tense relationships of Balanchine's dancers kept under so strict a discipline in so free an exercise pushes the spectacle to a high pressure point. Everything is so focused, compressed, packed, playful that it is as if the entire design were patterned on coiled steel or explosive fuels. Combinations of music in motion approach a fourth dimension that cannot be verbally defined.

With Balanchine, eye and mind translate or transform sight as sound. Superficies of scenery and costume, the ordinary appanage of theatrical decor, poetic pretexts, and, above all, the exhibition of self-loving and self-limiting personalities are consigned to more primary levels. His fourth dimension is beyond the primary three of plastic formality. Sight as sound, defined by dancers dancing a dance, spells an extension of what is possible to inspect as orderly occurrence on a super-humane plane. It is a severe statement and seems to deny chaos, chance and, in its paradoxical dialectic of determinism and free will, is an important notion to consider as this century hurtles towards its millennial crisis.

The Policy of a Ballet Company

IS IT POSSIBLE to define the "policy" of a ballet company? What is meant by "policy?" Webster says that policy is "a course of action adopted (especially in state affairs)"—and, further—"prudent procedure." *Polis* is Greek for city; metropolis is a great city; understood as a model or metaphor of a civic institution, a metropolitan ballet company may be thought of as pursuing policy, whether prudent or not. "Prudence" is "cautious or judicious anticipation or foreseeing."

Have ballet companies in the past had policies, determining directions consciously projected? If so, how did they relate to circumstance, the political scene, the historical background? The policy of cultural exposure in the North Italian Renaissance where ballet first constituted itself as a princely appenage was part of propaganda for competitive glory. Louis XIV enlarged its scope, making it a permanent branch of spectacular self-glorification in the aid of French imperialism, involving the finest national gifts in music, dancing and decoration. His example became a royal habit during the eighteenth century. In the nineteenth, with the construction of large popular civic opera houses, these were leased to private impresarios for commercial exploitation. Policy, if their manipulation may be dignified as such, was determined by the provision of suitable vehicles for a succession of star dancers. Glorification shifted from reflections of a princely patron to the *prima ballerina*, who, throughout the second half of the cen-

◊ Reprinted from *Playbill* (New York State Theater issue, Nov. 11–30, 1975), 3–4, 6, 9–10.

tury, except in Russia and Scandinavia, surpassed the male dancer, reducing him to a mere *porteur* or support.

The policy of the imperial Russian ballet was a hybrid of royal patronage and the need to fill subscription seasons by novelty and the revival of old favorites. Novelties were strictly formulated by recipe. Music served to propel steps within a restricted vocabulary; visual furnishing, while opulent was deemed satisfying if it appeared costly, but, as with music, bore no connection with progressive revolutions being conducted in Western Europe by symphonic and operatic composers alongside revolutionary painters and poets. Choreography, in many ways, was part of the visual upholstery. Steps given to the ballerina were ingenious needlework, emphasizing a unique capacity; the corps served as a uniform setting for a crown jewel. Music in Petersburg was in the hands of two ingenious and capable court composers, Minkus and Pugni; the grand operatic repertory included ballets as divertissements during which voices could find a rest, rather than as independent works with a primary interest. The important ballets that have survived, mainly with the three capital Tschaikovsky scores, still provide the principal star roles for late-twentieth-century performers. As for policy, politics or success, we must remember that both *Swan Lake* and *The Sleeping Beauty* were relative failures at their respective debuts. They violated the normal expectations of a sedentary public by their seriousness, complex scoring, adventurous dignity, their ambition to be considered something above light amusement. "Ballet" and "ballet dancer" were terms long associated with superficial entertainment, which was far less the case with operatic or dramatic performance. The rigid policy of the Russian imperial theaters was to provide spectacle that charmed, that gave immediate pleasure by visual brightness, and which, on occasion, offered diplomatic or patriotic service with the introduction of native or foreign national dances.

When Diaghilev brought the Russians to Paris in 1909, he established a policy of newness, of what would come to be recognized as the deployment of a permanent advance-guard, allied to music, decoration and choreography. This was a drastic departure from imperial policy. He brought *Giselle* as a vehicle for Karsavina and Nijinsky but it now seemed *démodé* to Parisian taste. He also presented a series of national dances, which to the West seemed a canonization of *l'âme slave,* the Slavic ethos compounded of mongol and tartar. As for ballet itself, novelty was incarnate in Fokine's early work with scores by Stravinsky, which, at the time, could not have been produced in Petersburg. The policy of Diaghilev's later seasons was determined by the fact that he was serving a Parisian public which dictated' world taste. Separated from a source of well-trained Russian dancers by the Revolution, he took over painters and musicians from the School of Paris in their most radical dimension, bullying and often baffling a public by outrage, caprice and the spirit of youthful shock and adventure. This was a rational policy in adapting materials at hand while compensating for those not available. Diaghilev understood how to irritate and satisfy an elegant concentration of taste-makers and taste-consumers. Dancing was at least effective but, as for choreography, it hardly compared with the brilliance of earlier seasons. Policy was shifted from Russia to France and England, as politics in the large worldly sense dictated. Seen in the perspective of half a century, it spelled novelty, discovery, daring and the continual definition of persistent modernity.

When, in 1934, Balanchine came to New York to found a school and company, the chief model was Diaghilev's inheritance as exhibited by the Ballets Russes de Monte Carlo, performing a number of his ballets produced between 1909 and 1929, with recent additions by Balanchine and Massine. America had seen no ballet on an international level since Nijinsky's ill-fated tour of 1916–17, and welcomed the Russian dancers more enthusiastically than before. Balanchine's first tentative efforts were towards the establishment of an "American" ballet, although these were received as an extension of Franco-Russian taste since there was little enough of a native authenticity to satisfy even the most sympathetic observers.

The problem of sounding an indigenous voice had troubled American writers and artists for a century. Whitman and Melville, however, unpopular their initial reception, had laid the basis upon which Mark Twain and Jack London would build international reputations. Whistler and Sargent outshone Winslow Homer and Eakins as far as Paris and London went. As for "serious" musicians, there were a number of German- and French-trained composers who had some historical interest, but they offered little intrinsically, compared to the great Europeans. Ballet, as seen by New Yorkers, was an Italian or Viennese import, and as in opera, boasted few native artists. When the first great American reputations arrived in the persons of Isadora Duncan and Ruth St. Denis, recognition derived from their presumed inspiration from Greece or the Orient. Yet popular theater, ragtime, jazz, musical comedy, the vaudeville circuits and above all cinema, increasingly gave a rich vein of indigenous character with intense personification of cowboy, gangster, the life of cities and the Old South.

Those of us in some way responsible for the foundation of "American" ballet in the early 'thirties sought this genre of sensibility far more than the atmosphere of the imperial scene. Balanchine, as many Russians, had felt the vitality of a new-found-land even before he left Russia. American jazz had penetrated to Petersburg after the first World War; Russia was in a crisis of revolution, and the artists who had been former servants of the Tsar were now proponents of Futurism, Constructivism and collaborators of Mayakovsky, Alexandr Blok and Eisenstein. When Balanchine came to Western Europe in 1924, this progressive attitude was supported by Diaghilev who, nevertheless, had refused to become Minister of Fine Arts for the Soviets; he preferred to conduct his own crusade for modernism free of the exigence of Bolshevik doctrine.

Thus when Balanchine arrived in America with a predisposition for its tempo, he found himself soon working on Broadway with Rodgers and Hart, in Hollywood with Sam Goldwyn and the brothers Gershwin. This would not mean a resultant repertory of standbys based on American rhythms and pretexts, although there were a number of ballets produced which labored under the constraint of folkloristic compulsion in token homage to what was hoped to be a growing national appetite. This kind of theater was far better served on Broadway or in Hollywood. But Balanchine, forging a policy which has been followed for the next forty years, was deeply touched by dominant factors within the American cultural complex, as distilled in Manhattan.

When one analyzes what was given by his early companies, first called "The American Ballet," later "The American Ballet Caravan," one can recognize, first of all, a particular type of performer who was magnetized by his gift and person. Many had already been trained by Russian teachers—Fokine in New York, and three ex-imperial ballerinas in Paris studios. Fokine had been in America since 1916, repeating his earlier successes on a compromise scale, but attempting nothing of permanence or with a local or contemporary flavor. The use of popular music, ragtime or jazz, for serious ballet seemed unthinkable. Russians in exile were victims of crippling nostalgia. Balanchine had been freed of such bewilderment, first by the revolution itself, then by Diaghilev, and now most powerfully by his attraction to what New York could best offer. What he recognized as especially characteristic was the force of the rhythm of New York, symbolized by athleticism, speed, extrovert energy, the reckless dynamism in its syncopation and asymmetry, and as well a kind of impersonal mastery, an abstraction of life symbolized by the grid-plan and numerical nomination of its streets and avenues. These elements he synthesized for his own purpose, and it became policy. His dancers were required to move faster, with more steps in tighter sequences than any previous corps. In compressing or eliminating mimicry and pageantry, he compacted the dance-element to a tightness of largely kinetic interest. His insistence lay in the direction of patterned movement rather than individual personalities; it was "choreography"—the map of motion—rather than any attempted equal balance or synthesis of music, movement and decoration which he welded into an unspoken but visually eloquent program. And from this policy was born a company.

To say that he made dance dominant in ballet is poor history, but in a sense it is true he forced the issue. Personal projection, visual opulence, as frames for a unique or superior performer, he rejected. Stars were discountenanced for artistic as well as economic reasons. His American partners had patriotic ambitions and the borrowing of foreign professionals seemed betrayal. This naive chauvinism was discarded after Balanchine soon enough established his own and his company's security. Now a phenomenon which came to be popularly recognized as a "Balanchine-dancer" commenced to be something of the darling of journalism. There was, however, a residual truth in the vulgarization of his concept of a ballerina as an athlete rather than an empress.

The archetypes of Louis XIV, Catherine the Great (even Queen Victoria), lurked in the minds of those who then determined the policy for nascent national ballets. It was a radical departure to employ the competitive kinetics of basketball and tennis as a physical criterion. The star as sovereign, as reigning queen of the dance, enthroned as an object purveyed as a commodity of known value, had served impresarios for a century. Balanchine was intent on creating a *company*, an organism, a *corps d'élite*, a democratic corps de ballet, a body of dancers, without hierarchical status or fixed table of organization which could demonstrate celerity, muscularity, interplay of sportive action, without reference to the prestige of former reputations. The policy of his company was involved primarily with the stuff of dance rather than the presentation of personalism. Freedom from the tyranny of stardom is not purchased cheaply. Star-reputations, secure and negotiable, command an easy audience. To insist on the quality of movement as such, rather than the expression of an attractive idiosyncrasy, was hardly courting popularity. But Balanchine proposed a new aristocracy, the election of an entire corps as a body of interchangeable soloists. Capable aspirants emerged from his schooling in an advanced stage of preparation, taught according to his aim at speed and control, a linear preoccupation and a highly plastic and emotional expressiveness. The level of efficiency required far exceeded the normal perfunctory services of the old corps de ballet. An inflexible, quasi-military code of achievement established in European companies, from prima ballerina assoluta, through principal and subsidiary soloist, down to the last *coryphée*, was abandoned as wasteful and self-restricting. If parts suited a new entrant into his company, Balanchine at once promoted a recent student to important roles. The company was an instrument of repertory in all its variety, not a frame for a reputation.

And for this kind of organism, a new repertory was mandatory. There were more dance-action, steps, combinations in the clock-time of *Agon's* duration than in many "full-length" ballets. Such concentration demanded re-education in an audience; without padding, repetition or fat, Balanchine's most progressive repertory (notably his Stravinsky ballets) was determined on a basis of analytical structure. In the fifty works with which he has provided the contemporary international repertory, all of which were first performed by his own dancers, a policy of concentrated yet generalized employment of an entire corps is presupposed. He has serviced a new territory of movement without recourse to revivals, although he has continually paid homage to his masters, Petipa and Ivanov, in recensions of their originals. His policy as to revivals laid no claim to claimed "authenticity" for which there was no truthful living witness. The older steps and sequences were used as a skeleton, fleshed out with the action of which his dancers were capable in their increased development. His ballets aimed to suit the dancers he had drawn to him; the map of movement came first; then the dancers, according to their capacity and temperament were fitted to it. But it was not personality that determined the primary policy; it was the abstracted, refined and essential material of dancing itself.

Classic Ballet: Aria of the Aerial

A RECENT WRITER in a counter-culture weekly suggests (more in sorrow than anger) that, for our 'seventies, dancing as a popular cult overtakes rock music of the 'sixties. This may or may not be as true of regional as of urban America, but on a grass-roots level, local proliferation of holiday *Nutcrackers* on some professional basis is astonishing. Parallel to this is the increased presence of "Dance" in colleges, with residencies for well-known companies. The number of young people now aspiring to become dancers approaches actors, singers or musicians, a condition unthinkable twenty years ago, while there is a new paying public which hopefully organizes economic support, even state and civic aid.

Dance includes separate families for teaching and performance: "ballet," "ethnic," "social" and "modern." For ballet, there is a single canon of instruction comparable to that which equips pianists, violinists and singers in fingering or voice control. Different emphases obtain but the alphabet taught is universally legible from long tradition, demanding the same criteria. "Ethnic," which includes social styles (more for fun than show), encompasses folk dance, recreation for amateurs and source material for theater. Formerly "national" dances, stage-versions of Spanish, Slav or "Oriental" were instructed, but today these, as balance or alternative to academic ballet, are largely replaced by "modern."

◊ Reprinted from *Playbill* (New York State Theater issue, April 27–May 11, 1976), 3–4, 6, 8–9.

During the 'thirties when "modern-dance" first asserted itself, an inheritance from Ruth St. Denis and Ted Shawn fragmented into main lines of apostolic succession. Forty years later, energy is lodged in the repertory of Martha Graham, her immediate heirs and theirs. Increasingly, with a use of the ballet *barre* and borrowings from ballet-trained instructors, "modern-dance" has lost some of its early antagonism to classic ballet. Stylistic lines blur and fuse. However, important polarities exist, so it may be useful to fix parameters of Ballet and Modern. Cursory definition involves oversimplification; generally it can be stated that ballet-training and performance accentuates the area of air, denial of gravity by leg-work in beats and jumps; brilliant multiple turns; speed in the stage-traverse; *pointe* (toe)-shoes; virtuoso acrobatics (attracting large audiences to opera houses) accompanied by orchestras of symphonic dimensions.

"Modern-dance" came into being partly as a reaction against such factors, with a basic rationale accentuating the solar-plexus as source of contraction and release; a response to earth's gravity and pull; "psychology-through-movement" with ideas from myth and social-protest. Stemming from Bennington College, then spreading to state normal-schools where it began to replace "Phys. Ed" (physical education) as a more aesthetic body-building, "modern-dance" acquired the fervor of a crusade, vaunting ethical superiority over "mere" (mindless) entertainment.

Along with such protestant policy, there were other determinants. Ballet instruction was then not widely available nor performances visible. Conditions of labor and production costs were prohibitive for unpaid volunteers. A modesty of visual and musical accompaniment made virtues of necessity, fast elevated into articles of faith. It was proclaimed that main differences between "modern" and ballet were between "principles" and "technique," as if one lacked skill, the other morality. Both had both. Rather, difference was and is between accidental idiosyncrasy against tradition, personalism versus collectivity, discontinuity as opposed to an unbroken line. "Modern-dance" opted for self-expressive "originality," defined by a few notable heterodoxies. Self-expression triumphed without providing either a cohesive teaching method or a repertory past individual utterance. "Modern-dance" lies among the minor verse of theater. When one counts how few "major" poets (or anything else) there are, how "major" so many "minor" ones, this seems no aesthetic limitation, although it may prove both a temporal and popular one.

No matter how close "modern-dance" approaches widespread acceptance, however flexible or eclectic its expanded idiom, essential contrariety remains. "Modern-dance" choreographers can compose for ballet-trained professionals with few limitations, but "modern-dancers" cannot slip from one technique to the other, lacking academic classic training. Few modernists start aged eight or nine, which is mandatory for ballet as for piano or violin virtuosi. Admittance to ballet-schooling (at its most responsible), is not licensed by simple ambition, but through expert opinion. Severe physical preconditions determine the ultimate chances of a classical professional; such "elitist" limitations need not deter "modern." In ballet, as far as doing-one's-own-thing goes, there is little scope for "originality" or improvisation. "Modern-dancers," since they start so much later, with minds more developed, are free to intellectualize impulses which have no bearing on acrobatic efficiency depending on synthetic method. "Modern-dance" training is based on a few isolated concepts tailored first to their unique inventors and restricted by such stylization, then adapted by a more or less liberated succession to their own peculiar needs and possibilities.

Ballet's vocabulary, by which strong executants magnetize big audiences, depends on muscular and nervous control deriving from four centuries' research in a logic combining gross anatomy, plane geometry and musical counterpoint. Its repertory is comparable to opera, symphony and classical drama. "Modern-dance" may be equated with the collected works of contemporary prose or verse writers. It has still to be proven that subsequent performances lacking their originators may long hold the intensity of their originals. "Modern-dance" is no longer a vanguard of reform. Far livelier in its current effect on both ballet and "modern" are influences from popular music, jazz and its mutations. Here, its risk lies in the very timeliness of novelty; transient slang fixated on a given epoch.

The root of ballet-training in the five academic foot-positions established some three centuries ago is not arbitrary. These determine the greatest frontal legibility and launch of the upper body as silhouette framed in a proscenium. Ballet-repertory was calculated for opera houses with orchestra pits, and balconies rendering the stage-floor a virtual backdrop for half the public. It is not the only form of theatrical dance; it is the most spectacular. Extreme acrobatism entails hazard which, overcome, sparks the most ardent audience detonation. Its filigrain of discrete steps; its speed, suavity, and flagrant tenderness; its metrical syncopation and asymmetry make visual superdrama on the broadest spectrum. In "modern-dance," focus is elsewhere. From its start, it was on and in central somatic areas of the body, rather than extension of peripheries. A prime distinction exists between Occidental and Oriental dancing: open against closed, centripedal against centrifugal; kinetic against (dominantly) static; fast against slow. This is oversimplification, but a like parallel might be set for ballet against "modern": aerial versus terrestrial.

From Denishawn down to today, the Orient, both in movement and morality, strongly influenced "modern-dance." From ideas via Emerson, Whitman and Nietzsche invoked by Isadora Duncan, with Denishawn's experience of Japan and India, first intellectual, then ethical superiority was claimed from religious precedent and temple practice. Ballet, with its vulgar connotations as frivolous luxury, sexual toy or musical bagatelle (until Diaghilev), offered a likely target for self-educated amateurs. Isadora was a puritan; she feared seduction of her students by the charms of Russian ballet. In the wake of war and disaster, German and Austrian poets, painters, musicians and dancers of the 'twenties and early 'thirties proposed valid experiment which gained prestige as a passionate vanguard. Serious ballet had been lacking in their countries for nearly a century. American tours by Mary Wigman, Kurt Jooss, Harald Kreutzberg corroborated and encouraged our own modernists. But, as Diaghilev himself said—the Germans had learned how to move as they forgot how to dance.

At the same time, classic ballet received fresh impetus with the arrival in New York of Diaghilev's heirs. America had seen no Russian dancers since 1917. Through painting by Matisse and Picasso, concerts by Stravinsky and Prokoviev, audiences were eager and prepared for "modern" ballets by Massine, Nijinska and Balanchine. This repertory was as much novelty as "modern-dance" and bore slight kinship to Pavlova's *Dying Swan*. However, the new ballets spoke with a Parisian accent and further spurred an opposition which was not only struggling for progressive form, but also a nascent national expression. From such tensions "American Ballet" was born.

It is not too much to claim that its present popularity began in commercial theater, on Broadway and in Hollywood. The strongest exterior influence on the development of the academic dance has derived (and still does, largely through Stravinsky) from jazz rhythm, beat, the shifting pulse and syncopation of styles and steps from ragtime to rock. "Modern-dance" unquestionably extended possibilities. Unorthodox use of the body in ballet, from Nijinsky and his successors was more an inversion of academic positioning than any radical extension of technique. The rehabilitation of theatrical elegance from commonplace habit came through Kern, Gershwin and Rodgers. Balanchine's insistence on the then-unknown credit "Choreography by" in 'thirties musicals gave a new coinage to the classical line, at once sleek, rangy, athletic and modish, whose prototypes were more Ginger Rogers and Fred Astaire than ex-imperial ballerinas.

That ballet has gained a mass-audience is evident. That "modern-dance" has its own is plain. What continues to distinguish the two are elements which have always been present and do not change. In ballet what attracts its public is a sharper focus on the execution of steps, clear components of dance-speech, not necessarily at top speed nor unbroken flow, but which proclaim capacity in flexibility, lightness, power, brilliance *off the floor*. Ballet simulates a conquest, against gravity of aerial space.

Grace and elegance are involved but in unwavering control, the convincing wizardry in ease which at once conceals and demonstrates effort. In "modern-dance" the torsion of exertion, the moist anguish of psychological contest supplies pathos. The style in its tragic or mythic aspect stays agonized and intimate. Ballet is open, broad, grandiose, courtly and considerate, not of the exposed self, but of skill in steps and partners in a company. Psychic nuance, the visceral unconscious upon which "modern-dance" depended, remains its prime self-limiting material. However, as it has developed through a third or fourth generation, present champions are prompted by pop music as well as Bach and Handel, for satire and comedy, increasingly a reaction from the solemn tyranny of their progenitors. But lacking any absolute acrobatic proficiency, it is doubtful whether continued use of the term "modern" holds much permanent contemporaneity. Its attraction becomes time-bound, a nostalgic mode, like "art-nouveau," "art-deco," "modern-art."

Dame Marie Rambert proposes that classic ballet offers a service parallel to *bel canto* voice-production for trills and roulades. For her, *"La Bella Danza"* is not a nineteenth-century stylization nor a period fashion, but a steadily expandable vocabulary of spectacular action, propelling unique and extreme capacities of the dancer's instrument. For the ballet artist, mastery of steps infers domination of space, as much above the floor as upon it. Limits explored are not those of extreme emotion but of expressive motion. Determined and defined, ballet is a continuous aria of the aerial.

The Performing Arts and Our
Egregious Elite

In 1930, when Kirstein had started writing about dance, there was little or no ballet in America; by 1977, when the following article was written, ballet was a fact of national life. In the wake of the cultural explosion, ballet was big time, big business, and big budget. Could a professed elitist, who had lived "the aristocracy of talent," accept and deal with popular (and institutional) success? In Kirstein's first thirty years of battling for the dance, the problem had not arisen.

In 1963, the Ford Foundation made an unprecedented grant—over $2 million—to the New York City Ballet, with additional funds to the School of American Ballet, in recognition of dance as a cultural force and of Balanchine's preeminence in the field. The following year the New York City Ballet moved into a brand new theater designed especially for dance—designed, in fact, for "Lincoln and George"—the New York State Theater, by architect Philip Johnson. In 1965, the Federal Government entered the picture, in the form of the National Endowment for the Arts, and with the proliferation of dance performances this engendered, the audiences across the country grew dramatically. The "dance boom" had begun. The New York City Ballet started to receive substantial aid from both the National Endowment and from the New York State Council on the

◇ Reprinted from *The Performing Arts and American Society,* edited by W. McNeil Lowry. Papers prepared for the fifty-third American Assembly. Englewood Cliffs, N.J.: Prentice-Hall, 1978, pp. 181–197.

Arts; this, in turn, stimulated corporate and individual support. Other companies were expanding at parallel rates. Balanchine's Stravinsky Festival of 1972, in addition to its overwhelming artistic merit, was a press agent's dream. Tickets were unobtainable; it had become chic to go to the ballet. By 1982, the operating budget of the New York City Ballet was $13,500,000, only a portion of it covered by grants. The remaining deficit was far too large a responsibility for a single person, even one with Kirstein's powers of persuasion. A Board of Directors and Development Department handled the fundraising; the Company had moved beyond the resources of the individual. In the winter of 1978–79, for the first time in its forty-five-year history, the New York City Ballet was almost continually "sold out"—thanks to the presence of a star (Baryshnikov) and the airing of the repertory on national television ("Dance in America" and "Live from Lincoln Center"). But both of these, along with the idea of real estate—the culture complex or arts center—as a stimulus to creativity, have always been anathema to Kirstein, so success has not been absolute.

Whatever he thinks of the vast new arena for dance—whether he finds the enlarged audience plebian or enlightened—there is no question that his efforts helped to bring it all about.

N.R.

THE METAPHYSIC of intellectual and moral energy is no simple matter. The human imagination, poetic or scientific, has few limits. It is impossible, and once one might have thought it undesirable, to try to control either. Imagination—lyrical, artistic, or mechanical—is the mortal enemy of habit and routine. Sir James Fraser, the great master of *The Golden Bough,* wrote: "Imagination works upon a man as really as does gravitation and may kill him as certainly as a dose of prussic acid." Habit and routine are the safe or accountable practice of all quadrupeds and most bipeds. Anything threatening habit or routine, those relatively safe paths by which we endure to survive our hazards of accident or circumstance, causes suspicion and fear in various kinds and degrees.

The scientist, since he or she is associated with metrics which impinge upon the necessity of maintaining breath and blood, is always protected and supported more than poets or artists whose imaginativeness, invention, or fantasy are both unmeasured and immediately unmeasureable. The measure used by lyric makers and their colleagues and partners, performing artists, is neither so obviously secure, safe, nor tidy. Their very ensign flags refusal to condone or accept habit or routine. Indeed, their egotistical, selfish, or reckless renunciation of safety, the proud or vain embrace of hazard or chance, is the first gauge of creative energy or artistic quality. Naturally this has always inspired suspicion, which can grow easily to something approaching fright. This fear, inchoate or focused by prejudice, is always to be triggered at some level, whether it is manifest by distrust of disorder, a rational protection from the impractical, spendthrift, or capricious, or merely a dislike of the unlikely or unfamiliar. It is only assuaged by flagrant signs of economic neatness, interpreted as the stability of institutions or artifacts which somehow have managed to survive previous shock, terror, blame, or failure. It was Saint Augustine among the early Christian fathers who laid down the fundamental ethic of distrust of the sensory imagination: "The devil insinuates himself in sensuous forms; he adapts himself to colors, attaches himself to sounds, abides in perfumes and flowers, lurks in conversation and clogs the channels of understanding." This was an echo of Plato's exile of artists from the ideal republic because of their danger to the stability of the state.

If some political recklessness may be tolerated, together with a bit of sanguine pessimism, one might start by attempting to define what the performing arts signify on the level of absolute quality, rather than auditing their dilution by demographic assignment or median societal acceptance.

The performing arts at a high qualitative level have been and always will be majestically urban phenomena, simply because the economic base of a repertory audience lies only in cities with centers which can attract and pay for them. The bigger cities have the better audiences, indeed the single big-scale publics which can afford prime producing institutions. By and large television so far has absolutely nothing to do with quality culture, except as it squirms uneasily to pay miserable dues to a substitute for live performance, whatever the size of the screen or the integrity of the choice of images. Our big performing companies can no longer travel widely as once they could since the costs of labor and transport are highly inflated, and local subsidy, even with some cautious aid from federal pittances, seldom sanctions the necessary guarantees. But television, once and for all, is not a substitute for live virtuoso performance.

"New York is not America!" This is demonstrable fact on any map. However, if the megalopolis is not capital and criterion of our culture good or bad, where else are they located? Ask any performing artist whether, if given the choice, he or she would prefer to remain loyal to the native hearth or risk an appearance on Broadway. Without the criterion of the highest professional levels, sustained by metropolitan audiences alone, there are few standards of quality left by which the face of a nation's culture can be estimated or, indeed, displayed.

Regions avid for capital evidence of the performing arts find it hard to match the hugely greater prevalence of absolute quality in the service of great libraries and museums of the visual arts. Objects of art, apart from historic or aesthetic value, have an immediately visible, riskless, negotiable, and marketable appreciation. Museums and libraries are warehouses of success. Whatever the mortal failure of a Blake, Van Gogh, Seurat, or

Cézanne in their lifetimes, they have become saints of success, canonized in their expensive endowed sanctuaries which now replace more orthodox sites of worship. There is neither danger nor hazard in an enshrined masterpiece whatever the initial cost in neglect or suicide. But the arts of performance always involve hazards, both moral and physical. Performers are also acrobats whose tendons may snap, or voices fail, or whose ill-assorted careers may founder on commercial mischance. Failure is unfriendly, but worse, magically unlucky, and while we as democrats prize our right to fail, even in building repertories and audiences, failure is finally judged as an unpaid debt, damning testimony to sloppy judgment or bankrupt operation. And should a performing arts institution by some miracle end a year in balanced fiscal condition, the state councils funding it may easily decide that it therefore needs no support. In fact, it may be penalized for a proper operation, since there are a majority of others in more desperate need whose very deficits inspire superior pity and terror.

Repertory institutions have a rule of thumb that one in three to five novelties may not add to the repertory past the season of their debuts. This third or fifth can be translated into waste, which rarely includes the excitement stimulated by risk, free press coverage which anticipates it, or the moral stimulation of the artists responsible. But its evidence is forgiven far less than failed litigation, bankruptcies of shops or banks, or surgical operations with drastic consequences. The allocation of artistic responsibility lies with individual, nameable imaginations or talents, artist managers or producers. This failure is focused in the field of operative fantasy. Their daring is unforgiven and the threat of it guarded against by those whose fantasies are satisfied by formulae. Courage and imagination in the act of invention are impalpables, two costly and feckless luxuries in the minds of those who recognize neither, but who by endemic apathy or ignorance are self-appointed guardians of the public purse. However, the chance of failure, the risk of unpopularity is treated as a moral naughtiness. The fright of failure is an active illness of our national health. A century ago in his essay on "Culture and Anarchy," Matthew Arnold wrote: "Our society distributes itself into Barbarians, Philistines and Populace; and America is just ourselves [the English], with the Barbarians quite left out, and the Populace nearly."

This fear of lyric or artistic imaginative risk is not to be mitigated by comparison with other common or popular services, for the performing arts are scarcely acknowledged as service, to say nothing of necessity. It has not proven useful to reiterate that museums, libraries, hospitals, and schools fail to run themselves as profit-making successes. These are bound to the self-evident necessities of life-maintenance; any granted expenditure is forgiven as prime need. These do not "lose" money; they are able to raise money and spend it. Rarely has so evanescent a property as artistic

136

culture been recognized as anything approaching first importance since the decline of the age of faith, except by artists, poets, makers, or inventors who are possessors of gifts, talents, vision, and energy different in kind from purveyors, maintainers, or manipulators. With their lurid "problems" or presumed "temperament" artists are deemed unstable (unlike psychotic statesmen or demented tycoons); hence a condign threat to the body-politic. When Plato in his wisdom exiled artists from the ideal republic, this was not an ironic attitude. We remember that Phidias was indicted for embezzling gold and ivory from work on his colossal statue of Pallas Athena intended for the Parthenon, and that the trials and tribulations of Richard Wagner, despite personal support from the greatest music lover of the nineteenth century, were colossal, persistent, and, befitting his talent, Napoleonic.

There are two threadbare statements which serve as keys to self-protective ignorance or apathy, and which are wielded powerfully by those whose self-centered criteria arrange the subsidies from which we starve. "I don't know much about art, but I know what I like." Boasting a seemly ignorance, both modest and honest, has its own mindless artlessness which, while not exactly endearing, is a locution which makes a whole world kin. Parallel to this is the declaration, when wandering through a museum gallery or marooned in a concert hall: "This [painting or tone-poem] doesn't do a thing to [or for] me." "Fortune," said Louis Pasteur, "favors the prepared mind." Clinically, the inability to attach meaning to sensory perception is called *agnosia*. In such a state the act of perception cannot be completed, so that a person, while capable of scanning or viewing an object, is unable, owing to lack of focused energy or illness, to recognize its essential nature. There is a common supposition that art has some heavy and overwhelming obligation to affect a blank or resistant field, unprepared by curiosity to enliven itself. The very instinct to disdain, whatever the vapid emptiness in the observer or listener, vaunts its own beefy innocence. Condemnation of the complex, multilayered, or unfamiliar is a proud assertion of the ordinary citizen's right to be simplistic and ordinary. It follows that everyone else should be equally and democratically passive and mindless. After all, as we say, who needs it? Art, the broad and deep practiced play of imagination, therefore requires no prior preparation, attention, or sympathy. We cannot trust our artists as we trust any banker or surgeon. And, as for the problem of elitism, the elite as possessing a discrete place or attitude (unlike blind prejudice or apathy) is clearly supercilious, superior, undemocratic. The terrified doubt of superiority, of failed claims, or unproven prestige lies, mental or moral, at the heart of opposition to the poetic process.

Metaphysically the problem of resistance to an imaginative elect is a question of will. In man, will is maintained as an agent of necessity, of survival. Each act commences with the energy or heat of volition, of will-ing. On higher levels, will is something more than choice between oppo-sites or alternatives. It can be directed by energetic focus toward a particu-lar creative or inventive target, even serving as a mighty tool toward personal ambition. But, alas, the average biped is a miserably weak and pitifully de-energized unit. This disturbing and distressing truth is one of the many obscene facts of existence, and one which an affluent, demo-cratic society both ignores and battens on, while the imaginative elite manfully labors against persisting conditions of apathy and ignorance. The gross consumer body forming our potential audience is indolent in thought, lukewarm in desire, and only exceptionally generates enough energy for a will strong enough to gain its desires, to say little of first being able to formulate what such desires might intend. It rarely wills but only vaguely wishes. It is restricted by habit, by the dross of received ideas, by setbacks, perplexities, and annoyance on daily levels. With the first hitch, inconvenience or discomfort, it abdicates and abandons the struggle to-ward the ideal or the more difficultly superior, the elitism of perfection which is the artist's main existence. Energy has not chosen it as a reposi-tory for magic. It behaves like a sleeper awake, and we must ever contrive to engage it at least in its minimum of wakefulness to support our fortu-nate or unlucky energetic chances.

Optimistically we can show that since the last three major wars there has been considerable public interest in the promulgation and hope for a more ideal situation to be enjoyed by the performing arts in the not-too-distant future. If not in this administration, then possibly by the next, or at least sometime in the new century. Almost every city in the nation with a population of half a million seems to be planning or has already built some sort of civic center which hopefully can house music, drama, or dance. Certainly facilities have not exactly improved parallel to the re-sources of the average provincial hospital; but we should be grateful for what we are given. But lest we congratulate ourselves unduly on such very often ill-planned accommodations in which local pride does nicely without expert opinion as to the needs of dancers' feet or players' dressing rooms, we may forget that until the close of World War I, artists like Duse, Bernhardt, Sir Henry Irving, Caruso, Pavlova, and the Diaghilev ballet toured even the tank-towns of the far and middle west, while today the most that widespread touring offers middle America is music-tents and the traveling circus.

While music training in the United States has enjoyed a comparatively long history in capital schools for virtuoso performance; although today there are few enough academies in the traditional sense which teach the elemental crafts of draftsmanship, painting, and stone-cutting; and ap-prenticeship in the drama still suffers perhaps from a lack of regional companies, there has been a wide quantitative and qualitative improvement in the instruction of the classic dance. A national school of music, parallel to the French or Soviet conservatories, is hardly our present need for the larger urban centers, and a dozen universities and conservatories have fairly stable, if perennially needy, continuity. At the moment, whatever the idealistic expectations of a few artists and educators, a national theater in terms maintained by British, French, or Russian governments, all of which include music, drama, dance, and film, is scarcely thinkable. And while we must all be grateful for Washington's Kennedy Center, both as it functions as a national ensign of cultural interest and as a magnetic center where our legislators can actually view live performances, it is more a very welcome booking house than a fountain of noncommercial productions on the highest creative and artistic level.

Certainly our Congress will not soon be ready to match West Point, Annapolis, or the Air Corps Academy with top educational facilities for training in drama, dance, music, or film. From the geopolitical aspect, the nation is too expansive for any single isolated central school, either in the Washington area or on neutral ground. But if, as one hears, the Kennedy Center is ambitious to maintain under its own roof a National Opera, Drama, and Ballet, these should require supporting academies as well as a coordinating bureaucracy for recruitment and massive budget to insure subsidies for production and touring. The cost of such a centralized effort on any absolute scale might well exclude any such support, at least for this century. It took the British, with their world repertoire, from the Elizabethans to today to achieve a national edifice, even though their new dramatic theater exists on the fringes of state bankruptcy.

Lacking a criterion of academic excellence, it will be difficult to canalize opinion in the direction which may even in the twenty-first century support the kind of selective and qualitative standards ensuring virtuoso efficiency, a pool of superior performers comparable to the training of the great technical and medical schools with their mandatory collegiate affiliations. Such a productive educational absolutism is unquestioned for the national defense and security but hardly as an appenage of culture. The majority of taxpayers are not disturbed that cash annually appropriated for arms (to say nothing of health, education, and social welfare) is seldom questioned either as to essential need or allocation on any qualitative basis. But what can justify any considerable fraction of even a billion dollars toward an indeterminate, unmeasured and perhaps unmeasurable across-the-board cost of national culture? The very act of proclaiming or subsidizing superior talent, on the grounds of quality rather than popular appeal, will be left to specialists who do their minimal best via the foundations or private donors.

Sooner or later the quality of education for the performing artist must come into question. The medical profession in the United States grew from the tradition of medieval barber-surgeon's guilds. Licensing was almost a question of self-election for generations. Abraham Lincoln's law office was not graced by a diploma from the Harvard Law School nor J. P. Morgan's from any business school. However, if the state started to qualify dance studios today to the same degree that dentists, chiropractors, or even lay healers are licensed and held accountable, possibly a large portion of the industry would be out of business. This is not to claim that present danger threatens unsuspecting children who are put on *pointe* at the age of four, although this is certainly more dubious as to future careers than premature baton twirling. But there are only relatively few first-rate teachers who have themselves never performed in public, who have gained their science mainly from observation, books, or peripheral instruction. It is only a gauge of the superficial interest of the gross public in virtuoso performance which permits anyone who wishes to set up a dance studio to start to teach young children in a corpus of information which has accumulated by trial and error over three centuries and which compares in complexity, subtlety, and practice with English common-law, *materia medica* or musical composition. The recent proliferation of regional dance companies, the broad and loose instruction of "modern dance" on whatever permissive, self-indulgent, or amateur basis, particularly in the colleges, calls for some critical standards and qualifications. Separations are not easily made between what is art appreciation, life enhancement, audience building, the amateur, dilettante, and modestly professional. It would be decent enough to equate the schooling of a professional dancer with that of an aspirant pianist, violinist, or singer, candidates for instrumental mastery, and these cannot start instruction in their hardy disciplines in late adolescence nor are they taught by those who have not themselves been professionally experienced. There exists in the minds of many Americans a notion of latent amateurism, the pride of the autodidact, the jack-of-all-trades, the pioneer improviser, which invests the optimistic philosophy of can-do. The universal mechanic was a cheerful ideal when the country was still to be conquered in its physical boundlessness. But now a residual amateurism degrades a recognition of standards, and yet at the same time secretes a distrust and a resentment of the strict limitations of a professional elite. It is as if the performing arts, an area inhabited by entertainers, have a less serious right to elevate their skills into a necessary service.

Part of this problem is of course taken care of by the process of natural selection, by personal suitability, obvious talent or the glaring lack of it. The survival of the fittest and loose, happily upward mobility magnetizes or canalizes superior energy past puberty. This is perhaps one of the chief advantages of an anarchic popular democracy. Our loose, uncoordinated, even unlicensed system may be ultimately wasteful in its disregard of an ultimate potential, but its awkward mechanism has proven more productive than the tidy regimentation of the British system which inhibits recruitment of dance students on the basis of a preposterous outworn nineteenth century syllabus, a chauvinist restriction on international instruction, and the severe societal limitation of an entrenched teachers' association. The needs of our regions and centers have to be balanced and reconciled, yet one may hope that the pressures of a national movement can be firmly directed toward the truths of virtuoso quality in teaching and performance, which has little to do with the blind will or wish to perform or with the support of a passive liberal-minded community to award "A for Effort."

The social sciences over the last half-century have not convinced us that they provide a metric which is much more than a choice of statistics. Investigations and reports concerning costs or conditions of the performing arts rarely penetrate into the radical humane reasons for their stimulation or resistance, except for the presumption that culture is somehow therapeutic.

Apathy and ignorance, energy and inertia, are not quantitative abstractions, and although they may be read as blanket numerical simplifications of persistent states of mind involving suspicion and resentment, they remain constants in any developed society. Weber, the famous sociologist, has imagined "we are moving from the simple legitimacies and irrationalities of traditional society to the desolation of instrumental rationality in a megalopolitan context." But however our present situation is offered or analyzed, any grand revelation pointing toward a solution of a permanent dilemma seems far away. Costs (labor, managerial, entrepreneurial, artistic) have to rise, along with the rest of the economy. Inflation is only more death and taxes. The sole consolation history has to offer is that there has never been an epoch which has not had its well-informed prophets of imminent doomsday. We are not now in a situation for despair, and it is a selfish betrayal for anyone to try to gain an individual point by pretending that the demise of a single performing arts institution means the end of civilization. This has been a happy cry of "Wolf, wolf!" by those who can best afford to hire Madison Avenue to save their skins.

Rather than the terror of costs, it is the fear of the free-wheeling, far-ranging imagination whose products cannot be anticipated or measured by negotiable values which is not to be legislated away either by votes or cash. Indeed, we have much for which we may be thankful. In some ways we are quite in luck. Western civilization has managed to take for its models birds and beasts rather than ants or bees. Our mechanical and industrial energy or ingenuity, our brute physical force derived from the centuries of marvelous amalgam of the cream of European immigration have given us an affluence, however feverish, which is fat enough to permit a fraction of its waste to support the fruitful chaos of unprogrammed discovery, invention, and, yes, creation. When we look at the state of our performance efficiency today, no matter what its ragged activity, compared with the deliberate retardation (or death) of the ancient patrimony of Russia or China, we can soberly congratulate ourselves on our freedom from the kind of bland maintenance which only promotes a tyrannical, organized, and exhausted stasis.

Nevertheless, we can never underestimate the millions of our own people who are taxed, and who must always resent any portion of their dollars being assigned to matters in which they find small delight. Yet even here art seems to protect itself, finding its own scale of survival on an interstitial level. The portion of the tax dollar likely to be spent on so impractical an action as the art of performance in theaters can hardly serve as a red rag to whatever bulls would smash our precious china shop. We are free to be poor, to conduct our poverty in private, free to fail, free to manage our improvisation, permitted to fool around with projections as long as they appear to satisfy the worst fears of our few but patient patrons. We live in a land fat enough to support our home-grown anarchy to which we are quite accustomed, and our abject respect for the name and category of "education" has its lucky as well as its specious aspect. All money raisers know that "education" is spelled "open-sesame," and that if art, or culture, can be identified with some general massive hope, it is that much less frightful. Many of our causes essential to the survival of the arts survive by some hygienic or ancillary attachment to a remote and often irrational "educational" process or service to the very young or the very old, where compassion forgives disquiet.

Finally, what the performing arts need is not "audience-education," but the continued, adequate subvention of professionally educated performers, producers, and their products which their long and arduous education displays and requires. Money for preparatory levels is well spent, but not unless it is balanced by the maintenance of those self-elected and self-surviving institutions whose unique responsibility is the growth and tender care of repertories which sooner or later become the prime resource and residue of education itself. "Audience-education" has unduly legitimized nonprofessional attitudes in both acting and dancing. This hardly affects a far more sophisticated public for both sport and music; there is no dilettantism in the professional ball player, pianist, or violinist. The levels of improvisatory or dilettante performance in the ancient crafts of dance and drama only leave students with false notions of the time, task, and talent which alone produce peak performance. The overall lack of primary physical qualification for a dancer can at once be recognized as ridiculous compared to conditions controlling candidates for highly professional "amateur" players of ball games. But ball games are serious business, with vast alumnae and popular support. Also, they can be televised to sell cosmetics. It is accepted that ballet is an ephemeral and special diversion, while the *pas de deux* is about its only formal fragment (apart from the portraiture of individual star personalities) which can be currently photographed with a quality which remotely approaches live impact.

If anything positive can come out of societal analysis in the next years relative to a reduction of resistance to the aid of our performing arts, it might be well to spend effort on particularization, on trying to pinpoint those areas most sensitive to possible improvement, namely what works toward a more just and conscious appreciation of the nature of peak performance and its preparation, its difference from mere diversion or entertainment, its otherness from self-indulgence and amateurism, its capacity to prove and improve the limits of physical and imaginative possibility. Continued confusion and, with it, impotence is caused by peripheral considerations, rhetorical and political, and while one has to continue to talk to the apathetic and ignorant, there are limitations which must be accepted both as permanent and even endurable.

The main problem is indeed one of "education," but an education in strategic or tactical policies rather than secondary or propitiatory ones. If live performances were more widely dispersed on a proper broad scale, if vivid virtuosic action was in some more continuous position to be made immediate, there would be small need to educate a public as to prime quality. The mass public may "know nothing about art," but they are, or can be, electrified past ignorance by authority in skill. They cannot be fooled or confused by the essence of peak performance whatever their ignorance of refinements of grace or technique. Ballet or opera may not "do much for or to" overwhelming numbers of watchers or hearers, but those who are a bit more than idly attached recognize the veracity of the virtuoso, and even their numerical orders are not contemptible. Audiences need to be "educated" not only by participation and attendance, but also by the need to recognize the exact processes by which performances come into being and are maintained, with money or without it, when indeed there are no audiences present to watch such preparation.

The performing arts may "entertain," although they have suffered grievously from hasty identification with entertainment. The dictionary includes among its definitions, indeed as its first one, but alas, italicized as *now rare:* "a. To maintain; keep up. b. To retain, as in service. c. To give reception to; to receive." The meanings of amusement or diversion, once subordinate, have become capital. Today, if people cannot pay for being entertained, the rational answer is that either they cannot afford it, do not want it, or do not deserve it. How much and/or how many really want or need it? If we want it enough, we could or should pay for it. Since persua-

143

sion on the scale of indeterminate necessity has so slight a clout, since other pressures are so much more urgent, is there much hope that we can do more than already has been done? We can console ourselves perhaps even in the relative unimportance of cultural prestige. In the United States, our prime complaint is not what we do, or how it is done, but how little we have for what we might do. Great Britain, despite or indeed because of its dependence on an Arts Council as a centralized authority, has to face the rage of Scotland and Wales and the provinces of Britain (which have not been propitiated by nominal promotion to "regions") for an over-emphasis on Greater London as the capital of culture and the seat of national and royal ballet, opera, and theater. The regions have little chance to witness shows they pay for presented in the home counties with anything approaching the panache of Covent Garden or the South Bank. Canada, despite its generous arts budget, has to pacify legislative rancor in hiring expensive alien performers to insure those foreign appearances in New York and elsewhere which make a national prestige, something upon which the young native institutions can one day be built. Russian support of the performing arts surpasses all others in fiscal terms, but their development has been catastrophic in the debasement of their own performance morale, restricted on every imaginative level, surviving only in a muscular limbo of mechanical activity. Certainly, admitting our dollar starvation, the United States lacks nothing in talent, executive, inventive, or technical. In potential, we are incomparably the envy of the world, and it is by no chance that Europe is increasingly staffed by American directors, choreographers, dancers, and repertoire just as New York has replaced the hegemony of Paris in the realm of the visual arts and architecture.

If one is impatient or greedy or just a worker in the field, progress in appreciation or development may seem in sad arrears; yet perhaps without diluting our energy we should be grateful for what we have and are. Our busy interstitial activity is more healthy and active and free of imposed conditions than many more ancient households. Consider the restrictions under which the Paris Grand Opera operates, with its unchanging nightmare of labor relation confusion, its haphazard dependence on a presiding minister or intendant who falls with each change of government, its entrenched chauvinism, all of which derives from the imperial patronage of Louis XIV but which still maintains a popular prestige as criterion of the world's lyric theater and ballet. Our pendulum seems to be swinging, however slowly, toward sympathy for the arts of performance. As appropriations increase at whatever snail's pace, and against whatever sluggish governmental encouragement, political and geographic distribution will be proportional, and with this inevitably comes spread and dilution. But in their supreme acrobacy or virtuosity, the performing arts cannot be diluted any more than professional sports will employ fewer prime ball players. And lonely, egotistical, hardy, willful, courageous, and talented individuals will continue to exercise their own priceless and indefensible gifts, no matter what support, or lack of it, allows.

Programs for development, platforms for policy and diplomacy, aid for formal lobbying in the Congress will unquestionably pursue their useful paths. One can only hope that an immediate virtual desperation may make common cause on attractive populist grounds yet not vitiate principles or standards. The performing arts with their essential specialization cannot be popularized out of intrinsic quality. This quality, muscular, mental, and moral, aiming toward perfection in practice, will never be reduced, whatever compulsive political demands may come for adopting one stance or another as the chronological moment requires. Some epochs are chronologically unlucky. Franklin Roosevelt's enlightened and productive public works project was the greatest arts patronage this country ever enjoyed. The Congress killed it, mindlessly, as boondoggling. The time was wrong, but the precedent remains. We are indeed luckier due to the examples and sacrifices of our predecessors, artists, and lawmakers.

However, if there is one single primacy which can be presently considered, accepted, and then fought for, it is the assertion or admission that there is in fact and deed an *elite,* that this elite, not only on account of its peculiarity but despite it, deserves to be legitimized, fostered, preserved, encouraged. The word *elite,* like so many others which were once unprintable or almost unthinkable, must emerge into the vulgate and colloquial, in the frank and full illumination of its veritable intention. For *elitism* does mean something definite, discrete, apart. It is not a dirty word, a loose epithet, a convenient demogogic handle left to the barbaric defacement of professional philistines. Elite is a word to be fought for. Around it has accumulated a dusty web of vague negatives which have come to affirm a positive pejorative, a fair justification for mindless unpopularity and tacit antipopularism. Similarly, the term "esoteric" once meant what was known only to a select and worthy few, unavailable to the commonality. Most specialists deal in esoterics—neurologists, astronauts, mining engineers, astronomers. Their specialties deal in fact rather than fancy or fantasy, and constitute them as an elite. But the esoterics of the artist are no less special, apart, difficult, and demanding of legitimacy.

The root meaning of the word *elite* is election, which implies also selection. The big Oxford dictionary first defines it as "a person chosen," citing an early example: "a bishop *elect.*" This involves further "the choice or flower of society, or of any body or class of persons." Election, selection, choice. Aristotle said man was a choosing rather than a rational agent. Who elects, selects, chooses? Who has the energy or capacity of rational choice? First of all comes a candidature. History or circumstance, at once or in eventual perspective, recognizes clear claims of peak accomplishments, personal or collective. But we must also admit that an elite is self-responsible, self-chosen, and in a rather lonely sense, self-serving. Who has the wit to choose? Only those who have been exposed to the vast possibilities in a range of choice. The commonality hardly appoints an elite; it merely confirms it, either by awe or acclaim. The very quality of difference, excellence, or superiority is so self-evident and proven by inherent capacity that finally, despite initial resistance which is almost a sign of its status, it elects itself. The elite is, perforce, an aristocracy; however impotent politically, culturally it is imperial. We know that to the Greeks *ariston* meant the best. It has become one of the ironies or paradoxes of our democratic dictionary that *intelligence* has, by recent historical accidental attachment, a meaning associated with sinister. *Shrewd, clever, ambitious* have all been reduced to negative epithets. These all connote or denote a presence of energy, rational or at least intellectual, and all act as offenses against apathy or inertia rooted in ignorance. The word *elite* is possible to use in a positive popular frame only if it is disqualified as applying to a suspect, localized, and hedged minority, with condign supercilious attributes. If the defenders, patrons, and promoters of the performing arts over the term of the Carter administration have one salient, modest, persistent duty or objective responsibility, it is to reason and clarify their claims to be associated with a legitimate elite alongside ball players, brain surgeons, or brokers. It is time for the inventive, lyric, poetic, creative elite to come out of their closets and declare themselves—their worth, their difference in kind, their capacity, their energy, and their strength. Most of all—their necessity.

Of course this last must sound more like a rhetorical boast or fantasy than a plank in a political platform which may soon be acted upon. Elitism should be a rallying cry for that band of brothers and sisters who bear the culture of their country, for it is this cultivation of the only memorable residue that marks and outlives their epoch which justifies their permission to perform and produce as free agents, whatever the risk or cost to their countrymen.

Part Two

Three Pamphlets Collected

LINCOLN KIRSTEIN

Three Pamphlets Collected

BLAST AT BALLET • 1937

BALLET ALPHABET • 1939

WHAT BALLET IS ABOUT • 1959

With a new Foreword • 1967

One of a series of republications by Dance Horizons, Inc.

1801 East 26th Street, Brooklyn, New York 11229

These collected pamphlets are for

VIRGIL THOMSON

on his seventieth birthday,

for telling me on my twentieth,

that ballet in America was not

a possibility but a necessity.

FOREWORD

The *Shorter Oxford Dictionary* tells us that "pamphlet" comes from a generalizing of *Pamphilet* or *Panflet,* from a twelfth century Latin comic poem, *Pamphilus, seu Amore,* so, at the very start, delectation was implied. We are further instructed that (as of 1642), the substantive "pamphleteer," means "a writer of pamphlets; often contemptuous,"—whether profession or product is not entirely clear. The three pamphlets here reprinted bridge thirty years to provide footnotes for some aspects of theatrical dancing in that period. Each was inspired by love of much ballet and contempt for most critics, feelings which, as years pass, increase. Also, as years pass, many problems here passionately proposed and sweepingly solved have become meaningless. New readers may well ask: why all the sweat?

Blast at Ballet (1937), named after *Blast!,* Wyndham Lewis' Vorticist Manifesto of 1914, appeared in an edition of one thousand, paid for by the writer, of which less than three hundred sold. Two or three hundred were given away to persons whom I hoped would be outraged. Barely noticed by the press, it turns up now and then in book catalogues at a flattering price. The two best things in it are in the Appendix: Gordon Craig's notes on Diaghilev, and Glenway Wescott's letter on the Gluck-Balanchine-Tchelitchev *Orfeo* at the Metropolitan Opera. There are other ghosts invoked or exorcised, who, active then, have faded. Explanatory notes, to give all their due, would by themselves make a book bigger than this. Pamphlets must trigger themselves from villainies, real or imagined. My villains were the then as yet un-Americanized Russians who formed, in my mind, a condign conspiracy to strangle the infant Hercules of American ballet in his cradle. Mr. Sol Hurok, in poor thanks for his heroic services, I cast as the wizard Kastchei. He must smile wanly should he recall an interview in which I presented him with this precious piece, prophesying the end of his sinister reign. In return, he later generously gave the New York City Ballet, the Chagall production of *Firebird* which was no longer wanted by the Russian company by which it was commissioned. The pamphlet was dedicated to the initials of Mrs. William K. Vanderbilt, the first of her generation to encourage an American ballet on the highest level of patronage. When one is sixty, eighty doesn't seem so *very* old. When you are twenty-five, it is simply: historic. In between memories of Nijinsky and Diaghilev, she forgot the name of a young man to whom she thought she might have once been engaged. I had been reading Dixon Wecter's book on American society as my homework. I recalled that name: Franklin Roosevelt's *father*. Mrs. Vanderbilt paid me the highest compliment an older person can pay a younger; she treated me with no mind to age or eminence. She was fascinated by the *idea* of ballet in America. We were both in league against "the Russians." Considering the talents and numbers of the Russians with whom I was then basing everything on, this now seems scarcely consistent, but even the oddest pamphlets have never been models of unalleviated justice.

Ballet Alphabet was printed by Mr. and Mrs. Martin Kamin, who for many years kept the best (and only) bookshop devoted to dancing in New York. I hope, but doubt, they recovered their costs. It has an article cribbed from Delsarte, on "Gesture," which has the virtue of compacting information otherwise hard to find, except as scattered through half a dozen sources difficult to obtain. It also includes technical gossip and information obtained from four graduates of the Russian Imperial (or State) Schools: Michel Fokine, Anatol Oboukhov, Pierre Vladimirov and George Balanchine. Gisela Caccialanza, herself a fine dancer, provided help on the Italian style in which she was schooled by her godfather, Enrico Cecchetti. I had briefly taken classes from Fokine and Vladimirov and had felt in my own body some of the basic muscular emotions by which dancers breathe. A footnote: Paul Cadmus' sketches were based on photographs of Michael Kidd, a talented young dancer in the Ballet Caravan.

"What Ballet Is About" was composed as the initial issue of Dance Perspectives, in gratitude to Al Pischl, for having the enterprise to start a new, serious magazine, along the lines of our own Dance Index. It is an addition to Ballet Alphabet and was graced by good photographs of the first Agon, by Martha Swope. These sadden me, since Diana Adams, Allegra Kent and Todd Bolender don't dance any more. Agon is still well done, but it has never been the same as when cast for the dancers for whom it was conceived. A gloomier thought: dance is the art of the momentary, immediate and evanescent. Its prose, read after the fact, is dusty. Here's an accumulation of three decades of dust. I hope traces of gusto can stop readers from sneezing. Marianne Moore, as usual, gives hope: "Gusto thrives on freedom in art, as in life . . . is the result of a discipline imposed by ourselves." The discipline of ballet produces freedom to dance which is a paradigm of all action, in its lyric essence. If anything rigorous remains here, it comes from associating with dancers, who, at the last, make all words dust.

L. K.

Washington's Birthday, 1967

BLAST AT BALLET

1937

BLAST AT BALLET

A CORRECTIVE FOR THE AMERICAN AUDIENCE

By Lincoln Kirstein

Acknowledgment

PART OF THE MATERIAL IN THIS PAMPHLET HAS APPEARED

IN A SIMILAR FORM FROM 1933 TO 1938 IN

Arts and Decoration
The American Dancer
Dance
The Dance Observer
The Hound & Horn
Modern Music
The Nation (New York)
The New English Weekly
The New Republic
New Theatre
The North American Review
Theatre Arts Monthly
The Saturday Review of Literature
Town and Country
Vogue

THIS PAMPHLET IS FOR

A. H. V.

TRUE FRIEND OF THE DANCE

WHEREVER IT'S FOUND,

AND IN PARTICULAR IN

THE UNITED STATES OF AMERICA

*Perhaps it will seem strange to austere Republicans that we occupy ourselves with the Arts while united Europe besieges the domain of Liberty. Artists do not fear the reproach of neglecting the interests of their country, they are free in essence; by their nature; the characteristic of genius is independence; and certainly in this memorable Revolution they have proved themselves to be the most zealous partisans of a Regime which restored to Man his dignity so long disdained by that class, which was the protectress of the ignorance that worshipped it.**

Description des Ouvrages de Peinture, etc., Exposes au Sallon du Louvre par les Artistes Composant La Commune Generale des Arts, le 10 août, 1793.

CONTENTS

PAGE

ADVERTISEMENT *165*

PART ONE

OUR BACK-DROP *167*

I. INTRODUCTION *167*

    1. Ballet in a bad time: 1938 . . . . *167*

    2. Ballet in a better time: 1909-1929 . . . . . *168*

II. THREE AGES OF MODERN BALLET: 1909-1939 . . . . . *169*

    1. The Golden Age: 1909-1916 . . . . *169*

    2. The Silver Age: 1917-1929 . . . . *171*

    3. The Age of Iron: 1930-1938 . . . . *172*

       a. Russian Ballet in America: 1916-1936 . . . . *172*

       b. The American Ballet at the Metropolitan Opera, 1936-38 *185*

       c. American Ballet in America: 1936-19-- *194*

PART TWO

THE GREAT CONSPIRACY *205*

I. THE MANAGER'S STAKE *205*

II. PORTRAIT OF THE PATRON *213*

III. THE FUNCTION OF THE CRITIC *220*

    1. The Historians *222*

    2. The Appreciators *223*

       a. On Ballet Photographers *224*

PAGE

3. The Journalists 226

   a. The Critic's Lexicon: John Martin 228

4. The Technicians 236

IV. OUR YOUNG DANCER'S IDEAL 238

PART THREE

PROGRAM AND MANIFESTO 250

I. BASIC PRINCIPLES 250

   1. The classic dance and American character-dancing . . 252

   2. Ideas and Collaboration 258

II. THE ORGANIZED AUDIENCE 266

   1. Postscript for conductors of symphony orchestras . . 267

III. AN ALLIANCE OF AMERICAN BALLETS 269

APPENDIX

APPENDIX 271

I. THE REPERTORY OF THE AMERICAN BALLET COMPANIES:
COLLABORATORS AND FIRST PERFORMANCES

   1. The Littlefield Ballet 271

   2. The Ruth Page Ballet 273

   3. The Ballet Caravan 274

   4. The American Ballet 275

   5. The William Christensen Ballet 276

II. EDWARD GORDON CRAIG'S MARGINAL NOTES ON THE "GOLDEN AGE"
OF SERGE DE DIAGHILEV 277

III. A LETTER TO "TIME," CONCERNING "ORPHEUS" AT THE METROPOL-
ITAN OPERA, FROM GLENWAY WESCOTT 281

Advertisement

THIS pamphlet will not be favored with many reviews in the public press. In the first place, pamphleteering is not a familiar method in America. Anything bound in less than semi-permanent cardboards seems scarcely worth the trouble of scanning. And then, as you will see, the people who will be most hurt by my tactlessness are the very ones who would ordinarily be obliged to notice it in print. As Sir Benjamin Backbite admitted: "To say truth, ma'am, 'tis very vulgar to print: and as my little productions are mostly satires and lampoons on particular people, I find they circulate more by giving copies in confidence to the friends of the parties."

If, for example, this present pamphlet had been published in the England of Sheridan's day, and it should not have constituted a basis for libel action, which I hope my section on dance critics might be interpreted to do—there would doubtless have been a few paper-bound responses immediately issued in opposition to my point of view, with attendant letters to the *Times*, or at least to the equivalent of the *Dancing Times*.

In America, however, we have a different and perhaps more efficient technique for handling impolite, uncomfortable or brutal Blasts. We ignore them. A wall of silence costs little to build and is extremely effective. However, as author of an irritant, I am perhaps more fortunate than several of my colleagues who have lately issued similar works affecting the press, radio and films. Our vocative dance public may be comparatively small but it is very passionately interested in questions of theoretical practice, artistic policy, and even commercial dance management. It is to them, then, above all others, that this pamphlet is addressed, and to young American dancers whose futures are so vitally affected by the setup herein described.

Since I do not expect to receive much printed expression of opinion I should be delighted to receive letters from private persons or groups, who are to any degree moved by my ideas, either towards correction, amplification or coöperation.

Lincoln Kirstein

PART ONE

Our Back Drop

I. INTRODUCTION

We are dancing on a volcano, SAID M. LE COMTE DE SALVANDY
AT A FETE GIVEN BY THE DUKE OF ORLEANS TO THE KING OF
NAPLES IN 1830.

1. Ballet in a Bad Time

Ballet, or the exact science of traditional theatrical dancing, survived
the French Revolutions of 1789, 1832 and 1848. Nor did the World War
kill it. It persisted during the Paris Commune of 1871. Its development
has been uninterrupted in Russia in spite of 1905 and 1917. If any form
of Western art is thought to remain in moderate health, then ballet is just
as healthy. It may lag behind poetry or painting in its direct reflection of
society, but not for long and not nearly as much as many might superficially think. It is still a form of art as practical and important to us as
the two other great formal contributions of Western artistic ingenuity;
aerial perspective in painting, and the symphonic form in music.

But ballet itself in America is in a bad way because Americans have
been led to believe that *Russianballet* is one single word. *Russianballet*
is not a single word. It is true up to now, there has been plenty of reason
given us for thinking so. But it is my purpose to investigate that here.
Russian ballet has meant world-ballet from 1910 up to about the year
1935. Yet, Russian ballet itself stopped being specifically Russian when
Diaghilev, its unique promoter, quit Russia in 1909. From 1914, it was
international ballet with an increasing French overtone. Its last direct
contact with creative Russia was in 1929, the season of Prokoviev's *Prodigal Son,* and of Diaghilev's* death. If, but only if the still surviving Con-
federate veterans represent the American standing army today, then the
White emigrés, their heirs and assigns represent Russian ballet today.

Traditional classic stage-dancing arose from a fusion of Italian and
French sources, from theatrical usage and folk-custom. In 1738, ballet for
Europe and the known Western world was *French* ballet and *only* French,
but who can name a first-rate French dancer within living memory? In
1838, the monopoly was Viennese, or else Italo-Scandinavian. Today
what Germanic or Italian ballerina has one seen? In 1938, we count off

---
*In this pamphlet I have used the letter *v* as a final letter, whereas the English use
the double *f*. But the *v* is simpler and phonetically closer to the Russian sound.

167

ten Russian and only Russian. This, only to show Russianballet has not always been a single word.

Ballet is in a bad time in America today because the blackmail of the Russian organization, primed by publicity and patronage, still works. The Russian-ballet repertory, itself a vitiated and dying formula, is coasting down-grade on the prestige it has accrued over the last three decades. Its sunset manifestations in their clouded glory seem more brilliant and familiar to our audiences than the young, crass, naive, but healthy form which marks the beginning of an American classic dance. Our audiences are hired and instructed to aid the charming dotard and starve the yelping child. That is why ballet in America is in a bad time.

2. *Ballet in a Better Time: 1909-1929*

Under the unique dictatorship of Serge de Diaghilev, ballet enjoyed a better time. Released by accident or design on the one hand from direct connection with the crippling bureaucracy of the Imperial Theatres on Russian soil, Diaghilev on the other, employing the highly developed apparatus of dancers, musicians and designers attached to the subsidized theatres, could operate in Western Europe with comparative freedom. The security of the Czar's personal subvention had provided working and practicing conditions which produced dancers and choreographers with the training of Fokine, Nijinsky, Karsavina and Pavlova. Diaghilev himself was a serious and completely educated man. The economic substructure backing his first venture in Western Europe was the Franco-Russian political entente. Russian music and dancing aided the military alliance which is still operating. But that very substructure, resulting in the World War, would separate his ballet from its native Russian earth forever.

The inevitable snobbish reaction against Diaghilev just after his death, felt and voiced by his artistic heirs, has now faded for good. He can be judged as he would now judge himself. Ten years have elapsed and there has not appeared in our contemporary Russian companies either a single musician, painter or choreographer of value unknown to him. There can be no second Diaghilev. His taste was his own, but his breeding, background, instruments and resources were part of an epoch that is forever passed. Beware the little men who seek periodically to revive either his own work or those aims proper to his time, and to him alone. The Diaghilev-period is an historic chapter in the history of Western theatrical culture; recent talk among the White Russians of its revival is no less archaistic and unprofitable, than to revive the Romantic ballet of 1830 to 1850, or the age of Noverre from 1750 to 1780.

II. THREE AGES OF MODERN BALLET

YOU HAVE THE PYRRHIC DANCE AS YET,
WHERE IS THE PYRRHIC PHALANX GONE?
OF TWO SUCH LESSONS, WHY FORGET
THE NOBLER AND THE MANLIER ONE?
YOU HAVE THE LETTERS CADMUS GAVE—
THINK YE HE MEANT THEM FOR A SLAVE?

Don Juan, CANTO III

1. *The Golden Age: 1909-1914:* Gods and Heroes

The success of the Russian ballet in Western Europe is a phenomena so familiar by virtue of the memoirs of Mme. Nijinsky, Svetlov, Prince Lieven, Arnold Haskell, Gabriel Astruc, Jean Cocteau and Calvocaressi, that there is no need to push through it again. In 1909, only thirty years ago, Paris and London had heard very little Russian music. Post-impressionism in painting was still an unearned investment of the picture-dealers, and dancing as represented by the ballet at the Paris Opéra, had all the bourgeois security of an official finishing-school for naughty girls. Three-quarters of the first great success of the Russian ballet lay not in any of its inherent perfection of music, decoration, choreography or dancing, nor in any new social or moral ideas, but rather in the *contrast* to everything accepted by Western Europe as theatrical dancing at that time, and for the last forty years. As long back as 1892 Henry Adams had written "his heart sank to mere pulp before the dismal ballets at the Grand Opéra."

No one, of course, would recklessly attempt to underestimate the large personal contributions of Stravinsky, Bakst, Benois, Fokine or Nijinsky. But let us at least grant them their historic due by considering them in their real place in their own time. There is no need to wrench them out of their realistic position and make them do double duty for all time and every place.

Petrouchka for example; let us take *Petrouchka.* Stravinsky's delectable orchestral score remains intact for concert at least, and the story in essence at least, is still useful. Benois' successive remountings of his original scenery seem thin, patchy, and creased today. As for Fokine's choreography: in the original production, he had Bolm, Karsavina, Nijinsky in the chief rôles. The fragments of character-dancing, the vignettes of coachmen and the moujiks were then brilliantly executed by top-rank character artists from the School of Moscow. Even the smaller parts, some scarcely more than walk-ons, such as the gypsy, the organ-grinder, or the drunken Barin, were taken by first-rate performers like Theodor

Koslov, Bronislava Nijinska, and Ludmila Shollar. The holiday crowds in movement were organized, a sizeable crowd and not a stray handful of accidental supers picked up an hour before curtain time.

Now we have none of this former glory. To be sure, the best dancers available take the leading parts. But do they convince us as Blackamoor, as Ballerina, or as Doll? Do we see them as archetypes of tragedy we have been led by all the writers to look for? Are our hearts broken when Petrouchka's pitiful fluttering mittens crash through his paper house? We do not and they are not, at least if we're honest. We view with rapidly diminishing interest a vehicle once propelled by renowned artists. We see famous costumes nearly identical to those carried by Bolm, Karsavina, Nijinsky, covering dancers approximating the original gestures once electrified by Bolm, Karsavina and Nijinsky. But now, it is all a ghostly double-exposure, a spectral blackmail that the Golden Age of Russian ballet still exerts on our inert eyes.

The repertory of the Golden Age of Diaghilev still whipped like a staggering cart-horse over the ballet-trails of the world today, includes also besides *Petrouchka*, the dances from *Prince Igor, Les Sylphides, Carnaval, Papillons, L'Oiseau de Feu, L'Après-midi d'un Faune, Le Coq d'Or, Thamar,* and *Schéhérazade.* Of all of these, *Cléopâtre* alone, with its preposterous hobble-skirts and belly-mirrors of the vogue of 1909, was howled off a Newark stage in 1937. The rest smugly remain. The indiscriminate, pot-flung color of Bakst, the caramel orchestration of Rimsky-Korsakov, Glazounov or Tcherepnin, the old dancers' galvanic, drugging physicality has been something for our fathers and mothers to tell us about, like Dewey's triumph after Manila Bay, or their first automobile-ride. Wonderful for them, but not for us. For us, if we leave off the rose-tinted spectacles obligingly provided by the Great Conspiracy of commercial manager, dance and music-critic, and ballet patron, we will see only a dismal carnival in a theatrical storage-warehouse. The fatigued world-worn troupes stamp out the mechanical tunes to which our ears have long since refused to listen consciously. Yet these relics of the Golden Age of Diaghilev are the very backbone, the chief mainstay of Russian ballet today. When we see them again let us recognize them for what they are. We may harbor for them among other nostalgic souvenirs of our remote youth, an affectionate warmth. But to think that there is anything here to instruct, nourish or enlighten us for what we ourselves as adults will want to do or see, is like going to be taught or advised by a darling old nurse, or a favorite scoutmaster.

2. *The Silver Age: 1917-1929:* Experiment and "Modern Art"

This is the chapter of the Russian Ballet that isn't Russian, and it is the most interesting chapter. That is, we assume *Petrouchka, Le Coq d'Or, Thamar, L'Oiseau de Feu,* and *Prince Igor* are White Russian-Russian; *Schéhérazade* is Russo-Persian; *Carnaval* and *Papillons* are Russo-Biedermeier, and *Les Sylphides* is Russo-ballet. For Russian, read Russian tea-room, with the tea in individual tea-bags and not a samovar in sight. The difference between Diaghilev's *Ballet Russe* and Baliev's *Chauve Souris* was negligible at many points of contact. The tea-room Russian soon enough tired even the Russians themselves, and Diaghilev commenced an age of experiment which though by far the most valuable contribution of his career both in paint, music, theatre and poetry, is almost unrepresented in the present repertory of the Russian Ballet companies. Many of these works, to be sure, might not weather revival and, as we have recently seen, revivals are increasingly exhumations. But as long as revivals pay on principle, let them revive this period as well.

With the departure of Fokine and Nijinsky, passed Diaghilev's Golden Age, and the youthful Massine was permitted direct contact with the international collaborators of the School of Paris. "Permitted contact" is correct, because at that time there was no thought of a dictatorship by the choreographer, even by those as distinguished as Fokine or Massine. Diaghilev was the only dictator of dance, decoration or music. Massine and Nijinska worked with Erik Satie, Matisse, Stravinsky, Juan Gris, Picasso, Prokoviev and Derain. Revolutionary cubism hit the ballet with its ton of bricks and horrified the old-guard ballet-ballet lovers, which was Diaghilev's earnest intention. Social-satire, American jazz, the everyday continental vacation and boulevard life of the nineteen-twenties; dada, neo-classicism, the falsely naive, the falsely archaic, and decorative folklore no longer of Russia, but now of England, Italy, France or Spain were all exposed to the caprice of Diaghilev's ingenious combinations.

Why, with the exception of pieces deliberately old-fashioned at their very birth, such as *Le Chapeau Tricorne, La Boutique Fantasque, Cimarosiana,* or *The Good Humored Ladies,* is this experimental period unrepresented by the self-styled heirs of Diaghilev? Were the works of the Silver Age less amusing than those of the Golden Age? By no manner or means, and quite to the contrary. Nijinska's *Les Noçes* and *Les Biches,* Massine's *Parade, Mercure* or *Ode,* Balanchine's *Le Bal, Barabau,* or *Le Fils Prodigue* would be a great deal more fun to see today than the rabble-scrabble and bobtail we're stuffed with instead. Only these ballets do not *represent* the *Russian* ballet of the "original" period. *Les Noçes,* it is true, was admirably revived in London and New York two years ago, but its starkness and the fact that it demanded a largish chorus were seized by the direction as an excuse to end its appearance once and for all. *Les Noçes* and these others are not considered sufficiently antique. They might destroy the picture carefully constructed by idolatrous historian, wise ballet-manager, and lazy patron for the public's consumption. Remember the manager thinks the public is a stupid beast. *Russian ballet, Russian ballet, Russian Ballet*—repeat it ten times before each performance. What? A house-party, a steel-factory, a movie lot in *Russian* ballet? What would Petrouchka think, what Schéhérazade, what the Sylphs? The more sprightly inventions of Diaghilev's Silver Age, even lacking a large part of the original Imperial schooled dancers, Bakst's decor, and the political prestige, were the real contribution of Diaghilev to contemporary theatrical art. These represented the institution of ballet faced with the world we lived in. Maybe some of the ballets were half- solutions, part-failures, mere *succès d'estime* or scandal. They were, and still would be however, neither as preposterous, muddy or dull as the others which still stick like cinders in our eyes.

Don't think for a second all the Russian dancing artists themselves prefer the older repertory. Don't think their old-world hearts beat in dedicated sympathy to the tunes that pop-concert, radio, and school-band have worn bone-clean. Very often Zobeide's slave appears to be dying his death of ennui, a far deadlier sword than Shah Schariar's, and his ennui, dear manager, critic, and dear patron, is transmitted in its unadulterated wallop to us, blind as we are—the patient, hopeful watchers in the darkened house. Lord Chesterfield once remarked of two people dancing a minuet: "They looked as if they were hired to do it, and were doubtful of being paid."

3. *The Age of Iron: 1930-1938: a. Russian Ballet in America: 1916-1936*

Most of the original Diaghilev troupe came to the Americas in 1916. Otto Kahn, one of our entirely disinterested and understanding patrons of every sort of creative expression from opera to pure poetry, lost a very substantial sum of money on it since he undertook to fulfil the obligations of the Metropolitan Opera Association, with whom the contract was signed. Financially the tour was a disaster and prevented dancing being shown on a scale worthy of its scope in America for almost twenty years. The Italian intendancy entrenched at the Metropolitan Opera House were terrified lest Diaghilev with his experience in presenting Russian opera and ballet should not by chance alone supersede them, operatic hacks of whom the Scala was well rid. It was vitally necessary to them that his tour should fail, and on a commercial basis, fail it did. The routing and back-tracking, the placing of badly paying engagements and conflicting dates, safely secured the margin of their sabotage. Not only was the Diaghilev troupe pioneering in theatrically undeveloped territory, but aside from the big towns, it was pioneering in a vacuum where up to that time only a circus could have prospered. In our deep South, the negro slave in *Schéhérazade* was forced to put on all sorts of new and peculiar tights, colors and characterizations. The young dancer, Gavrilov, frequently appeared in *Le Spectre de la Rose*, although Nijinsky's name was usually on the program. Few in the audience were any the wiser. When people from the South and Southwest tell you, "Yes, of course we saw Nijinsky dance; he was incomparable," it is just as likely that they *thought* they saw him, even if they didn't. For example, though long announced, he did not actually appear in Boston, due to passport difficulties. However, the effect was always the same. Even then the press-agent knew his business.

And although the great tour was a failure financially, it rocked a widespread minority of interested people all over America to their imaginative foundations. There is a curious little poem to be found among the juvenalia of Hart Crane, with a mispronounciation of *Daphnis et Chloë*, to fit a rhyme of *Cloh*, testifying to his amazement, his rapture at the Russian ballet. Likewise, other painters, poets, musicians, and stage artists all benefited from the Russians' first American visit. Robert Edmond Jones, for example, received his first great impetus towards his remarkable career, by his designs for Nijinsky's *Tyl Eulenspiegel*, and for the unproduced *Mephisto Valse*.

But far more than the Russian visit, Americans have benefited by the Russians' stay. Michel Fokine, Jove of the Golden Age, remained in New York, and has taught with his unique pedagogical mastery many of the best of the present generation of American-born dancers for the last twenty years. The choreographic works that he has created since 1914, seem minuscule in comparison with his influence as a source of choreographic information, style and theatrical presence. It is exactly as if our contemporary poets had had for the last two decades personal contact with Browning or Tennyson, or our musicians personally could have talked to Tchaikovsky or Debussy, our painters to Monet or Renoir. Few have been aware of it, because many of the more conscious ones have been thrown off Fokine's teaching by the shabbiness of the productions he has himself arranged here, by their down-at-the-heel repetition with no dancers but weak pupils of his own, performances which even in comparison to his works in the Russian troupes have been shameful. I remember, only four years ago, seeing his rearrangement of a ballet to the Tannhaüser *Bacchanal,* danced on a raised square platform erected in the middle of a remote Brooklyn armory, with the amplifying system which provided the recorded music placed under the shadow of a large field-gun. It was miserably stamped out by his students, and yet it had a certain interest, for it was full of the bas-relief gesture which he insists Nijinsky took from him for *L'Après-midi d'un Faune.*

Other dancers of the Golden Period trained in the Russian Imperial academies before the war, who later settled in America, were: The Bekeffis, Bolm, Bourman, Gavrilov, Koslov, Kobelev, Kotchetovsky;—later, Novikov, Mordkin, Oukrainsky, Pavley, Shollar, Simeonov, Tarasov, Vilzak and Vladimirov. These have taught and produced ballets in the Russian tradition from Washington to Los Angeles, from Houston to Chicago, and from Hollywood to New York. Since their arrival, American dancers of our generation have naturally accepted Russian teaching as normal. Before, it had been primarily the Italian pedagogical tradition of Albertieri, Bonfanti and the school of Milan, favoring a small, detailed dancing-style and almost completely discouraging the male dancer. The actual training our dancers have received from the Russians, with the possible exception of Fokine, Bolm, Balanchine and Vilzak, who had each in his different way danced or created ballets quite apart from Diaghilev, was what the older artists themselves had been taught by the Imperial Russian School masters during their own adolescence from 1900 to 1910. These teachers continued to profess the technical groundwork which made possible the great late-nineteenth century repertory of Petipa, Ivanov, and Gorsky. It was excellent training as a theatrical basis, even if it may seem to us needlessly rigid today. Some influence from Fokine's early period may have been apparent in their own lessons, but general Russian instruction of American pupils has hardly even been touched by the choreographic experimentalism of the Diaghilev Silver Age, from 1917 to 1929. Most of these teachers had left Diaghilev by 1916, for America. Fokine himself, has considered every subsequent innovator in choreography as a rank upstart. Massine's symphonic work was mere *Wigman sur les pointes;* Balanchine's creative effort, which Fokine had influenced in the old Petersburg School, was *La mort de l'Art et la décadence de la danse.* Fokine pays his respects to the talents of Serge Lifar in an amusing and malicious article published in the London *Dancing Times* for July 1938. Separation from the source of development of the advance-guard movement in the dance tended to crystallize and age the elder Russian teachers' own ideas before their time. Imaginatively, they became fixed in their own first great golden period. They were heroes of the Golden Age, not only to their pupils, but to themselves as well. They naturally instructed their little American pupils to emulate them, the only real dancers in the only real florescence of dancing they had ever known. This was only logical, but Russian dominance in the American teaching profession has further intensified those notions of the American audience which are susceptible to the blackmail by the traveling Russo-International ballet troupes. It is obvious that older Russian teachers should prefer *Petrouchka, Prince Igor, Les Sylphides,* to more recent choreography. They recall the good old days before their long separation from their lost homeland. But there are half a dozen Russian teachers of the younger generation in America who encourage and applaud the efforts of their young American proteges, with a devoted and unselfish interest which is characteristic of the best traditions of the Imperial Schools. After the debut of Fokine's first ballet, he received a card of generous praise from Marius Petipa, who after three-score years, and still a Frenchman, had become the fountainhead of the Russian classic dance.

On the whole, however, this historically inevitable Russian groundwork has been more than advantageous for America. The Russians have been proud of their American pupils, and if they have made them memorize Cossack or Persian dances from the repertory of their own youth, then they have also mounted for them their idea of Navajo and Mexican numbers as well. Petipa early in his Russian career invented what was then a surprising novelty for the Marinsky Theatre—a Russian ballet, that is, a work with a native folk subject. By school recitals, or semi-professional performances with local student ballet-companies, our Russian teachers have stimulated sectional interest and local pride in American dancing. They have, by their association with the renowned Diaghilev, given the dancing profession a dignity and a prestige which it never enjoyed before. Without their aid, direct or indirect, the recent Russian ballet tours would have been as much a failure as the first one.

In spite of numerous proposals, Diaghilev never would return to America, and this country at large has never subsequently seen the influential experiments he activated by collaborations with the School of Paris. However, the music has mostly been heard in our concerts, the painting has gone into our Museums, even the great part of actual sketches for costume and decor of his last period, from the collection of Serge Lifar, now reside in the Avery Memorial at Hartford, Connecticut. And of course, there were many American tourists in London and Paris from 1922 to 1932.

After the death of Diaghilev in 1929, his choreographers who seldom, it is true, had ever worked for him all at the same moment, disbanded.

Massine came to America from Italy, worked unsatisfactorily at the old Roxy Theatre, but on the side, mounted the first American stage performance of *Le Sacre du Printemps* in his own version, with Leopold Stokowski and Martha Graham. Nijinska went to South America, Balanchine to the Theatre Royal in Copenhagen, Lifar to the Paris Opéra. Boris Romanov, who had been working in Monte Carlo, Italy and South America, was later to replace Balanchine at the Metropolitan Opera in New York.

The Monte Carlo Ballet, founded in 1932, was a reassemblage of forces in the name of Serge de Diaghilev. The direction consisted of René Blum, long interested in the direction of the theatre of Monte Carlo, and of Colonel de Basil, an alleged ex-Cossack concert-manager. They made Balanchine ballet-master, entrusted him with the formation of a troupe. He requested and received Massine's coöperation. The ballets *Cotillon* and *Concurrence*, by Balanchine, and *Jeux d'Enfants* by Massine, were new. Later came the large symphonic works of Massine. Yet as a bridge with the past, were also included *Les Sylphides, Prince Igor, Petrouchka*, and *Les Matelots*, as well as *Le Beau Danube*, which had not been created for Diaghilev originally, but for *Les Soirées de Paris* of Count Etienne de Beaumont.

From now on we are all on pretty familiar ground. The Monte Carlo Ballet was substantially the late Diaghilev ballet, except for the apparition of the much heralded new baby-stars: Toumanova, Riaboushinska, and Baronova, whom Balanchine discovered in the dancing-schools kept in Paris by the four last great Imperial Ballerinas. It was a working ballet mechanism in every particular, complete with its own slight novelty and some success. It delighted the Diaghilev audiences who feared that with him, his ballet was dead. It only lacked the one vital element to make of it a genuinely creative enterprise—Diaghilev himself.

To remedy this lack, after realizing the entirely retardative and dominantly commercial aims of de Basil, which took most people five years to admit, George Balanchine, Diaghilev's last choreographer-in-chief, with Boris Kochno, Diaghilev's close aide for the last period of his life, and Vladimir Dimitriev, for the last five years director of the School of American Ballet in New York City, founded *Les Ballets 1933*.

It was not any easy task, for after a single season the Monte Carlo Company had appropriated unto itself the prestige of the "true" mantle of Diaghilev. However, when the first nights of both companies arrived in June of 1933, the actual hereditary distinction of Diaghilev was found to be resident not in the old Châtelet, the scene of the triumph of *Les Sylphides, Igor* and *Petrouchka*, but in the newer Champs Elysées, the stage of the scandal of *Le Sacre du Printemps*. The creators of the 1933 Ballets, were mostly an amplification of the Silver Age collaborators: Derain, with his marvelous Etruscan decorations and clothes for *Fastes* and *Les Songes*, and the musicians Sauget and Milhaud. Pavel Tchelitechev set his white, hysterical and crystalline stage for *Errante*, with Charles Koechlin's splendid orchestration of Schubert's *Wanderer* fantasy. Among the artists who had not worked for Diaghilev were Christian Bérard (subsequently designer of Massine's "symphonic ballets") ; the dancers Tamara Toumanova and Tilly Losch of the Vienna Opera; the German poet and creator of contemporary epic-drama, Berthold Brecht, and his composer-colleague, Kurt Weill; the surrealist architect, Emilio Terry, and the brilliant young German stage desginer, Caspar Neher. Their dozen or so evenings of ballet in London and Paris in the summer of 1933, were in reality, the swan-song of the Diaghilev period. Here was real artistic discovery, real theatrical invention, true collaboration on Diaghilev's own ground, even without him. It could not have been greatly different even had he been alive to supervise the scene, for every new talent of the day with the possible exception of Salvador Dali, and the surrealists (who had refused on idealogical grounds to be included), was somehow involved. Significant and novel ideas in music, dance, poetry and social-comment were presented. Nothing as powerful, influential or original as this has happened in the world of theatrical-dancing since that time.

If the responsibility for the success of *Les Ballets 1933* was due to any one person, it was to their choreographer, George Balanchine. He is not a person easily described. I had first remembered seeing him in 1926, during Diaghilev's London season, not in the "modern" ballets which he was then helping to create, but in mimed rôles such as the enchanter Katschei in *L'Oiseau de Feu*, and the Corregidor of *Le Tricorne*. He invented something extremely personal and distinct for parts which can so easily be ciphers if only filled by a dancer for the sake of the printed program, while having no connection with the rest of the action.

Balachine had been with Alexandra Danilova and Tamara Geva, Diaghilev's last connection with the Russian academic tradition, now continued in the State Schools of Leningrad, which after the 1917 Revolution still employed the masters of Imperial days. Balanchine had danced at the Marinsky Theatre for seven years after the Revolution, ever since he graduated from its ballet-school, and had only left Russia on a summer-vacation tour to dance with a small troupe organized by Vladimir Dimitriev, a singer of the State Opera. Failing to obtain a passport to perform in Japan and China, they found they would be permitted to work in Germany and France. Diaghilev signed them for his own company in London, and they did not return to Russia. It was the midst of an age of experiment in the West, and it seemed too exciting a chance to pass up. Balanchine at once become a choreographer of the Russian Ballet in Western Europe, and later when Massine left, its last ballet-master.

In spite of Balanchine's phenomenal American success in the popular genre of musical-comedy, he has tended to remain in the minds of the serious dance public as at best a choreographer's choreographer, and at worst as a perverse and mysterious talent. That is, in his serious work he has been found not to be interested in producing ballets which have any interest other than that inherent in music, or in the dancing as it stems from this music. He has always avoided crass pageantry, showy stage pictures of living models, pictorial build-ups, and parades in which there is no *dancing* as such. For that reason he has never had the obvious popular fame of the Russian ballet-ballet choreographer. He has, nevertheless, an extraordinary instinctive gift for finding the quality of coherent gesture to fit the exact shade of quality in the chosen music. His movement is a continual homage to music; the better the music the more effective is his choreography. I have come to feel that music unduly tyrannizes him, but then I am not a trained musician nor a trained dancer, as he is, and hence, have less right to speak of it. Balanchine's greatest pleasure is derived from his collaborations with the scores of Gluck, Mozart, Chopin, Liszt, Tchaikovsky, Stravinsky, Prokoviev, or Hindemith. Balanchine has an inborn choreographic sense so acute as to amount almost to that of a painter's extra gift, giving him an eye so delicate that he can see color spectre past the range of his fellows, or a musician hearing more delicate and quite different sounds that the rest of us, even with some musical training. Balanchine's employment of the material with which he chooses to work is not only exceptional musically, but from the plastic results he obtains. His choreography is not ever literally narrative; it seldom tells a consecutive story. It weaves, however, a dominating but eventually a climactic and profound atmosphere which is frequently romantic, but just as often so odd in its romance as to seem a genre of romanticism the like of which has seldom been seen before. It is the poetic romanticism not of a Rousseau or Chateaubriand, but of the cruel tales of E. T. A. Hoffman, Grimm or Andersen; the sombre verses of Lenau, Heine and Hölderlin, the cynical self-contempt of Byron and Poushkin. It is a romantic attitude divested of sentimentality. It is an atmosphere at once nervous, individual, spoiled, tender and tragic. Balanchine utilizes no ordinary academic pantomime. Instead he amplifies and broadens ordinary conversational gestures from our familiar lives to connect and correlate the specifically danced portions of his design. If he is deeply moved by his music, Balanchine visualizes amazing cross-currents and short-circuits of representational emotion. These representational fragments are not literal, and hence, have to be watched more closely than the ordinary corroborative mimicry which is easily familiar to superficial audiences. The dancers clutch no fists nor beat any brows, nor point at, nor manually identify each other by vigorous threats or parries. Nor are his gestures "symbolic"; they do not *symbolize* anything; they are in themselves deeply and completely lyrical. They are like the statement of joy or grief in German *Lieder*. The printed words may quietly say that the postman is coming with a message from my love. But Schubert's horn-call annihilates the verses and at the same time, makes them sing and burn in an emotional counterpoint. Balanchine's choreography for Gluck's *Orpheus*, with its grave, sonorous sensuality; for his nervous, tender and diabolical games in *Cotillon;* and for the controlled hysterical transparent nightmare of *Errante,* are to me as wonderful in their way, and in a parallel way to the floating melodic line of Schubert or Mozart. The gestures have a quality of independent rightness exhausting the motor impulses in the music and in the lyrical substructure of concepts on which the music is founded. I have never seen anyone who can approach his mastery of the poetry of dance pattern in a symphonic form. I do not mean by his utilizing the symphonies of Brahms or Tchaikovsky, but in his orchestrating dancers to move in his given space, as sounds exist in their given time in a symphony.

When Balanchine uses solo figures moving against the choral background of his corps de ballet, with this background not visually muted, but with gestures controlled by their further distance from, and hence, less importance to our eyes, as in his *Serenade,* I always think of the uses of the piano against a string-background in the Beethoven or Chopin piano concerti. Balanchine is too fine a musician to succumb to the literal transcription of an entrance for a solo dancer to correspond to the entrance of a solo instrument. He would never have been so naive as to reiterate the individual air-turns of the opening of the fourth movement of Massine's *Choreartium,* where a brave attempt is made to connect the dance-steps with the initial ascendant chords of Brahms, only up to the place where the symphonic structure becomes too complex for a choreographer to follow literally—at which point he simply abandons the note-for-note pattern and just turns the ballet into what Arnold Haskell calls "being effective." Balanchine would never be guilty of the niggling closeness to Mozart's intervals, which makes Fokine's *L'Epreuve d'Amour* look like a literal translation from the Franco-Chinese. Balanchine's musicianship is essentially, not literally poetic. He uses his music with the utmost tact as well as with the utmost freedom. The divisions in his corps de ballet do not have to correspond to exact divisions to strings, brass and wood-wind. His patterns are not musical "visualizations" but movement created in and from tonal cadence and harmony. The dynamics of his broad movement are not correspondents but equivalents to the dynamics of his orchestra. In any given Massine danced symphony, you will find four entirely dissimilar stage-pictures, each one having been conceived, as far as the underlying quality of gesture goes, apart. In a Balanchine symphonic work, he will take a certain grain or quality of movement, rather like a chord based on the original theme of an orchestral piece, and exploit this grain to its utmost. The grain, for example, in his *Mozartiana*, had a curious feeling of outthrust, expectant, bold and capricious high-stepping wilfulness. This grain, chord or quality was never lost, however much it may have been developed on the original statement. He chooses his scale and makes his pattern change on a consistent texture. I know of no one else who has the skill both to hew to the music, and to create a musical counterpart to such a degree. Watch the running, fresh, transparent tone of *Serenade*, or the abrupt, brusque, pettish deliberately delayed motor intervals in *Concurrence*. It is hard to realize the extent of the theatrical information and specific dance experience which has been accumulated, rejected and assimilated to produce the purity and sophistication of Balanchine's best works.

My admiration for his inventive genius or taste has never for a second faltered, whether or not I have agreed with his interest in a special subject-matter or rather in his lack of interest in any subject matter whatever. I think he has more to teach a young choreographer about formal gesture in the developed classic tradition than anyone now working in this field. He continues to amplify the range of possibility in the classic dance to such an unfailing degree that he seems a mine of choreographic information. The more you take from his ideas of movement as model, the more there is to be taken. He is here to be used by Americans of less experience, and from the moment I saw *Les Ballets 1933*, I knew he should be used by Americans in America.

Les Ballets 1933 was an international European and not a specifically Russian effort. In one sense it was an end of an epoch; in many others only a beginning. Of its collaborators, the Germans are, of course, all exiled. Bert Brecht continues to influence the American stage. His version of Maxim Gorky's *Mother* was produced here in 1935. Marc Blitzstein's labor opera, *The Cradle Will Rock*, bears its dedication to Brecht. Kurt Weill composed music for *Johnny Johnson*, for the Group Theatre, for Reinhardt's *Eternal Road*, and is currently in Hollywood where he has been actually the first composer of note permitted to orchestrate his own films. Caspar Neher works for John Christie at Glyndebourne, for whom this year he designed the revival of Verdi's *Macbeth*. Sauget's opera, *La Chartreuse de Parme*, based on Stendhal's novel, is in preparation at the Paris Opéra. Milhaud is making ready his huge *Christopher Columbus*, for the 1939 World's Fair in New York, in collaboration with the French Government. Pavel Tchelitchev's enormous dialectical painting, *Phenomena*, has just created its scandal in London, preparatory to an American exposition, and he has designed the new Hindemith-Massine *Nobilissima Visione* (St. Francis), a collaboration Diaghilev had indicated, but which he did not live to present. Bérard, last year designed *La Symphonie Fantastique*, and this year, Beethoven's "Seventh" for Massine, besides sets for the Comédie Française. Derain invented the chinoiserie pastiche for the Blum-Fokine-Mozart's *L'Epreuve d'Amour*, besides frequently collaborating with Serge Lifar at the Paris Opéra. Charles Koechlin just completed an able sound-track for Henri-Cartier's Spanish documentary war film, *Return to Life*. Thus a brief indication of results stemming from *Les Ballets 1933*, an effort small in scale but rich in possibilities, and in the normal tradition of Diaghilev's anti-academic experiment.

Compare it to the subsequent record of the collaborators of the so-called Russian Ballet. The decor by André Masson, for *Les Présages*, was for a while abandoned, only after its full hideousness had been allowed to baffle the world for two seasons, but now the Australians will get a chance to look at it. Three obscure White-Russian Parisians were responsible for the tepid back-cloths and clothes for *Choreartium*, which even Arnold Haskell, de Basil's most passionate apologist, could not stomach. Jean Victor-Hugo did his usual clever pastiche of his own old sets for Cocteau's *Romeo et Juliette* again for the wealthy musical amateur, d'Erlanger's opuscule, *Les Cents Baisers*; Dukelsky's (Vernon Duke's) fatuous score for *Jardin Publique* received two complete extremely expensive decoratings and costumings in two seasons, was a failure in both, and junked in a third.

The musical collaboration of the de Basil Ballet, however, was more distinguished than the inheritance of *Les Ballets 1933*. It included Brahms, Tchaikovsky (four times), Berlioz, Beethoven, with revisings of Händel, Scarlatti, and Rimsky-Korsakov. The unqualified distinction of these composers has not been questioned for some time. A gesture in

181

the direction of American folk-lore was conceded in the concoction of *Union Pacific*. The published libretto signed by Archibald MacLeish, had little connection with what we saw on the stage; but the costumes and scenery were both by American Broadway designers. Music was by the talented Russian, Nicolas Nabokov; choreography as usual, by Massine. Arnold Haskell placidly hailed it in London as "living tableaux from Currier and Ives prints," but that was a forgivable lapse; he had probably never seen any. It was as authentically American as English jazz, the average French notion of New York, or Puccini's *La Fanciula del Far West*.

The one new choreographer presented by de Basil entirely *faute de mieux*, has been David Lichine. His first five ballets: *Nocturne* (1933) ; *Les Imaginaires* (1934) ; *Pavillion* (1936) ; *Le Lion Amoureux* (1937) ; and *Les Dieux Mendiants* (1937) were failures indistinguishable from one another, and scarcely remained in the repertory long enough to be seen. The capriciousness of Balanchine's latter perversities for Diaghilev was presented seven years afterward, undigested and without comment. The Tchaikovsky *Francesca da Rimini* (1937) was an unwieldy and retardative spectacle based on visual memories of the Italian Renaissance as seen by a Hollywood decorator. It could easily have been presented without surprise by numerous pupils of Fokine, who had, indeed, himself staged it in Russia in 1915. Lichine is a flashy dancer with a very weak technical basis. As a performer he is a good showman and an excellent grotesque mime. However, his selection as a dance-designer is only an indication of the thin end of the Russian ballet's choreographic strain. He has just mounted *Protée* to Debussy's *Danse Sacrée et Profane* for harp and orchestra. The scenery is by de Chirico, and the whole piece is consciously or unconsciously formulated as a revival of the neo-classicism of the 1920's. Here is the Diaghilev decorative formula reduced to its ultimate absurdity: a revival of a revival of a revival, Russian-Greece, 1938, superimposed on Paris-Greece of 1922, which itself was a double-exposure of Roman-Greece, Louis Philippe's Renaissance and Picasso's post-war classicism.

Except for the dubious quality of the innovation of Massine's symphonic ballets and the fine dancing of certain principals, notably Massine himself, Toumanova, Danilova, and Shabelevsky, the artistic heritage of the official Russian Ballet has been almost completely bankrupt.

I cannot pretend that watching the Paris and London season of *Les Ballets 1933* was an unheralded revelation to me, nor that I immediately took them for *my* private and personal Golden Age of Ballet. I had been seeing every Diaghilev season since 1925, with Pavlova, the Swedish

Ballet, Bolm's and Mordkin's troupes in between times. As a matter of fact, I have never as yet seen anything on the stage comparable to what I imagine it could be under the proper circumstances. All my time and energy is devoted to realizing what I imagine. Rather than discovering everything new and wonderful in *Les Ballets 1933*, I did, however, find much of a healthy creative direction, which after the long interregnum since Diaghilev's death seemed almost more satisfactory than novelty.

I will not permit the rest of this résumé to become irritatingly personal because I am not myself irritated, either by what has happened to me or because the general economic, artistic or political situation is what it is. Even if I accidentally became involved with the ballet business in a very personal capacity, I refuse to let this fact disqualify me from writing about it. The question of my personal prejudice will naturally arise from my readers, and I would hesitate to plead any more unselfishness or objectivity than anyone else. However, our record stands in spite of us and will be regulated and attested by other remoter historians. I do claim that my actual connection with this narrative fits me, rather than strips me of a chance to be frank about it.

Since I was very young, I had always wished to be connected in some way with the ballet. My parents did not allow me to see the original Diaghilev Company when it came to Boston in 1916, not because they thought it was something the young should not watch, but probably because a nine-year old's wishes weren't taken very seriously. For this denial I harbored a deep-seated resentment against them for years, formulating revenges and astounding retributions. I thought of running away to become a dancer, and watching my astonished family, who as a matter of fact would not have minded, across the footlights on the night of my successful debut. Only lately have I been glad, for my many present reasons, that I never myself saw the real Golden Age, but only its faded echo. It somehow separates me as a worker in this art, instinctively and essentially from its deadliest period. As Max Beerbohm wrote in 1906 of the dancing of Adeline Genée, "For all men the time of their fathers is the most delicious time of all; just near enough to be intelligible, just far enough to seem impossible. I am glad I never saw Grisi, never saw Taglioni."

My education was accelerated and intensified, however, by an intense exposure to the Silver Age of Diaghilev, and to the public and private lives of Paris, London, and the Riviera in the 1920's, which was the essential subject matter of the works mounted under his direction. Even then, I never wanted to live "abroad," and I began early to translate into American terms the experimental artistic formulae I saw worked out

183

every summer; creative formulae for the most part already affected by American ideas in music, clothes, books or architecture. So when I saw *Les Ballets 1933*, I felt here was a point of contact and a place to start. I was lucky in arranging for its prime-movers, Balanchine and Dimitriev, to come to America, and I have been continually fortunate in working with them.

Over the last five years since we founded the School of American Ballet together, I have learned many things; every mistake, every error in judgment, every false-step, seemingly at the time a disaster, has in compensatory retrospect proved inevitable and for our own best education. With the aid of Edward Warburg, who has involved himself more whole-heartedly in the support of ballet in America than anyone since the late Otto Kahn, we made the start of it financially possible. Strangely enough, almost the very last letter Mr. Kahn wrote was one to us expressing pleasure, interest in, and hope for our new venture.

There have been other ballet-schools founded in America before us and probably many will be founded after, but I think few have started with such complete plans, or with such a root-grounded base of organization or instruction. The bulk of the teachers are still Russian, with one distinguished American member of Pavlova's company. The Russian State School pedagogy is still incomparable. Only now, after five years, our own pupils are beginning to be in a position to teach themselves and other younger generations. At the present in our winter and summer courses we have nearly two hundred students from all over the country.

The first performances of the American Ballet Company in New York City and on tour in 1935, pleased many people and disappointed others. I think it was John Martin who called it *Les Ballets 1935*, and with some reason. Balanchine, since he had brought over with him the costumes and scenery, remounted *Mozartiana, Errante* and *Les Songes* from his 1933 repertory. However, *Les Songes* had a witty new score by the American composer, George Antheil. The most popular ballet produced was *Alma Mater*, a satire on our recent college days, which Eddie Warburg arranged with Balanchine to Kay Swift's comic music and John Held, Jr's perfect costumes. I personally liked *Transcendence* best. This ballet had a strange history: to music by Liszt, with remarkable painting by Franklin Watkins of Philadelphia, it independently anticipated both Frederick Ashton's *Apparitions*, Nijinska's *Well-Beloved*, and Massine's *Symphonie Fantastique*, all ballets on the same theme, all produced within a year and a half of each other, by choreographers working independent of one another. In *Transcendence*, the Fokine-trained St. Louis-born dancer, William Dollar, made an unforgettable impression. As a

184

ballet based on the life of the virtuoso Nicolo Paganini, with overtones from "The Golden Bough," it was a perfect example of Balanchine's framing an individual artist of exceptional and very personalized gifts. *Serenade* was one of Balanchine's most beautiful lyric works, in the uniquely human manner that only he can realize.

b. *The American Ballet at the Metropolitan Opera House: 1936-1938*

The remoteness of the auditorium of the Opéra is nearly negligible for those people who possess their own carriages; but one cannot deny that the less opulent classes of honest citizens which the spectacle attracts, are constrained from coming more from the difficulty of getting in, than from the trouble of getting home, due to a lack of public means. The net loss cannot be valued, for this reason, at less than the sum of sixty thousand livres. The deficit, since 1783 and up until 1785 is then, the result of an infinitude of false operations to which the Direction has not had the power of opposing.

Memoire Justicatif des sujets de l'Academie Royale de Musique en reponse à la Lettre anonyme qui leur à eté adressée le 4 septembre, 1789.

It is as hard work as any other to create from scratch a ballet school and a ballet company. It is unwise, as in any other work to go too fast, because you'll have to pay high for your high speed later on, but it is almost impossible to resist the temptation to permit oneself to be pushed "ahead" if people are willing to do it even if, on a considered basis you aren't ready for it, and it really isn't "ahead." When Edward Johnson assumed the intendancy of the Metropolitan Opera Association, ending the Italian succession, he asked the American Ballet to come in, create the opera ballets and present their own repertory. The invitation was so unsuspected, the opportunity seemingly so wonderful, there was scarcely a thought of refusal.

Balanchine withdrew the American Ballet from the Metropolitan just three years later. A tabloid columnist said it was just another case of "You can't fire me; I quit." Possibly, only it was not quite so simple as that. The whole arrangement with the Metropolitan was hopeless from the very start. Although Balanchine had long created opera-ballet successfully for London, Copenhagen, Monte Carlo and Paris, the particular situation in New York was something no one could foresee.

Perhaps Opera Houses are the same all over the world, have ever been the same, and will ever be so. Perhaps we were wrong to expect anything else. Indeed Thackeray had his Mr. Cox, the shop-keeper, visit the London opera of 1838.

After the aperture, as they call it, comes the opera, which, as I am given to understand is the Italian for singing. Why they should sing in Italian I can't conceive; or why they should do nothing *but* sing. . . . . Fancy old men dressed in old nightgowns, with knock-knees, and dirty flesh-colored cotton stockings, and dabs of brick-dust on their wrinkled old chops, and tow-wigs (such wigs!) for the bald ones, and great tin spears in their hands mayhap, or else shepherd's crooks, and fusty garlands of flowers made of red and green baize. . . . Such dirt, darkness, crowd, confusion and gabble of all conceivable languages was never known.

As for myself, I was so enchanted to work in the dusty labyrinth of that palatial mortuary under the cracked gilt plaster, powdery scenery, and bundles of rotting costumes, that my *zeal* exceeded a crusader's. I had not yet learned the first rule of diplomacy: *Surtout point de zèle.* We all naively believed what they said when they asked: "Give us something fresh in the ballet, something new." Everything proceeded on our part with a fatal and precipitate enthusiasm.

For example, we decided to put a little Egypt into *Aida*, an opera the locale of which is ostensibly Egyptian. It is indeed a fact that this opera had been written for a Khedive, was first heard in Cairo, but since then, Verdi's original ideas have been somewhat improved. As we all know from having frequently watched it at the Metropolitan, *Aida* is a concert of duets and choruses sung in fancy-dress, with two real horses in rubber-boots, twelve real negroes somewhat paler than the made-up Nubians of the ballet, a brass-band in horn-rimmed spectacles marching on the stage, decked out by amazingly rickety canvas representing the wrecked interior of the Scala Theatre before a recent renovation. We did not wholly permit ourselves this realistic picture in the beginning, but we quickly learned. Balanchine's acrobatic divertissement for the "Victory" dance, his *danses du ventre* for the priestesses based on religious sculptures at Sakkarah, at Beni-Hassan, and from La Fage's archeological engravings, were a scandalous failure. Balanchine rearranged these same dances three times after his initial try, and finally signed them "*after* Petipa," *after* which official silence gratefully closed over them. But we might have known after our first *Aida* that we were through.

For the *Tannhaüser* Bacchanal, Balanchine read Richard Wagner's correspondence, his printed stage-directions, and Isadora Duncan's adventures in her own novelties at the Bayreuth Festival. No one else on 39th St. had this information, if so the Metropolitan stage had never been sullied by the results of this patently pornographic research. *Tannhaüser*, had we the brains to think it out, should have been arranged in pre-Duncan dancing-school drapes, on the symmetrical pattern of the academic French opera. Balanchine's Bacchanale was so convincingly orgiastic that although they used to turn out almost all the stage lights, still the paying-guests in the boxes who infrequently arrived early enough to see it, objected, and from their point of view, rightly so. They were cosily attached to the moth-eaten vision of Leda's stuffed swan and Europa's plaster-of-Paris bull. The dancers were somehow and unaccountably alive. The same confusion arose over the dances in *Lakmé, Samson,* etc., etc. Yet some of the opera-ballets, oddly enough, were a success with parts of the public, some of the newspapers, but hardly with any of the box-holders, and after all, who runs the Metropolitan? Balanchine's *Carmen* divertissement, for example, always saved the opera after the Met's favorite Carmen lost her voice. Even the management admitted that. The "Kermesse" scene in *Faust,* for absolutely no reason, was highly praised by the newspapers. I think Balanchine must have composed it in a deep sleep.

It was soon discovered that due to the cost of extra rehearsals, it was wholly unfeasible to present our own ballet company, one of the main reasons we had been invited to enter the Metropolitan in the first place. During this epoch, however, the Metropolitan found enough money to rehearse and present two entirely new operatic works by American composers. The first, *Caponsacchi,* by Werner Hagemann, was longer and more embarrassing than *The Man Without a Country* by Walter Damrosch.

Yet Balanchine arranged *The Bat* to Strauss' *Fledermaus* music, which the orchestra already knew, and could, hence, play without extra rehearsal. *The Bat* must have been performed nearly as many times as Massine's *Le Beau Danube* and always pleased the public. Keith Martin's pretty costumes helped, but it was never one of my favorites. William Dollar mounted the Chopin F-Minor Piano Concerto as a ballet. It was a remarkable piece of invention with respect to the mood and form of the music, all the more so, since it utilized forty dancers, and was this fine artist's debut as choreographer. This piece was also chosen since the orchestra had it in repertory. It was presented only on Sunday evening "gala" concerts, and was never noticed by the critics of the daily press. John Martin was invited to a piano-rehearsal (there was no "dress" rehearsal permitted), since he had other duties at the time of the actual performance, but caretakers at the door forbade his entrance, since they could not believe a critic of the *Times* could legitimately want to see *dancing* at the Met. I don't blame Mr. Martin for never coming back. This, however, was only an indication of the official attitude at the Metropolitan towards the position of its American Ballet Company. Then, I guess it was, that Balanchine indulged himself in a fanciful interview with a morning newspaper reporter. He said music critics knew nothing about dancing, and not much more about music, as they were continually proving in their columns. That fixed him, and with him, the American Ballet as a possible collaborator with the Metropolitan Opera Association.

The *coup de grace* was, however, reserved for our production of Gluck's *Orpheus*, in the spring season of 1936. It is too long and too special a story to tell here; I am reserving it for a detailed study elsewhere, when I can print pictures. We were, naturally, all eager to put into immediate action all our theatrical ideas we had developed from Diaghilev's day to our own tenure at the Metropolitan, concerning the proper contemporary presentation of lyric drama. These ideas were in essence revolutionary, and hence, unsuitable for the Metropolitan. The Metropolitan is scarcely the place for experiment, even in an "experimental" spring season. We knew that even at the time, but there was little enough to lose and everything to gain by going ahead. By a curious relaxation of the general managerial inertia, or on account of it, or because everyone was so preoccupied with postponing their much publicized reforms promised ever since Johnson took over, or because Mr. Warburg agreed to divide the expenses for new scenery and costumes, we were permitted to stage our *Orpheus* with chorus, soloists, orchestra, and stage crew of the Metropolitan Opera House. It was by way of being a reckless manifesto designed, rehearsed, and produced within three weeks' time; but as Whistler replied when the Lord Justice asked just how long it took him to paint a certain landscape, "My whole life-time."

After considerable study and discussion of the legend of Orpheus and Eurydice, we decided to present what was most living for our epoch in the Orphic myth. We saw it as the eternal domestic tragedy of an artist and his wife, with Love himself a male angelic embodiment, with real feather wings and real muscles for flying, not a girl androgyne, which was the tradition of the Paris Opéra. Balanchine also had suggested that the singer who sang the rôle of Orpheus while Lew Christensen danced, should not have a woman's voice, in the Franco-Italian tradition of the *castrati*, but instead a tenor. This replacement had long been achieved in the Russian Theatres. Instead, the Metropolitan permitted the dancer to be a male (which even Paris still refuses), but insisted his voice should remain female.

We saw Hell as a concentration-camp with flying military slave-drivers lashing forced labor; the Elysian Fields as an ether dream, a dessicated bone-dry limbo of suspended animation, and Paradise as the eternity we know from a Planetarium arrayed on the astronomical patterns of contemporary celestial science. The movement was danced and mimed in some of Balanchine's most accomplished erotic patterns, touching and electric encounters, and noble plastic groups. Attic vase drawings, themselves, and not polite dancing-school scarf dances, in his love-knots and amorous garlands had really come to life. Pavel Tchelitchev's scenery and costumes, which in tonality and atmosphere recalled Massacio, Piero della Francesca, and our everyday work-clothes, clad pseudo-Eleusinian mysteries equal in dignity and grandeur to Gluck's superb score.

The actual production was a complete failure; a failure echoing with dog-howls of triumph from an opposition that was already vocative; partly outraged box-holders, partly the displaced professional Italian claque. It was a complete official failure because it was neither a castrated Puvis de Chavannes mural, nor yet an archeological 18th century reconstruction; it treated the emotion of love in an adult manner, and the theatre as an adult occupation, both serious mistakes in such a house. It was only presented twice. It offered the music critics the best chance so far to ask those rhetorical questions which rank them as *Messieurs les Ennemis*, the hardy perennial complacent censors of new life. They demanded with Olympian satisfaction: "Who are these unknown presuming persons, who have been vouchsafed the sacred scene of this great house, etc.?" Indeed, the audience, in several places had tittered because the human flesh of the dancers was designed to be seen in loving contact. *Orpheus* is about love, and sex does enter it. We made a triumphal arch for love to enter, but the shy-eyed and weak-minded were very upset. The critics loathed it because it made them think. Rather, it didn't quite make them, because most of them were incapable of the function. However, the act of thought was indicated, and they punished us for their incapacity to face it.

Orpheus, then, was a complete failure except for the forty dancers who performed it as a conscious dream; the few artisans and stage-hands who created the wonderful ritual objects, the crystal lyre of Orpheus, the white ghastly whips of the military Furies, and the white-silver branches of the Shadows which the dancers handled. A few American painters, poets, architects, writers, musicians, actors, and stage-directors on seeing it at both performances have never forgotten it. Take it or leave it, here in 1936 was an attempt towards living theater. The critical disdain was effective. When the Met announced *Orpheus* for a new production for the season of 1938-39, the press release stated it had not been in the repertory (of the regular season) for fifteen years. The American Ballet was rewarded for the production of *Orpheus* by never being allowed to create even a suspicion of such an arrant indiscretion again. But the genteel mockery of the Metropolitan management politely continued. Still agreeable and tantalizing requests were forthcoming from the General Manager's office for "something fresh, something new." Sometimes back-stage we could not avoid encountering Mr. Edward Ziegler, the ironic and able controller of the mechanics of the Metropolitan management. We feared his smile more than his wrath. It is indeed Ziegler, more than any other man, who makes the Met work. Hence, he is a miracle man. His candour about the ballets' chances was delightful; here at least, was a genuine realist. He knew to the ground the difficulties of the conditions under which the opera was conducted, and had developed a manner of cold-steel, the only manner which could be effective in such a house. But sometimes he would discuss the dancing. I still occasionally recall with fright the look that would freeze his face when he permitted an icy criticism to crack his lips. Heinrich Heine thus described M. Duponchel, director of the Paris Opéra in 1835; "To judge from his outward appearance one would take him for the overseer of the Père Lachaise cemetery rather than for the director of the Grand Opéra."

There is to be found in the September 1938 *American Dancer* an interview with Mr. Edward Johnson on "What is Wrong with Opera Ballet?" The remarks credited to the General Manager of the Metropolitan Opera Association are recognizable for their scrupulous good taste. His recent unpleasant experience with the American Ballet is never alluded to once by name. This is, for those who know, a mute rebuke for the outrageously frank tirade of which Balanchine delivered himself when he shook the dust (no metaphor) of the Met from his heels. Mr. Johnson says that the trouble with opera-ballet is that it usually tries to compete with big-time Russian ballet when it should be only an incidental and indistinguishable cog in the complex mechanism of traditional opera production.

Even in the face of such handicaps, choreographers complain that they are not given the opportunity of rehearsing their ballets. It can clearly be seen that this is impossible. It is for this reason, therefore, that intact ballet groups are engaged. Ballets must be previously rehearsed to such an extent that they can fare alike with musicians, choristers, and singers while in the Opera House.

The American Ballet learned to its sorrow that the Metropolitan found it indeed impossible to afford the ballets' necessary rehearsals but there is one single point in our favor, of which we could never convince the Metropolitan general management. This was concerning the age of the dancers. They had specified that the dancers must be "fresh, charming and youthful," and hired our ballet on that basis. Hence, in most cases, these dancers were quite new to 39th Street, their average age being not over twenty-one. Unlike the musicians, choristers, singers and supers, they had not been repeating identical stage-business for the last twenty-five years, until they could move automatically like trained somnambulists in a noisy nightmare. Our young dancers were continually thrown on the most famous operatic stage in America, so badly rehearsed from a musical standpoint, that on one occasion during a performance of the Polka from Smetana's *Bartered Bride*, the ballet found, to its grief, that the orchestral score had had cuts made in it from a previous production, which were not restored for the present one. The rehearsing had been done in the studio to save money. When the dancers were approaching their climax on the stage, the orchestra stopped suddenly. The conductor had forgotten about the cuts, and the dancers were left in mid-air. The critics wrote that the dancers couldn't keep step. The publicity department of the Metropolitan agreed, and naturally enough, gave no extenuating explanation.

Why did the Metropolitan imagine they wanted "freshness, youth, novelty" from our ballet, in the first place? Quite simply, because they thought that it would be cheaper and easier to hire a troupe with a repertory already rehearsed and proven, because the ballets in this repertory could be utilized as part of the general operatic program without extra cost (except for rehearsals, which were "impossible"). But the physical conditions (the lack of rehearsals, clean costumes or proper shoes), attendant upon the production of ballet-divertissement in the regular operas themselves, were so unjust that the box-holders became prejudiced against the American Ballet as an entity almost from the start. Hence, they gave it little or no encouragement to demonstrate what it could do, independent of the singers, and with a decent presentation. The Metropolitan was continually embarrassed by Balanchine's integrity as an artist when he attempted to defend the rights of his troupe. It was, after all, the dancers who were ultimately to suffer, not himself, as he had plenty of work for the future on the outside. The mechanism of the Metropolitan is so antiquated even with all the extra-musical odds in its favor, that I understood only too well how much the ballet question pricks them. But they give it less thought than new uniforms for their ushers.

However, I refuse to be silent in the face of the genteel if hurt accusations, the well-bred blame which the Metropolitan now levels at Balanchine and his ballet, for treatment over the last three years. The Metropolitan Opera Association, as a specimen of inert survival, is a diverting relic. It inhabits a physical plant in which all the effort of an extremely efficient, technical staff is forced to manufacture an eighty per cent efficiency out of a mechanism not capable of fifty. They could have sold the building and land five years ago to house them well in a new place, but they waited for a "better" price. The market dropped, and they are still waiting. If the single voice of Kirsten Flagstad were removed from their box-office attractions, I, for one, would not tremble much to think of what would happen to their receipts. They have created a popular German repertory entirely on the basis of one great voice and two composers, Wagner and Richard Strauss. Their seven-dollar top, their comparatively short season, their heavy subsidy, their lack of any French, Russian, or Anglo-Saxon repertory or singing actors, their contempt for American singers and composers of our generation, and for any music since 1914, is only compensated for by a persistence of the accrued prestige of by-gone glory, and the persistent interest of the box-holders in the value of the real-estate if and when the house can be sold.

But I still think that given half a chance, ballet even by Americans, would please an opera-house audience if the atmosphere were a trace less snobbish, and if it were given only half the physical consideration, for example, that Radio City Music Hall's ballet automatically receives. The Music Hall is almost as difficult a mechanism to operate as the Metropolitan, with a new stage show every week, with two large dance troupes beside chorus, orchestra and soloists. Yet Miss Florence Rogge, the ballet-mistress, is treated like a human being, and she produces work in return which is of a superlative average quality, and whose popularity increases year by year. Under proper conditions ballet would be as useful to the Metropolitan as Serge Lifar's weekly Monday evenings of ballet have been to M. Rouché of the Paris Opéra since 1930.

At the same time and before this, there was parallel activity in the ballet in other parts of America. In Philadelphia, Catherine Littlefield had been long working with the Philadelphia Opera Company. She had been subjected to similar European sights and sounds as all the rest of us. Among other works, she redesigned Stravinsky's *Apollon Musagète*, and recreated Poulenc's *Aubade*, both of which had been presented in Paris by Balanchine before. She staged the first complete choreographic performance in America of Tchaikovsky's *La Belle au Bois Dormant*, the last act of which in one way or another has long provided the Russian

Ballet with *La Mariage d'Aurore.* Miss Littlefield also presented Ravel's *Bolero,* and his *Daphnis et Chloë,* not seen in America since Fokine's version in 1916. Her performances had the excellent musical background of the Philadelphia Symphony Orchestra, with Leopold Stokowski's or Alexander Smallens' direction, and were enthusiastically received.

In Chicago, Ruth Page occupied a similar position. She had worked in Monte Carlo with the Diaghilev Company. She had danced in Bolm's production of *Le Coq d'Or* when he presented it in the Metropolitan Opera House without acknowledgments to Fokine who surely should have been, but was never asked to be *maître de ballet* there, on account of the Italian supremacy. Page created the rôle of the Dancer in the League of Composers' American debut of Stravinsky's *L'Histoire d'un Soldat.* She has toured extensively in America, the Orient and Europe with Harald Kreutzberg, alone, and with her own company.

Mikhail Mordkin, one of Pavlova's most famous partners and an experienced artist of the Golden Age, mounted for his own company of professionals and pupils, perhaps the oldest ballet of which we have any clear record, Dauberval's *La Fille Mal Gardée,* and also revived *Giselle,* both in his own rather than in their original version. He also produced other dance works to the music of Glazounov, Tcherepnin, and the stock Golden Age Russian musicians, to subjects from Russian fairy stories, Poushkin, etc.

In the far West, in Portland, Seattle and San Francisco, William Christensen, an American dancer of Danish tradition and Italian training, working with the orchestral conductor, Willem van Hoogstraten, produced dance versions of Enesco's *Rumanian Rhapsody,* and Tchaikovsky's *Romeo and Juliet.* Adolf Bolm of the Diaghilev Company, mounted for a John Barrymore film, *The Mad Genius* (vaguely supposed to have been based on the life of Diaghilev and Nijinsky) Mossolov's *Steel Foundry,* as a "modernistique" ballet, and later staged it completely for the Hollywood Bowl. As early as 1922, with the Chicago composer, John Alden Carpenter, he had presented Herriman's famous comic-strip character, *Krazy Kat,* as a ballet, and in 1928 had given the world première (before Diaghilev's) of Stravinsky's *Apollon Musagète.* Bolm has frequently worked with American music by Carpenter, Griffes, W. G. Still, Eicheim, besides Bach, Ravel, Rimsky, etc.

Fokine, on the other hand, in his long career has never created a single work on a contemporary subject, and has scarcely ever invented on an historical or traditional American background, although he has been located in New York for nearly twenty-two years. In September 1921, however, Fokine designed a new ballet for *Get Together,* a revue at the

193

New York Hippodrome. It was "The Thunder Bird," in one act, adapted by Vera Fokina from an old Aztec legend. The music was an arrangement of selections from the works of Balakirev, Borodin, Glinka, Rimsky-Korsakov and Tchaikovsky.

Over a number of years, the League of Composers in collaboration with Leopold Stokowski and well-known American or Russian-American dancers and designers, presented works in the gamut of Diaghilev's repertory. Stravinsky's *L'Histoire d'un Soldat, Le Sacre du Printemps,* his *Les Noçes,* and *Oedipus Rex* were all given their first New York (and frequently Philadelphia) performances. So was Prokoviev's *Le Pas d'Acier,* de Falla's *El Retablo del Maese Pedro,* and Schönberg's *Die Glückliche Hand.* The productions were admirably presented from a musical standpoint, but the dancing and mise-en-scène were seldom successful, as there were neither first-rate collaborators nor a permanent dance organization to execute them. They frequently were second-hand reworkings of Diaghilev's ideas, but without his apparatus or, above all, his taste. Hence, these American productions gave many people who had not seen the Russian Silver Age, a false or confused conception of the work actually being done at this time, or shortly before, by the School of Paris.

This, then, was the activity of Russian Ballet on American soil, either by Russian dancers or by Russian choreographers with American dancers, or by American dancers with choreographers under the influence of Russian notions. At this epoch Russian ideas in ballet were as dominant as German standards in music at the end of the last century, and Italian of the century before. It was a normal historical development, a necessary appropriation to our techniques and imaginations of certain standards and tendencies important for our future. I think in no case was there any competition intended with the "legitimate" Russian ballets. These efforts of our American Age of Iron were considered as individual initial solutions of our immediate personal problems. They were accepted by the local intelligentsia with the patronizing air of parents at a dancing-school's graduation recital, which perhaps they rather were. Only, they seldom considered the performers as their own kids, but rather as those of the poor people next door. Yet many audiences and local folk who had never been able to see ballet before, liked them. They wanted more of them. And these audiences formed the basic nucleus of the mass public for the popular future of ballet in America.

c. American Ballet in America: 1936-19---

The American Ballet Company returned gloomily to the Metropolitan

Opera House in the fall of 1936, primed with rumors of all sorts; threats, admonitions and tacit warnings. Something palpably had to be done if they were to be allowed to stay even another year. The Metropolitan management, distressed over receiving hardly less than equivocal notices in the newspapers, and by no means satisfactory services in the opera ballets in return for their entirely uninterested collaboration, made it quite clear that Balanchine and his troupe were there on sufferance only. Something plainly had to be done. The result was the American Ballet's Stravinsky Festival in the spring of 1937.

Balanchine had always had an admiration for Stravinsky bordering on filial idolatry. One of the first things he had set for Diaghilev had been a restaging of *Le Rossignol* (1926) in Monte Carlo, with the English baby ballerina Alicia Markova (Alice Marks) as the Nightingale. In 1928, with Stravinsky's close collaboration, he had mounted *Apollon Musagète* for Serge Lifar. In Russia, as far back as 1922, he had worked on *Pulcinella*. Stravinsky's generous homage to Balanchine as dancer, musician and choreographer, may be found in the composer's memoirs. Balanchine now decided that it should please the Metropolitan Opera management, establish the American Ballet once and for all as a major institution in the American theatre, and in order to give himself a great personal happiness, he would mount two Stravinsky ballets unfamiliar or unknown to America, and one new work to be written for the occasion. The Metropolitan stage would be used, the Philharmonic orchestra would play, and the composer himself would conduct.

From the very first I was, in company with our older colleague, Vladimir Dimitriev, opposed to this ambitious scheme. I felt that as great a dance-musician as Stravinsky is, he had already had his due from his own Russians, that he would never lack a chance to produce his own work, and that the ballets, chosen to be mounted were every one in a different way retardative. Balanchine wished to produce *Apollon,* for which both he and the composer had a considerable personal affection. He wanted to present *Pulcinella,* but Massine had then announced it for his own immediate production, and since he had originally designed it in 1920 with Diaghilev, Balanchine now stepped aside, though Massine has not yet (1938) reset it. *Petrouchka* and *Firebird* were too familiar to be considered. He felt *Le Sacre du Printemps* was not possible as ballet-music today. Nijinska had just done a fine production of *Les Noçes* in *New York,* and *Le Rossignol* was known as an opera at the Metropolitan. *Renard* and *L'Histoire d'un Soldat* were too small for a large house. So inevitably *Le Baiser de la Fée* was chosen, Stravinsky's homage to his master Tchaikovsky, and Balanchine's to the choreographers Petipa and

Ivanov. The new ballet was *Jeux des Cartes*, or "The Card Party," upon which the composer was engaged when Mr. Warburg approached him. I disliked the idea of this dictatorship by a musician, even if the musician happened to be Igor Stravinsky. For Balanchine, on the other hand, music as always was his prime-mover. He considered the dancing nearly incidental. Balanchine said he would almost prefer to be the conductor of an orchestra for dancing, as much or more than being a choreographer. Anything Stravinsky chose to do was O.K. with him. It was more than O. K.; it was a direct commandment whose fulfilment was joy.

The Festival was admirably rehearsed, ably presented, brilliantly received, and almost paid back its considerable cost in two nights. Lew Christensen in the rôle of *Apollon* achieved a human nobility and technical mastery which he had promised in *Orpheus*. His distinguished interpretation of this difficult part was more golden baroque, more the Apollo Belvedere than Serge Lifar's dark, electric, archaic animalism of nine years before. But at last here was an American dancer with his own individual classical attitude, using his six feet of height with a suave and monumental elegance which was wholly athletic, frank, musical and joyful, and wholly unlike the smaller-scaled grace of the Russian prototype. Martha Graham thought it held the most beautiful contemporary ballet gesture she had seen, and said so. So did a few others. "The Card Party" was ingeniously worked to the regulations of Stravinsky's very rigidly indicated libretto. In spite of witty music, fascinatingly orchestrated, dainty perversions of Rossini, Delibes and Stravinsky himself, I found the literal unfolding of a poker-game according to Hoyle, undramatic and even flat. The audience, however, thought they adored it. A poker-game; marvelous; poker is such a definitely American game; *The Poker Party* must be an *American* ballet. Balanchine's choreography was tricky as the game itself. It was difficult to dance, and it was very well danced. At least three Broadway revue producers wanted to whittle it down for their own shows. *Le Baiser de la Fée*, with Alice Halicka's tender decorative investiture, was a touching evocation of the early period of the Romantic ballet of the 1830's, the lost epoch of Philippe Taglioni's *La Laiterie Suisse* or *La Fille du Danube*. Balanchine recalled the Marinsky Theatre of his youth, only his choreography was not a reproduction of, but a sophisticated comment on the school of Petipa and Ivanov, turned towards an epoch in the dance fifty years before their time. A Russian friend, sitting in what would correspond to the Imperial loge at the Metropolitan, said: "I can't help it, and it may be terribly depressing, but it reminds me of Petersburg, 1914, before the Revolution." But no, it was only New York, 1937, a long time before another revolution.

John Martin, the suggestive dance-critic of the New York *Times*, even said he liked *Le Baiser de la Fée*, that it was the best thing Balanchine had done since he had been in America. Of this, much more later. The evening of the première was a great success. The congratulations were colossal, Stravinsky beamed, and the result was completely zero, although it did prove this American Ballet Company was a splendid technical organism. For me, however, it was a triumph in a vacuum. It had been hoped that in the next season at the Metropolitan the three Stravinsky ballets would be presented as part of the regular operatic repertory. Such, however, was scarcely the case. When Mr. Warburg, having paid for everything else, refused also to pay for the Metropolitan's additional rehearsal time necessary for presenting the ballets, the plan understandably fell through. *Apollon*, since it had only a string orchestra and hence required (so the Metropolitan considered) next to no rehearsal, was actually given twice in the regular operatic season of 1937-38. The least interesting of the ballets from a popular viewpoint (although my favorite), was dealt its death blow by the excruciating orchestral performance which the Metropolitan permitted it to receive.

The only tangible result of the Stravinsky Festival seemed to be that the American Ballet did return to the Metropolitan in the Fall of 1937 for its third and final year. In the summer, Balanchine took the company to Hollywood and successfully mounted two ballets for *The Goldwyn Follies*. I did not go. I was neither disillusioned, disappointed, alienated nor sad, with either Balanchine or the American ballet. I knew that my service to this American Ballet was over because there was absolutely no chance for the young dancers in whom I was more and more interested, getting any opportunity to perform in the kind of dances which I wished them to create. Balanchine had Hollywood and his enormous popular success on Broadway. Rouché of the Paris Opéra was always after him to return, and he had agreed to collaborate with Massine's new venture while protecting the integrity of his own American company. His future was more than assured. He had done much to instruct and influence our American dancers who worked with him.

So I organized a small troupe of dancers from our own school, which had been incidentally very successful, and from among those of the American Ballet proper who were dominantly interested in classic ballet choreography applied to native themes. We found in Frances Hawkins an energetic and humorous independent manager, who heretofore had only worked with the "modern" concert-dancers, Martha Graham and Harald Kreutzberg. In six weeks we made a little repertory and gave our first performances in July 1936, at the very centre of the bitterly anti-ballet, "modern-dance" school in Bennington, Vermont. That debut was a nightmare, although the Bennington audience was a great deal more patient, tolerant and interested than many other people for whom we would dance when we became much better known.

"The Ballet Caravan" has been in microcosm a permanent laboratory for classic dancing, by, with and for Americans. So far we have given over a hundred performances from Skowhegan, Maine, to Havana, Cuba, and are embarking on our first transcontinental tour in 1938-39. It is a company neither as old nor as large in repertory or personnel as the Littlefield Ballet or Ruth Page's troupe, companies dedicated to the same principles and working along the same general directions. The story of the Philadelphia Ballet or of the Chicago Ballet is probably in every way as instructive and entertaining as my story, only the creation of the Ballet Caravan is an important part of *my* story, so I'm telling it here.

I intended to create a small company of good dancers which could one day be amplified into a big company with a similar repertory. The music was to be good enough to serve both, and it did. The dancing was to be a foundation for further developments, and it is. Realizing the danger Diaghilev risked at never having more than two choreographers at his disposal at one time, and only five in his entire career, I started off by mounting four works by four different dancers. The first season of the Ballet Caravan with a tour in New England was of not much interest except to the dancers and myself. It was more of a hard vacation than work, a feeling-out for our future. But William Dollar's dances for Ravel's *Valses Nobles et Sentimentales,* and Lew Christensen's to Mozart's *"Haffner" Serenade* are still in our repertory. Elliott Carter's *Pocahontas* offered too many technical problems of stylistic handling to be immediately successful; the music was so good that now, two years later, we are reviving it with all the means we have at our disposal.

For the second season we mounted our first American works successfully, and appeared with the Philadelphia Symphony orchestra. Our musicians, while they are all native-born Americans, had everyone of them been exposed to the School of Paris, directly or indirectly, through Nadia Boulanger, the heirs of Erik Satie, *Les Six,* and the principles of *musiquette;* or else they had refused to be affected by the Franco-Russians and were hence influenced in reverse. Each of them used American folk-material. Robert McBride had long played and arranged for a jazz band; Paul Bowles knew Kentucky and Mexican folk-songs from first-hand; Virgil Thomson, the composer of *Four Saints in Three Acts,* had just finished music for the United States Government film, *The Plough That Broke the Plains,* and would soon start on *The River;*

Elliott Carter, Jr. had studied with Loeffler, Piston and Gustav Holst, and had conducted a workers' chorus all over France. All of them were in the lively traditions of *les Jeunes*. They knew and loved Russian ballet as much as I did, shared my opinion of its uses and abuses, wanted to collaborate on American subjects.

The American subject-matter gave me a lot of thought. I had only a small company, so that anything involving pictorial pageantry was out of the question. Trial and error had showed me the danger of competing with the Russians on any ground at all upon which they might choose to perform. Finally, there must be no Spanish, Russian or Italian manual pantomime or character-dancing. We needed something that would seem familiar to our hoped-for audiences, something with which they could feel at home, and yet something in which our specifically American-styled dancers could be shown to their best advantage. The familiarity of our subject-matter must never duplicate the familiarity of the Russian formula. The American classic style should never be dulled by a veneer of Russian glamor.

Just as there is always a literary diction like Tennyson's as opposed to lyric speech created from the vernacular of our every epoch, by poets like W. B. Yeats or A. E. Houseman, so is there an opera-house post-Imperial ballet-ballet style in dancing, as differentiated from that simple stage elegance which always distinguishes a true classic dancing-artist, whether he or she be Russian, Polish, Danish, French or American. Due to the effective blackmail of the Russian Ballet, the only *style* which is now recognized as legitimate, is a stylization stemming from the specifically *Russian* ballerina. Some idea of Soviet Russian style as opposed to the Imperial Russian style could be gained from watching the remarkable performance of Wachtang Chabukiani of the Bolshoi Ballet at Carnegie Hall three years ago. He was an exultant acrobat of extraordinary physical power and nervous strength. His effects were broad rather than refined, but his vitality was intoxicating, like the pictures of demonstrating athletes one seems in newsreels of Moscow May Day parades. The post-Imperial style-type springs from Fokine fragments for Pavlova, as exemplified in her popular "Death of the Swan." Pavlova herself was probably not responsible. Only her diluters appropriated a certain half-shut-eyed, strangling, ecstatic agony of beauty felt-to-be-unbearable, peculiar to this one short number, and developed it as a consistent manner of stage-behavior. I have seen Tamara Toumanova in the Grand Variation from *La Mariage d'Aurore*, for example, when if you let the activity of her eyelids or nostrils serve as any symptom, you might have thought that she was fighting off a syncope or some other more intimately painful shock. The Russian ballerina has gotten to be considered some faintly fairy creature, some celestial Grand Duchess vouchsafing an aerial apparition to her enslaved terrestrial fans. She is bent on being remote, bloodless, apart, glittering with crown-diamonds, socially aristocratic, with a sex-appeal as artificially frigid as it is definitely provocative. This style is a reflection of the society of pre-war Russia. Its present use echoes the maintenance of the lost Imperial myth by Parisian White Russians. It is a style that needs overhauling, since it is no longer an index of human dignity, but rather a decorative hangover and a sentimental imitation. It's all very *vieux Russie;* tiny champagne suppers for two, crushed vapors of snowy tarlatans, and bubbly sentimental toasts quaffed from pink ballet-slippers. This is the vulgar cliché that has been far too long hammered into the eyes of most of our audiences. It makes dolls of the dancers, only perhaps a wooden puppet would be less irritating. One recalls the remarkable notes of the German romantic poet, Heinrich von Kleist (1777-1811) when he visited in company with a brilliant young dancer a provincial marionette theatre.

And what advantage would this puppet have over a living dancer?

What advantage? Above all, dear friend, a negative one, to wit, it would never behave affectedly. For you know, affectation is shown when the soul (*vis motrix*) is at a point other than that of the centre of gravity of the movement.

Now, the dancers I have to work with in my own small troupe can put on some very droll imitations of Russian ballerinas of the antique genre if they have themselves performed well that night and someone is giving a party afterwards. But it is not *their* style. Dancing style is merely a heightening, a theatricalization of the personal gifts of the artist, a conscious projection of their delight and security in their work, a direct and transparent reflection of their essential value as human beings, which takes its color from their training and from their environment. The style of the Russian dancers whom we are now privileged to see, echoes the faded aristocracy of the Imperial schools or its Parisian reflection. The style is not a simple affectation. It is an accurate reflection, and for thirty years has framed the most intense and vital lyric theatre we have had. The American style will not imitate the Russian, but instead be its equivalent for our time and place. Our legitimate reflection of a Democracy is of necessity not distant, but immediately intimate. There is *pride* in both styles, the awareness of the human body in all of its super-human released essential energy. I leave with my readers their choice of future style in the dance. The choice ultimately depends among other things on which political or economic system has the best bet in America. Amer-

ican style springs or should spring from our own training and environment, which was not in an Imperial School or a Parisian imitation of it.
Ours is a style bred also from basket-ball courts, track and swimming
meets and junior-proms. Our style springs from the personal atmosphere
of recognizable American types as exemplified by the behavior of movie-
stars like Ginger Rogers, Carole Lombard, or the late Jean Harlow. It is
frank, open, fresh and friendly. It can be funny without seeming arch,
and serious without seeming pained. These actors or dancers like them,
wish to establish a direct connection, approaching personal intimacy or
its theatrical equivalent with their audiences, like Helen Morgan perched
on her piano, or Paul Draper appearing not as a dancing-entertainer,
but as an artist-guest and host from his own dance-floor.

The Russians keep their audience at arm's length. We almost invite
ours to dance with us. Anyone of us would like to know Fred Astaire,
since we have known other nice, clever, happy but unassuming boys like
him. The same is true of Paul Haakon's clean, manly brilliance, his
brilliant apparition like a pocket-Hercules; Buddy Ebsen, a contemporary Daniel Boone or Davy Crockett, seems to have just hoofed out of
the sticks; and Ray Bolger is the eccentric dancer's paragon for the "Tin
Man of Oz." These dancers have the American style, and so has the
cynical footwork of Donald Duck and Popeye, the Sailor. It is this kind
of feeling we will have to find and accentuate in order to provide American dancers with their best background, and American dance audiences
with their best entertainment.

> You can't expect a cowboy to agitate his shanks
> In etiquettish manner in aristocratic ranks,
> When he's always been accustomed to shake the heel and toe
> At the rattling rancher dances where much etiquette don't go.*

Partly because The Ballet Caravan was touring the Maine and New
England Coast, partly because I had a great fondness for Melville's
marine narratives, we pursued our American subjects with *Yankee Clipper*, which chronicled a farmboy's adventures in the ports of the world
and on a merchant-ship of the "fifties." Eugene Loring did a charming
job of parodying the native dances of Argentine, Japan, Bali and Africa.
He put his Tahitian girls on toe-point. The folk numbers were episodic,
like a newsreel-travelogue. The Adagio for the farmboy and his Quaker
girl recalled Balanchine, as was only natural. Lew Christensen's *Filling
Station* had the benefit of Virgil Thomson's music and inclusive stage
information and Paul Cadmus' comic-strip clothes. This was a ballet

---

*J. B. Adams. (Songs of the Cattle Trail and Cow Camp, by John A. Lomax.)

with a contemporary background. It started out quite differently on an idea I had the year before. This was to have been called *Bombs in the Ice-Box,* or *Everyone is Equally Guilty.* It would probably have been a very flat American danced imitation of Auden and Isherwood's *Dog Beneath the Skin* or *Where is Francis?* It would have required a gigantic frigidaire full of rubber-tubing and tear-bombs, a swing-session of gas-masks, and a hero-surgeon who with a miner, a fireman, an aviator and a diver (the four elements) destroyed the war-mongers. All these bad ideas, however, resulted in some good ones. *Filling Station* has only a few characters, but each, either alone or in combination, has its reason for being, each represented an actual facet of American civilization. Each was a recognizable social type, and each had its choreographic climax treated in a manner to heighten each individual dancer. Lew Christensen's choreography had a virtuosity and showmanship to which his long years of training in big-time vaudeville had accustomed him. The two truck-drivers' tumbling act was a sure-fire hit. The group dances in which he freely used the Big Apple were simplified past any actual resemblance to a dance fad which might date it in six months, as our repertory almost must last us for many seasons.

Now we are working on Aaron Copland's *Billy the Kid,* Elliott Carter, Jr.'s *Pocahontas,* and a contemporary treatment of the Minotaur legend, more modern Nazi than ancient Greek, with music by Charles Naginski, who sometime after starting our ballet, won the *Prix de Rome.* Our plans include works based on the subject-matter, if not on the actual plots used by Melville, Hawthorne, Mark Twain, Whitman, Henry James, Stephen Crane, Hart Crane, Thomas Beer, or James Farrell; folk or popular material that is comprehensible to all of us whether we've read these particular writers, or have ourselves had experiences on this continent which they have already recognized. Our treatment, we hope, is moral rather than rhetorical, although there is plenty of work to be done along this line. By moral, I do not mean ethical. By moral, I mean having some connection with the manners and behavior of men and women with whom we are familiar, as directly or indirectly displayed in theatrical settings which have a real, not a rhetorical or decorative relevance to ourselves.

Consider *Billy the Kid,* for example. Instead of take a picturesque cowboy legend and making it the tragedy of an individualistic, romantic desperado, *à la* early "Western" serial movies which, following the Russian formula, would have been the obvious thing to do, we saw the Kid's life as only a fragmentary, if symbolic, incident in the expansion of our vast frontier. Billy's career was doomed, not by implacable fate, but by the collective necessity of establishing law and order so that people could live in a new place in peace. Billy was used as the symbol of an order of reckless individuals which, however charming or picturesque, was doomed by the historical process of the developing Frontier. Billy was not a tragic poet but a little bad-man, like others we know and even like, and are forced to shoot to keep them from shooting us first. Realism in the ballet may be an anachronism. I, for one, haven't the slightest intention of adapting the means of the realistic theatre to the lyric stage. Only a realistic historical attitude can be used for far more powerful lyrical ends, because they will be truer ends for our time and place, than a persistent prejudice for a romantic, story-book, unrealistic and essentially decorative ideal as exemplified by the "poet" of *Les Sylphides*.

Coincidental with our activity, Catherine Littlefield had been working on a series of ballets with American subjects which she later presented in Europe with considerable acclaim. Although Isadora Duncan and Ruth St. Denis had toured abroad two decades before her, Miss Littlefield took the first contemporary classic ballet company from America to Paris, Brussels and London. She had arranged the dances for Carlos Chavez' *H.P.* (Horse Power), with decor by Diego Rivera. Her *Terminal*, set in a railway station, *Let the Righteous be Glad*, a negro ballet, and her *Barn Dance*, gaily conceived as an integrated suite of American square-dances, have been particularly appreciated.

At the same time, or slightly before, Ruth Page in Chicago had presented *Hear Ye, Hear Ye*, a court-room ballet with tabloid-burlesque and night-club interludes, to the music Aaron Copland had written especially for her. She also presented George Gershwin's *American in Paris*, with the virtuoso tap-dancer, Paul Draper, who had been benefitting by strict classical ballet training. Recently, Ruth Page's *Frankie and Johnnie*, score by Jerome Moross, has been the big hit of the past Chicago season. Catherine Littlefield is preparing her *Ladies' Better Dresses*, with the composer Herbert Kingsley, as well as a satire on *Café Society* (Ferdy Grofé) for immediate production.

In San Francisco, Portland, Seattle, Los Angeles, Pittsburgh Washington, Boston, Baltimore, Newark and Detroit there are the first healthy signs of local American ballet companies. In Rochester, New York, Thelma Biracree has mounted several ballets by younger American musicians at the Eastman Conservatory of Music, on subjects ranging from Anthony Comstock's vice-crusade, Ladies' Day at a Ball Park and Haiti voodoo, to dictatorship and Mexico. Before about 1870, there was scarcely a permanent endowed civic symphony orchestra in America, and yet we all are familiar with the presence of an endowed orchestral institution in almost every one of our fair-sized cities. Now, it is not too much to hope with some encouragement and the employment of taste and efficiency on the part of the companies themselves, that we may be able to have one day as many ballet organizations as there are orchestras. All sorts of reciprocities and collaborations are open to alliance between ballet-company and orchestra. The literature of dance-music and its subsidiary tone-poem is extremely attractive to popular audiences. American ballet in America is rapidly approaching the proportions of a national movement. And all this in spite of my inconvenient villain, the "Great Conspiracy."

Our future in dancing, however, is by no means assured. We can no more believe that Americans can create ballets to cancel the Russian repertory's popularity in the next five years, than we can hope for peace in Europe for a same length of time. But the question of time happens to be the most important. Now, not five years from now, is the time to encourage our American companies, since lack of interest, or consistent setbacks can kill their initial efforts without too great pressure. This is what the managers of the Russian troupes count on; not consciously, perhaps, because consciously, they would never admit any competition whatever. We are naturally grateful for the tours of their international companies, who from the snow-balling of their accrued prestige have dug our groundwork for us. I, for one, want to see Massine create for many years to come, because his choreography has always elements for our instruction, his great dancing always fills us with delight, and his appreciation of theatrical values is a model for the young American dancer. The question is now, at this moment, and within the next five years, whether or not there's enough backing, private interest or public energy for both. Or will the "Great Conspiracy" manage to draw the teeth of an American Movement by consolidation and compromise. Can the appropriation and Russification by flattery and pigeon-holing of our best young American dancers proceed? Can the Russian companies Americanize themselves in every way but the essentials? Will the "Great Conspiracy" succeed?

PART TWO

The Great Conspiracy

I. *THE MANAGER'S STAKE*

The promotion of ballet in America may be a nervous excitement full of frustration and love for some of us, but for others it's big business pure and simple. As a matter of fact, it's pure business for both, because no one any longer has independently enough cash to take dead losses year after year on the scale Diaghilev, Ida Rubenstein, or Rolf de Maré of the Swedish Ballet did. Russian ballet in America has paid extremely well, considering the fantastic complexity of the organization needed; boat-fares back and forth, train-fares across the continent, the reams of publicity bought on the line, and the over-balancing size of personnel and machinery. The Russian Ballet has been treated in our Provinces like a road-show, a circus, an old-time "Ben-Hur" production, because that's been the only way up to the present that a mass-audience can be hooked. The general impression one gets from talking to dance-managers is that ballet costs a fortune, brings in a fortune and loses a fortune. This partly arose from the mythical rumor that although Diaghilev in his first Paris season made two million gold francs, he lost three and went on doing so for twenty years. In America, the dance-managers behave as if they were patient but feeble-minded altruists; unfortunately for them, the ballet's got into their blood; they seem doomed to haul it back across the wide ocean year after year, to satisfy their own exigent artistic hunger. They somehow have to drag it all over America for seven or eight months, playing one or two-night stands because America just simply *needs* it. However, the managers are not, to say the least, feeble-minded. Their actual financial stake in presenting such a complex attraction as ballet is ridiculously small, because they are not in reality either general-managers or even impresarii. They are booking-agents, pure and simple. They are more than safely backed by two of the chief concert, music, radio and entertainment monopolies, the Columbia Broadcasting System and the National Broadcasting Corporation. There is a persistent belief on Broadway, difficult to ground, that these are one and the same company, and their rivalry is on the same pattern as the Standard Oil Company of New Jersey's earnest competition with its arch-enemy the Standard Oil Company of New York. Maybe the same banks backed both at the beginning. In any case, the monopolies control so much money budgeted for direct and indirect advertising, that they do not mind setting aside what is for them a relatively small amount to be spent on a prestige build-up accruing from the exploitation of music or dance attractions. This money is not really risked, but rather administered by these managers who are allowed to place "their" attractions through the booking facilities of the monopolies.

It is a waste of time talking to people who, supposedly interested in the so-called Fine Arts, nevertheless refuse to soil themselves by understanding the basic economic background which conditions the very painting, architecture, theatre and dancing to which they pretend they are so passionately attached. No one who honestly cares about the dance can afford to be lazy-minded about the concert-management racket. I am not calling for an economic Holy-War at the moment, since I am a realist, but I do call for an elementary historical and economic comprehension on the part of our dance-loving audience. The position of the monopolistic dance-managers is exactly parallel to that of the men who "made" such great railroads as the Central Pacific. In the words of Louis Hacker: "They achieved great wealth not because they were mighty enterprisers, taking risks with their personal fortunes and hence gaining well-earned rewards, but because of the bounty and, incidentally, the cheating of the government." For "government" insert Broadcasting Companies. As far as "cheating" goes, the definition of this word will be left to the District Court. The fact that the concert-managers don't make as much as the quarter-billion Archer Huntington and Leland Stanford took, does not eliminate them from our suspicion or excuse them from our disdain. We may not assume that the Huntingtons or the Stanfords did nothing in return for their plunder. Tammany Hall served many poor New Yorkers very creditably as an agency for quick relief for some years. All I wish to imply is that the price paid for these services has been too high, so high, in fact, that it would be cheaper to find other agencies, even if we have to go to the trouble of creating a new one or limiting the old.

Last spring, only because he happened to be a close friend of a friend of mine, I was permitted to interview the general-director of the greatest of these monopolies. I told him somewhat more angrily what I am writing here. He listened courteously but without interest. He explained frankly that his whole concert-bureau division which controls the dance and music attractions for his organization, grossed no more than eight or ten million dollars a year. Hence, it was maintained more for the benefits of its incidental publicity prestige-value than to make much money directly. He even humorously admitted that he didn't know the names of the dance-managers who had arrangements to book their important attractions through his companies' large resources, the very well-known names in the trade, about whom I was complaining. I pleaded with him desperately for some encouragement for our young American artists, but he could scarcely be expected to be impressed. I withdrew, frightened and vengeful, but patently helpless. The grotesquery of the situation nevertheless continues to appal me. Here we have an important part of our cultural lives entirely, if indirectly dependent on radio-advertising. Its very existence is made possible only through booking-agencies sponsored as a mere side-line by radio and movie monopolies which are so large that their sole interest in the original music or dance attraction is to use it in the flesh as a purely incidental aid for selling radio-time to national advertisers of coffee or cigarettes.

Recently our Federal Government has instituted a civil anti-trust action, *United States of America* v. *Paramount Pictures Inc. et al.*, entered in the Federal District Court of Southern New York. The Government is attacking the eight major motion-picture producing companies, together with their numerous subsidiaries, as well as one hundred and thirty-two executives. This is a major effort to break the monopolistic control of every means of production, distribution and exhibition which prevents an independent film operator from making a tiny living. It is an attempt to curb or regulate the vicious practice of block-booking. The case will unquestionably be protracted, but it may eventually have serious repercussions in radio, and hence indirectly on the entire field of concert-management, where the principles of block-booking are equally poisonous. Perhaps, as the Broadway cynics say, the Government is, in reality, only trying to force Hollywood to "regulate" itself. The situation is very complex. There are reports that the independent operators themselves are worried over the effects of a possible Federal legal victory, since it would throw them into violent open competition with an enormous head-start, by virtue of their capitalization and past contacts, in the hands of the big companies, even should the Government force them to break up. Now, at least, they know from which tables the crumbs will fall. If the tables are turned anything might happen.

There was a letter recently published in the theatrical trade-paper *Variety*, dated August 11, 1938, which succinctly analyzes the entire situation from the point of view of films. But even if one substitutes *"dance-attractions"* for *"films,"* no other word need be altered. This letter was signed by Leo F. Wolcott, president of the Allied-Independent Theatre Owners of Iowa and Nebraska. That is, this letter represents the attitude of an ordinary provincial distributor on whom the very life cash of the great monopolies depend.

Because of the many abusive and evil trade practices forced upon the independent exhibitors by the motion picture trust such as unreasonable film rentals, block-booking, percentages and designated time, threats and coercion in selling, circuit expansion with consequent protection or non-availability and many others, the independent exhibitor has his back squarely against the wall, fighting for his very business existence. *It has been proven time and again that the monopolists in this industry do not willingly or easily relinquish the grip they hold.* In view of this, it would be remarkable indeed, if anything short of the full success of the Government's projected anti-trust action could correct the present situation.

We have seen round-table conferences before, resulting apparently only in greater monopoly and we are frankly skeptical that the lasting reforms so urgently needed in this industry can be accomplished without government action, or at least common consent decrees.

The italics are mine.

All this may be rather tiresome reading for the disinterested ballet-omane, who only occupies himself with the purer aspects of the developments of Massine's symphonic achievements. But if he is only a little distinterested, it shows he has really no serious interest at all, for the future of dancing in America may not be settled in a theatre in London or Monte Carlo, but in a District Court in New York.

There is no use inveighing against the system of radio sponsorship or monopoly in American business here, but to put it rather crudely, that is why some people favor both the Roosevelt's, Theodore's or Franklin's, trust-busting policies. The ramifications of the twin Broadcasting Companies, control directly or indirectly through their concert bureaus of the "Community" or "Civic" systems almost the entire musical and dance-life of millions of metropolitan and provincial Americans. For their economic convenience, "dance" is always considered a part of "music," just as one might consider a violin is the only stringed instrument in an orchestra. There seems to be room for only one *kind* of dance, just as only one *kind* of musical virtuoso is allowed on a "series." Dancing itself, which has as many categories as there are instruments in a band, is not deemed worthy of a series of its own which, if handled right, would pay as well or better than the *hors d'oeuvres* which are now stingily offered. This is a situation which has naturally arisen from our general competitive economy. I do not think it is of any interest to complain of it from an ethical point of view. But realistically speaking, the managers, due to the greedy necessity of quick returns on an investment which they themselves only risk on paper, have an inevitable tendency at first to exhaust, then presently to destroy public interest in each ballet attraction which they undertake to present. It may also be true that without the managers, provincial Americans would see little or nothing of foreign attractions; but the price they pay for this, over and above the price of their admission, is by way of being hardly ever permitted to choose what they prefer to hear or see from their own native attractions. The dance-managers will tell you that a metropolitan audience seldom and a provincial audience never, knows what it wants to hear or see. It serves their purposes to believe this, and if possible, they will always keep both selection committee and the audience itself in convenient ignorance.

The managers feed the provincial selection committees or local managers their clippings of the criticism of their attractions by the New York dance and music reviewers. Mainly on this basis are the provinces sold. Take for example, any small town in the Middle West. The Entertainment Committee of a local Woman's Club has signed up exclusively, as they usually must, with one or the other broadcasting company's booking divisions, for, let us say, six concerts during their season. The Club offers to their town the whole course at a figure lower than if one bought tickets for each individual concert. They will receive, perhaps, a soprano, a lecturer on world-affairs, a symphony orchestra, a virtuoso instrumentalist, a travel lecture, and a single dance-attraction. They will not receive any soprano, any violinist or dance-attraction other than the one owned and operated by the monopoly. This artist or other attraction must correspond in importance to the category of the size of the town requesting the attractions. If the committee should by some evil chance not exactly desire one or two of the attractions offered, but rather a third, or else one on some other list, they are told they won't be able to get any if they won't take the lame-duck; because the lame-duck has been awarded a contract in one of the manager's off-moments, and the unlucky contract must write itself off. If the small town should by some rash error request an artist handled by another monopoly, or by an independent manager, the least the committee is made to feel is as if an indiscretion had been committed which is something nice people (in the big city) just rather not think about.

The competition in "concert" management, the moral slugging and back-stabbing is vicious, bitter and relentless as it is in all other forms of our competitive monopolistic commerce. For an independent manager successfully to sell his one or two attractions in territory controlled by the two monopolies or their subordinates who will not hesitate on occasion to combine against him in order to share the preservation of their monopoly, this independent manager must be prepared to encounter every form of blackguarding and intimidation up to physical violence itself. And he does encounter it, every inch of his way. If on occasion, a big manager booking through one of the monopolies' resources smiles with favor on an independent operator by tossing him a few crumbs when one of their own dates has accidentally fallen through, it is only because this same independent manager may be counted upon to ripen certain attractions generally considered difficult or unfamiliar, taking all the risk for his pioneer work, but only so that in the end his attraction will be snatched up by the monopoly after sufficient time has passed to insure a reasonably safe success. The managers themselves actually assume next to no risk. Why should they? They easily operate on prestige funds set aside by the parent broadcasting corporations. Even a European attraction has to assume the guarantee for its own existence before it is ever brought to America; and it can hardly ever expect to be clear of this obligation, labelled advanced royalties, slapped on by the manager to pay the boat-fare. No use in complaining about the weather or because you happen to have blue eyes. These are facts faced by every American working in the dance in America today. It is a different, but not an easier story, for aliens. Without a doubly sure margin of capital put up by a new attraction either in work or cash, the monopolies will not touch a native product because the artistic monopoly of Russian ballet in America can still be further exploited; and it it easier to prolong this exploitation even until the companies are run straight into the ground, rather than to encourage a single American troupe whose future is dubious. Can you blame them? I can and do, not because I think they're heartless bullies, but only because they're bad business men.

Ethically, I am not perturbed, for from a casual point of view the managers are charming men, their morals no worse than the boss of the company who sells you cigarettes, electricity or automobiles. But economically and from an attitude of material realism, I consider them short-sighted.

Take the particular case of the Ballet Jooss, for example: When this talented German exile won the international choreographic prize awarded by Rolf de Maré at Paris in 1932, he had made himself a small repertory, the focus of which was *The Green Table*. Jooss was brought to America, shoved into a Broadway theatre with a stage that was hardly small enough for his troupe, and forced to play *The Green Table* for six weeks straight. When the Russian Ballet itself came for its first season its manager was bright enough to run it for only ten days. It was even hard to give away seats for Jooss after his first fortnight, which was scarcely a disgrace for the novelty of this kind of attraction; but the manager wanted to be able to sell Jooss to the sticks, on the slogan "Direct from six weeks on Broadway." Jooss' splendidly trained and rehearsed company naturally made warm friends all over America, and these friends, like Jooss himself, wanted to see a logical and normal extension of his work. Everyone wondered what would happen—one ballet, two ballets, three ballets *after* his first and only success, *The Green Table?* But his knowing managers decided that Jooss was to be claimed for *The Green Table* and for that alone. It was a convenient saleable tag. That was all there was to it. Jooss worked for six months preparing a new ballet, his *Prodigal Son.* I am not interested for the moment in the artistic merit of this particular piece. But after one look at it, the manager decided that was not the kind of ballet which audiences who had been taught to like *The Green Table* would like. Hence it was summarily withdrawn, after a single New York performance, before anyone including Jooss himself had a fair chance to know whether it was really a good ballet or a bad ballet. I saw this same eminent manager at the dress-rehearsal of Serge Lifar's ill-fated debut in New York City. He personally insisted on so many alterations not only in Lifar's choreography, but in the lighting, costuming and program arrangement, that it was surprising that a highly strung, self-respecting artist like Lifar could appear at all.

The manager's place should never be in a position of artistic censorship. The manager is not an artist, but a booking-agent. This is not a snobbish criticism. It is merely a logical acceptance of the rôle which he has chosen for himself and for which he is too well paid. Extensive creation of repertory, presentation of the artist for whatever he or she may be in their own unadulterated essential personality, is the only method of exploitation possible if any permanent test for an extended commercial success can be expected. Ask anyone what chance Jooss or Lifar has in America today. They will reply, "Yes, but we've seen *The Green Table,*" or "Yes, but everyone said Lifar's *première* was so badly done." Whatever else the monopolies may or may not be, they are not lazy. They work hard for their cash, and it is perhaps curious that in so many cases they should be willing to milk an attraction to death so quickly, purely on the strength of a convenient selling point.

The commercial handling of the Russian Ballet in America has been efficiently exploited from nearly every point of view. The technical difficulties of routing sixty people around this continent, with supplementary musicians to be picked up in every town, with any amount of scenery and wardrobe, with all the details of publicity and box-office, is no easy task. But in order to sell the *Russian* ballet, it has been ordained that all ballet on this continent should be *Russian,* or else it isn't really ballet at all. They feel they are vindicated in this policy by the success of such a "Russian" spectacle as Fokine's *Coq d'Or* last year. But few people outside of New York and all over America, realize that the size and complexity of this production prohibit it from ever being shown to the country at large. At best, ten big cities have a chance to see it. For the hundreds of small cities which make the bulk of time on tour, they can always sling them *Les Sylphides,* or *Petrouchka, Schéhérazade* or *Prince Igor.* The small cities are finally sick of being sold, tired of being treated more patronizingly, for example, by the Russian ballet than they are by Helen Hayes, whose performances of *Victoria Regina* in Topeka or Houston were identical to her appearances in Chicago or New York. It is difficult to give good performances of large dance works in towns that have small theatrical facilities, but the point is this: The productions of the Diaghilev ballets, and those built on the same formula, still in the Russian repertory, were designed to hang in such big houses as the Champs Elysées Theatre in Paris, or Covent Garden in London, where their initial reputation is made. The present technical mechanism, just as the present economic policy, and artistic attitude of the Russian ballet does not any longer apply to the general needs or practical uses of the American theatre. But the sticks are notoriously five or ten years behind New York, although unfortunately for the managers, movies, radio and the ballet tours themselves have taken a tuck in the lag.

Sooner or later, after all our hard ditch-work and pile-driving is done, the managers will turn to our American companies and try to assimilate them on their own conditions. If Russian ballet still can be made to hold together, yet if the available Russians happen to be all in Australia or South Africa at the moment, it will not be difficult to tack a couple of Russian names onto a pick-up American company. They will be able for some time to come to find someone who remembers enough echoes of the Imperial repertory to slap it on a stage. The Mordkin Ballet announces for the present (1938-39) season *Voices of Spring* (Strauss), *Lac des Cygnes* (Tchaikovsky) and *Trepak* (Tcherepnin). He further states "there will be also new leading dancers from Leonide Massine's Monte Carlo troupe, including Nina Stroganova, Vladimir Dokoudovsky, Kari Karnakovsky and Tania Dokoudovska." It is significant that the Mordkin Company is the only native American (sic) troupe to be handled by one of the two large concert-management monopolies. Although Mordkin has been in America for years, one does not think of him as yet caring to qualify as the head of an "American" ballet.

And there may be some money in Russo-American ballet companies, but not for long. I only hope that when the time comes for the monopolies to turn their attention to our stripling American troupes, we will have the popular support or else the good luck to be able to resist them. They will need us badly, and naturally we will always need them, at least for *our* lifetime. But if we can survive independently up to the point of our being over-hauled, we ought to be able to hold out enough longer to get as clever lawyers as they've got. We all know the hard history of ballet in America; we've been making it and we've been paying for it. We will be to blame, not the managers, if we can't name our own terms at that juncture. And ultimately speaking, which is all in our favor, the managers don't care. They'll be big about it if they can, without much risk, clean up on our dancing. What difference does it make, ultimately speaking, and even to them, whether it's an American or a Russian company? Shucks, if the boobs want American ballet, let 'em buy it.

And then a warm, nostalgic glow will gently suffuse them. They will bend back in their swivel-chairs and allow themselves vague and gentle reminiscences of all their contacts and all their contracts with dancers dead and gone. They will tell you how much they lost on Mordkin, on Isadora Duncan, Pavlova, on Shan-Kar, and on the Russian tours. They will point to the framed photographs (and "framed" is correct) of all the artists they have "managed" over the long decades, with affection and genial amusement. They will be talking out loud about the artists, but they will be thinking inside about convenient bankruptcies, broken contracts, legal "reorganizations," artists snatched from their lists and artists they've been able to seduce from their rivals. And they will smile, partly to themselves. What the hell, it's not been such a bad game, after all. In their small way they have been art-patrons, too.

II. *PORTRAIT OF THE PATRON*

IS NOT A PATRON, MY LORD, ONE WHO LOOKS WITH UN-
CONCERN ON A MAN STRUGGLING FOR LIFE IN THE WATER,
AND WHEN HE HAS REACHED GROUND ENCUMBERS HIM
WITH HELP?   *Samuel Johnson: 1755*

Patronage of the arts either by states or individuals, once meant the provision of money towards certain creative ends. The Roman Catholic Church, the Medicis, Louis XIV, the Esterhazys, Ida Rubenstein, derived pleasure in the productions of painting, sculpture, architecture, music or stage-works for which they paid, for a variety of public and private reasons. Some delighted in a product in which they themselves had no part except the capacious enjoyment of achieved beauty. Others preferred to participate, and still others to pay for a frame in which they could themselves shine, or could be illuminated by reflected glory. The patrons of Diaghilev included at various times: Baron Dimitri Guinzbourg, the Comtesses de Greffuhle, de Noailles, and Polignac; the Aga Khan, Otto Kahn, Sir Basil Zaharov, Lord Rothermere, Mesdames de Euphrussy, Chanel, Misia Sert, the Marchioness of Ripon and Etienne de Beaumont. Most of these influential but cultivated people genuinely loved the ballet. It was their opulent pleasure to permit Diaghilev to employ their money as he desired. There were few conditions attached. Frequently these patrons would detest the results which their money made possible. The givers were his devoted personal friends; the gifts, mostly genuine expressions of their affection or admiration.

Ballet-patronage continues with the Russian Ballet today, but in an altered form to fit the time. When Diaghilev was given money to stage opera or ballet, he spent it staging operas and ballets. He did not extract even a modest commission for their presentation, because he produced only what interested him to produce, and his pleasure demanded no surplus profit. He died bankrupt, and it is well known that Mme. Chanel even paid for his funeral. But in recent years ballet-patronage has operated differently.

For example, when *Union Pacific* was in consideration, that benevolent despot Colonel de Basil, implored a committee of American ladies to subvention this new ballet, which was to be *their* new ballet, as a private and personal enterprise. This was an efficient system used subsequently on other works. A sum was collected, just about enough to mount two large ballets of the same size. Yet to this date, neither the composer of the musical score nor the author of the libretto have been awarded their extremely modest royalties in full; although for three years the work must have been produced in America alone, some seventy-five or eighty times. The accident of the choice of the Baron d'Erlanger to write tepid music for *Les Cent Baisers* by Bronislava Nijinska, or for this season's *Cendrillon* by Fokine, is only explicable on the face of an elegant amateur's wanting to hear his music performed up to the point of being willing to pay for it. Diaghilev never accepted cash to produce works he did not deem worthy of production, even though he might have kept part of it to produce other works which interested him, any more than Fortune Magazine takes money for industrial surveys it considers news-worthy, from the corporations it chooses to describe. This kind of ingenious, if fragmentary, patronage by trifling amateurs to which de Basil assented, did little to enhance a growing repertory. Since it was based only on personal considerations of social prestige or economic convenience, the ideas in the dancing or artistic quality were inevitably secondary.

When the inevitable cracks became too apparent in the fabric of the contemporary Russian organizations for hiding even under its official veneer of glamor, when after seasons of bickering, threats and back-breaking tours of nightmare insecurity had culminated in a spectacular stabbing in Chicago, and a bigamy in Louisville; when even the cold sense of the dance-managers could no longer prevent an open split be-tween Leonide Massine, the chief artistic mover, and de Basil, the mo-tivating commercial energy, then came the call to auxiliary committees of American ladies who, fluttering on the fringes of Russian "first nights," had not been previously marshaled to their own best uses. A rear-guard of resident White Russian night-club colonels and a dapper composer left over from Diaghilev galvanized by the ballet-managers' busy press-agents, summoned thrilling emergency meetings at impor-tant homes to enlist the aid of one and all in the preservation for Amer-ica of the glorious tradition of Russian ballet, which seemed, heaven knows why, vaguely to be in some threatened condition.

The American female patron is an engaging specimen, young or old. She is utilized singly and in the herd as peripheral aid, on the one hand by the commercial-manager; on the other, by the ballet-organization it-self. She can be counted on for a certain amount of social-column space attendant upon her apparitions at *premières,* and she can always be ex-pected to know someone who knows someone who would be willing to ask someone who knows the president of General Telephones for a little cheque. She herself is a comparatively "poor" woman. She has given up her second car, and done without an extra man-servant. But she has a proprietary air about Ballet, "our" ballet, she calls it. Her father-in-law, or her uncle was a trustee of Juilliard Foundation, or of the Metropolitan Opera Association, or of the Philharmonic Society. She herself, has no longer time for music-lessons but a divine young Russian emigré, fright-fully attractive and talented, is coming or has just come to play his new score for her, which Massine absolutely must be made to do, and he in-sists, that to really understand it, she must take up her playing again. You can see even Massine's job is no cinch either.

Music indeed is very often the bait or link which lures or binds a female patron to a Russian ballet. Her training and experience in the arts has been mainly musical. From this one might have thought that during the last five years she might have interested the Russian directorate in one single American composer. Yet who, with the exception of Hindemith, whom Diaghilev had approached ten years before, were even the new foreign composers: Jean Françaix (*Beach*), Vladimir Dukelsky (*Jardin Publique*), Nabokov (*Union Pacific*), Karol-Rathaus (*Le Lion Amoureux*), the Baron d'Erlanger (*Les Cent Baisers* and *Cendrillon*). In America, Catherine Littlefield had worked with David Guion, Ferdy Grofé and Herbert Kingsley; Ruth Page with Aaron Copland, Jerome Moross, W. G. Still, and Gershwin; the American Ballet with George Antheil, Kay Swift and Henry Brant; the Ballet Caravan with Paul Bowles, Elliott Carter, Copland, Robert McBride, Charles Naginski and Virgil Thomson. The female patron may be forgiven for not having heard among the names of all these younger American composers anyone save that of George Gershwin. Yet have the Europeans written scores intrinsically more significant or even more danceable than the Americans? They decidedly have not.

However, there are indications that the female patrons are weakening and may be in the market for an American or two. Last year Mr. Vladimir Dukelsky, in his dapper personality as "Vernon Duke" the Broadway songster, organized his *High-Low* Concerts, a tasty series at the St. Regis roof, which Muriel Draper promptly named the *New Low* (in Vulgarity). Duke attempted to veneer the younger American musicians with enough social glitter to make them passable to the international set by having "portraits" of well-known people set to a piano and oboe, or hiring a blues-singer to "swing" a few eighteenth-century songs. There is a special kind of Russian *hors d'oeuvre* which they make out of how-you-say? Indian sweet-corn and sour-cream. It must be about the only Russian *hors d'oeuvre* that isn't absolutely divine.

However, even though one pretty, idle, nervous woman may be unimpressive, an aggregation of idle, pretty, nervous women exert a certain furtive levy on retired bank-presidents, corporation lawyers, or indulgent husbands, and on an occasional unsuspecting but ambitious social-climber. The actual stake of the patrons is even less than the manager's, because these girls don't even work. But they do exert a kind of penumbral pressure, and serve a definitely useful function for the "Great Conspiracy." Their personal taste is no real taste, but merely a light preference for an amalgam of erroneous memories of the Golden Period of ballet, fashion-photos from the last two numbers of Harper's Bazaar, and whatever they can retain from the program-books of occasional Friday afternoon concerts in Carnegie Hall. To them snobbery in its fancier forms is no more alien than fleas to a dog. But congregated to back the

Ballet Exhibition, to buy boxes for the Ballet Benefit, to add their little ounce of obstructionist atmosphere to the general economic confusion, they are reliable enough. For them, New York is still a province of Paris, and the rest of America is its dirty back-yard. If they should be humanly sweet, or handsome, or well-meaning, or even for a moment or two genuinely and selflessly interested, then it is even harder for the serious artist to bear. For ultimately speaking, they are idle women, and we are occupied with work.

The plight of the ballet-patron, like the Policemen of Penzance, has not been, at least recently, a happy one. Due to the late unpleasantness in the world of Russian ballet, descent from Imperial days has been like the Greek Orthodox Church itself, split. But where is Rome, and where Byzantium now? There are the Montagues of the house of Colonel de Basil, and the Capulets of the house of Mr. Serge Denham. The managers (here, Hurok Attractions, Inc.) oscillated nervously, which was quite understandable, before finally passionately espousing the colors of the Capulets. There were a lot of Montagues who wouldn't mind being Capulets, and some Capulets weren't so damn sure, themselves. The managers and the Committee of Patrons arranged a desperate merger to fuse the family's interests, and at first they blandly operated without the consent of either Romeo or Juliet who, very much alive, resided together in the furious person of the artistic dictator, Leonide Massine. As far as dictators go, it is far more legitimate that Massine hold a whiphand, than a hitherto obscure if agreeable Russian called Serge Denham, whose only claim to fame, aside from a decent reputation on Wall Street, is his recently expressed interest in dancing. Mr. Robert Pitney, America's number-one balletomane, is quoted as questioning, upon the mention of the unfamiliar name of this director of the bigger Ballet Russe: "Hum, Serge Denham? denim, serge? . . . Then it *must* be made up out of whole cloth."

The American female-patrons were treated to quite a gamut of hysteria following the daily developments of the great world-ballet serial-thriller, and the attendant publicity was not stinted. With one troupe at Drury Lane and another at Covent Garden, picture their confusion. Even today they resent. any direct question as to whose colors they really sport—because they are not absolutely sure with whom Tania will be dancing, or where darling Baba's heart lies. But if de Basil is exiled today or Denham dethroned tomorrow, their hearts won't exactly break. Arnold Haskell, the manager's darling of the British tours, very recently was claiming de Basil as the unique figure fit to assume Diaghilev's cloak in the present distressing anarchy of ballet. His Cossack steel-eyed strength, his efficient use of the psychological knout was widely publicized as just what the doctor prescribed. Less than a year ago de Basil was the Stalin of ballet. Later, due to his regrettable but understandable misunderstanding of our so difficult, how-you-say, English language, de Basil accidentally disposed of the commercial rights of some of the more popular ballets in his repertory a couple of times to the different combines, which, as the English Courts of Law later decided, was an excess of efficiency. Yet this seems to me no worse than anything else de Basil did during his remarkable dictatorship, when one recalls he was only stopped by an hair-breadth from mounting Scriabine's *Le Poème d'Extase*, with an ecstatic libretto by the spurious mystic, Dimitri Merejekovski, and that he had never at any time any interest in dancing at all. Now, de Basil has been remanded to the caviar-industry, and Mr. Haskell is taking a reef in his Mosaic prophecies of the fulfilment of the contemporary Russian ballet's manifest destiny. Arnold Haskell is the Neville Chamberlain of ballet-spokesmanship. It will perhaps be a difficult yet not insurmountable task to explain the inevitable and necessary return from his Elba of the redoubtable Cossack Colonel. Judging, however, from the models of the "realistic" notes recently issued by Downing Street on Spain or Czechoslovakia, we can be confident of the logical and tactful formulation of Haskell's policy.

The Managers have, through their busy press-agents, developed quite an agile technique for catering to the American female-patron. Ballet-balls, ballet-teas, and matinee ballet club-specials with Russian-salad plates are sagely scheduled. Cards are issued for "open" dress-rehearsals. The female-patron's professional advice is occasionally requested, *en passant*, during an entr'acte—"What would Madam like to see in repertory tomorrow? How did Madam think Tania looked last night?" What difference does it make to the managers as it is always the same repertory and Tania either looked tired or else she didn't? The stage-door is usually open to them, and the poor Russian dancers, lonely enough in their eternal vagrancy, are not averse to having an expensive shoulder on which to sob. For the female-patrons are genuinely sympathetic: "My dear, what that little dancer told me about her life, why Siberia—, escape, Shanghai, Monte Carlo—, why it was incredible! You never read anything in a novel so fascinating." As we know, they don't read much.

Seriously speaking, as for ballet-backing, private patronage in America is almost a thing of the past. Even though I know of two or three spectacular and devoted exceptions to this rule over the last few years, nevertheless, and for the immediate future here at least, the reliable patrons must be the anonymous mass-audience of ordinary people all over the country, who will not interest themselves in ballet for either acquired prestige or direct publicity, but because they love it as theatre and pay as much for it as they do for any other form of theatre. This unquestionably is the way it should be. Either the ballet must keep itself, as it did, for example, in Europe from 1830 to 1850, and pay brilliantly,—or as it has in England and America from 1934 to 1938, and pay (due only to the "Great Conspiracy") less well, or else it is not worth our time or trouble.

There is an increasing and definite economic connection between art forms and their popular reception. No private patronage can much help that reception if the dance form itself lacks inherent interest, nor can an idle and fragmentary private patronage long fetter the form with its own narrow restrictions of inertia or idleness. There is not much use talking about State patonage in America for a long time to come. The recent Fine Arts Bill offered in Congress was laughed out of the House of Representatives, when an anti-New Deal Congressman brought down the House when he gave a crude imitation of a toe-dancer. However, there may eventually be a source of theatrical patronage from a field which may at first seem surprising. Many of us would not be a bit surprised if, in the next five years, some of the large labor-unions would directly occupy themselves with presenting works of independent theatrical excellence. The activities of a great organization such as the International Ladies Garment Workers Union, with its enlightened social and cultural program, has already successfully made its debut on Broadway with the production of its phenomenal revue hit, *Pins and Needles*, of which at the present time, some three or four companies are simultaneously touring the United States. Our best labor unions are in an excellent position to take the place of the Medici. Organized working people have been taught by their unions something more than elementary economic defense tactics. They have been taught to respect the cultural monuments of the human spirit as standards of human behavior. The creative theatre is a weapon as well as a recreation. Dancing may be also discovered as not the least of its defenses.

III. THE FUNCTION OF THE CRITIC

EDGAR DEGAS SAID THAT THE MUSES NEVER DISPUTE ANYTHING AMONG THEMSELVES. THEY WORK ALL DAY, ENTIRELY APART. WHEN EVENING COMES AND THEIR TASKS ARE DONE, ON FINDING THEMSELVES AGAIN TOGETHER, THEY DANCE. *They do not speak.**

There are several ways of considering the function of an art critic, whether his field is paint, music or the dance. Some people would have him explain and clarify for his general public by a technical, historical or dialectical analysis, the work under discussion, which from its very particular or original values might seem temporarily difficult to appreciate, and then to enhance this appreciation as the essence of the work is clearly revealed. Others would have him simmer down the essence of the work of art to its diluted lowest-common-denominator, showing its superficial resemblance to the origins from which it had sprung, and then to offer the public a vulgarized secondary version which removes the obligation of having to make up one's mind about the fresh original. Both these attitudes presuppose that the critic is mildly interested in what he is criticizing, and that if he finds something that pleases him he will praise it and induce others to share his pleasure; or if not, he will attack it and illuminate its sterility. But we have a third sort, who actually dislikes what he writes about, and whose interest is, however active, entirely negative. This sounds like an anomaly until we realize that too many of the dance-critics in America are not by experience or by profession critics of dancing at all, but usually music-critics who have been ordered by their editors to cover a given dance-attraction as a scheduled "musical" assignment. Here is another sinister alliance in our "Great Conspiracy."

The music management-bureaus find it convenient to sell dance-attractions as *music*-attractions; hence, the indirect commercial uses of the music-critics who have continually to be primed. The ordinary music-critic has a tolerant contempt for dancing. He chooses to think of it as a secondary accompaniment or tertiary complement to music, with which he may or may not be familiar. If he knows the music he will not perhaps bother to learn as much about the dancing and will assume that the dancing is "not as good as" the music, since he has less information, instinctive or acquired, about it. The critic must at all costs maintain the superior prestige of the *music* as such, over and above any dancing whatever, in order to insure the superiority of his own position. Hence, the music-critic usually *hears* the dancing. He seldom if ever allows

---

*Degas, Danse. Dessin. p. 11 (Paul Valèry).

himself to *see* it. The mediocre orchestral presentation of the Russian ballets has only furthered his disdain, should he have been a conscientious musician. But even had they a good orchestra instead of a bad one, such thinly informed pen-pushers as Samuel Chotzinoff of the New York *Post*, having once half-humorously voiced their ignorant dislike for dancing, would still be necessarily contemptuous on principle. There have been a few startling exceptions to this, exceptions which set the general average only in a blacker light. Heinrich Heine's and Théophile Gautier's correspondence and daily reviews, Stendhal's notes on the dancer Salvatore Viganò, or Carl van Vechten's notes on the Diaghilev Golden Period are excellent models. One remembers with gratitude the late H. T. Parker of the old *Boston Evening Transcript*; Margaret Lloyd of the *Christian Science Monitor* is very able and informed, but far too kind and gentle, even to me. For me, as with Blake: "Damn braces, bless relaxes." I am grateful for three intelligent younger critics—Jerome Boehm on the New York *Herald-Tribune*, Walter Terry of the Boston *Herald*, and Edwin Denby of the quarterly, *Modern Music*. The last two have actually danced. Lucile Marsh of *Dance Digest* has for a long time courageously defended our American dancers. Ruth Howard of *The American Dancer* has been actively interested in sensible national legislation in favor of our dancers. Anatole Chujoy in *Dance* has caused Agripina Vaganova's important technical treatise to be run serially, and is an ardent advocate of choreography by Americans. He is also one of the few Americans who has a reading knowledge of Russian, and is a devoted visitor to all dance studios. Albertina Vitak of *The American Dancer* knows good dancing because she is a good dancer. Ann Barzel of Chicago writes occasional letters to dance magazines. Some newspaper should employ her permanently. Her taste is excellent, and her wit is acid and true. Chicago, indeed, is favored with more critics who have a real interest in American dancing than New York. Claudia Cassidy of the *Journal of Commerce*, Eugene Stinson of the *Daily News*, Ashton Stevens of the *Evening American*, and particularly Cecil Smith of the *Daily Tribune* are all worth reading. In Los Angeles Isabel Morse Jones of the *Times* maintains a consistently high standard. John Rosenfeld, Jr., of the Dallas *News* is my candidate for the ablest younger generation dance critic in the country. In Washington, Glenn Dillard Gunn of the *Herald* formerly of Chicago, and Ray Brown of the *Post* are both reliable. In Pittsburgh, Dr. Frederick Dorian of the *Gazette* is both a scholar and a journalist. In Hartford, Theodore Parker of the *Courant* is particularly friendly to American dancers. In Spingfield (Mass.) A. L. S. Wood of the *Union* is articulate and accurate.

In the farthest flung towns, strangely enough, one frequently finds the best critics. Personally, I would prefer to be reviewed by any critic rather than those in the "big" cities. For example, in Lewiston, Maine, Charlotte Michaud stimulates communities who have little chance to enjoy stage dancing. Page Hosmer of the Tacoma *News Tribune,* Elizabeth Hylblom of the Colorado Springs *Gazette,* Ilmar Grondhal of the Portland Morning *Oregonian,* and J. W. Sayre of the Seattle *Post Intelligensia* all appreciate our native efforts. In San Francisco Alfred Frankenstein on the *Chronicle* and Alexander Fried on the *Examiner* are far more open-minded and intelligent than their colleagues on the *News* and the *Call Bulletin.*

And above them all, there is Ernest Newman, the distinguished music-critic of the London *Times,* whose style is as urbane, knowing, witty and generous as his analysis is profound and full of common-sense. Theatrical dancing does not frighten him, and dance-music does not seem to him an impure or a secondary form. Read for example, his notice of Paul Hindemith's score for *Nobilissima Visione* (St. Francis, July 24, 1938) and Massine's symphonic treatment in general.

1. *The Historians*

In the realm of writers about the dance as a special art-form, there are three main divisions; the historians, the appreciators, and the journalists. I personally prefer the historians. These are writers who may or may not have been professional dancers, but who all at least have had a direct participation with the dance-stage and with the dance-works they describe. They have written the history of their theatrical epoch from first hand observation, because for the most part they have collaborated in creating that history. One can reread Calvocaressi's *Memoirs of Opera and Ballet;* Prince Lieven's *Birth of Ballets Russes,* and Ninette de Valois' excellent practical book on her work for the British National Ballet. Cocteau's, Stravinsky's, Lifar's and Astruc's memoirs are invaluable marginalia. The composer, Constant Lambert's *Music Ho!* was the first realistic study, and remains almost the only clear-eyed British book on the policy and aesthetic of the Diaghilev Period. In a slightly different category are Cyril Beaumont's invaluable bibliographies. He is the eminent English book-seller and publisher, who has done more to dignify the historic literature of the dance than any man of his epoch, by issuing such works, for example, as translation of Théophile Gautier's collected criticism, Noverre's letters, André Levinson's *Taglioni,* besides a recent large and fascinating anthology of ballet libretti. In America, the Kamin

Bookstore exercises a similar highly useful function with its shop and publishing headquarters in New York City. From the work of all these writers and editors, specific information may be obtained as to definite facts and events concerning the actual production of dancing in theatres. They do not set up too many aesthetic or qualitative judgments. They have been busy with practical problems, and we turn to them for aid in the solution of our own theatrical needs rather than to know gossip or personal opinion about a certain contemporary dancer in a certain personal situation.

2. The Appreciators

Great Britain is particularly lush in the ballet-appreciators. Hardly a month passes when some new work of enthusiastic appreciation is not issued by writers who are also usually critics of paintings, or films, or of literature. The English seem to exult in an unreleased and self-indulgent enthusiasm for ballet-ballet, which is due in part to their physical insularity, to their traditional suspicion that Paris is always patronizing them from across that Channel. Yet the ballet in Paris, aside from Lifar's Mondays at the Opéra, is barely popular enough in France today to warrant a Russian season once a year. Nowhere in the Western world today is there such an avid audience for classic dancing as London, and it is surely most fortunate for their own young national movement of British Ballet. But the ballet-appreciators, no matter how well-educated they are, and they have a general literary and artistic background that puts nearly every American writer to shame, do little or nothing to make dancing simpler to see for ordinary people who would like it anyway after being exposed to it once or twice. Either the appreciator constructs *recherché* baroque verbal panoramas of beloved ballets, as Sacheverell Sitwell treated Diaghilev's production of *La Belle au Bois Dormant* in his *Dance of the Quick and the Dead,* or else they erect vague philosophic systems of personal esthetic values, an ample sort of ballet epistemology as Adrian Stokes does. Stokes' two little books, *Tonight the Ballet* and *Russian Ballets,* have many good things to say about dancing; but in general, his particular passion and correspondences are too apparent; he is *personally* so convinced of his unique definitions that his descriptions read as if he were recording his own spiritual and emotional progress. The succeeding ballets he has seen and described are almost epigraphs for an autobiography. However, the ordinary British blanket-acceptance of the Russian phenomena as an aspect of divine artistic revelation has been recently tempered by the suggestive studies of Rayner Heppenstall,

Caryl Brahms, and A. V. Coton. Contemporary English prose-style, as far as most dance-criticism goes, has unfortunate models. Instead of basing their statement on a Coleridge, a Matthew Arnold, or even an I. A. Richards, their paragraphs are predominantly pre-Raphaelite. Markova and Toumanova are framed in pearly periods which but for Walter Pater could never have appeared. Yet the appreciators are always doomed to lose out in the end. They try to paint with fatty words what happens in time on a clean stage. They make of their word-painting a competitive indoor-sport, like bridge or badminton. You feel them earnestly forcing their pens: "We'll make you *see* it: we'll *make* you see it." As a matter of fact, even their most detailed and rhapsodic appreciations are usually unintelligible unless you *have* already seen the ballet, and if you have already seen it, there is hardly any need more than an enjoyable if superficial corroboration, to read the libretto after you get home from the theatre. And as a matter of fact, they merely supplement the candid camera. But in combination they'll have to do for us until we're given actual films of complete ballets.

a. On Ballet Photographers

Recently the candid-camera has invaded the field of ballet documenttion. The candid-camera in the hands of most news-photographers and the average eager amateur, is the worst liar in the photographic family. Under the guise of an objective and frank reporter, the candid-camera distorts, alters, and ultimately destroys the very dances it pretends to document. In the first place, the candid operator has usually to stand in the wings, on one side of the stage. At best, if placed in a prompter's box, he is too near to include the whole stage-picture, and from his seat he is too far away. Hence, nearly every shot is an angle-shot to start with, snapped from a place where no one in the audience has ever seen the ballet, and from where the choreographer never intended it to have been seen. If a considerable number of candid shots could be reproduced in sequence, an approximation of a record of motion might possibly be obtained. By a considerable number I mean fifty, not twenty. But lacking this, the ballet snapshot is usually seized out of its legitimate context, to accentuate an accidental if spectacular leap, or some astonishing motion only effective in a camera print, but which has little or no connection with the ballet as it is seen by an audience in the intended procedure of its performance. There has been recently published in England an extremely expensive album of such photos called *Ballet in Action*, by Merlyn Severn. Its blurb assures us:

The vast majority of ballet photographs published are not, strictly speaking, ballet photographs at all. They are pictures of one or more dancers in pre-arranged poses which may even bear only a vague resemblance to the poses actually used in the ballet in question. They are consequently of little use in the serious study of choreography, none at all in analyzing the style of individual dancers.

This book changes all that. Miss Severn's photographs, which it is not too much to say have revolutionized the art of ballet photography, were all taken during actual performances by the ordinary stage lighting.

Now Miss Severn may have spent time and effort on stage and in dark room, but her published efforts are not worth a tenth of the sixteen dollars they cost in this country. Ordinary stage-lighting is wretched illumination even for a fast candid film. The lack of any range of color is rendered more miserable by the falsification of chromatic values in the coarse-screen grain of black and white snap-shot. Instead of receiving a representation of startling accuracy we have only a record of arrested physical strain. Compare, for example, any old "posed" photo of Nijinsky in *Le Spectre de la Rose* and Miss Severn's shot of a contemporary dancer in the same rôle, with his face constricted in an agony of effort like a runner collapsing at the end of a hundred-yard dash. We are not, as a matter of fact, nearly as conscious of this strain when watching him across the footlights as in looking at the candid shot. The very reverse of her blurb's boasts are true. Any posed, static picture of a ballet, if arranged by a sensitive photographic craftsman or the ballet's choreographer himself, tells far more of the spirit, atmosphere and essence than a casual and accidental performance picture. It makes very little difference if the actual poses are included in the ballet or not. In neither case is any movement actually transcribed. But, by careful lighting and conscious arrangement, a designed approximation of the essential movement can be achieved, impossible in the broken hurry and accidental angling of a candid close-up. Looking over Miss Severn's coarse-textured and blurred plates, one sees only the clipped mistakes in technique of her suddenly betrayed subjects. It is true that the leaps seem incredibly high, higher than they do on the stage itself, because they are shot from far below the audience's eye-level. But for the most part, we have a permanent record of lazy legs, sloppy arms, indeterminate gestures which are only preliminaries to an absolute climactic position. These climaxes which she never records, or at least never selects to print, are the honest salient foci in ballet design. All others are diminishing movements departing from the climaxes, or crescendant ones approaching them. If we take Miss Severn's surface records as basic fact, we find the ballet troupes she photographs have a technical equipment so loose, ill-rehearsed and awkward that we can scarcely recognize them.

The posed photos of the Golden Age of Russian ballet are often very fine. The prints of Walery, Gerschel, Fisher and Bert may seem superficially old-fashioned in their decorative accessories or pre-war framing, but these craftsmen and others of their generation in Warsaw, Paris and Petersburg, were careful to light and arrange Nijinsky, Karsavina, Pavlova and Fokine in positions which were the summation, the highest common denominator of a kinetic sequence. Baron Gayne de Meyer's brilliant sequences of *Le Pavillon de Armide, Carnaval, Faune* and *Spectre* are particularly impressive. Taken twenty years ago, they seem as fresh as done today. Man Ray's portraits of Lifar in *Apollon Musagète, Jack-in-the-Box,* and *Barabau,* however, "posed," give a true impression of these ballets' movement. George Hoynigen-Huené and Cecil Beaton in London have made some splendid still-groupings of the Monte Carlo repertory. In New York, George Platt Lynes' numerous plates of the artists and productions of the American Ballet and the Ballet Caravan serve as a magnificently lit and complete visual record of their work, and yet hardly a plate is a literal transcript of actual choreography. All of it was posed by photographer or choreographer against backgrounds representing but not reproducing stage conditions. Maurice Seymour of Chicago has done good static portraits of the contemporary Russians on their American tours. None of these are candid operators. The candid camera is a facile fibber. One has to question its eye just as much as one must perforce be cynical of the writings of most ballet journalists. Perhaps, if a candid-artist used his eye, instead of his trigger-finger, he could get some good selective shots. But it takes more than quick fingering. Barbara Morgan and Paul Hansen have done some fine shots of Martha Graham, and Richard Tucker of Boston demonstrates by his conscientious work that there is nothing the matter with the candid-camera itself, but only the ordinary uses to which it is put.

3. The Journalists

The journalistic critic of the ballet is the hardest for a worker in the dance to tolerate. He it is who, combining the functions of historian and appreciator issues stop-press reports for the benefit of an audience whose latent hysteria it is his task to incite. It is he who must report or invent the juicier details attendant upon the lives, fortunes and private honor of the ballet dancers, directors and other collaborators.

Arnold Haskell of the London *Daily Telegraph* knows the ballet well enough, and it is not so much the sense of all of what he says, as the way he says it, that makes most of his writing so invincibly exasperating. He has assumed, consecutively, since his early monographs on Trefilova and Karsavina, the attitude of devout neophyte, inspired crusader, tender lover, and evangelical guardian. Book after book from his facile hand appears and the illustrations and format become annually better and better. His letter-press couched in the stylized apology of a helplessly obsessed yet sympathetic family friend, reads like an elder brother's letter to a schoolgirl about the facts of dance-life. He has nary a real disapproval, and has mastered the subtleties of critical evasion to the point of fastidious diplomacy. One can never be quite certain which current ballerina is to be the recipient of his unimpeachable accolade as sole guardian of *true* "classicism." For years, with his quiet yet burrowing energy he has played his game of critical tag; now Toumanova, no—now Baronova; no,—now Danilova; no, now one of our own English dancers is *it*. Both his reader and his ballerina were kept in an agony of delicious indecision, rather like sophomores waiting to be tapped for a college sorority, as Haskell groomed his catalogue of allusive parallels to great dancers of the past, his current comparisons with our own.

His extended biographical study of Diaghilev stands in that most trying category of first-rate subjects treated in a second-rate fashion. Arnold Haskell was discreet when he should have been surgical; genteel when he might have been honest; at all times styleless and dull when he had an unparalleled opportunity to recreate brilliance, human complexity and tragic splendor. Think of what Marcel Proust, or lacking him, what André Gide, Levinson, or even Harold Nicolson might have done with the same material.

Yet Haskell's last book *Ballet* is a remarkable piece of publishing. By no means a small book, it can be bought in America for less than half a dollar. It is clearly written, well organized, has excellent pictures, and is in every way his best work. In it he shows traces of a comprehension of the economic structure of Russian dancing. He betrays an approach to a new (for him) realism, accentuated by his knowledge of the break-up of Russian ballet, and a new, very honest and admirable passion, his devotion to the young national British ballet. Yet he still accepts *Schéhérazade, Carnaval, Igor,* and the dreary rest of them, on their face value; for him Fokine is still a criterion, and the future is anticipated only in terms of the familiar past.

In America we have of course our ballet journalists, yet they are not necessarily much improvement over our British cousins. There is no one here, for example, who is as experienced, as educated in dancing, or who writes as popularly as Haskell himself. Our methods are a little more high-pressure. We want immediate results in terms not of books published, but in minutes on radio-stations, inches in gossip-columns, pictures in the Sunday Supplements. Irving Deakin is an American version of Arnold Haskell. But he has neither Haskell's information, taste, nor devotion. He has been pursuing one of the most curious crusades in the rococo history of recent ballet journalism. He has dedicated his pen to proving that Adolph Bolm, preëminent Russian character of the Golden Age, was responsible not only for Serge de Diaghilev's initial success, but for the present happy status of ballet in America as well. This curiosity is not clarified even when one reads on his blurbs that he is "incidentally" Bolm's son-in-law. In his books which are pasted-up riflings without acknowledgment from every other writer on the dance since Noverre, in his radio talks and in his articles, he is a past-master of ballet-cliché and theatrical vulgarism. He is our "Great Conspiracy's" greatest journalistic conspirator.

a. The Critic's Lexicon: John Martin

When Mr. John Martin addressed a sell-out audience on the night of "Modern" Dance, which followed the Evening of American Theatrical Dancing at the Center Theatre in New York, given under the auspices of Dance International 1900-1937, he blandly assured us that what we were about to see was not *theatrical,* its scenery was not really *decor,* its costumes were only vesture for motion, its music mere aural scenery. The "modern" concert dance was relegated to a level distinctly superior to that of simple theatre-stage framed by an ordinary gilded proscenium. By his inference dancing became not simply a diverting or evocative spectacle but rather an autobiographical rite celebrating the psychic impulses of its individual dancers. In a review of the New York première of the American-Wigman follower, Hanya Holm's composition, *Trend,* Mr. Martin praised Arch Lauterer's ingenious and massive constructivist setting as having "no smack of decor." Last summer (1937) Mr. Martin was alarmed by certain "decadent" (i.e., theatrical) overtones he sensed in young Anna Sokolow's anti-Fascist dance work. Last year (1936-37) he detected in Martha Graham's a "neo-classic" tendency, and this year (1937-38) he found her perilously "surrealist."

The technique of dance-criticism lies chiefly in the use of the critic's vocabulary. In the field of dance the critic's vocabulary has often to be borrowed from another art. In architecture we can talk in terms of structure, material and function, calling Georgia grey, Vermont or Indiana limestone, lally columns, t-beams or soil-pipes by their specific given names. That is, these terms mean the same thing to everyone. Similarly in painting and music. The theatre, however, employs for its own uses architecture, poetry and music. Hence, its critical language, while more amplified, is also more vague. The vocabulary of dance criticism borrows the idiom of fine arts and literature, but the problem is not simple even when one is armed with this combined ammunition, primarily because the dance critic, like his colleagues the drama critic and the sportswriter refer to an event passed forever before anyone reads of it, an event largely interesting only to those who saw it at a certain already vanished performance, and much of whose interest depends on the quality of that particular performance. To combine an analysis of subject intention with a factual description of what actually transpired in a broad enough frame to be something more than a mere news-report, calls for a technique which is very developed, a vocabulary, in other words, which is precise.

I wish to consider the vocabulary of John Martin, the well-known critic of the New York *Times.* By his energy and interest in dancing he has almost single-handed created a place for the dance-critic in New York, and hence, in America. His job has not been easy, for on the one hand he has been assailed by the ballet-managers for his contempt of ballet as a theatrical form, and on the other, by a large section of young dancers in this form who fear his influential opposition to the future of their art. He is incorruptible, and this is no idle homage, for in the last two years I knew very well at least one powerful ballet-manager and one ballet-patron have done their best to have him displaced from the position he has done so much to dignify. The maintenance of this position and personal attitude testifies to his editors' complete faith in him. I myself was forced to resign as ballet-critic from "The Dance Observer," an anti-ballet monthly, because I had written an attack on Martin which they refused to print. My bread and butter luckily didn't depend on it, but I was given a fair taste of what it feels like to be under fire, even in journalism. I have even heard of Martin's being proposed for a permanent chair of the Dance at Harvard. His presence at a college might easily prove more useful than his expression of continual irritation at his necessity to report the activity of our unfolding theatrical dance. My disagreement with Mr. Martin is the sincerest form of flattery because there is hardly any other name in the American field which represents the expression of a conviction based on preference rather than on second-hand reading.

Looking over his several published works, I assume Mr. Martin opposes his use of the words "health" to "degeneracy," "degeneracy" to "decadence," "Neo-classicism" to "classicism," "classicism" to "romanticism," "naturalism" to "realism," "realism" to "surrealism," and "aristocracy" to "democracy" in his idiosyncratic system of values, and that he can tell you exactly what he means by each and every epithet as well as the next man. But lurking in these categories there has become more and more apparent an insidious alignment of chapter-heads which has assumed a censorious attitude which is less in the analytical structure of an Aristotle than in the ethical strictures of Saint Augustine. We discover on the negative side "decadent," "neo-classic," "surrealist," "theatrical," "aristocratic." Under "theatrical" we find "decor," "ballet," "ballet-audience," "ballet-impresario." On the positive side we find "impulse," "inspiration," "heroic type," "integration," "inevitable," "logical," "democratic." Yet there seems to be no hard and fast adherence to these perilously equilibrated lists. For example, Mr. Martin found Hanya Holm's *Trend* less closely related to mere "concert" dancing than it was to "theatre" (i.e., Greek tragedy). I mean, in short, that this antitheatrical bias which I have long sorrowfully observed in Mr. Martin has now shifted its attack from the ballet even to include Mr. Martin's personal protegé, the "modern" dance, and in particular the creations of its greatest worker, Martha Graham, because he feels her work increasingly theatrical, in his terminology "decadent."

As long ago as 1933, Mr. Martin in his book "The Modern Dance," complained that all dance had meant in the past the *ballet*, and ballet had meant only the *ballet-d'action*. Yet Mr. Martin should have known very well that the *ballet-d'action* or ballet dominated by eighteenth century dramatic pantomime was a reference in common use only as long as J. G. Noverre's immediate influence was felt. The *pas d'action*, a pantomimic number in mid-nineteenth century ballet-form is something quite else. There is all the difference in the world between Noverre's *ballet d'action*, ca. 1780, Vigano's *choreodrame*, ca. 1820, Manzotti's *azione coregrafica*, ca. 1870, and Fokine's *choregraphie*, ca. 1910. Martin also stated (p. 4) that there weren't half a dozen artists who could employ the classic dance properly, although he has since had occasion to mention Massine, Danilova, Spessivitza, Markova, Semenova and even Paul Haakon, who were all performing at the time (1933). He stated (p. 38) that in the old ballets the floor-plan was the *only* consideration, when he must have meant that most of our exact information about steps danced in the old ballets are derived from engravings of floor-patterns. He forgets that the visual and musical synthesis in antique ballet was due to such costumers as Berain and Bouquet, and musicians like Lully, Rameau and Gluck; but it is true that this combination of the dance, music and decor does "smack," as he says, of theatre. It was in fact a theatrical synthesis. He states (p. 107) that music developed and dancing stood still for "hundreds of years," although he grudgingly admitted a little earlier that great dancers did successively enlarge their technique's idiom. No use to call his attention to Noverre, Gardel, Angiolini, Gioja, Blasis, Perrot, St. Leon, Stepanov, Ivanov, Petipa, the Taglionis, Elssler, Manzotti, Fokine, or the more recent Russians—a name of primary historical importance to each decade, if one wished to cite them. In Mr. Martin's two books, historical data was included only as a condemnatory resumé; facts were rearranged and selected to present an apparently objective case against theatrical dancing which almost rivals the ingenuity of the Third Reich's *Kulturkammer.*

By 1936 Martin's anti-theatrical bias was firmly developed. In *America Dancing* (p. 56) we learn that by our early nineteenth century, the poisonous infiltration of foreign theatrical-dancers managed "pretty thoroughly to supplant the simpler English style of theatre-dancing." Following this, the French, Italian and Slav dancing-masters accomplished their invasion. He continues:

It is interesting to note each of these influences was occasioned not by any demand from the American field, but by political conditions in the homeland.

That is, committees of Boston or Philadelphia society-folk did not send over their boats for dancing-teachers. Which is the same as to suggest that the "pure" Massachusetts Indians ought to have felt a deep intuitive impulse to invite the Puritan Fathers over for the sole purpose of giving exhibitions of Playford's Country Dances. Mr. Martin finds it convenient to forget the facts. There were theatrical-dancers in Williamsburg, Virginia, as early as there were stage-plays; there were ordinances against dancing in Boston as early as 1684. By 1794, in Charleston (S. C.), pantomimes in which dancing had important parts were more popular than the plays themselves. Nearly every well-known international dancer has appeared in America since before our revolution, playing before the same kind of American audiences which made theatrical-dancing in Europe a continuous popular form. In an article in the winter 1937-38 number of the *North American Review*, Mr. Martin concedes the fact that the de Basil ballet grossed a million dollars on its transcontinental tour, which in his context means that this enterprise had (strictly) commercial implications, which are alone responsible for its inexplicable

success. Yet in another paragraph, we are confronted with a most perfect example of this critic's lexicon (p. 239) :

This is what is sometimes called the classic view as opposed to the romantic,
the aristocratic as opposed to the democratic. On its basis kings and courtiers
have maintained ballets for their diversion, and today wealthy men of this
opinion, whose tastes do not run to the outdoor life, keep companies of dancers
instead of polo ponies.

Here we have in full flower a priggish jeremiad tailored to a categorical prejudice. Qualitative distinctions are colored by blind personal
irritation. There are few ballet companies "kept" by kings and courtiers
today unless government subsidy of the Vic-Wells, the Paris and Bor-
deaux Operas, the Scala at Milan, the Bolshoi and Marinsky Theatres
can be considered mere bureaucratic prostitution. Native American ballet companies in Chicago, New York, San Francisco and Philadelphia
to a surprising degree manage to pay their own way, keeping many
dancers under long-term contract, and traveling far more, for example,
than the "modern" concert-dance groups. That wise-crack about the
outdoor life and polo ponies is on the same level of fancy pet that makes
Mr. Martin fill our ballet audiences with the "usual silver-haired dowagers with their bald-pated escorts" (p. 249). I don't like dowagers any
better than Mr. Martin, but there aren't a million dollars' worth of diamonds alone to give the big Russian companies their annual forty weeks
of work, worse luck for them. Mr. Martin must learn that New York is
not America. People who like ballet in the United States today are, in
cross-section, people who like the legitimate theatre. This Mr. Martin,
even after the recent Center Theatre performances, the de Basil tours, the
present high commercial value of foreign dance-attractions, refuses to
admit. Mr. Martin recognizes, as I do, the degeneracy, decadence and
snobbery which vitiates too much ballet today. But with this difference.
From his consideration of the situation within the confines of Russian
ballet, he arrives at the decision that *all* ballet is equally infected. Hence,
he believes as he leads many other people in his audience to believe, that
all ballet is Russian ballet, thus qualifying for charter membership in
the Great Conspiracy. It is unjust to blame a large art form for its misuse. Does one attack architecture as a whole because people still build
bad imitations of Gothic churches, or music, because students still turn
out watered Brahms? Mr. Martin does not care to realize that classic
ballet is an exact science of theatrical movement and gesture, created by
masters down to their pupils for four centuries. The vocabulary of classic ballet has been formulated by trial and error, brilliant experiment
and great personalities, just like the history of homeopathic medicine

There is a *materia choreografica* just as there is a *materia medica.*

I submit Mr. Martin is, and has been consciously naive, temperamentally prejudiced or baldly ignorant about theatrical dancing. That he detests the theatrical element in the dance is his privilege, that he continually attempts to wreck it, is his right; but in so much as dancing happens to take place (even today) in theatres, and is in the minds of most of its audiences a theatrical form, I feel he must find some new terms to cover his dislike. He is the chief critical name in this country whom provincial selection committees and dance-managers have respected, and his word has gone far in influencing students of theatrical dancing in America. At the present, theatrical values in the dance, whether in the developed classic ballet or in the "modern" dance, are dominant values, and increasingly so by every indication. The "modern" dance, for example, has in numerous recent programs begun to call itself "modern" ballet, and Martin a very parfyt knight of purity smells theatrical taint even among such schismatic Modernists. Mr. Martin is upholding the banner of an imaginary anti-theatrical purity, an ideal and not a true purity which, if it were analyzed, could be broken down into dance forms that have already outworn their sojourn in the antique categories of the "interpretive," and "expressionist," and "absolute" and the "abstract."

Many critics at a certain age in their active development, start to defend their initial or past enthusiasm with a conservative philosophical barrage which employs an *avant garde* vocabulary to blackjack the future. This is the conservative attitude of "Redder Than the Rose" or "More Royal Than the King." It permits Mr. Martin to boost dismally retardative productions such as Fokine's recent remounting of *Le Coq d'Or* as all that is best in contemporary ballet.

Le Coq d'Or was a pompous and successful gift-book spectacle. It was an exact evocation of taste and tendency, which first blossoming in the Golden Age of a quarter of a century ago, has been reappearing ever since in diluted forms via Russian tea rooms, White Russian Folke Crafte Shoppes, night-club peasant "numbers," etc. Fokine's production was slick with the syrup of opera-house pantomime in which a fat King comically pats his jelly-belly, whereupon a self-conscious chuckle of inane amusement flickers through the house. John Martin called it "fine, healthy, full-blooded art," and found it "expansive, lusty, colossally humorous." After this judas-kiss from such a canny critic, one is hardly surprised to find little or no dancing in *Le Coq d'Or.* We cannot carp at Fokine's perennial competence. But his false-naive spirit, the placid silliness of his pantomime, the rigid sterility of the symmetrical parades, the weakly balanced surprises, the warmed-up buffoonesque fragments we know so well from every one of his works since *Fire Bird, Islamey, Schéhérezade, Thamar, Prince Igor,* down to *Don Juan,* slung together to comprise a *Fokiniana*—these we hate. And we also hate the critical accolade which from prejudice or ignorance hid the historical background of such a work as *Le Coq d'Or.*

Rimsky's opera was for a considerable time banned in Russia. The police of Nicolas II were quick to understand the contemporary use of Poushkin's satire on a do-nothing czar. The basic Russian fable has life, and is a definite social comment. The Queen of Shemakhan, the Lady in Red was well known as the symbolic precursor of revolutionary change. Fokine pulled the teeth of the tale and made it an infantile bed-time story when in reality it was a wise fable for grown-ups. It was within the function of a dance critic to illuminate this discrepancy. But Martin, no doubt tired of protests from his continual bad notices of the ballet was relieved to find something which he could praise without risk. Hence his critical conscience could rest untroubled at the cost of a modicum of creative information.

Similarly, Martin praised Balanchine's archaistic *Le Baiser de la Fée* as what a contemporary ballet should best be; that is, old-fashioned by definition, confined to the expected familiarity of what he thought he recognized. But even here he was wrong, and probably more from ignorance than prejudice confused the stylistic frame of a late 19th century revival with that of a far earlier epoch. Recently, in his Sunday section of the New York *Times,* Martin devoted almost his entire column to Balanchine's creative work, the first time he has troubled to consider it since the choreographer came here five years ago. In that time he has mounted some half dozen new works besides as many more new versions of older ones not seen before in this country. Did Martin discuss or analyze any of these, even to condemn them? Not at all. Instead he chose to laud Balanchine's incidental dance-numbers for Broadway musical comedies. I am second to none in my admiration for George Balanchine; indeed, I was the original pretext for his coming to New York; but no one who loves him or his art can pretend that the numbers he turns out every year for an *On Your Toes,* a *Babes in Arms,* an *I Married an Angel,* or *The Boys from Syracuse* are much more than competent or agreeable time-filling. Nor does Mr. Martin actually believe otherwise. By complimenting a readily misunderstood artist on his hack-work, he patronizingly knifes him in the back, so that Balanchine may be permitted to merit no serious attention as a genuine creator in the contemporary dance. That very number in *I Married an Angel* which Mr. Martin found so inventive, witty and so gracious is an easily recognizable hash of fragments from *Errante, Le Baiser de la Fée, Mozartiana,* and other well-remembered Balanchine ballets, already presented in the "dream" sequence of *Babes in Arms,* only here whittled down to a vulgarization which Broadway, and I am forced to admit, Mr. Martin as well, can digest without cramps.

If Mr. Martin's prejudices against theatrical values in dancing were sifted down to their psychological origins perhaps the clinical results would read something like this. Mr. Martin started out by being an actor. Somewhat accidentally he found himself on a newspaper, not as a critic of theatre, which was his background, but instead as a dance critic at a time when dancing was hardly recognized as worthy of an independent reporter. Martin's courageous attempt to separate dance from theatre in the mind of his readers led to a confusion based on his justifiable attempt to separate dance criticism from theatrical criticism. It forced him, perhaps unconsciously, but after his first few steps with an increasing logic, to defend and further those elements in the dance which had the least connection with the "legitimate" theatre. Hence, we find him as the consistent defender of the ephemeral amateur, the lay dancer, the grand spawn of experimental "Modernists." Column after column has he awarded to serious discussions of young dancers, who after receiving the benison of his attention, have vanished from the scene, seldom to reappear. On the one hand he has always encouraged new "modern" dancers, and his encouragement has gone a long way to providing them with whatever security the subsidies of interested Foundations, Schools or Fellowships have been able to award. On the other hand, he has created a whole alumni of semi-professional dancers, who can only point to a couple of tentative solo-recitals and a long notice by John Martin as the sum of their claim to fame. By this encouragement they have come to consider themselves artists too important for mere subsidiary "group" work. They either attempt to form their own "group," or remain in expectant and ambiguous isolation, or else, knowing nothing better to do, they presume to "teach." This may be an encouragement on Martin's part, but I doubt if it is a service.

If the specific theatrical elements are analyzed which he most dislikes, we find that it is most of all "sentimentality." I have yet to find a definition of the word which means approximately the same thing to most people, and which is not a personal opinion. If it means indulgence in a specious emotion for its own sake, a mawkish projection of emotion when no emotion is called for, then it is hard to know what Martin is talking about. In reference to dancing he seems to mean any overt expression of physical emotion, directly expressed, not "abstractly" rendered, as "sentimental." That is, *sexuality* or its dancing transcript is "sentimental" as in Martha Graham's Puritan duet from her "American Document." But *sensuality*, as lavished in any given Fokine opus of the Golden Age, he finds not "sentimental" but "lusty," "vigorous" or "healthy." Remove a gesture from essential reality, disinfect it from the physical, robe it in rhetorical decoration, then it can pass Martin's antiseptic muster. The anti-theatrical basis is essentially an anti-physical bias. Martin like many others who deeply suspect the sources of physicality, is shy-eyed. It would be curious to discover that Martin is innocent of a conscious dislike of theatrical dancing, since he has a temperamental blindness to it, and hence has never seen it at all.

4. The Technicians

What dancing in America needs today and what it will certainly get when the art of ballet is permitted to develop, is a group of critics who are neither historians, appreciators, or journalists. We need the honorable craft of dance technicians. We need newspaper men, poets, or novelists who can look at physical movement on a stage and translate their objective impressions to print without irrelevant autobiographical comment, personal prejudice, or an eye on the advertiser.

In Russia there was a whole class of technical amateurs of ballets, at their worst retired soldiers or men about town, and at their best a number of accomplished and learned commentators, the well-known character-dancer Lopoukov, the classic ballerina Vaganova, Valerien Svetlov, the aged Muscovite enthusiast Volyinsky, the historian Pleschaev, and Prince Serge Wolkonsky, the last Intendant of the Imperial Theatres. Anything Fokine or Massine have committed to paper is nearly as valuable to us as Noverre's own writing, because anyone who has been responsible for creating a theatrical epoch knows certain valuable things about his own intentions which may not even appear in the finished work. Even Serge Lifar's growing bibliography holds elements of historical interest if you forgive his egomaniacal conviction that he, not Fokine or Massine, invented Diaghilev. Even so, he has done work for ten years in the medium on which he writes which is a qualification not shared by many more voluminous writers. Best of all Russian criticism are the albums of caricatures by the two dancers Serge and Nicolai Legat, realistic cartoons of excruciating detail, and tenderly vicious familiarity, which gives us an almost complete picture of the two chief lyric theatres in Russia around 1905. We recognize clinical portraits of many of the dancers of the Golden Age of ballet in Western Europe, as they emerged from the embryo of their school training. But there are others, equally great dancers in all the curious mannerisms of style and technique, who never left Russia, and there is also portrayed the entire staff of the opera-house organization down to the last major-domo, wig-maker, machinist, and conductor. André Levinson's ballet criticism, most of which remains untranslated into English except in the excellent publication of *Theatre Arts Monthly* and Cyril Beaumont's *Taglioni*, had a ferociously difficult vocabulary, but he meant what he said, he knew what he meant, and his information both historical and by his own visual experience was colossal. Levinson wrote French like a foreigner, which he was. His vocabulary was precise, even in its utmost flights of the recondite. But compare a page of his with one by Paul Valéry. In this great academician's recent work, *"Degas. Danse. Dessin',"* we are given in the simplest yet most eloquent prose many a profound, witty and surprising technical analysis on art in general, drawing and dancing in particular. Levinson was a technician for technicians or historians, Valéry for the general audience of poetry at large.

One of the very best small books on ballet in recent years is the all too little known *Russian Ballet Through Russian Eyes* by Vladimir Kameneff, published in London in 1935. The author is obviously a technician, but he is also a creative critic in terms of dancing. He has a gracious, almost courtly style appropriate to his epoch and his origin, which gently renders such angry pens as mine discourteous and gauche. But under his deliberate elegance are steel claws. His questions eviscerate not only the vitiated ballet of the period of de Basil, symphonic or otherwise, but his analyses of the English ballet critics are models of able counter-attack. I am somewhat younger than Mr. Kameneff and hence, not as agreeable. If any readers are displeased with the tone of this pamphlet let them consult his book, a study by a Russian of Russian ballet; a Russian of the old school who loves ballet better than his memories.

Most American sport-writers have a real love for the sports they report. They are not impressed by them as Sport with a capital "S," as some ballet-critics are eager to be dazzled by ballet as Russian-Ballet. Sport-writers do not sentimentally fear or distrust any game as an exhausting form of exotic exercise, although they may detest bad form or style in whatever sport: golf, tennis, yachting, boxing or polo. Yet many of our dance- and music-critics write as if they are afraid of the dance or music with which they are confronted. They do not allow themselves to regard the spectacle with clean eyes. Either they are ignorant or sloppy, or else they are too busy discovering outstanding, heretical differences in new expression from their rigid conception of the basic form as they were originally taught it, and as they have lazily decided it may as well always remain. Sport-writers can usually play the games they describe with some amount of efficiency. Paul Gallico let Jack Dempsey knock him out to learn what it felt like. Hence, their bodies as well as their brains feel from actual experience what they are writing about. Many dance-critics cannot play the piano or read a note of music. It would, of course, be too much to expect that most dance critics should dance. However, the great Russian analyst, Volyinsky, took up the technique at the age of seventy for his professional purposes. Haskell has worked at the *barre,* and others have attended classes enough to make up for lack of actual physical application.

One can no more expect ballet-critics to praise everything they see any more than sports-writers personally must like individual runners or teams of tennis-players whose performance they are assigned to describe. We need ballet-critics who write about dancing with the lack of preciosity which Ring Lardner described baseball, Paul Gallico boxing, or John Tunis reported tennis. In some paragraphs of Ernest Hemingway's "Death in the Afternoon" he approaches great technical dance-criticism. In the military histories of Captain John W. Thomason and Colonel Liddel Hart, notably the lives of J. E. B. Stuart and "T. E. Lawrence," there are descriptions of the movements of individuals and troops, men, horses and machines, which are models of vivid pictorial exposition without personal bias, but which create an intense emotional response.

The technical critic of any art is occupied with the net efficiency or practical beauty, which turns out to be almost the same, of various physical results needed to gain a desired visual or audible end. They can also, by their technical analysis, judge the quality of those means and resultant ends; they cannot help to do so justly, at least by inference, if the presentation of their picture is technically complete, and if their historical background roughly coincides with their own visual or aural experience.

IV. *OUR YOUNG DANCER'S IDEAL*

The most dangerous thing about the "Great Conspiracy" in the world of ballet, is not that there has been such a conspiracy, which was historically inevitable, but that it may still operate on our next dancing generation. The female patrons of the Russian ballet will disclose to you their plans to interest American, yes, actually my dear, *American* painters and musicians, by annual competitions for music and scenery, to start possibly as soon as 1940. When you ask about what use they have now for American dancers, or by a daft chance, American choreographers, their confusion is only equal to their uncertainty as to *which* Russian ballet they are now connected with. "Americans may have some painters and composers for Us; but dancers, well, no, not just yet."

Hence, the American dancers already assimilated into the Russian companies are usually obliged to change their names from Peterson to Petrovsky, from Billings to Bilinsky. In the Diaghilev troupe, for example, Patrick Kay became first Patrikieff, then Anton Dolin, Hilda Munnings was Sokolova, Alice Marks, Markova. Their public naturally expects a *Russian* ballet. And so our provincial Russian-American dancing teachers or their imitators instruct their pupils to be Russian dancers, or at least try to impose upon them their semblance of a Russian, or at least a continental style. I remember when in the first year I worked with the American Ballet, a boy from Maine, born of French origin, but whose family for generations had been called Carter, asked me to pronounce it *Cartier* because it was, as he said, "Not exactly more foreign but, well, you know, softer."

During the tours of the de Basil Russian Ballet across the United States, auditions have been held in many cities to acquire new members for the troupe. Not a few Americans have been chosen to appear with the Russians. Yet of necessity, the printed record in the program has had to have been appeased. Shirley Bridges of Rochester, New York, is still visible under the veneer of "Adrianova." "Nina Radova" is Vivian Smith of Cleveland. "Kyra Strakova" was known in St. Louis as Patty Thall. Marcel Leplat of Seattle is the excellent mime "Marc Platoff." The late "Mira Dimina" was Madeleine Parker of New York. The dancers appearing with David Lichine (née Lichtenstein) in his latest ballet *Protée*, labelled Lerina, Sabinova and Denisova (by any chance Leroy, Sabin, or Denis?) were reared by June Roper, a dancing-teacher of Vancouver. If these kids, born and bred on this continent are considered able enough to hold their own in a Russian organization, then they are good enough to appear dignified by the names with which their parents blessed them.

Lacking a consecutive native tradition of renowned artists, we have logically enough appropriated Russians for our models. But there is a definite limit to our necessity for so doing much longer. If we continue this imitation, our young dancers may soon find they lack an inherent local magnetism which their increasing audiences expect, from a familiarity with a parallel native style as developed in movies and musical-comedy.

If we would learn from the results of persistent adherence to an alien tradition in our arts, consider the parallel field of sculpture. The insistent maintenance of the so-called "Greek" ideal has blinded too many competent American sculptors to the real beauties of an American physique. The Greek athlete had proportions and animal qualities determined by his sun, air, land and sea, and by the variants of military and physical training he underwent some three thousand years ago. He was transcribed by his great sculptors into an heroic type so powerful that it came to serve as a universal model for all times and places; and yet, how very rarely does one feel that in any of our contemporary classic sculpture (I am not speaking of academic "modern" sculpture) is there anything more than a pastiche or a dilution of Athens, Rome or Florence. Our classic sculptors have been blinded by their first version of Hellas, or its reworking under the Rome Empire or in the Renaissance. Their eyes and hands have no longer any real creative elasticity. Yet the human body is as beautiful here as it was thirty centuries ago. They cannot seem to adapt their preconceived preference for the Greek plastique to the new requirements which the creation of a specifically American archtype requires. Even in athletics our own best bodies are less rhetorically heroic than those we see in sport-photos of athletes demonstrating in Scandinavia, Russia, or in the Czech *sokols*. Plastically, American bodies are more compact and cast an aura of a somewhat more familiar intimacy than the more baroque European physique. Our muscular development is not monstrous or bulgy. We are always more surprised by the brilliant efficiency of one of our swimmer's, runner's, or tennis-player's technique, than by his or her anatomical endowment or personal "beauty." Don Budge, Glenn Cunningham, and Jesse Owens have the motor style of champions, and yet, except in action, we hardly think of them as especially Phidian, or Michelangelesque, perhaps not even then. Their ranginess is no less *intrinsically* beautiful than the particular antique quality of the winner of the first Olympian game. Only, these American athletes have their own particular value, due perhaps to California climate and inter-state University tournaments. Sports and dancing, at least in matters of national style, have many common elements. Our rowing style, our running style, and even our boxing style have assumed definite local characteristics which indicate the direction which our developed dancing style must one day take as well.

If we would pursue this parallel closer to theatre let us investigate the influence of Constantin Stanislavsky's "method" on native-born American actors. This great Russian stage-scientist developed a technique for projecting an approximation of spontaneous emotion. Russian and American actors have utilized his researches and developed from them a "universal" system, best demonstrated in New York City by performances of plays by the Group Theatre. Stanislavsky created his attitude from the basis of collaborations with such realistic prerevolutionary playwrights as Tchekov and Gorki. This fragmentary "naturalism" seems to us to-day as accidental and stylized as the "unreal" cloak-and-sword dramas of Edmond Rostand. It was the tendency of a period in reaction against official theatrical taste of its particular epoch.

Yet this Russian formula has been appropriated by certain over-intel-lectual American stage directors who were dazzled by a first vision of the Moscow Art Theatre, as their blanket panacea. The principle of "breaking-down" any given actor by inducing essential emotional con-flicts, so that private "suffering" is projected as public "sincerity" has its underlying, yet deceptive logic. Stanislavsky himself worked for a cer-tain high-bourgeois strata of nervous, volatile, francophile slavs of a decade when the influence of Zola, Flaubert and Antoine's theatre were dominant among Muscovite students and amateurs.

When we go to a play by the Group in New York, based on the Stanis-lavsky method, we persistently recognize the identical stock character-izations: the kindly old character-actor (Jewish or Italian), the frus-trated young man (boxer, medical student, revolutionary), the aging or adolescent young woman,—suicidal, maternal or resigned. The Bronx is close enough to Moscow as it is, without slipping into an easy double-exposure. Instead of the transplanted Russian method giving elasticity, which is hard enough to get in any repertory company, since the same actors have all to be found parts, it produces rather a rigid formulariza-tion. It is the same as in the Gilbert and Sullivan repertory, when Katisha of "The Mikado" is Buttercup in "Pinafore," Lady Jane in "Patience" and Mad Meg in "Ruddigore." What has all this to do with dancing, pray? Just this: The Stanislavsky technique is a specifically Muscovite method, applicable to the particular repertory of a particular epoch. Classic ballet training is an international technique, traditional and *not* epochal, whose most recent great period happened to reach its epopée first of all on Russian soil.

The fact of the matter is that no American can even pretend to be a Russian dancer, and few want to be. Surely no American dancer can get even to first-base in a Russian company. They are, it is true, able to swell the ranks of the corps de ballet, and every so often they are awarded a small solo. Remember the case of young Roland Guerard of Phila-delphia, who had about the most faultless pure classic technique in the original Monte Carlo Company. His "Blue Bird" was a superlative aca-demic accomplishment, and not like Lichine's, a flashy fluke. Yet Guerard has hardly ever been permitted to appear, except in the provinces where the ranking soloist was saving himself for the big cities.

The managers have spent too much money publicizing their three or four first-rank solo Russian names. Russian names aren't easy for strangers to remember, and no confusion will be risked by the addition of a Smith, Brown or Jones, no matter how well they may dance. At least not yet. Soon enough, probably, and perhaps too soon when the American ballet-drive starts in earnest, I can easily imagine that the managers will one day insist Lichine change his name to Little, Danilova to Daniels, and Massine to Mason. But that's perhaps not a grave threat at the present. Neither American dancers with Russian names, nor Russian dancers with American names will help much to create the American ballet for which we hope. That rests entirely with the developing invention of our native choreographers.

Every cultivated Russian choreographer feels Poushkin, Dostoyevsky or Gontcharov not as written literature, but as if they were chronicles of their own personal histories. They are *themselves* Onegin. They *are* Pierre Bezukhoi. They *are* Oblomov. They *are* Raskolnikov. The national monuments resident in the Skazki, Lomonossov, Poushkin, Tolstoi, Blok and the rest, utilized by Tchaikovsky, Moussorgsky, Rimsky, Borodin, Stravinsky, Shostakovich, Nabokov or Prokoviev, are their *essential* subject-matter, and if Russian choreographers aren't allowed to translate it into ballet terms with the national Russian background they breathe through, instead of a superimposed American background, we can have reason to expect Evgeni Onegin at the New Orleans' Mardi Gras, Ivan the Terrible at the Siege of the Alamo, and the Snegouroutchka by the shores of the Sky Blue Water. Massine's *Nobilissima Visione* (St. Francis), with Hindemith's great score and Tchelitchev's amazing decor may more than likely prove to be a revelation as the most fascinating danced work of this decade, but I want to see our American Gods and Heroes as we know them, canonized by our vision of them.

American dancers have earned the right to be *American* dancers. In the films, on ball-room floors, and on the musical-comedy stage, they are encouraged to be American, to develop freely in their own personal and national style. But in the realms of the "serious" dance they are not yet permitted to come of age. The old Russian names can still be worked, and it naturally pays better if the Russian monopoly is tightly held. When threatened by a new movement, the Monopolies will undoubtedly compromise by the inclusion of American dancers or ideas, as long as they can exert an ultimate control. And as long as they exert even the least taint of control there may be some slight chance for individual

Americans, but for the future of the best interests of American dancing, there will be no future at all.

Not that our immediate aspect is by any means hopeless. Quite the reverse. In the last few years, as the appendix to this pamphlet shows, the veritable American repertory has reached more than adolescent proportions. We may have to pay for an aggressively nationalistic period at present to offset the recent drag of Russian blackmail, but if so, it will be only a transient and healthy reaction. American folk-lore or historic atmosphere drawn from our national epos, from Pocahontas and Conestoga wagons, down to Harper's Ferry, Lindbergh and Corrigan, are rich veins to be mined for ballet-material. But there should be no reason why we will not be able eventually to present our American comment on England, France, Italy, or on Russia itself for that matter, just as the Russians have admirably done. But it will be *our* time's comment, a new comment, and a comment we only can achieve.

Parallel to the line of folk-lore or historical atmosphere, there will also emerge in our expanding American repertory a series of works to older music; works of a dominantly choreographic nature which will be used to develop and amplify our own ideas of the traditional classic dance. The literature of the dance-suite of the epoch of Bach and Händel are full of remarkable dancing-music, for these forms logically emerged from seventeenth and eighteenth century court and social-dances. Just because they have been for the last two centuries held sacrosanct for use in concert-halls alone, is nothing against their present or future legitimate employment as dance-music. Ernest Newman who is surely a music-critic for musicians, says "I have never been able, as a balleto-mane, to see anything sacrosanct either in the symphony or in Brahms and Beethoven. . . . The whole trouble has arisen because a few people insist on bringing their concert ears with them to the ballet theatre." The idiom of classic traditional dancing, the vocabulary of its movement and gesture has so enormously developed since the time of the music's composition, and particularly in the last thirty years, that the pieces can today receive a genuinely complementary and contemporary treatment, impossible if an attempt is made to present the music and dance archeologically in the strict period of their origin.

The Passacaglia, for example, offers superb chances for cohesive choreographic production with its melodic statement, developed variations, and eminently dramatic recapitulation. It has recently been used for an extended composition by the "modern" dancer and choreographer, Doris Humphrey. The so-called "modern" dance has among its four leading teachers no common basic technique except what John Martin calls a common "attitude," although through the teachings of Louis Horst, all of them share a considerable background in the basic dance-forms of the 17th century from which the sonata and the symphony were later developed. It is almost a paradox that so much of the formal compositional elements (apart from the idiosyncratic gesture) of the "modern" dance is almost academically rooted in these pre-classic dance forms. The architecture of their dancing is frequently well thought out. But just as often, due to too much respect for Sarabande, Pavane, Courante or whatever, they seem on the stage undramatic and flat. I have never understood the blanket acceptance by the "modern" faculty, of the pre-classic musical forms and their blanket rejection of the style of classic traditional gesture which was the close historic parallel of these very forms.

Music by Bach, Händel, Gluck and much more as late as Weber, Mendelsohn and Schubert, is, I feel, infinitely more suitable for contemporary stage-dancing than the large romantic symphonies which Massine has been recently appropriating. In the first place the older classic music is, if not actually written for dancing, then close in origin to basic dance-forms. The big bang-up symphonies with all their extra-musical prestige, their monumental literary history, their record of interpretations by famous conductors, will inevitably overbalance the dancing to compete with a visual production.

Personally, I have no ethical objection to Massine's use of any symphony he chooses to have played for his ballet-accompaniment. It saves him the trouble of collaborating with any living composer or commissioning a new score, and if the symphonic partition is reasonably familiar, the music-critics, at least, will immediately recognize the chief themes. They can hum them comfortably to themselves during the course of the dancing, and the harsh, fresh dash of unaccustomed vision will be made soothing and tolerable by one more hearing of the oft-heard noises. Only, and again only personally, I have not cared for extra-illustrated gift-books since my twelfth birthday. Even Gustave Doré's remarkable interpretations of Dante are superfluous, and Arthur Rackham's Shakespearean pixies are perfunctory. Massine's symphonic pictures are to me, at least, gratuitous illustrations, or vignettes, free fantasies on well-known themes. Anyone can shut his eyes during a performance of Beethoven's "Seventh," particularly if they have been only half listening to the sounds, and let moving tableaux form behind their eyelids. Perhaps you will see the first movement as the Creation of the world. Maybe, the second shows an Entombment; the third, the Marriage of the Earth and Sky; the fourth, the destruction of a Sodom or a Gomorrah. Why not? Your guess is as good as the next guy's. Except that

the "Seventh" of all symphonies is a work of such consistent dance texture that these cheerful or lugubrious chromos seem an affront even
tailored by such a dressmaker's edible talent as Bérard's. In any number
of movies, it is very easy to have the sound-track dub in a recording of
the Ride of the Valkyrs for a forest-fire, or the second theme of the first
movement of the Cèsar Franck Symphony for a death-scene. Massine has
a right to embellish the old music-masters, but it is scarcely a creative
act when he does so. It is, pure and simple, an inferior act; the act of
illustration.

But from a purely technical point of view, Beethoven's "Seventh Symphony" played by the required number of Union Local 802 musicians,
is a possibility only in a dozen of the largest cities in this country.
Otherwise the sacred "Seventh" is performed on a scale reduced to less
than half the size of Beethoven's most ordinary demands. To this sort
of sacrilege, our music-critics, otherwise vestal virgins of their muses'
fire, discreetly wink. Arnold Haskell lays any criticism of Massine's
symphonic treatment aside by blurting that whatever the legitimate objections may be, at least *"Massine got away with it."* That is, if a Russian
does it, it's all right. But catch an American or even an English choreographer (though God knows we don't want to) mounting a ballet to the
Cèsar Franck, the Schubert "Unfinished," or the Sibelius Seventh (as
nothing can probably stop Massine from doing) ! If one of our choreographers should do it, the critical howl would be unanimous, a field-day
for the nifty music-boys: "Vulgarity, lack of due technical consideration; confusion of the media; no respect for musical values." Oh Yeah!
Well, let them clean their eyes and ears, coldly watch Massine's version
of Beethoven's Seventh, or Tchaikovsky's Fifth, when they see them for
the next time, and then ask themselves a few cold questions.

But whatever one may think of Leonide Massine as a creative choreographer, there can be little question of his remarkakble personality in
the execution of character rôles. He bridged the difficult gap between
his youth and his maturity, so that he has never seemed an aging juvenile
but always and only a mature male artist. Having danced so much in his
life, it is impossible that he should not have acquired polish, presence,
physical control. But he adds to the technique of experience a charming
personal overtone, an idiosyncratic stamp of very strong flavor. Force
and shyness, fire and tenderness which simultaneously mock each other
in an exquisite theatrical urbanity, give a certain tragic or at the least
an ironic quality to his vivid performances. It is almost as if he were
making sober sport of his own interpretations while dancing them up to
the hilt. It is almost as if he mocks or at least draws attention to the

transient essence of dancing itself, and yet by his vivid activity demonstrates its mercurial permanence.

If, as I believe, an American ballet repertory will be built on the twin basis of native historic themes and contemporary traditional choreography to classic music, there will be unquestionably a third strain contributing much more to the technical development of classic dancing than to the ideas or subjects treated. This will be the two-fold contribution of choreographic elements *apart* from the traditional classic dance; on the one hand, from popular vaudeville, revue-dance, and popular jazz or swing music; that is what we could call American character dancing—our parallel to the national dances of Spain, Italy or Russia; and on the other, from certain aspects inherent in the "modern" concert dance. There is no American composer now writing who is in any way conscious of his time or place, who has not been affected by jazz. Hence, any serious music written as setting for contemporary themes will call for an understanding of basic contemporary dance-forms from the Two-Step, Tango, and Rhumba, to the Lindy Hop, Shag, or Suzy-Q, and their combined spontaneous use in the Big Apple or one of its variants, which are essentially a contemporary improvised Quadrille or square-dance. A salient feature of American style is the presence or at least the appearance of the presence of spontaneous improvisation. When a Russian accomplishes a difficult classic variation with their suave mastery of technique, one assumes they have done it hundreds of times before. When an American dances well one almost feels he or she is making it up as he goes along. Vaudeville training capitalized on this feature and made it one of the most attractive in the American theatrical idiom.

I have long been suspect as an enemy of the "modern" or "concert" dance, and with a single exception still vigorously am. I have always found to hate in most of it a persistent, arbitrary, priggish and doctrinaire avoidance of theatrical elements, a refusal to accept the traditional classic dance as a basic theatrical instrument. I have been irritated by its prejudiced rejection of the form of ballet as a decadent hangover of feudalism. I have been contemptuous of its general intellectualization and clannishness, divorced from the physical needs of our modern stage. But in the last two years I have been forced quite in spite of myself to recognize that there are some definite elements emerging from *one* "modern" dancer, which can be plastically important to all American classic dancers. I still feel, however, that these elements are largely useless without a profound groundwork of traditional ballet-training. I am not yet reconciled to dancers starting their professional training after the age of twenty-one. I do not think that a mere desire to dance is enough to make a dancer, or that six weeks at Bennington is a blanket diploma towards a professional stage-career.

Indeed last winter I talked to the charming directors of the Bennington School concerning their plans for establishing in New York a permanent Central School for the Modern Dance, extended along the lines of the six-week summer course they have so successfully conducted over the last five years in Vermont, and which they are transporting in its entirety to Mills College in California in July 1939. Although they knew perfectly well my attitude towards ballet training versus the "modern" dance, since my troupe had been invited twice to give performances and demonstrations at Bennington, nevertheless, they are very broad-minded women and we discussed the possibility of a Central School both on an ideal and a realistic basis. And I had only one really fundamental disagreement with them, which lay in the difficult problem of such a school's moral responsibility for the future professional employment of dancers which it undertakes to train. The ultimate obligation must rest with the dancers when they choose their school. While I realize no serious school can "guarantee" either professional standing or even a temporary job, nevertheless, the question of future employment inevitably enters in. A student with three or four years of ballet-training can reasonably expect to dance in half a dozen of the independent ballet troupes, in musical-comedy, in films, or at worst, in opera-ballet. A dancer with only "modern" training can merely attach herself or himself on a highly impermanent basis to one of the four or five "modern" teachers for occasional individual performances, or for infrequent tours which are rarely more than a month or two out of the twelve. It is perfectly true that able modern-dancers can find positions to *teach* the "modern" dance at State Universities, Physical Education Colleges, etc. I have always maintained the modern dance may be incidental physical training for laymen, but it is no pedagogy for the theatre. We discussed this problem for some time and at the end of the talk, one of the directors asked me: All right, but don't you think it would be better to have in *existence* such a central school rather than to have none at all? And I was forced to admit that even here, something was probably better than nothing, because in spite of the past, no one could tell what might happen in the future. Yet the problem remains. What chance of a *stage* career has the ordinary "modern" dancer?

One can almost forgive John Martin everything he has ever written or said, up to his remark on the Bennington School of the Dance, in his column of August 21st, 1938 (The New York *Times*). He says the School "must certainly have done much to break down the old notion that professional and lay dancing are entirely different activities instead of merely different levels of the same subject." A dilettante, by this token, is some one whose interest is not unlike, but only whose energy is unequal to the rigors of a vulgar professionalism. It's all very well to have one great big happy family in the "Modern" Dance, although its very lack of professionalism up to date is just what has doomed it to a universal popular failure.

As far as classic ballet goes—there are no *lay* ballet-dancers any more than there are *lay* heart-specialists or *lay* plumbers. The trouble with psycho-analysis is that there are still *lay*-analysts. One of the troubles of the "modern" dance is that you never can tell who is a *lay* dancer. Ballet-dancers are theatrical dance-specialists as well as artists. That is their only dignity on which to base any self-respect or collective security. An earnest will-to-dance or six jovial weeks in the lovely Vermont hills are not enough guarantee either to make your living as a dancer, or to be considered a serious artist. The Ballet is a serious art, craft and science. Incidentally, it may also help a person to have a better body, or at least a better educated body. But instruction in ballet has nothing to do with Physical Education. Let the "modern" dance take care of that. The "modern" dance may prove preferable to Swedish gymnastics. It may educate a lay-audience to watch other "modern" dancers, but the amateur spirit, outside of croquet and stamp-collecting, only induces further amateurism on the stage, however healthy, vigorous, and good for the nerves and digestion it might incidentally prove.

Nevertheless, particularly in the more recent work of Martha Graham, I have been deeply impressed by a use of a lateral breadth in her leaps and in her extended profile which is far more satisfactory for some athletic American dancers than a complete adherence to the perpendicular stylistic rigidity of the Russo-Italian pedagogy. In Martha Graham's finished work as in her strict professional classes, I can find nothing inimical to the developed classic dance as expounded, for example, by George Balanchine's *Apollon* (1927), in the second movement of Massine's *Choreartium* (1934), or even in Nijinska's *Les Noçes* (1922). Graham does not use the virtuoso pirouette turn on half-toe or in the air common to acrobatic ballet, nor do her girls wear toe-slippers. Yet she has no root-prejudice against their use, and she admired Bronislava Nijinska's *Les Noçes* as "modern" dance. Objections to turns, toe-work and beats are mere decorative details in comparison to her recognition of the essential five positions of the feet, the pelvic turn-out, and the complete linear extension which is the legible basis of good ballet-training.

Graham has developed an idiosyncratic gesture which is the reflection of a superb personal, feminine and native human quality. Her dancing vocabulary has moral and almost didactic overtones. Graham is a New England Purtian; there is something in her face and figure which recalls New Bedford sailing-ship figure-heads as well as the surface-finish, economy and suavity of Shaker architecture and wood-carving. Her philosophical links are with the Concord Revolutionary moralists, Emerson and Thoreau, with Whitman and the painter Albert Ryder, far more than with Mary Wigman, Nietzsche, or Richard Wagner. Graham has as little to do with Central European post-war dancing as Isadora Duncan with Michel Fokine. Any connection between them was independent and accidental, with the contact over-emphasized by superficial historians. Graham's contribution is unique and uniquely personal. I have always felt one of her most difficult characteristics was her frightening originality, her independence of *any* tradition whatsoever; but like Blake, she has had to create her "own system or be enslaved by another man's." In her intense effort to create and cleanse our native American dance idiom of its rhetoric and exoticism, its merely decorative accretions at the same time, and to find for it a way of its own, she has explored some dead-ends and has offered numerous manifestoes which she has later superseded, like any consistently creative artist. But recently her ideas have begun to be the equal of her technique, her impulse has been apparent in its theatrical fulfilment as in its intellectual inception. Virtuoso technique and decorative atmosphere to a remarkable degree the recent ballet has had, but ideas in general or particular have been almost completely lacking. Graham has ideas in plenty for the classic dancer as well as her own pupils. To a badly-trained, a part-trained, or to a self-indulgent or stupid classic dancer, Graham's method might prove disintegrating to the point of complete destruction. However, to an instinctive, clean, conscious or well-trained classic dancer, Martha Graham has much to offer. The personal frame her theatre makes is specifically her own, and cannot be appropriated undistilled by the ballet, which is a far more sophisticated, collective, complex and impersonal form. But her sense of a projected physicality, her spinal integration, her sense of controlled entrance, and the deep human color of her dancing style, is a purer and frequently deeper repository of essential classicism, even if it may be a narrower one than the easily accepted and much more superficial idiom of school-ballet.

PART THREE

Program and Manifesto

I. BASIC PRINCIPLES

THE ART OF LIVING IS MORE LIKE WRESTLING THAN DANCING.

MARCUS AURELIUS

What is there to be done in general, and indeed, what is there for us to do now? There is everything to be done. We must first of all, with the materials already in our hands, create a ballet repertory which will sufficiently interest a large public to support us on some more or less permanent basis, to permit us to continue without too much dictation from the dance-managers. We must create a repertory which will not only displace the existent Russian programs, but which can keep abreast of them in ideas and invention. To do this, we must not underestimate their very real powers. They are masters of the theatre, and past masters of dancing. Even in their decadence they have more knowledge of stage values in their toes than most of us have in our whole bodies. They have a basic experience from producing works with the collaboration of the best wits and talents of their generation, from their earliest youth. They have a discriminating taste which has been so dominant that we have come to think of it as infallible. The Russian dancers have their individual formula for effective stage-presence so well worked out that the assurance of a brilliant personal apparition has been frequently more than enough to save an otherwise boring ballet. They have, in fact, everything it takes to make great theatrical dancing except intellectual energy, moral stamina, and a reserve supply of native dancers.

These three desirable qualities might seem *sine qua non* for a healthy young movement, facing a future of vast possibility. But for a decadent old movement, reclining on its piled-up prestige, they are, realistically speaking, negligible. After the first opposition, the initial sales-resistance to a new idea or direction has been overcome, both seller and buyer are somewhat exhausted from their mutual struggle. The Russian Ballet as the seller, forced its unfamiliar wares on the Western World some thirty years ago. Within ten years these wares were fairly universally accepted, and the buyer, in the form of the audience, settled itself down to seeing what it expected to continue to be shown. A certain inertia pervaded both parties, and it was Diaghilev's great gift to pinch both buyer and seller

250

out of their tendency towards an imaginative apathy. But Diaghilev has been dead ten years, and apathy has finally prevailed. Of course, the automatic physical energy persists, but the recent split in the Russian Ballet's economic set-up as well as the signs of more imminent strain, show how shaky even that is. You can beat water till it foams, but even so it's never cream. The top is off the Russian Bottle. Now it's up to us to whip our own cream.

What can we do? A great deal. First of all, we can make ourselves conscious of the economic situation as it actually is. We can realistically marshal and inspect our own forces and feel our own power. For we have a lot. We must investigate recent history and the more remote past once and for all, to salvage from it whatever is immediately useful to us. We must consider every element which might go into the construction of great theatre in terms of dancing, and then construct a program for ourselves which although it must be elastic enough to include the unexpected, shall primarily be strong enough to stand the shock of our necessary experiment and our inevitable mistakes. We must be conscious of ourselves in the world in which we dance. The age of interior-decoration, even in ballet, is over. Period-rooms and period-ballets seem equally the tiresome and tricky left-overs of the nineteen-twenties. If we should mount works with an historic background, let them have a pressing connection with our present lives. Let this connection be more significant than the archeological reconstruction of correct costume or antique dance-pattern. Dance for the sake of Dance alone is no longer any more a tenable law for us than art for the sake of art. But certain dances, even without definite subject, can be more than merely agreeable divertissement. With the aid of great music and worthy gesture, they can always be a monumental testament to the powers of the human being expressed through his or her human body. A dancer actively released in his legible freedom, springing in space, is as satisfactory a witness to the irrepressible and indomitable instinct to human liberty as anyone can find. There are many ways to pay homage to liberty, equality and fraternity. Great dancing is not the least of them.

I am submitting first a program for our basic uses, and then a manifesto towards our immediate action. Neither is final, as I have worked entirely alone and only on a basis of personal experience. I invite comment, amplification and signatories, should they be forthcoming.

1. *The classic dance and American character-dancing.*

I submit an unalterable and fundamental basis for a national American ballet, training in the international classic traditional theatrical dance. If anything would render me more sure of the common-sense, collective usefulness and early instinctive preference for a professional attitude to be gained from a constant connection with classic dancing, it would be the spectacle of the last twenty years of experiment in the field of the "concert" or "modern" dance. The "concert" or "modern" dance was called into being to purge the theatrical tradition of ballet. From Duncan and Dalcroze to Wigman and the American "modernists," the net result has been education, not for dancers, but for the lay audience in elementary aesthetic principles, *away* from, not *towards* the theatre. Isadora's principle may have been far beyond mere roofed-in theatre, and Wigman had her extra-theatrical and ego-centric interests, but I am assuming from reader and audience an essential, immediate and constant interest in theatrical ends. That is, dance is done in theatres, is part of theatre, and is paid for as theatre. Towards theatrical ends I cannot recognize any means for a dancer less complete than whole-hearted training in the classic dance.

It is hardly necessary to indicate for dancers an historical background of traditional classic dance training. But for laymen, by "classic" dance, I mean a system of fundamental instruction for dancing comparable to an understanding of cadence, harmony and counterpoint in music; form, value and color in paint; structure, material and function in architecture. The roots of this instruction were first of all to be found in the social-dance books of Milanese dancing-masters of the late Renaissance. Their categories remain essentially the same today as, for example, the essential divisions in the anatomy of Vesalius, or the architecture of Vitruvius. Four centuries of work in France, Italy, Scandinavia, Poland and Russia have put flesh and muscle on the original bare skeletal structure. *Tradition* only means a *handing-down*. Great dancers, ballet-masters, musicians and costumers have each and everyone added their individual contributions, as in the brother dynasties of physicians, architects, and poets. There is, as I have said before, *materia choreographica* just as there is a *materia medica*.

In T. S. Eliot's remarkable essay "Tradition and the Individual Talent," he specifically spoke of English poetry and its relationship to criticism both French and English. Yet on a rereading its cogency is startling, turned on the field of another verse, the poetry of physical movement.

Tradition cannot be inherited, and if you want it you must obtain it by great labour. It involves, in the first place, the historical sense, which we may call nearly indispensable to anyone who would continue to be a poet beyond his twenty-fifth year; and the historical sense involves a perception, not only of the pastness of the past, but of its presence; the historical sense compels a man to write not merely with his own generation in his bones, but with a feeling that the whole literature of Europe from Homer and within it the whole of the literature of his own country has a simultaneous existence and composes a simultaneous order.

The experiment of cubism in painting has been loosely compared to experimental "modernism" in dancing. But cubism was a logical, traditional development, while the modern dance was "original." In the first place, no one any longer puts quotes around cubism, and yet because the exact degree or species of "modernity" in the dance is difficult to allocate under the general word "modernism," this term still remains an ism in quotation marks. The pictures of Nijinsky's *Le Sacre du Printemps* appearing in the *Illustrated London News* during the season of 1913 were labelled "cubist ballet." The superficial angularity of the gesture, even clothed in the pseudo-Scythian clothes of Prof. Roerich, seemed to the caption writers somehow related to Picasso's or Kandinsky's experiments. Yet had the *News* wished to be exact they might have called it a *Fauve* ballet, a ballet under the influence of the post-impressionist followers of Gauguin in the naiviste and exotic, ca. 1905. The "modern" dance has had little or nothing to do with cubism or abstract painting. The cubist method was an analytical method for breaking down representational rendering into shapes or forms which had a precise balance in their given frame. It was also an historical criticism of the vaguely composed, accidental snap-shots of the French Impressionists. It was a strong solvent which by way of Cezanne's previous researches reinvestigated the whole tradition of western pictorial composition. Cubism was a natural development in the classic tradition of French painting. Its validity was as much in its comment on impressionism, which had become a stuffy academy, as in its serving a new basis for subsequent painting for the neo-Romanticism and surrealism which followed it. And above all, we are left with some great individual cubist and abstract panels by Picasso, Braque and Mondrian.

The "modern" dance has left us, to begin with, not one notable composition to which one can refer like any of the half-dozen outstanding ballets of innovation in the Diaghilev repertory. Unlike cubism, the "modern" dance was not a traditional outgrowth of the rest of western classic theatrical dancing. It was a radical revolt from it, so violent at its outset that the base was rootless, or rather, only rooted in the idiosyncracies of the few leading personalities who professed this attitude. Nijinsky's gestures for *Le Sacre* seemed "original," yet they were really only the classic five positions adapted to their reversal. The turn-out was turned *in*. The classic dance was turned inside out. It was not thrown away. It was the reverse of the medal, not a different coin. As in politics, it is more legitimate and easier to affect party policy *within* the movement by a participating member, than to purge it from *outside* by however violent a criticism.

The aim of the "modern" dancer by and large has been to deny any traditional residual material whatsoever, to attempt to erect instead an *original* system which they felt might be more applicable to "our" time. They forgot that even "our" time is the cumulative result of other times, and has its connections with a continuous logical lineage. Nevertheless, the "moderns," on an idiosyncratic basis of personal preference and individual prejudice created as many "schools" of the "modern" dance as they were dance-teachers, having no more connection with each other than with their enemy, the theatrical dance, except in what John Martin called their "attitude." This attitude, reduced to its minimum verbosity, was quite simply a fundamental opposition to the tenets of classic ballet.

The reason for this fundamental opposition was not too hard to discover. None of the Modern Dancers had ever seen progressive ballet, as represented by the Silver Age of Diaghilev, until they were too fixed to alter their prejudice against it. This bias in the first place, had been gained from hearsay, and was then necessarily maintained out of a compensatory jealousy for their own considerable technical inadequacy. The dance- and music-training of Jacques Dalcroze, already formulated by 1910, towards making students and children conscious of audible rhythm and visible gesture, has more to teach us today than the entire results of the individual artists or choreographers he subsequently directly or indirectly affected. The Central-European dance, as represented by von Laban, Wigman, Bodenweiser, Trudi Schoop, their pupils in America, and even Jooss, has had a diminishing theatrical effect, not on the basis of its various individual ideologies but purely and simply on the basis of its lack of a comprehensible or consistent *technique*. Technically, the "modern" dance if taken in a pure dose does not offer a complete enough training for any serious theatrical dancer.

Take the case of Kurt Jooss, for example. He calls his choreographic works *Ballets*. But he makes an academic doctrine out of his avoidance of the culminating accents and emphasis of traditional classic ballet practice. He uses an aerial profile, a fluent extended silhouette, the gracious openness of plastic style which serves the basis of the academic dance, and which was founded among other influences, on the Italian baroque plastic arts—the *contraposto* or anatomical opposition of Giovanni di Bologna, Michelangelo and Bernini. But he stubbornly avoids the use of toe-shoes, air turns, brilliant beats, or acrobatic turns on the floor. Hence, his choreography, however magnificently rehearsed as it has had the unique good fortune of being able to afford, always seems muted, toned down, a simulacra; one is pleased by his smooth finish, yet one always expects something *more.* His own academic ideas are not significant enough to compensate for a lack, not of technical polish which his dancers surely have, but of the maintenance of theatrical tension or interest by technical virtuosity which his dancers surely have not. And why not? Partly because von Laban's early prejudice against the classic Russian training was a Prussian chauvinist hang-over that was transmitted blindly to Jooss, who later had to try to rationalize this inherited opposition. Partly because, purely by accident, Jooss does not have the patience to instruct up to the peak ultimate of classic method. Mostly because, as an "innovator" he has had to have some point of difference with the rest of the dance-world; so this has been it. His work has suffered for it very much over the last three years. Jooss has, through the patronage of Mrs. Elmhirst, enjoyed an unparalleled chance for creation. His own ideas, as testified at least by *The Green Table* (1933) are full of meaning to us. Yet why does nothing more come out of it? I think because Jooss has been fighting the chimera of traditional classic theatrical dancing. His opposition to the tradition has channeled his energies away from the full aims of dance-theatre.

A dancer must ideally be capable of everything. In Russia, where such things are valued more, dancers are speaking actors, sometimes singers, as well as acrobats. Why do people like dancing, anyway? Because they see in the flesh men and women with two arms and legs just like themselves, moving in air with the heightened, coördinated logic which represents for them their most-hoped-for possibilities, a denial of earthly gravity, an ultimate freedom of action, a super-human domination of flesh and earth. By definition, the dance is acrobatic. The dancer's only tool is in his or her proper human body. This tool is a universal instrument, capable of infinite articulate use. But all its uses must be theatrically legible. The bodies' activities must be able to be watched clearly by an audience seated at some distance from their actual moving. This is where theatricalism comes in. Classic ballet training provides first of all substructure for acrobatic brilliance, then the motor logic of a readable silhouette. By the trial and error of over four centuries stage-dancers have come to know the moving balance and axis of aerial and terrestrial excitement. By brilliance they create interest, tension, and accelerative excitement in their watchers. This information has become a strict science and an honorable craft. It can be taught. Our classic traditional dance training teaches it.

And the classic dance instructs us in something else which is even more necessary. This is a classic *style*. The frame, the outward glow, the final polish which it is impossible to superimpose on a structure anything less than solid, does, however, add the ultimate stamp which sets finished dancers in the aura of their accomplishment. The style may be a Russian style, which we have known, or an American style, which we may come to know; but in any case its importance cannot be overestimated. It is what the ignorant-eyed see first. It is what the knowing-eye sees first and last. It is what sells dancing to people all the time.

Parallel to the daily regimen of dancing exercises based on the five fundamental classic positions of hands and feet which are the equivalent of finger-exercises for a pianist or a singer's vocalized scales, the Russian pedagogy has developed a very complex instruction in character-dancing. The basic ethnic steps from Hungarian, Spanish, Polish, Italian or Cossack national forms were given a broader theatrical treatment for stage use. Simple turns became pirouettes. Leaps were filled out with foot-beats. The basic gesture founded on custom, earth and weather, were italicized for legibility in theatres. This whole department of the dance served as a "natural" and useful complement to the "artificial" academic classic tradition. The two lines crossed and recrossed. There was a whole intertwined genre of Italian, French and Russian operatic dancing known as the *demi-caractére*. "Spanish" hands or "Hungarian" heels were mixed with toe-work. Folk-influence enlivened the colder, purer, and more arbitrary foundation.

Americans have assimilated European character-dancing in the past and can learn it well. Arthur Mahoney's Spanish numbers have an astonishing authenticity and effectiveness. Paul Haakon's Russian sailor-dance from Glière's *Red Poppy* is a perfect example of character-dance for theatre. William Dollar's Czardas in Balanchine's *The Bat* had an ecstatic, almost desperate fire that came perhaps from the fact of his own Hungarian ancestry. But there is always the element of *tour de force* in an American dancing, however ably, authentic dances of other lands. Somehow the fact of the Russians having been born on earth shared by the rest of Europe makes their dancing of a *farucca* or a *tarantella* less strained.

It is only recently that Americans have discovered we also have our own character-dancing which can serve us theatrically better than any Russian or Spanish. And this is not the dance of the Sioux, the Hopi, or the Navaho, nor the square-dance of the Tennessee Mountaineers. Our character dancing is a vital contemporary manifestation, not an exotic left-over. Since the tradition of "eccentric" dancing descending from the days of buck-and-wing minstrel-shows vanished with four-a-day vaudeville, we have not been very aware of dancers employing "popular" dance - forms consciously. American character - dancing has stemmed from a double strain, one from vaudeville or musical-comedy, the other from social-dances in ball-rooms, barns, barracks, gyms or dance-halls. Buster West's American sailor number, Buddy Ebsen's hick fast flat feet, and of course such fine Negro teams as Buck and Bubbles have been continually paralleled by a "smoother" tradition stemming from Irene and Vernon Castle, Moss and Fontana, Veloz and Yolanda, and above all, Fred Astaire and Ginger Rogers. These "social-dancers," even though they frequently dance on ball-room floors instead of on a stage, take over from annual popular dance fads numerous new forms and tricky steps, and theatricalize them by adding specatcular lifts, or free fantasia on jazz steps with astonishing tap cadenzas, as Paul Draper does. The recent wide-spread interest in Charleston, Black-Bottom, Suzy-Q, Lindy Hop, Shag and Big Apple testifies to our inherent love for popular music and dancing on an intimate, or at least on a familiar basis. The ancestors of the Big Apple trace themselves back in an unbroken lineage to Bunny Hug, Turkey Trot and the Negro Cake-Walk. The complexity and ingenuity of "swing" band-music is equalled by the variety and invention of steps which the dancers create to accompany it. The Big Apple is a communal expression, recalling square-dances of the mid-nineteenth century which from the *contredanse* later developed into the *German* and *Cotillon*. The Big Apple is a kinetic *dance*, which the static, ordinary two-step of the 'twenties hardly ever was. Elements of rhumba and tango, fragments of negro, Mexican, Cuban and Argentine gesture and movement are embroidered into a consistent fabric of motion whose spontaneous flow fits the personal mood of the improvisor.

This material offers an American ballet-choreographer as rich material as *gopak, saltarello* or *bolero,* with the added advantage that our dancers have enjoyed these dances as part of their own experience from their earliest schooldays. They are able to perform stage versions of them with conviction, not as an imitation of a form they have seen done by Russions or Spaniards, but rather because the quality of their jazz and gesture is as familiar to them as the kids with whom they first danced at high-school prom, Saturday night socials, or in the summer-dances on the Mall in Central Park. These social-dances must necessarily be redesigned for the stage, and can be hung on a structure of classic technique for their greatest stage effect.

We are all of us familiar with the splendid stance, the proud spinal carriage of the Spanish gypsy. We easily recognize the jack-knife spring and release of Cossack knees. We have known the brilliant play of pantomimic flirtation in Italian peasant-dances. Let us also recognize our own native detachable snake-hips, our rangy legs, our educated feet. Our arms and fingers wave and snap in a special way. Our shoulders hang as no other people's shoulders hang. Our classic theatrical style will find an added authority and flavor from the essential qualities of American national dances.

2. Ideas and Collaboration

A ballet, no matter how rhetorical or how transparently atmospheric will, upon inspection, always be found to contain some substratum of *ideas*. This will be less upsetting to old-school balletomanes than at first appears. For them at least ideas may be all very well, in their place (in libraries possibly), but why drag them into dancing? Don't brush the gold-dust from the wings of the Sylphs. But take *Les Sylphides*, for example, a ballet in which it is usually assumed no idea has ever been permitted to penetrate. This suite of dances is framed as a decorative revery recalling the style and forms of Romantic Ballet in 1840. The corps de ballet float in the dreamy tarlatans of Taglioni's time. The single poetic young man represents, for the purposes of 1909 or 1939, the dance-maddened, or at least the dance-inflamed male dancer of the tradition of the romantic epoch, when the male dancer's position was anomalous. The ideas then in *Les Sylphides*, are decorative ideas about dancing itself, framing Fokine's stylized gesture which was his own invention, and except for final or accentual poses had probably very little to do with Romantic Ballet of the "forties," considered archeologically. I have always thought of ballets in the genre of *Les Sylphides* rather like still-life in painting. The French accurately term such work *nature-morte*, dead-nature. The still-lifes of Chardin, to take representatives of the greatest, are much more than formal arrangements of vegetables and kitchen-utensils. Aside from their dazzling display of the technique of the application of paint, the seemingly accidental choice of carrots or copper kettles patently testify to the homely domestic virtues, the peasant honesty and solid "human" values witnessing the rights of common-men at the period directly preceeding the first middle-class French Revolution. I mean that while there may be more apparent social *ideas* in a Chardin than there are in *Les Sylphides*, yet when you realize the choreographer Fokine was creating a work of art in the taste of the audience of the Imperial Russian Theatres, for retired generals, court chamberlains and visiting French and English diplomats, for the bureaucratic families all of whom were educated in a taste for the delicious charm of the epoch of their grandparents and the quaintness of the opera-houses of 1840, in fact, when you realize every ballet is thus a reflection of the concepts of the choreographer faced with the conditioning of his audience, then perhaps *Les Sylphides* can be thought to have its social implications too.

It is perhaps harder to find ideas, social or otherwise, in Russian-Russian ballets or in the oriental-Russian pseudo-exotic ballets. *Schéhérazade* and *Thamar* are pure exotic decoration, having little or nothing to do with genuine fantasy or fabulous invention. The emotion indicated is rhetorical and literary. If a memorable dancer's performance has been accidentally attached to the skeleton of the choreography, it is good luck, just as if some good dressmaker may have incidentally clothed the dancers. The ideas behind most of the ballets of Diaghilev's Golden Age are comparable to the extra-illustrated *editions de luxe* of Pierre Louys or Anatole France, which French booksellers in Paris and Petersburg tricked out with water-color pornography. The basic ideas reflected the delicate vacuity of the taste and education of Leon Bakst, for the Golden Period was dominantly pictorial. Bakst appropriated the style of any historic epoch he capriciously chose—romanticized it without respect for its inherent historical meaning, and served his riflings piping hot with a terrific palette of tomato-red, chrome yellow and sapphire high-pressure paint-guns borrowed from the methods of the French Impressionists.

It was Nijinsky, in *Jeux* (1913) who first permitted a little material from immediate life to penetrate into the Russian Ballet. A young artist, he was then feeling his way. He used only three dancers because he wanted the action to be clear of group helter-skelter or Fokine's pageantry. He was trying out a new *kind* of gesture and a new *kind* of subject-matter. Its decorative frame was a tennis-game. Its emotion was the three-angled love and play that Noel Coward popularized twenty years later. Sport, chic, the playful surface physicality of the twentieth-century received here its initial apotheosis. *Jeux* itself was not a popular success, in spite of Debussy's beautiful orchestral partition. Yet here the Russian Ballet for the first time stopped being not only Russian, but what was far more serious, it threatened to cease being exotic. It commenced to be slightly human.

Not until Jean Cocteau and Pablo Picasso entered Diaghilev's cabinet in 1917 did the ballet become human again. In *Parade*, Satie and Massine, with ideas inherited from Guillaume Apollinaire and the Cubist painters, faced the choreography with American rag-time, the infantile world of the modern "child," the fantasy of Chaplin films and the three-ring circus. Later came a series of "modern" ballets: *Les Biches*, Bronislava Nijinska's delightful houseparty, *Le Train Bleu*, *La Pastorale*, *Les Matelots*, etc. Even in the Monte Carlo Company there was Massine's *Beach* (1933) for a couple of seasons, a late rehash of all the old sport material. But very soon the contemporary subject-matter lost any claims to a human treatment. Instead, it became as decorative and exotic as any other period piece, Versailles, Poushkin, or Persia. Only this new "period" was, perforce, the present. Massine's *Le Pas d'Acier* was Diaghilev's *hommage aux Soviets* by way of Prokoviev. It may have shown an aristocrat's good-will toward the new Russia, but it was not very deeply felt. The material was a second-hand treatment from the early Eisenstein and Pudovkin films. It had a certain brash energy on first sight but it did not survive.

Decorative treatment of dance-material developed a succulent technique of presentation. Persia was no longer revived by way of Bakst's extra-illustrations. Now a gifted painter like Picasso viewed an ancient Greece through his cubist spectacles; or he cast away cubism and saw Delphi through the decalcomania windows of a Paris suburb under the Third Republic, with overtones of Pompeii stencilled on the Rue de la Paix. This decorative attitude became a parlor-game of historical attribution. It served the dressmakers and fashion magazines well, because it had an immediate edible perfection of conglomerate taste which has always been and still persists as the strongest point of Russian Ballet.

Massine swung his attention on America in *Union Pacific*. He collaborated with an American poet and American designers—but his basic *ideas* were entirely decorative. He took over the material of building a transcontinental railway. It was surely epic, cinematic stuff, yet he cut it down to fit the familiar formula of Russian-ballet decoration. Any life his choreography had was in the vitality of its character-dancing. The dancers may have been costumed like children's picture-book Mexicans, Chinese coolies, Indians, or roving gamblers, but they danced nice Russian national dances, complete with Spanish arms, Hungarian feet and Russian boots. A decorative treatment of dancing ideas is of no use to us any longer. Audiences are too accustomed to the formula for further interest. It only attracts the surface eye which has already been surfeited.

During this season (1938-39) we will have a chance to inspect the works of a Russian ballet purged of the sinister coloration of Colonel de Basil. I do not think, however, there will be much alteration in its creative temperature. To be sure, we will get a chance at the ballets Fokine made some time ago for the René Blum troupe. Gluck's *Don Juan* contains considerable viscid pantomime in lush opera-house taste. Mozart's *L'Epreuve d'Amour* is one of the many pastiches which have been saved by the bell of André Derain's decorative taste. Massine gives us his latest symphony, now the Seventh of Beethoven, decor again by Bèrard, the whole thing rather *en série et sur commande*. Massine also produces his *Gaité Parisienne*, the last edition of *Le Beau Danube*, with his big character solo, this time clad in Peruvian dress. This is the same number we have loved since the Can-Can of *La Boutique Fantasque* (1919), the Mazurka of *Le Beau Danube* (1924), the Barman's dance of *Union Pacific* (1934), etc., etc. It is still a splendid number and it is proper that Massine should occasionally change its costume and scenery.

Bogatyri (Russian Heroes) to Borodin's symphony, has Gontcharova's decorations. Massine's story "is based on the brawling, fabulous heroes of Russian legend." All right, why not? As for *St. Francis (Visione Nobilissima)*, Hindemith's score and Tchelitchev's decor at least guarantees a provocative spectacle. The essence of Saint Francis might be a lovely point of departure for a vital lyric work. It will be interesting to discover whether or not Massine has created a human character and invented a mood, or has only designed decorative fragments from Byzantine or early North Italian painters. Lifar returns to New York in *Giselle*, his greatest rôle. Perhaps this reconstitution of the choreography will give us a clear museum headlight on the original romantic ballet for which *Les Sylphides* has been doing false service so long. His *Icare* with its much manifestoed percussion band, will hardly convince American audiences as a radical departure. Even before Mary Wigman came here, our "modernists" have been dancing to drum accompaniment for a decade.

No; I am afraid Massine's bigger and better Russian ballet is just the perennial *Ballet Russe*. One imagines working conditions may be happier, hence the morale of the troupe higher. But we want a new *idea;*

a new *use* of paint or music, a *feeling* in gesture you can't better derive from the actual paintings of Giotto, Constantin Guys, Christian Bèrard, or Genia Berman. Neo-Romanticism is as collapsed as cubism. A Byzantine style is no substitute. *Le Martyre de Saint Sebastian* happened in 1911, and d'Annunzio died last year. Yet the application of a decorative *style*, any style, is the only formula left for them. Russian-ballet is still interior-decoration. The style of the Russian ballet is still pre-war and there is not much satisfaction in the fact that it shies before a second rather than tags after the first World War.

It is not that theatrical decoration, scenery and costume must necessarily be cancelled out, or that the ballet will take suddenly to a bare stage, like the Mercury Theatre's *Julius Caesar*, or Jed Harris's *Our Town*. Not at all. Scenery and costume will find a new and more interesting use if they are the *frame* and not the *excuse* for the dancing. Every theatrical idea has a superficial skin and an essential heart. The Russians for the last three decades have been anything but heart-specialists. They cannot afford to be. They have capitalized on the fact that due to their voluntary or involuntary exile they have either broken hearts or no hearts at all. The Russian Ballet long ago lost contact with a home-base. Instead they have been serving up decorative skin-treatment of whatever temporary home-base might serve them for the moment. This is matter for sympathy rather than for blame, but it merely shows why we who live in one place musn't imitate them.

Literal transcription of factual notions, incident, gesture or movement, is not for the dance any more than is interior decoration, in whatever epoch's style. Literalism in ballet is perhaps further from the essential lyric truth than even superficial decoration. It is for us to find an essential lyric truth in contemporary gesture grounded on our ideas, by study, research, taste and also our instinct. I can't tell any choreographer what he should do, but perhaps I can illuminate the general problem by telling a few things I have myself seen done.

When we were planning to mount a ballet on an every-day subject, which finally turned out to be "Filling Station," we first of all searched for a basic fable that would already be familiar to most of our prospective audiences, on which we could make our own comment. We couldn't find one ready-made. We looked into Aesop and La Fontaine, trying to reclaim an old fable with modern implications. No use. We had to make the whole thing up ourselves. It wasn't as if we didn't know what our ballet was about. We did. It was about work, today. It couldn't be put in a factory, on an open road or on a farm, because we didn't have enough dancers to suggest a mass of workers. Work-gestures and movements which in themselves may be beautiful in contact with actual machinery, if taken away from the machines and transcribed into literal pantomime, seem affected or naive.

We chose as locale a gasoline Filling Station. It was both cross-roads and way-station. It would be a logical place in which work could be done and where different kinds of people could meet. The locale once chosen, the hero was naturally the Filling Station Attendant. His name was Mac. He was both presiding genius, master of ceremonies, and first classic dancer. The character of the Filling Station Attendant was described by the virtuosity of his opening variation. His acrobatic brilliance showed him capable of treating any emergency that might come up, with brilliant resourcefulness. He was the type of self-reliant, agreeable and frank American working-man. His dancing was styled to announce him as such. I had wanted him to be interrupted by two little girls who lived like stray cats around the Filling Station and who were friends of his, but as the composer Virgil Thomson pointed out, these two had no real logic. They were useless decoration. The two truck-drivers, Roy and Ray, however, were not. They would be normally passing along the highway by Mac's station. It would be a natural place to stop off and break their haul. Lew Christensen saw them as tumblers and described them as if they had been vaudeville knockabout-comedians. Paul Cadmus clothed them in the zipper-front jacket that mechanics always wear in the open, but instead of ordinary canvas or leather, the work-clothes underwent a theatricalization into velvet, silk lastex and cellophane. He stencilled handprints in grease and oil on their trousers, and stuck a lilac in Roy's cap. It was soon apparent that the truck-drivers had come in for a definite reason. They were seeking refuge from the State-Trooper who was chasing them for speeding. After his warning and speedy departure, a family of ordinary motorists arrived on a dismal waltz of domestic life. The Husband, a combination of Caspar Milquetoast and Mutt, just as the Truck Drivers were paired as Mutt and Jeff, had already asked his way. His Wife, in green-blonde hair, summer slacks and sinister green-celluloid visor, chivied her little girl, who was a nightmare twin of Shirley Temple or Little Orphan Annie. Her toe-work was indicated as the prize-number of a spoiled child's dancing-class graduation exercises. To these representatives of the proletariat and the middle-class were added the Rich Boy and the Rich Girl, a drunken couple dropped in from the nearby Country Club. The number that described them was a pie-eyed classic adagio gravely built on a ball-room rhumba. The ensuing group-dance was a sublimated Big Apple. The *pas d'action* was the chase of the gangster who held up the station, based on movie-serial hurry-up music. The processional at the end was a reprise of the rhumba, *We won't get Home until Morning,* and *Hail, Hail.* At the end, the Attendant, Mac, was left in his empty station, turning on the radio, spreading his tabloid across his knee, waiting for the next thing to happen.

So, lacking a modern myth, we made one up, and discovered that it was already in existence since everyone immediately recognized it. Any success we may have had was due as much to our method as to our material. The handling of both was by a complete collaboration of painter, choreographer and musician. Each was of the same imaginative generation and provenance. Each respected the spine of classic dancing which was our language. Each knew as well as his own name the comic-strip, the movies, the manners of highway and suburb on which the pantomimic gesture was founded. The field of these ideas was like particles of energy waiting to be polarized into a specific channel. It was hard to say afterwards which of us had which idea first. We put to conscious use a set of corresponding concepts based on a tradition of American social humor with the tradition of international theatrical dancing. The traditional classic dance was grafted on American character-dancing. It may sound, written out here, doctrinaire, arbitrary and formularized. The element of fun, for example, which is present in the dancing, can't be indicated in a description either of the ballet as performed or as it was in preparation.

All sorts of collaborations are open to American ballets of the future. These collaborations will not be a mere haphazard juxtaposition of a convenient composer, a fashionable designer with any given ballet-master. Every talent has its close correspondent in the parallel fields. Certain designers have an essential sympathy with certain ideas which are best furthered by treatment with a particular personal selection of a musical gift. And first and last, the idea at the root of it all must be worthy of the most exhausting collaboration into which it can be plunged. Very often the selection of an idea is only an accidental choice of a ballet-master. Perhaps, due to the combination in an ensuing collaboration, it turns out to be a success, but very often and perhaps in spite of collaboration, it is a failure. The ballet-master cannot be expected to know or do everything. His or her particular job is the arrangement of dance pattern and gesture on the basis of a previously chosen plot. In the late Diaghilev ballet and in the early days of the Monte Carlo Company, Boris Kochno was the gag-man. Much of the atmospheric strangeness of Balanchine's *Cotillon* (1932), for example, can be traced to his pungent poetic talent, a poetry of ideas verbally rather than scripturally transcribed into terms of dance by way of the choreographer, rather into terms of verse by a poet. Jean Cocteau had this valuable and elusive gift, and perhaps to a lesser degree, Jean Louis Vaudoyer, who was responsible for the original idea of Fokine's enchanting *pas de deux, Le Spectre de la Rose.*

The poet of the written word can easily serve the ballet-master, not only as author of a written scenario, a vocal sound-track or a program-note, but during the actual rehearsals and production of the ballet. That is, if the poet can think in terms of theatrical dancing. Some poets and painters have a genuine gift for visual imagery which can be almost immediately transcribed into ballet incident. We remember how Lumley, the Director of the Queen's Theatre in London, had commissioned a ballet-scenario from Heinrich Heine, on whose work Théophile Gautier had based *La Sylphide.* Heine worked with erudition and enthusiasm. He produced *Der Doktor Faust, Ein Tanzpoem.* It was, due to a variety of reasons, never produced. Heine wrote from Paris in 1851:

The ballet master regarded it as a dangerous novelty that for once a poet had actually composed the libretto of a ballet, whereas up to that time, such products had always been delivered by dancing monkeys mimicking the poet's craft, in collaboration with any worthy literary hack.

Personally, I should welcome a working arrangement with young English and American poets of our persuasions. W. B. Yeats has always been absorbed by dancing, and has conceived several plays for dancers. His verse abounds in dance imagery. Christopher Isherwood and W. H. Auden have shown, from their verse plays, a clear lyrical sense of realistic fantasy and fabulous truth. Auden's "Dance of Death" was dedicated to its first dancer. Among our own writers I think of two. Muriel Rukeyser, author of "Theory of Flight" and "U. S. 1" can be of value to classic dancing. James Agee, author of "Permit Me Voyage" and a remarkable movie-scenario, "The House," published in "New Letters in America: 1937," could vitally aid contemporary choreographers. Glenway Wescott has composed an ingenious scenario based on the life and works of Audubon, the great American naturalist, which is too elaborate for most American companies to undertake, but which could make a fortune for the Russians. E. E. Cummings' published ballet scenario "Tom," based on the Harriet Beecher Stowe novel, is already equipped with a score by David Diamond, the gifted young American composer. I could even imagine Pare Lorenz, the instigator of the two fine U. S. Government films, "The Plough That Broke the Plains" and "The River" turning his eye to classic dancing. Anyone can "write" a ballet-scenario. But it takes a genuine poetic vein to be of any use as a collaborator in the theatre. A poet must be patient enough to be educated by the choreographer, and willing enough to conform to the stress and strain of the collective method.

II. *AN ORGANIZED AUDIENCE*

As has been indicated in this pamphlet, there is much at odds in the contemporary condition of our theatrical-dancing. I have presupposed the fact that my readers are to some degree interested in setting these odds to rights. But what is to be done? What can a mere individual do in the face of economic monopoly and entrenched commercial management? Hasn't the general situation always been virtually the same? Doesn't everything (dancing included) get done in spite of, rather than by aid of everything (or anything) else? After all, isn't our job rather watching the ballet than worrying about it.

Nevertheless, I am assuming, because my future depends on it, as well as the professional lives and artistic futures of certain dancers to whom I am personally attached, that in every city in America with a population of fifty thousand, there are at least half a dozen people interested in the presentation of American ballet in America. If they felt the same way about it, these might add up to quite an energetic force. To them I address a series of tentative suggestions which would materially benefit the development of ballet in America, not on a visionary but on a purely immediate and realistic basis. First I will briefly list them, then submit a plan whereby these suggestions, or others more feasible, can be put into effect.

1. The definite *separation* of dance-attractions from music-attractions on the commercial dance- and music-managers' seasonal block-booking schedule. That is, instead of listing a ballet-company in the same general category as a violinist, soprano, or symphony orchestra, they must list a ballet-company with perhaps a solo national-dancer, a "modern" dancer, or another ballet-company. This might even involve the coöperation of two or more managers from different bureaus.

2. The creation of a definite provincial American *circuit* for dance-attractions as such. This would take a little money for publicity. But if the program were worked out with a trace of care a contrast, and even a sense of competition could be created, with half the attractions remaining as foreign artists or troupes, and half from the native product, such as, for example, Mr. Joseph Mann's series at the Washington Irving

High School, and Mr. William Kolodney's at the New York Y.M.H.A. has done successfully for several years. This might easily depend on

3. *An annual or semi-annual season* of the American Ballet Companies in at least three centrally located large cities such as New York, Chicago, or San Francisco, in order that the provincial press and local section-managers could make use of the prestige of the reviews from the larger centralized capitals. This might easily depend on

4. *Coöperation with local symphony orchestras.* This season (1938-39) the Ballet Russe de Monte Carlo is appearing with at least eleven of our largest American orchestral organizations. It will unquestionably take some convincing their conductors that our American repertory is as musically distinguished as the Russian, which it is, or that Americans dance as well as the Russians, which they do. There are very few top-rank native-born conductors. The acceptance of the American repertory, in turn, might depend on

5. *The Commissioning* of American Ballet orchestral scores under the auspices of a local sponsorship, and with the interest of a local orchestral conductor. The more progressive sub-divisions of the big broadcasting companies have recently paid a number of our younger composers to write pieces specially for broadcasting orchestras. It would be possible for Women's Clubs, Garden Clubs or other local cultural groups, under a direction suggested immediately below, to occupy themselves with awards not only for music, but also for decor and costumes. If an orchestral conductor felt that there was a considerable interest in these commissions among individuals and groups who more than likely were also actively interested in the maintenance of the orchestra, there would be a new incentive to perform the works.

1. *Postscript for Conductors of Symphony Orchestras*

Aside from the organization of the Philadelphia Orchestra, which has so splendidly coöperated with the Littlefield Ballet, as well as other visiting companies, there has not been a great deal of interest on the part of our American conductors to play with any dancers except the Russians. Perhaps they scarcely realize that the American companies can serve them, that they already have in orchestral partitions which can be played tomorrow, a standard repertory of considerable musical distinction, entirely apart from contemporary works which the various ballet companies have commissioned for their own uses.

In chronological order of composition here are some two dozen works with choreography by only half a dozen American companies which should interest many orchestras to play, and their publics to see. Indeed, quite a few of them are at the present time in their current orchestral repertory.

Bach: Miss Littlefield has made a ballet to the first two Brandenburg Concerti. Adolph Bolm has used Bach, as well. William Christensen's company dances to the B Minor Suite. The Ballet Caravan dances to the Goldberg Variations, orchestrally arranged for them by Nicolas Nabokoff, Professor of Music at Wells College, Aurora, New York, as well as composer of *Ode* for Diaghilev, and *Union Pacific* for the Monte Carlo.

Mozart: Both the Mordkin Company and the American Ballet use the suite of dances arranged by Tchaikovsky for small orchestra and known as *Mozartiana.* The Ballet Caravan dances *Encounter* to the "Haffner" Serenade. The Christensen Ballet uses *Eine Kleine Nachtmusik.*

Chopin: The Littlefield Ballet in *Moment Romantique,* employs a set of dances which would be a welcome change to hear after the eternal *Les Sylphides.* William Christensen has composed a *Chopinade.* The American Ballet uses the F Minor Piano Concerto, with choreography by William Dollar.

Schubert: The American Ballet's *Errante* is his *Wanderer* fantasy magnificently orchestrated by Charles Koechlin, the distinguished master of the Paris Conservatoire. Ruth Page's *Love Song* is a series of short pieces chosen for their dancing quality, arranged by Wesley la Violette.

Tchaikovsky: The Littlefield Ballet employs most of "The Sleeping Beauty," perhaps the most brilliant theatrical dance music ever written. William Christensen has mounted the "Romeo and Juliet" overture with great success. The American Ballet's *Serenade* (for strings) was frequently performed at the Metropolitan.

Ravel: Both Ruth Page and Catherine Littlefield have employed the *Bolero,* each quite differently. The Ballet Caravan dances to *Les Valses Nobles et Sentimentales,* brilliantly orchestrated by the composer.

Stravinsky: Ruth Page danced *L'Histoire d'un Soldat;* Catherine Littlefield and Adolph Bolm, *Apollon Musagète;* and the American Ballet to *Apollon, Le Baiser de la Fée* and *Jeux des Cartes.*

This is only a small choice from the far larger repertory contained in my appendix, but any conductor can see that several interesting programs could be constructed on this basis alone. It is not perhaps easy to conduct for ballet. There is always likely to be a confusion between the choreographer and the orchestral conductor over the tempi, particularly if the composer of the score is not present. A pure orchestral treatment differs slightly from a choreographic one. With a ballet company, the conductor descends from his customary elevated place on the podium, and the orchestra itself shares the interest with the dancers, rather than with the conductor alone. Certain theatrical effects are demanded which the composer may or may not have indicated, but these differences can be resolved with a little patience. Nevertheless, the appearance of a ballet company with a symphony orchestra is a sure way to interest a larger public in the purely musical activities of its local organization.

III. *AN ALLIANCE OF AMERICAN BALLETS*

The suggestions proposed above depend entirely on our ballet companies and their audiences being organized into some active entity which can make their wishes realized. At present there is no similar organization in the dance field except the tacit alliance of dance-manager for utilizing their publics, and the promise of *The Ballet Guild, Inc.*, with headquarters in New York City, which, employing the services of the "patrons" I have recently indicated, will back the interests of Russian companies in America.

If every American Ballet Company could join in a strong combination with each other, much might be gained. The field of foreign attractions, due to the world situation, gets smaller every day. The management monopolies will soon turn to us, but they will only turn at the very last moment. In the meantime we can sink or swim. I propose we swim together. I propose we continue to get along *in spite of* the monopolies as we have so far done, even should they make proposals to us, as they are now beginning to do. I propose that the American Ballet Companies pool their resources and set up *their own* independent management office, which will be entirely occupied with furthering their particular interests, by building a national circuit and stimulating a national audience.

Every native local company could find backing for such a scheme. In every city exchange performances could be arranged, exhibition of prints, paintings and programs could be held, a national bulletin could be issued, and a national dance archives established. If the American Ballet managements could be organized into one powerful agency, the critics might be more respectful or at least more open-minded, and the patrons might think twice as to the object of their patronage.

Our audience awaits us. An alliance of American Ballets should have close connections with lay organizations on a broad basis. Whatever this base, let it be democratic, realistic and creative. Let the patronage be directed toward good lyric theatre, and let our dancers have the liberty, incentive and security to do what they best can do, and alone can do, which is to dance well on our stages.

APPENDIX

THE REPERTORY OF THE PHILADELPHIA BALLET

All Choreography by CATHERINE LITTLEFIELD

BALLETS ON AMERICAN THEMES BY AMERICAN COMPOSERS

	Music	*Designer of Scenery*	*Designer of Costumes*	*Date First Performance (All World Premieres)*
*The Snow Queen	Murray Cutter	A. Jarin	P. T. Champs	Phila., Dec. 28, 1935
*Barn Dance	Folk tunes arranged by: John Powell, David Guion, L. M. Gottschalk	A. Pinto	S. Pinto	Phila., April 23, 1937
*Terminal	Herbert Kingsley	A. Pinto	S. Pinto	Paris, France, June 1, 1937
*Let the Righteous Be Glad	J. Donath (Arrangement of negro spirituals)	A. Pinto	S. Pinto	Phila., Dec. 13, 1937
*Parable in Blue	M. Gabowitz	George C. Jenkins	Lee Gainsborough	Phila., Dec. 22, 1937
*Ladies' Better Dresses	Herbert Kingsley	R. Starke	Joy Michael	Chicago, November, 1938
*Café Society	Ferdy Grofé	Carl Shaffer	Carl Shaffer	Chicago, November, 1938
*The Vacant Chair (*The Meschianza*)	Tibor Serly	(Not decided yet)	(Not decided yet)	Phila., March, 1939

*(Indicates the ballet is still in regular repertory)

BALLETS TO MUSIC OF FOREIGN COMPOSERS
(Philadelphia Ballet)

	Music	Designer of Scenery	Designer of Costumes	Date of 1st Performance
*Daphnis et Chloe (3 scenes)	M. Ravel	A. Jarin	J. Pascal	Phila., Mar. 31, 1936 (American premiere)
*The Sleeping Beauty (5 scenes)	Tchaikovsky	R. Deshays	Lee Gainsborough	Phila., Feb. 11, 1937 (American premiere)
*Bolero	M. Ravel	Lee Gainsborough	Lee Gainsborough	Phila., Aug. 3, 1936
*The Fairy Doll	J. Bayer	A. Jarin	P. T. Champs	Phila., Dec. 28, 1935
*Prince Igor (Polovetsian Dances)	Borodin	A. Jarin	(None)	Phila., Mar. 31, 1936
*Moment Romantique	F. Chopin	(None)	(None)	Phila., Aug. 3, 1936
*Viennese Waltz	J. Strauss	A. Jarin	P. T. Champs	Phila., May 13, 1936
*Classical Suite	J. S. Bach (Brandenberg Concerti, 1 and 2)	R. Deshays	P. T. Champs	Princeton, N. J., Nov. 6, 1937
*The Minstrel	Debussy (Menestrales)	A. Pinto	S. Pinto	Haverford, Pa., Oct. 25, 1935
*Poème	M. Ravel (Pavane)	(None)	(None)	Phila., Dec. 8, 1936
Aubade	F. Poulenc	R. Deshays	J. Pascal	Phila., Mar. 5, 1936
Fête Champêtre	Lully, Gretry & Rameau	A. Jarin	J. Pascal	Phila., Mar. 31, 1936
Romantic Variations	Saint Saens	(None)	J. Pascal	Phila., Dec. 8, 1936
The Prodigal Son	Cesar Franck	(None)	L. Galpern	Phila., Dec. 8, 1936
Home Life of the Gods	E. Satie (Mercure)	L. Galpern	L. Galpern	Phila., Dec. 8, 1936
*Fantasia	Johann Strauss (Perpetuum Mobile)	Mary Fales	Mary Fales	Chicago, November, 1938

THE REPERTORY OF THE RUTH PAGE BALLETS

All Choreography by Ruth Page

	Music	Designer	Auspices	First Performance
Frankie & Johnnie	Jerome Moross	Paul du Pont	Chicago Federal Theatre	June, 1938
American Pattern	Jerome Moross	Nicholas Remisoff	Chicago Opera	December, 1937
Americans in Paris	George Gershwin	Nicholas Remisoff	Cincinnati Opera	August, 1936
Love Song	Franz Schubert	Nicholas Remisoff	Chicago Opera	October, 1935
Hear Ye! Hear Ye!	Aaron Copland	Nicholas Remisoff	Chicago Opera	November, 1934
Gold Standard	Jacques Ibert	Nicholas Remisoff	Chicago Opera	November, 1934
La Guiablesse	William Grant Still	Nicholas Remisoff	Chicago (Century of Progress Exposition)	June, 1933
Iberian Monotone	Maurice Ravel	Nicholas Remisoff	Concert (Chicago)	April, 1932

THE REPERTORY OF THE BALLET CARAVAN

Ballets to Classic Music	*Music*	*Costumes*	*Choreographer*	*First Performance*
Encounter	W. A. Mozart ("Haffner" Serenade)	after J. G. von Schadow	Lew Christensen	Bennington, Vt., July, 1936
Harlequin for President	D. Scarlatti (Sonatas)	Keith Martin	Eugene Loring	Bennington, Vt., July, 1936
Folk Dance	Emmanuel Chabrier	Charles Rain	Douglas Coudy	Burlington, Vt., August, 1936
Promenade	M. Ravel (Valses Nobles et Sentimentales)	after Horace Vernet	William Dollar	Bennington, Vt., July, 1936
Variations	J. S. Bach (The Goldberg Variations)	Walter Gifford	William Dollar	Athens, Georgia, April, 1938
Ballets to American Music on Contemporary Themes				
Pocahontas	Elliott Carter, Jr.	Karl Free	Lew Christensen	Middlebury, Vt., August, 1936
Yankee-Clipper	Paul Bowles	Charles Rain	Eugene Loring	Saybrook, Conn., July, 1937
Show Piece	Robert McBride	Keith Martin	Erick Hawkins	Bar Harbor, Maine, August, 1937
Filling Station	Virgil Thomson	Paul Cadmus	Lew Christensen	Hartford, Conn., November, 1937
Billy the Kid	Aaron Copland	Jared French	Eugene Loring	Chicago, Ill., October, 1938
The Minotaur	Charles Naginski	Leslie Powell	Erick Hawkins	New York City, January, 1939

THE REPERTORY OF THE AMERICAN BALLET

All Choreography by GEORGE BALANCHINE

	Music	Costumes and Scenery	First Performance (All New York City)
Ballets to Classic Music			
Mozartiana	Mozart (Tchaikovsky)	Christian Bèrard	March, 1935
Serenade	Tchaikovsky (Serenade for Strings)	Jean Lurçat	March, 1935
Errante	Schubert (Koechlin)	Pavel Tchelitchev	March, 1935
Transcendance	Liszt (Mephisto Valse-Elegie)	Franklin Watkins	March, 1935
Reminiscence	Godard (Brant)	Sergei Soudeikine	March, 1935
The Bat	Johann Strauss (Fledermaus)	Keith Martin	February, 1936
Concerto	Chopin (F-Minor Piano Concerto)	(Practice-tunics)	March, 1936
Ballets to Contemporary Music			
Alma Mater	Kay Swift (Choreography by William Dollar)	John Held, Jr.	March, 1935
Dreams	George Antheil	André Derain	March, 1935
Apollon Musagète	Igor Stravinsky	Stewart Cheney	April, 1937
The Card Party	Igor Stravinsky	Irene Sharaff	April, 1937
The Fairy's Kiss	Igor Stravinsky	Alice Halicka	April, 1937
Opera Ballet			
Orpheus (complete)	Gluck	Pavel Tchelitchev	April, 1936

THE REPERTORY OF WILLIAM CHRISTENSEN

Choreographer of the San Francisco Opera Ballet

	Music	Costumes and Scenery	Auspices	First Performance
Ballets to Classic Music				
Chopinade	F. Chopin	J. C. Taylor		Seattle, Wash., July 28, 1935
Capriccio Espagnole	Rimsky-Korsakov (*Capriccio Espagnole*)	Harriette Meyers	Portland Symphony Orchestra	February, 1936
The Bartered Bride (*Three Dances*)	Smetana	J. C. Taylor	Portland Rose Festival	June 8, 1936
Coeur de Glace	W. A. Mozart (*Eine Kleine Nachtmusik*)	J. C. Taylor	Portland Symphony Orchestra	December, 1936
Sketches:				
Divertissement	Gounod	San Francisco Opera Company Costume Department	Santa Rosa Symphony	November 9, 1937
Rosamunde	Schubert			November 9, 1937
Dance Chinois	Tchaikovsky			November 9, 1937
Tarantella	Rossini-Resphigi			November 9, 1937
Romeo & Juliet	Tchaikovsky	Helen Green (Costumes) Armando Agnini (Scenery)	Sacramento Symphony	March 3, 1938
A Bach Suite	J. S. Bach (Suite No. 2: B-Minor)	Armando Agnini		San Francisco, Cal. April 20, 1938
In Vienna	Johann Strauss	Helen Green (Costumes) Armando Agnini (Scenery)		San Francisco, Cal., June 20, 1938
*A Midsummer Night's Dream	Mendelssohn	J. C. Taylor		Portland, Oregon, July, 1938
Ballets to Contemporary Music				
Rumanian Wedding	Georges Enesco (First Rhapsody)	J. C. Taylor	Portland Symphony Orchestra	February, 1936
Brides on Strike	Godfrey Turner			In Preparation

*Choreography of "A Midsummer Night's Dream" by Lew Christensen, with William Christensen's dancers.

II. GORDON CRAIG AND THE RUSSIAN BALLET

The great English stage designer Edward Gordon Craig, whose theatrical writing, suggestive designs and theatrical productions have so profoundly affected our "modern" theatre, was the only critic of eminence who, from the very start, held out against the Russian Ballet. In *The Mask* for October, 1911, was published an article signed by John Balance called "Kleptomania," on the Russian theatre. It was a cold-blooded analysis of the Russian dancing and stage decoration, and is unique in its realistic attitude. In 1937, I acquired through a London bookseller part of Craig's library. In a bound volume of the French illustrated theatrical revue *Commoedia Illustré*, for the early Russian Seasons of 1909 to 1914, Craig had written in pencil the following notes, ideas which were later organized in *The Mask* article. Anything from Craig's mind is of interest to the theatrical worker. These notes are doubly so from their historical and contemporary analysis. These penciled notes *were written in 1913.* There are later comments indicated.

1. (*In the front of the Volume.*)

1911 to 1913—Showing perhaps (better than) as well as, any other document exactly what was happening in the new movement as expressed by the following men and women:

Fokine, Nijinski, Karsavina, Mad. Fokina
Bakst, Roerich, Visconti*(?), Bolm
D'Annunzio (?), *Antoine*, Ida Rubenstein
Rheinhardt, Maria Carmi (Princess Matchabelli)
De Max
Jean Morax
Bernhardt (?), Tellegen.

(I question some of these as representing anything in the new movement. The names *italicized* are the principal figures.)

(Note how Meyerhold was overshadowed in these years—in Paris!)

E. G. C. 1935

Now we have at a glance more clear idea *how·much* of (and what class of thing) the new movement got into the great city of Paris.

We know that Isadora Duncan got in and left her mark but her presence was unable to prevent the pandemonium which a big city seems to crave for.

But there are some important people who did not go to Paris:

---

*Scenic designer: Designed decor for Fauré's opera *Penelope*, Monte Carlo. 1913.

Stanislavsky's company of actors
The Irish Players from Dublin
Dalcroze's company of dancers

Still, even all these as visitors would have amounted only to a passing fashion and made Parisians "rave" for a month or two.

But Appia, not a word of him, and he is the greatest scenic figure of the new movement. Of E. G. C. we do not hear either—not to be with D'Annunzio and Bakst in Paris is lucky. To be left with Appia and the others is a good sign.

This "new movement" amounts to nothing when you've considered carefully what (there) is in this volume.

Why nothing (?). I will tell you in two words.

It's a *new theatricalism* which the whole thing amounts to.
—a new falsity
—it is beliefless—

In this volume you can see what their method was.

They thought they could imitate so well as to deceive us into believing it was creation.

They went to see the Indian statue's pictures dancers and did an Indian affair.

They went to see the Egyptian statue's pictures dancers and did an Egyptian affair.

They went to see the Grecian statue's pictures dancers and did a Greek affair.

They went to see the Turkish statue's pictures dancers and did a Turkish affair.

They went to see the Italian statue's pictures dancers and did an (Italian) affair.

The list is as long as the list of nationalities.
They had no belief in themselves and in principles.
They put on and put off anyone elses' *belief*.
We will do it "like this" they said on Monday
We will do it "like that" they said on Tuesday

They could do it anyway.
They were not doubtful if they could manage it.
They were sure of themselves, very.
Very sure they could disguise anything.

How far were they successful(?)
They disguised everything and created nothing
We believe that is to have failed. (E.G.C.—May 1915.)

2. *Notes on illustrations in the text.*

On Bakst's costume design of Ida Rubenstein, martyred as Saint Sebastien. *Sickness.*

On Bakst's color sketches for Le Miracle de Saint Sebastien: *Compare photograph:*
All is lost.

Costume is not dress (but only) a cover. Costumes is that which uncovers the Soul.

The flesh and bones are the costume of the Soul. Reveal them then— without exposing that which is mute and must remain so. *E. G. C.*, 1911

On four photos (Bert) of Nijinsky and Karsavina in *Le Spectre de la Rose:*

These four photos are charming indeed and represent all that is best in the Russian Ballet.

And yet Karsavina seems to be the very essence of insincerity and of vanity of a dull kind.

—but Nijinsky!!!

On a photo of Vera Fokina:

Possibly the best brains of the group. Her fat hands and whole person well under control and does not make mistakes.

On a photo of a Dancer designed by Leon Bakst for the Paquin (dressmaking) Pavilion at the Exposition of Turin 1911:

The awful effects of following the footsteps of Isadora Duncan.

The mixing of art-dressmakers-royalty-naked ladies-dancing and prostitution.

If pleasant things each in their own place how unpleasant when mixed in this friendly fashion.

All for commerce!

This kind of thing it is which makes us hate and wage war on commercialism. And this is only the fringe.

On a cover in color of *Commoedia Illustré* for June 1, 1912, showing Karsavina and Bolm in costume for *"Thamar"*:

Senseless if you will consider for a moment.

On Nijinsky's costumes for *Le Dieu Bleu* (Bakst):

Compare this first with the Indian plate 30 in Coomeraswamy. (The Mirror of gesture) after with the photographs facing (Nijinsky photographed in the finished costume).*

On a color plate for the decor of *Le Dieu Bleu* (Bakst):

The worms on the twig are rather unconvincing.
(The sketch) Not a bit like the result achieved. I saw it in 1912.   E. G. C.

On photos of dancers in costumes for *Le Dieu Bleu:*

Some good dresses.

On the dancer Baranovitch II:

Stupid woman, good dress.

On sketches by Roerich for *Le Sacre du Printemps:*

Roerich is the best of the Russians as decorators of painted scenes and costumes.

On the description with illustrations of *La Pisanelle* or *La Mort Parfumée*, words by D'Annunzio (Italian), music by da Parma (Italian), decor and costumes by Bakst (Russian), dances by Fokine (Russian), musical direction by Inghelbrecht (German)

And interesting this series of pictures, for it shows how much or how little the great Meyerhold could do without his own theatre, his own company and his liberty.   E. G. C., 1915

On a review by Louis Delluc of *La Pisanelle* (20 June, 1913)
"Is there nothing about Meyerhold?"
(The review had mentioned all the collaborators except the director-in-chief.)

*Craig's intention was to show how little the dead photo resembled the highly stylized sketch.

280

3. *Notes by E. G. C. in* The Art of Nijinsky *by Geoffrey Whitworth (1913), with Gordon Craig's bookplate. Florence 1913.*
On a quotation from the article on Ballet published in the Encyclopedia Brittanica (1910 page 1).
Only in an atmosphere of *ceremony, courtesy and chivalry* can the dance maintain itself in perfection. Right. (Italics of E. G. C.)

Page 9: The young Nijinsky soon *began to manifest the character of genius.* (Italics of E. G. C.)
and later on he blazed them by deserting the ranks of the Russian Ballet in Diaghilev's personal direction.

Page 17 and 18:
Nor must we forget the liberating force which sprang from the art of Isadora Duncan, whose heroic practice has done far more than any precepts of philosophy to widen our ideas as *to the intellectual and spiritual possibilities of the dance.* (Italics E. G. C.)

Not that—Isadora Duncan has not dealt with the dance intellectually, nor spiritually—but personally. The age saw to that!

III. *A LETTER TO* TIME

Mr. Glenway Wescott, the distinguished American novelist, wrote the following letter to TIME Magazine, after reading their review of the American Ballet's production of *Orpheus* at the Metropolitan Opera House in the spring of 1936. The letter was printed, with cuts. It is here reprinted entire.

May 30, 1936

To the Editors of TIME.

SIRS,

Though in an unhappy mood of revolt against the press, I think I know a good job of disapprobation when I see one. TIME is to be complimented upon its brisk descriptive damning of Balanchine's *Orpheus and Eurydice.* Critics of the daily papers indulged in obscure epithets, and bigotted defence of what they term tradition, in the ferocious diehard manner. TIME's policy, I believe, is to report the response of the public to such a performance in the spirit in which it reports the performance, as news; not to give individual opinion of its writers. In this case it failed to note the existence of two camps, two mutually exclusive views of the future of opera and ballet in New York. I submit what follows as information rather than resentful protest.

The present *Orpheus,* the only original undertaking of the opera association this season, gave as much pleasure to a certain public as offense to the critics. Readers of the various commentary up to date, including Time's, could have had no inkling of this. Yet, attentive to the American Ballet's young reputation, and admiring Balanchine and Tchelitchew, we crowded the Metropolitan. By virtue of the strange new scenes and twentieth-century dances, I was more deeply moved by the ancient myth and 18th Century music than ever before. I know that some thirty or forty persons of my acquaintance also were not disappointed. To what extent the enthusiasts are in the minority, no one knows. Minority groups have in the past had powerful effect upon public taste in matters of art and entertainment. If our enthusiasm were to prove sufficiently contagious, the Metropolitan Opera Association would have to give us what we want, or fail. It seems to me that readers of Time should be reminded of this possibility.

Alas, the guardians of tradition are suspicious as well as skeptical. Many of those who are paid to give opinions of such things as performances at the opera house evidently believe that mere citizens who pay for their seats are less inclined to be sincere than themselves. Therefore, since I speak of myself as fairly representative of a group or class, perhaps I should somewhat identify or characterize myself as an opera-goer. I am indeed what of late has been called by an ugly new name, *balletomane.* However, I am one who has believed that the Russian school of dancing has had its day: which has made me dubious of the effort of the company directed by Balanchine. Incidentally, working with these young Americans, he has adapted his imagination to make the best use of their native beauties and aptitudes; and this *Orpheus* is the only ballet I can think of that Isadora Duncan would have approved whole-heartedly. Balanchine is a very great man, I think. If I were to make a list of the dozen most exciting and inspiring things I have seen in the theatre, three of his choreographic works would be on it: *Apollon Musagéte* (Stravinski) and *The Prodigal Son* (Prokofieff) and *Errante,* revived at the Metropolitan this season. But by this general admiration I am not at all disposed to admire all that he does; quite the contrary. *The Bat,* for example, bores me. Need I add that I am not in anyone's pay? I did not receive complimentary tickets for *Orpheus,* nor do I know anyone who did. Now may I repeat that it gave me greater satisfaction and interested me more than any other art-event of the past season? I saw it both times it was given. I hope it will be given again. And I should like to see developed at the Metropolitan a new type of operatic art, uninhibited, unconventional, as suggested by it. I know that many people are of my opinion. Nothing has been done, and there has not even been time, for the curiosity of a great many more, who never set foot in the opera house at present, to be aroused. And I understand that it needs new patronage.

Perhaps I should admit that I and my friends have no great pious respect for the Metropolitan as a high place of operatic tradition, a temple, an academy. We go there for pleasure, nothing else. Also we have all heard that its vaunted tradition is no longer profitable. In the recent film, *Mr. Deeds Goes to Town*, the hero, asked to be chairman of the board of directors of an opera house, and informed of the deficit that he is expected to make up, remarks that evidently it is time for them to try some new kind of show. It would seem so. The banal repetition of nineteenth-century works amid tumbledown scenery, with no attempt at novelty except the expensive importation of phenomenal foreign singers, at a loss to the owners of the building, who annually campaign for funds as if operatic entertainment were a charity, cannot go on forever.

We honestly believe that—with its obvious faults corrected, given rehearsals that could not be provided for out of the spring budget, sung to a simple English libretto, under livelier orchestral direction—Balanchine's *Orpheus* would be a fine and sufficiently popular addition to the regular repertory. If Mr. Johnson and the deficit-ridden board of directors pay attention to the tradition-ridden critics, or even to TIME's anonymous impressionist, it may now be given up as a bad job; the money spent, the experiment only half-made. Perhaps the future of such public art as opera here is hopeless. It sometimes seems that we are a conventional, provincial people: in awe of artistic reputation built up abroad; credulous, docile; pathetically respectful of aged opinion. There is defeatism in the mere faithfulness to tradition. Advertisement is expensive. We have no aggressively young critics. It is hard to see how art can flourish without some form of free publicity. The older generation wins with a sneer its fruitless victory; the younger loses with a sigh.

The New York *Times'* Mr. Downes characterizes this production as impudent and pretentious and meddlesome. *Cavalleria Rusticana* was also given that night: indifferently sung, with the usual academic posturing, in old musical-comedy costumes, in glaring lighting, against a brightly daubed backdrop; and Mr. Downes praised this as competent, conventional, and comforting. His choice of adjectives, and the contrast between the two productions, makes the issue very clear.

In respect to art, when there is real difference of taste and a new division of opinion, it is not easy to be impartial. I am happy to admit that I am not. Time's reporter, for instance, says that the dance of the three principals together at the end of the opera suggests "a Japanese tumbling act." No doubt this comparison was scornfully intended. Yet it might be read as a compliment. For to those of us who find classic operatic pantomime ludicrous and of waning significance, the acts of acrobats often seem very fine. No doubt inadvertently, Time has taken sides with the powerful old guard as against a merely potent young generation.

GLENWAY WESCOTT

BALLET ALPHABET

1939

BALLET ALPHABET

A PRIMER FOR LAYMEN BY

LINCOLN KIRSTEIN

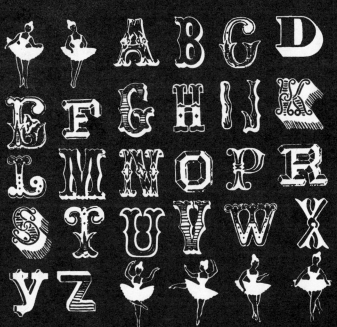

DRAWINGS BY PAUL CADMUS

FOREWORD

THIS book is intended to provide a foundation for the more common terms in the vocabulary of contemporary theatrical dancing. It is a practical reference work for laymen with few scholarly pretensions. While arranged in alphabetical order to be read piece-meal, it was conceived consecutively. Most readers will have some familiarity with the huge literature of the dance. For those who have not, the important definitions somehow manage to appear first, explaining and supplementing each other.

A general historical background is indicated, but space is too limited to render this either an encyclopedia or a biographical dictionary. Naturally, the opinions of a single author seem polemical when not strictly personal. The only polemics which may have crept in are the result of objective stage-experience, not of pedantic class-room prejudice.

The size of this book was limited by a desire to make it widely available. It is the author's intention one day to compile a more complete iconographic dictionary of the dance. As a visual art, its literature suffers grievously from having inadequate graphic representations for comparison. Ideally speaking, the only valid criticism of dancing would be motion-picture films taken from the dim past down into our own day. Lacking this, we must suffice with a few schematic diagrams.

The drawings by Paul Cadmus are generalized representations more to indicate the classic style than to serve as models for instruction. Absolute positions are only metaphysically absolute. Practically, they apply to the given bodies of particular dancers. These drawings seek an average, not alone of specific positions, but also of the various accepted academic canons and tastes.

Corrections, additions and suggestions for further headings in possible future editions would be appreciated.

LINCOLN KIRSTEIN

CONTENTS

	PAGE			PAGE
Academy	293	Grace		334
Adagio	296			
Air	299	Jeté		336
Allegro	300			
Arabesque	301	Lesson		336
Arms	302	Libretto		338
Assemblé	303			
Attitude	303	Maître de Ballet		339
		Mannerism		340
Balancé	304	Notation		341
Ballabile	304			
Ballerina	304	Opera-Ballet		344
Ballet	305	Opposition		346
Ballet-Blanc	307			
Balletomane	307	Pas		349
Ballon	307	Pirouette		350
Barre	310	Plié		352
Battement	310	Pointes		352
Batterie	310	Pose		354
		Positions		354
Cabriole	311			
Choreography	311	Relevé		357
Classic Ballet	311	Romantic-Ballet		357
Corps de Ballet	312	Rond de Jambes		358
Croisé	314			
		Tour en l'air		358
Dance	314	Turn-Out		359
Developpé	315	Tutu		360
Divertissement	315			
		Unions		361
Echappé	316			
Effacé	316	Variation		362
Elévation	317			
Enchainement	318	Youth		362
Entrechat	318			
Entrée	320			

Feet	322
Floor	323
Fouetté	323

| Gesture | 324 |

Illustrations

Plate 1.—between pages *307 and 310*

Plate 2.—facing page *320*

Plate 3.—facing page *332*

Plate 4.—facing page *346*

A

ACADEMY: school, method or body of instruction which is also a standard of ideal excellence and residual practice of an art or science. Academies of dancing in Western Europe owed their origin to renaissance revivals of antique Greek precedent. Poets, scholars and artists banding together for professional purposes established the Academy of Saint Cecilia in Paris (1570) and the Accademia della Crusca in Florence (1582), which investigated music, prosody, diction and classic metric. In 1661, an impoverished poet called Perrin received letters-patent from Colbert, Louis XIV's minister, granting him privilege to plan a French Academy of Music and Poetry, based on Italian models. In the same year, a group of dancing-masters requested and received permission to establish an authorized Academy for (preponderantly social) Dancing in the Louvre. These last two ideas were the direct source of the Italian composer, J. B. Lully's Académie Royale de Musique, in which dancing had an important function as an aid to productions of ballet-opera. The *maître de ballet*, Beauchamps, was its first director from 1671 to 1687. The French academy, expanding throughout the eighteenth century, became a model for the world persisting today as L'Académie Nationale de Musique et de la Danse.

Only a little later, under German influence, a theatrical school was founded in the Kremlin. The first Russian theatre was built in 1703. In 1735 the Empress Anna Ivanovna ordered all her infantry cadets to be taught dancing, and this was the origin of the great Petersburg-Leningrad Academy. The school at Moscow, which has suffered a certain snobbish criticism at the hands of the Petersburgeois as a home for acrobats and vulgarians, was not founded until 1809, yet at present, seems to have surpassed its ancient rival. Both schools were instructed by aliens for many years. The descendants of the Italian, French, and Scandinavian masters are responsible for the great dancers of our own day. Russian masters did not start to instruct their own pupils until around 1890.

There was always a ballet school in Stockholm in the eighteenth century, but when Rolf de Maré was organizing his Swedish Ballet in 1920, he was obliged to include dancers from other countries. The Royal Danish Academy boasts a more ancient tradition. Galeotti, a follower of Angiolini and Noverre, headed this school from 1775 to 1815. The Bournonville family, Antoine and Auguste, were in control, off and on, from 1816 to 1877. The great "romantic" ballerina, Lucille Grahm, was trained in Copenhagen, and there are many charming photographs of Danish dancers as Valkyrs in *tutus*.

Individual Milanese dancing-masters had been renowned since the fifteenth century and schools were established by 1640. However, the permanent Imperial Dancing Academy connected with the Scala Theatre was not opened until 1812 under the impressario Benedetto Ricci, although the Scala itself had opened in 1778, producing five ballets in its first season. Its greatest efflorescence came with the intendancy of Carlo Blasis from 1837 on, throughout the greater part of the century. The Italian Academy was responsible for the greatest influences of the nineteenth century classic dance, just as the French had been in the eighteenth, and Russians in our own day.

An academy is the life-blood of ballet. It economically provides all materials necessary for a mastery of technique. It holds the accumulation of residual information of generations of pedagogues and practicing artists. It develops early habits of discipline, providing in its complementary training, actual apprentice performances, the practical basis for a stage career. It establishes a standard for style, proficiency and instruction. Usually situated in a capital, it feeds the provinces.

An academy, to be worthy of the name, must provide a complete education for its students in all attendant fields, and its connection with a working theatre must be elastic and secure. In London, the Vic-Wells Opera and Ballet established a school in alliance with its theatre in 1933. America, as yet, has no real academy. Schools connected with our opera houses have the advantage of some stage-practice in however debased a form, but the instruction provided is only commensurate to the possibilities of production which are inferior, and the length of the seasons which are short. Academic standards in private schools are higher, but the results are difficult to gauge as few schools feed directly into permanent companies.

"The idea of an Academy is extremely important in the foundation of an national artistic tradition. In the beginning, a genuine aid and rallying point for creative energy, it often disintegrates into rigid bureaucracy. Then its standards are useful only insomuch as they precipitate against official rigidity, all youthful violence and ambition of talents, which usurping its authority, cause envy, contempt, and reform. A good academy is not by any means an anomaly, although recently there has not been much proof of this view."

In Paris, to become qualified, as a dancer at the Opéra, children start not much later than nine years. Students stay in the *classes supplementaires,* three years in the first and two in the second. At thirteen or fourteen they enter the *classes des quadrilles,* consisting of some fifteen boys and twenty girls. By yearly examinations the *corps de ballet* is chosen from the three groups.

At the present, the finest schools in the world are probably in Russia. Not only do they enjoy large state subsidy, economic security and work on a variety of stages, but also artists who are not suited for the large cities may find ready employment in numerous provincial theatres, not only as dancers but as teachers and choreographers. The Moscow State Choreographic Technicum is divided into the *Semeletka* (Preparatory High-School) and *Technicum* (University Technical Course). *Semeletka* is for seven years, *Technicum* for three. All courses are free at all times. Half the students qualify to receive pay as dancing-workers during the first or second year of instruction.

One hundred and ten persons are on the pedagogical staff, including eight instructors, in the various subjects, fifteen pianist accompanists, doctors, artists, costumers, etc. The Moscow State Academy is under the control of the Bolshoi Theatre, which is directly governed by the Central Commission of the All-Union Executive of the Socialist Soviet Republics.

In 1938, according to an article by W. G. Raffe in "The American Dancer" (September, 1939), 215 students were enrolled in the *Semeletka* and 20 in the *Technicum.* The elementary course has a large proportion of deserters who even go back to ordinary civil life, while the entrance to the technical course is extremely difficult.

Children from the age of nine are proposed by their parents or day-school instructors. All are annually examined by a special medical and psychological commission. There are seven courses, each of a year's duration in *Semeletka*. Eleven different subjects are taught in varying dispositions of time. The chief emphasis is naturally dance-practice, but languages, fine arts, anatomy, and history are also required. The standard and practical efficiency are equally very high.

In the *Technicum,* advanced students are taught as dancers and choreographers. Fencing, plastique, anatomy, piano, counterpoint and harmony are also mastered as well as political history, economic geography, art, literature, and Leninism. A trained dancer has an education equivalent of any other college-bred person, and the superior of almost any other stage artist in the world.

ADAGIO: From the Italian, *ad agio,* at ease or, at leisure. English teachers use *Adage,* the French adaptation, while Americans prefer the original Italian.

"A correct execution of an adagio is the *ne plus ultra* of our art; and I look on it as the touch-stone of the dancer." Carlo Blasis (1829).

1. Group name given to a series of ballet-exercises to slow music, calculated to develop sustaining power in a dancer, particularly by balance on one foot, and by held extensions of arms and legs.

2. Portions of a ballet in which girls perform, supported by male partners. The so-called "grand" adagio is the emotional climax of the classic dance, in which the ballerina, aided by her cavalier, achieves combinations of steps and positions of which she would be incapable alone. It was the function of the male partner of the early nineteenth century to display the ballerina to so great an advantage, even to effacing himself, that it resulted in his temporary disappearance from Western European stages from about 1845 until the Russians returned him in 1909. Even in the Grand Adagio of *Swan Lake* (Petipa: Ivanov, 1872), or *Aurora's Wedding* (Petipa: Sergeev, 1890-1921), the

male dancer is scarcely more than a mere *porteur*. He bears and braces. Yet even in such apparently insignificant rôles the male partner has his considerable theatrical responsibility. Much stage experience, as well as physical strength is demanded to carry a girl in those artificial leaps, by whose aid she seems to fly slowly over the stage at a single bound. A girl is often little enough aid, and either from ignorance or lack of consideration, frequently resists the man's upward thrust. Some good partners have an instinctive physical tact which enables them to gauge at once the girl's center of gravity. They know just where to hold, achieving an initial grasp without fumbling. Their grip has to be firm because they are holding, not solid flesh, but an exterior layer of costume which may slip in a shift of weight. Dancers, who, from habit or preference, have frequently danced together, come to have a sense of each other's physical presence, which translated into terms of dancing, is revealed to an audience as an exquisite mutual awareness or super-human courtesy. The big *adagio* of the classic Russian repertory may be considered as highly conventionalized love-scenes, in which the climax is not an actual embrace, but the most delicate support or adjustment of weight, which enables the ballerina to accomplish spectacular feats of sustained balance or elevation with the least *apparent* aid of her partner. The characteristic stage-gallantry of the male partner in adagio need not necessarily echo the feudal courtesies of European courts. Tenderness, playful solicitation, and a subtle, teasing flattery are the twentieth century equivalents for the devoted, dazzled, chivalric plume-sweeping behavior, of the nineteenth century *danseur noble*. Indeed, in certain Samoan tribes, the men sometimes make their gestures studiously clumsy and grotesque in order to accentuate a contrast with the fluidity of the woman dancers.

3. The term *Adagio* has been appropriated from the ballet stage by variety artists who perform acrobatic numbers. "Adagio" acts are sometimes strung on a series of dance steps, or consist of a team of tumblers who hurl themselves into the air to be caught by a partner or partners. Adagio dancers sometimes base their act on a dramatic pretext: a slave and her master, a snake charmer and his cobra, or the Moth and the Flame.

The man slings the girl by an arm or a leg in a series of vertiginous turns. The main difference between the Adagio dance of variety and the dancer of an Adagio in ballet is that the interest of the former is in a mechanical display for its own sake, while in the latter, acrobatic features merely enhance an expression of the dramatic relationship between the characters whom the dancers represent.

Supported Adagio of the ballet, as we see it today, did not come into existence until the last quarter of the eighteenth century, although men and women had appeared together professionally since the middle of the seventeenth. The ballet costume of the early eighteenth was a theatrical version of contemporary court-dress, except that both men and women wore higher heels, larger wigs, and fuller skirts. The stiff male skirt was called *tonnelet* (diminutive of the French *tonneau:* a cask), and while of knee-length was nevertheless calculated to immobilize the legs, even though it lent a kind of artificial monumentality to the figure as a whole. It was almost a physical impossibility for two wide-skirted dancers to clasp each other. Also, intimate physical contact did not suit the conventions of divinity with which the tradition of Court-Ballet endowed their chief protagonists.

Reforms in costume suggested by Noverre long before 1760, and only accomplished by the French Revolution, as well as the popularity of the waltz as a theatrical form borrowed from the ball-room (ca. 1800), laid the ground-work for our contemporary classic adagio. The waltz replaced the minuet, and other mincing or deliberate court-dances, for it involved rapidly moving couples more or less engaged in each other's arms. Weber's apotheosis of the Waltz,—the famous "Invitation to the Dance" (1815), has served for Fokine's inspired *pas de deux—Le Spectre de la Rose* (1910). *Spectre* is scarcely the conventional supported adagio but in the development of the genre, the more deliberate and dramatic duets, such as in *Swan Lake* (Petipa: Ivanov: 1872), could scarcely have come into existence without the presence of a more active idiom supported by such a swinging waltz.

A considerable impetus must have been given the department of Adagio by the tours of famous dancing couples in the first third of the last century, though the dances executed were by no means all in slow time. A man and a woman was about the smallest touring unit around which a local *corps de ballet* could be rehearsed. The visiting pair, in all probability, had their own numbers which were offered purely as *divertissements*, or which might be adapted for insertion into a given dramatic repertory. The great Italian choreographer, Salvatore Vigano (1769-1821) traveled all over Europe with his wife, Maria Medina. The Neapolitan ballerina, Brugnoli (whose fiery execution was to influence Fanny Elssler), and her partner, Samingo; the French duo—M. Albert and Mlle. Heberlé, were followed later by Paul and Marie Taglioni, Perrot and Grisi, Cerrito and Saint-Léon.

Marie Taglioni's brother married a German dancer, Amélie Galster. They made their American debut in *La Sylphide* (F. Taglioni: 1832) in New York City in 1839. In our own day, our parents still recall the wonderful partnership of Pavlova and Mordkin in their *Autumn Bacchanal* (Fokine: ca. 1914). Every such personal collaboration unquestionably added new means of handling, balance, innovations in support and greater freedom in the purely danced sections of Adagio. Outstanding examples in our contemporary repertory are the variation of Apollo and Terpsichore (*Apollon Musagète:* Balanchine: 1927-37) and the meeting of Saint Francis with the Lady Poverty (*Nobilissima Visione:* Massine, 1938).

In the preface to "The Dance of Life" Havelock Ellis, who understood all dancing perhaps better than any other Englishman, apologized for his slowness in writing. He quoted the sculptor Rodin: "Slowness is Beauty." "Certainly it is the slowest dances that have been to me the most beautiful to see, while in the dance of life, the achievement of a civilization in beauty seems to be inversely to the rapidity of its pace."

AIR: While the dancer's natural element is always air, a specific reference to the aerial sphere suggests that the movement executed, to a greater part, is off the surface of the floor. Conquest of aerial space is our dancers' most spectacular problem. They have at their disposal a whole vocabulary of movement, *la danse d'élévation,* which applies to it; leaps, battery, *tours en l'air,* etc., symbolic testimony of the triumph over space.

From the earliest study of dancing as a science or conscious accomplishment, the two divisions of earth (floor) and air (*terre* and *air*) have been established. Guglielmo Ebreo, the Jewish dancing-master of Pesaro (ca. 1430-1500), called the third and fourth of his prerequisites, *Partire del terreno* and *Aiere.* A contemporary, Antonio Cornazano of Piacenza, refers to the former as *Compartimento di Terreno.* By this we understand the dancer's estimation of the limits of his floor. *Aiere* identifies the quality of dexterity or lightness as well as the rising and falling of his body. Dr. Otto Kinkeldey of Cornell, who is responsible for our knowledge of these matters, tells us the words *elevato movimento* and *dolcie et umanissimo relevamento* explain *aiere.* Here at last is the suggestion of elevation and even a hint of the classic ballet exercise, the *relevé,* which is so important as ground-work for the attack on space.

Thoinot Arbeau, the orchesographer (1588), reaffirmed the categorical distinction between the *basse danse,* in which feet were kept close to the floor, and the more active *haute danse.* Throughout the eighteenth century there was a gradual theatrical conquest of air paralleled in the field of science by the development of lighter-than-air craft. Indeed, the balloon ascension of Montgolfier (1783), with its ornamented sphere, and ceremonial inauguration, had elements of spectacle in it, and was the subject of a ballet by von Starzer and Asplmayr in Frankfurt a.M. during the same year.

The *danseur d'élévation* or aerialist has always captivated the public. It is Nijinsky's conquest of air (ca. 1910) that is recalled, not his individual characterizations or his choreographic innovations. He was compared to a bird, but arms are not wings, and the flight of a man is not aided by air pressure, but succeeds in spite of it.

ALLEGRO: A term encompassing all lively movement, or that portion of ballet-exercises in which such movements are stressed. The study of *allegro* is the foundation of a brilliant rapid manipulation of the body, particularly the feet. The most essential attendant quality is that of *ballon.*

ARABESQUE (see plate 2): A pose of the classic theatrical dance, taking its name from a style of renaissance leaflike ornament, in which the dancer's body is supported on one foot either straight (*tendu*) or half-bent (*demi-plié*) with the other in the air, extended at right angles to it, and the arms composed to further a harmonious horizontality, creating the longest possible line from toes to finger tips.

Marie Taglioni (1804-1884), the great sylphe of the nineteenth century, was noted for the purity of her *Arabesque,* which gave momentarily static impressions of her hanging in mid-flight. In our own day Anna Pavlova, in her extension on toe-point, supported the pose for what seemed an extraordinarily long time. When an *Arabesque* comes as a sudden colon, or semicolon in an *enchainement,* the dancer appears to be resting on a crest of motion or music, and is propelled in the minds of the audience off in further imagined flight. A feeling of effortless suspension can be gained by a dancer's final *Arabesque,* posed at the end of a variation, just before quitting the scene, a finality rendered breathlessly infinite.

Although Compan's Dictionary (1787) does not include a definition, the *Arabesque* is a more or less "natural" dance position and can be found in various approximations of contemporary academic correctness throughout the long history of dance iconography. In the twenty-fourth plate of Lambranzi's "New and Curious School of Theatrical Dancing" (1716), Scaramouche is revealed at the rise of the curtain, as a statue on a pedestal *en arabesque* more or less *plié,* and three plates on, very *tendu.*

The etymology of the term itself is derived by association through a genre of architectural decoration, to the Moors. Carlo Blasis (1829) writes "Nothing can be more agreeable to the eye than those charming positions which we call *Arabesques,* and which we have derived from antique basso relievos, from a few fragments of Greek paintings and from the paintings in fresco at the Vatican, executed after the beautiful designs of Raphael.

"*Arabica ornamenta,* as a term in painting means those ornaments, composed of plants, shrubs, light branches and flowers, with which the artist adorns pictures, compartments, frises, panels. The taste for this sort of an ornament was brought to us by the Moors and Arabs."

In "Letters on Dancing," by E. A. Théleur (1832), an interesting book, not sufficiently well known, there is this note: "I have not succeeded in discovering the authentic origin of the *arabesque* attitudes, but am inclined to think we borrow them from the Spaniards, who for the most part do their steps with the same arm and foot. They, I conjecture, copied them from the Moors who, in the eleventh century infested this country: this leads me to suppose that they derive their origin from the Arabians, and are thence called *arabesques*."

But Carlo Blasis, as usual, is probably right.

ARMS (see plate 4): Arms give meaning and emphasis to head and upper body. Yet few dancers possess "naturally beautiful" arms. By "naturally beautiful" is meant the capacity to instinctively establish a gracious angle of the arms in relation to the position of head and shoulders, this angle to be taken and locked without tentative readjustment. If an arm comes too close to the head, the space between tends to diminish, if seen from a distance, and the expressive separation of head and arm is lost in a confusing identity. The arm, of course, controls manual gesture, but it must be considered as a whole, not as a mere shaft onto which an expressive hand is attached. The upper arm and forearm are naturally broken by the elbow joint. In the pure classic dance, but not in character-dancing or "modern" plastique, this completely destroys its grand style.

Although there are traditional established *positions* for the arms, their designed movement or carriage (*ports de bras*) is only rigid in its adherence to a gracious or open style, and exercises achieving it are never arbitrary, but at the discretion of individual teachers. It is as true today as in 1760 when J. G. Noverre wrote that "The *port de bras* must be varied as the different sentiments which dancing can express; set rules become almost useless; they must be broken and set aside at each moment, or by following them exactly, the *port de bras* will be opposed to the movements of the soul, which cannot be limited to a fixed number of gestures."

The position, opposition and carriage of the arms are perhaps the three most difficult things in dancing, as Carlo Blasis understood in 1829. "Few artists distinguish themselves by a good style of action in their arms, which deficiency generally proceeds either from the mediocrity of principle they receive from bad instructions or else it originates in their own negligence, believing as I have known many to do, that if they possess a brilliant mode of execution in their legs, they can do very well without the fine additional ornament of the arms. . . . When the arms accompany each movement of the body with exactitude, they may be compared to the frame that sets off a picture. . . . Take care to make your arms so encircling that the points of your elbows may be imperceptible. Beware lest they be jerked by the action and reaction of your legs."

ASSEMBLE: From the French for together. A step in which the feet are brought together, frequently finishing an *enchainement* of other steps. The *assemblé* is a kind of colon, semi-colon or period to a choreographic phrase. It serves to reunite after movement, the two feet, together, side by side.

ATTITUDE (see plate 3): From the Italian *attitudine,* a manner of holding the body.

This position was first demonstrated graphically by Carlo Blasis (Milan: 1820), who claimed he had invented a new dancing position from the famous renaissance bronze of the Flying Mercury by Giovanni da Bologna (1524-1608).

"On one occasion, performing the part of Mercury, I took, as I turned in my pirouette, the attitude of the statue of Mercury by J. Bologne. This fine position is very difficult to stand in. Unless a dancer is naturally arched he never can do it well, and the pirouette (*en attitude*) loses its effect. The body must lean forward, and the right arm develope (*sic*) itself almost entirely. The leg that is in attitude must be bent, and by its motion accompany the rounding contour of the position of the body. To render this attitude yet more graceful let the dancer stretch out his left arm, in which the *caduceus* is held; this takes off the angle at the elbows that it would otherwise present, and gives the pirouette much more elegance."

In a portrait by Jean Raoux in the Museum at Tours, Mlle.

Prévost is shown as a Bacchante, her outstretched arm holding grapes, on half toe, *en attitude*. It was she, who with Balon, mimed and danced *Les Horaces* for the Duchesse du Maine in the fêtes at Sceaux in 1708.

B

BALANCE: The *pas balancé* of eighteenth century social-dancing has come down in our ordinary class-room usage to be simply, *balancé*. It is an alternation of balance, or slight rocking from one foot to the other, usually in the same place.

BALLABILE: A group evolution of dancers usually employed as the end of a scene or grand finale of a ballet, in which members of the whole company lose their individual identities and are swept into mass formations. The term is derived from the Italian *ballare*, to dance. The plural is *ballabili* and was used, though not invented, by Carlo Blasis before 1830.

BALLERINA: Originally an Italian word meaning girl-dancer. It has come to signify in every western tongue an outstanding female soloist in a traveling company, a ranking principal in an opera-house, as well as a symbol for the whole art of classic dancing. There have been famous soloists ever since the foundation of Lully's Opéra (ca. 1670). A ballerina is created first by her own impetus and talent and is then fostered by commercial management which always needs prominent individuals on whom to focus publicity. It is necessary to canalize the generalized curiosity of the public to some degree with single personalities in a company. The ballerina is usually a not unwilling proxy. It is assumed that for these purposes she is more beautiful, more technically capable, and more exciting than any one else in the troupe. The possession of these qualities is frequently a myth, which can be upheld for a sufficient time to permit publicity to consolidate her official status. A ballerina with looks and *authority* need do little but appear.

The two greatest examples of the ballerina are Taglioni (active 1825-1840) and Pavlova (active 1909-1929). They resembled each other in their mineral remoteness, general ethereal super-human atmosphere and weakness in character rôles. They both dictated the dancing styles of their epoch, and both survived the efforts of choreographers to transform their individual personalities into expressions of dramatic power. Rival ballerinas gain reputations by specializing strictly in a chosen style. Taglioni was challenged by the fiery Elssler, who on occasion dared attack her faery rôles to suffer a prejudged failure at the hands of Taglioni hierophants.

It is said that a ballerina is born, and like a princess, can never rise from the ranks. Yet every mother assumes her dancing daughter is bred for it, and it is true that a child appearing as a prodigy has some advantage. This can be maintained only by discipline and judicious training which in our day of short-term commercial investment is more difficult than when Imperial subsidy established permanent theatrical security. Yet Alexandra Danilova, perhaps the most accomplished of Russian dancers today, while well known in the late Diaghilev repertory (1925-29), has only recently in the years of full maturity elevated herself into the rôle of a preëminent ballerina. She has gained this indisputable position by an accumulation of stage-experience so that in every successive season she appears more brilliant, sensitive and interesting. The careers of child-stars are frequently brief, and are in fact an extended decadence.

BALLET: From the Italian *ballare,* to dance.

Ballate were songs to accompany dancing in Tuscany of the thirteenth and fourteenth centuries. Not only minor poets, but even Dante and Boccaccio composed them. Later, in the high-renaissance, the Medici princes themselves wrote *canzon a ballo,* or dance-songs. *Balleti* is the diminutive, hence *ballet.* Dance-songs gradually acquired theatrical characteristics and so it is not surprising that when the Medici went to Paris in the middle of the sixteenth century, they took not only dancing-masters, but the term with them as well. The English *Ballet* (with a hard final *t*) refers to a short, rhythmical song, distinguished by Gastoldi and Thomas Morely (ca. 1590). The word *Ballad* is a cognate. Dr. Samuel Johnson stated in 1755 that a ballet is "an historical dance." Elsewhere he says, "History is a narration of fact."

Generally speaking, a *ballet* is a theatrical representation achieved through terms of dancing. Father Menestrier, writing in 1682, made this differentiation in speaking of certain Egyptian and Greek forms, "I refer to these dances as Ballet, because they are not simple dances like any other, but rather *ingenious representations,*" that is, dancing consciously contrived as spectacle.

Mark Perugini, the interesting author of "A Pageant of Dance and Ballet" (1935), makes his own definition which can stand for our time: "A ballet is a series of solo and concerted dances with mimetic actions accompanied by music and scenic accessories, all expressive of a poetic idea or series of ideas, or a dramatic story, provided by an author or choreographer."

What is commonly accepted as the first ballet in our understanding of the word is, *Le Ballet Comique de la Reine* (1581). In an introduction, its author, an Italian in the train of Catherine de Medici named Baltasarini, stated that "a ballet was a *geometric combination* of several persons dancing together."

John Weaver, in his "Essay Towards a History of Dancing" (1721), divided "Theatrical or Opera" dancing into three types, "the *serious,* the *grotesque,* the *scenical.* Serious dancing differs from the Common dancing usually taught in schools as Painting (House-painting) differs from Limning (Portraiture). For as the common dancing has a peculiar softness which would hardly be perceivable on the stage, so stage-dancing would have a rough and ridiculous air in a room when on the stage it would appear soft and delightful."

The Encyclopedia of Diderot and d'Alembert (ca. 1772) tells us that "Ballet is action explained by a dance." It goes on to trace the origin of dancing, repeating all earlier errors and confirming the confusion that persists into our own day that dance and ballet are identical. However, if we understand that the dancing is specifically *theatrical, spectacular* and done *to be seen,* the subsequent definition, probably by Cahusac, explains the eighteenth century conception. "A ballet is a picture, or, rather a series of pictures linked together by the action which makes the subject of the ballet. The stage is, as it were, the canvas on which the composer (choreographer) renders his ideas, the choice of music, scenery and costumes are his colors; the choreographer is the painter." All action, however, is not dancing, and in recent years, the most important developments in ballet have been to transform mimed action or pantomime into dramatic dancing, eliminating dumb-show and elevating the ballet into an independent art form, completely expressive in its own terms.

BALLET-BLANC: A ballet whose girls are clad in white tarletan. Generally speaking this refers to contemporary ballets like *Les Sylphides* (Fokine: 1909), the various *Chopinianas*, in which the "Romantic" atmosphere of the epoch of Marie Taglioni (ca. 1830) is revived by eliminating male dancers save a single soloist, and equipping the ballerina and *corps de ballet* in long gauze skirts, satin bodice and butterly wings which Eugène Lami first provided for *La Sylphide* (P. Taglioni: 1830).

BALLETOMANE: Franco-Russian term. Literally, a ballet-maniac or enthusiast for theatrical dancing.

"In Imperial Russia," writes Rayner Heppenstall, a distinguished British sympathizer, "Balletomania was by way of being a definite polite career, alternative to the Army and Navy or Diplomacy. Such and such an emigré, wishing to account for his social worth, will tell you that his father was a great general, a great statesman or indifferently a great balletomane."

It is generally considered that rabid public balletomania is not so much the fault of the art as of the class of society whose idleness or frustrations affords them hysterical compensation. There is no doubt, however, that the consistent apparition of the maniacs at ballet performances tends to prejudice many laymen against dancing, who ignorantly identify it with such flagrant approbation.

BALLON: The dancer's balloon-like quality of lightness or bounciness; the suave rise and fall of knees and feet in a sequence of steps. *La danse ballonné* is a genre based on leaps and broad movements, in which considerable air and floor-space is covered. Marie Taglioni (1804-1884) was the exemplification of this style for her epoch. André Levinson, with the precocity of his unique precision, defines it as the *"legato* of

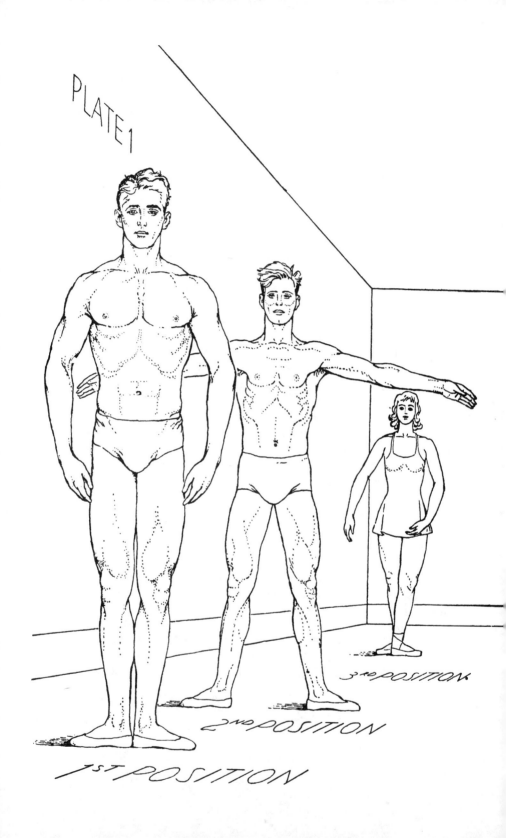

PLATE 1

3RD POSITION

2ND POSITION

1ST POSITION

4TH POSITION

4TH POSITION

5TH POSITION

great *paraboli* described in the air to a waltz movement, or the slow advancing of *developpées* in *adagio,* sustained by the singing of the (violinist's) bow." Carlo Blasis said in 1830: "Observe the *ballon:* nothing can be more delightful than to see you bouncing with graceful elasticity in your steps, scarcely touching the ground and seeming at every movement on the point of flying into the air."

BARRE (see plate 3): The bar, usually of wood, fixed opposite mirrors along the walls of ballet-practice rooms which students use in the first part of their daily lesson. This bar enables them to perform certain exercises with a maximum correctness, removing the need for sustained, unsupported balance. The bar thus provides an ideal criticism of faults, as well as aiding a weak dancer to become stronger.

BATTEMENT: Beating is the action of the extended or bent leg. There are *grands battements,* the straight lift of the leg to front, side and back which is a preparation for leaps. The *petits battements* are *battements degagés, frappés, relevés* or *tendus,*—separate or disengaged, full out from the knee, struck, raised on half-toe, or extended from a *plié.*

BATTERIE: "Generic term applied to all movements in which the feet beat together or one foot beats against the other. *Batterie* is divided into *grande batterie;* large battery; and *petite batterie;* small battery, according to the elevation, large or small. For instance: a *cabriole* is an example of *grande batterie* and *entrechat quatre* is an example of *petite batterie.*"
Cyril Beaumont's definition in his Franco-Italian Dictionary of classic dance terms (1931) can scarcely be improved.
A familiar demonstration of *batterie* is the sequence of *brisé volés* in the male section of the "Blue Bird" variation in *Aurora's Wedding* (Petipa: 1890). The *pas brisé volé* means the breaking step in flight. The swinging of the body in air from side to side suggests in the "Blue Bird" actual flying. Marie Taglioni (1804-1884) executed a new type of *brisé volé* in *La Sylphide* (P. Taglioni: 1830), which was later widely imitated and incorporated into classic idiom.

310

C

CABRIOLE: Derived from the Italian *capriola:* caper or goatish jump. In the seventeenth century, it referred to numerous jumps. It is now particularized. The dancer, raised off the floor while jumping, beats one foot against the extended length of the other. It can be executed to the side, back and front, while in each case the dancer's head faces the public to avoid an oblique angle, which would tend to diminish the full effect of the jump, although the actual visage may turn to the focus of action indicated by the dramatic expression of a given ballet.

CHOREOGRAPHY: Choregraphy, or as it is written today, choreography, meant in the time of its invention as a dance term (ca. 1700), the notation or stenographic record of dance steps. By corruption and association it has come to signify the design by a dance composer of dance patterns which comprise ballets.

It is the most important division of stage-dancing, since it regulates all that the dancers do. Its science is difficult to acquire and its practice, rare. There may be a hundred good dancers to a generation, and but half a dozen choreographers.

As in other arts, there are different levels of creation: choreography may be interpretative or decorative, or more importantly, inventive and creative. To "interpret" or illustrate music, or to decorate a stage with period revivals, however charming, is less interesting than the creation of lyric drama where dancing may not necessarily be a sole end in itself, but where it can be preëminently an arrangement of ideas particularly suitable to expression in dance terms.

CLASSIC BALLET: The classic dance is not merely a department of theatrical-dancing opposed to the "romantic," but rather a central line, or governing attitude which links the *purest* developments in traditional stage practice, whatever the epoch. To be sure, purity is comparative. In the vocabulary of step and gesture accumulated over the last five hundred years, there have been many "impure" influences, affecting the idiom from individual personalities, from exotic or national dances, from circus, music-hall and ball-room. But in the large residual body of expression, there is a basic-speech, founded on the five absolute *positions,* which demonstrate the human body on the stage in its grandest development by activity which is possible only in terms of dance, without reference to mimetic or associative gesture. As the residual information of medical practice is *materia medica,*—so in dancing it is *materia choreographica.* Its basic kinetic speech praises the body as free agent in air whose broadest extensions or highest leaps are its extreme lyric definition. The classic style is clean and open, grandiose without affectation, noble without pretension. Any idiosyncratic comment on it appears as offensive mannerism, which, however charming in a character-dance, destroys the linear purity of classicism.

"Classicism," wrote André Levinson, speaking of the ballerina Trefilova (ca. 1929), "tends towards geometric formula, but at the supreme moment, breaks and avoids it." Experiments in optics show that the line of least visual resistance is not necessarily the shortest distance between two points, but rather a long, easy curve which the eye may pursue with a gentle flow. This extended line is the property of every classic ballet position from *arabesque* and *attitude* to the more freely plastic *ports de bras.*

The classic dance may be rapid, but never brusque, jagged or broken. The classic line is sustained, serene and melodic, whose mercurial grace never disturbs its formal consistency unless it is dissolved on the metallic surface of technical incompetence or instinctive bad taste.

CORPS DE BALLET: A group of dancers used as chorus to project principal artists and to contrast by their mass evolutions, individual variations of soloists. In the classic repertory at least twice as many girls as boys are required and the men, except for their rôle of *porteurs* (in support), are usually restricted to the activity of the *premiers danseurs.* Although there is no fixed rule, even in our contemporary repertory, a general critical convention ignores the *corps de ballet.* It is snobbishly assumed they are ragged, badly trained, old, tired, partly as superficial proof of familiarity with the working mechanism of the profession, and partly because the *corps* of most traveling companies are too hard worked and under-rehearsed to be impressive.

In the subsidized state theatres, a formal hierarchy was recognized as iron-bound as the ranks of a peerage. The dancers farthest from the public performed their tasks almost anonymously, *près de l'eau* (near the fountain), since a jet of water was the familiar property of ballet back-drops. In Paris (ca. 1930) the company comprised forty *quadrilles*, twenty *coryphées*, seventeen *petits sujets*, sixteen *grands sujets*, three *premières danseuses*, three or four *étoiles*, and five *mimes*. The men were eighteen *messieurs du ballet*, three *premiers sujets*, three *grands sujets*, two *premier danseurs*, and four *mimes*.

Do soloists in large companies emerge from a *corps de ballet?* Infrequently. Soloists are usually "discovered" in school and elevated at once to positions of preëminence. To be sure, token emergence may occasionally prove that merit is rewarded. A *corps de ballet* somehow is usually a richer proving ground for boys and for girls.

A fair technical equipment is a prerequisite for a member of a *corps;* talent is not demanded, though experience may be gained. An ambitious chorus-member is a continual embarrassment to stage-managers, and a threat to principals. The work is no harder than in other jobs, and in large companies, at least, it has the advantage of a certain monotonous security.

Recently, particularly in the work of Diaghilev's choreographers, there has arisen the problem of the dissolution of the chorus, or at least the democratization of the *corps de ballet.* That is, drilled regimentation in the older repertory has been abandoned for a more broken background pattern. This naturally puts more responsibility for expression on individuals in the *corps.* The more disintegrated or specialized the choreographer, the greater the necessity for having a calibre of dancers who consider themselves more in the nature of soloists than of hacks.

The notion of having a troupe consisting entirely of soloists is a pleasant and democratic one. If it can be accomplished in practice without having the most advertised dancers desert, it may result in a competitive hysteria which even strong disciplinary measures will fail to correct. A horse once raced always wants to run. The fight back-stage is so bitter that the slightest chance to grasp a straw of prestige is not easily ceded, and a choreographer is faced with having ordinary dancers either refuse to learn certain rôles or else give so little coöperation that they may be almost useless.

CROISE (see plate 4): From the French *croiser,* to cross. A position of the body in which the dancer faces the body obliquely to the audience. The term also is used in connection with others, as *croisé en avant.* This means, the moving leg is nearest the footlights, opened to front *fourth* position, on the ground or in the air.

D

DANCE: *Dance,* the English word, is close to the French *danse;* deriving from the antique high-German *danson,* to drag, or stretch. In Middle English *danson* becomes *daunce* or *dawnce;* in Swiss and Dutch *dans;* in Danish, *dands;* in Spanish and Italian, *danza;* in Portuguese, *dansa;* in modern German, by the modification of Grimm's phonetic law, *tanz.* The Russian is close to German. The original Sanskrit root is *tan,* stretching; the Greek is *tenein,* and from the Latin *teneo* come tension, extend, intense, sustain, maintain, etc.

"But first," wrote John Weaver in 1721, "it will not be improper to explain what dancing is, and in what it consists. Dancing is an elegant, and regular movement, harmoniously composed of beautiful *Attitudes,* and contrasted graceful Posture of the Body, and parts thereof."

"Dancing according to the accepted definition of the word, is the art of composing steps with grace, precision and facility to the time and bars given in the music, just as music itself is simply the art of combining sounds and modulations so that they afford pleasure to the ear," wrote J. G. Noverre in 1760. Dancing as defined by Diderot and d'Alembert in the Encyclopedia (ca. 1772) is "Ordered movements of the body, leaps and measured steps made to the accompaniment of musical instruments or the voice." Desrat's Dictionary of Dancing (1895) says, "Dancing is the action of moving the body in harmony with a determined measure, and in allocating a given expression to the movements."

Perhaps the most complete contemporary definition is André Levinson's, quoted by Cyril Beaumont in his "Miscellany for Dancers" (1934). "Dancing is the continuous movement of the body traveling in a pre-determined space in accordance with a definite rhythm and a conscious mechanism." (*La Danse d'Aujourd'hui:* 1929.)

In a recent American radio program, *It's Up to You,* thousands of persons were polled to find out the twenty "happiest" words in our language. The first five were *healthy, laughter, home, love, peace.* The eleventh was *money,* the twentieth *dance.*

"Dancing," wrote Havelock Ellis in "The Dance of Life" (1923), "has forever been in existence as a spontaneous custom, a social discipline. Thus it is finally that dancing meets us not only as love, as religion, as art, but also as morals."

"All human work under natural conditions is a kind of dance. . . . Work differs from the dance not in kind but only in degree, since they are both essentially rhythmic. . . ."

"The dance lies at the beginning of art, and we find it also at the end. The first creators of civilization were making the dance, and the philosopher of a later age (Nietzsche), hovering over the dark abyss of insanity, with bleeding feet and muscles strained to the breaking point, still seems to himself to be weaving the maze of the dance."

DEVELOPPÉ: From the French, to develop or unfold. Ballet step and dance-exercise in which the leg employed is slowly raised and unfolded from its ordinary standing position to desired complete extension in the air.

DIVERTISSEMENT: A single number, or a suite of numbers calculated to display individuals or groups of dancers, through short dances, unrelated by a dramatic reason, which are sometimes hung on a plot pretext of festival or wedding. In classic ballets, such as *Coppelia* (Merante: 1870) or *La Belle au Bois Dormant* (M. Petipa: 1890), they occur as celebrations leading up to a finale. A kind of graduation exercise or vaudeville atmosphere pervades the demonstration of address and personality by favorite artists in old favorites. Considerable technical skill is necessary to reclaim divertissements from the realm of band-concert taste.

The best known contemporary example is *Aurora's Wedding,* composed of fragments from the Diaghilev revival (1921) of Petipa's original *Sleeping Beauty.* It makes up in recognizable familiarity what it lacks in essential interest. The eyes of the audience hum it like the Blue Danube. Hence, if some of the soloists are proficient, or at least showy, this is the ballet in which the *corps de ballet* can relax from their labors and think about packing. A series of *divertissements* may, however, be worked out with some ingenuity if composed for special occasions, which is in the tradition of their origin. The Ballet comedies of Molière (ca. 1660-1670), with danced interludes as important parts of the plot, survive in revivals of *Les Facheux* (Nijinska: 1924) or *Le Bourgeois Gentilhomme* (Balanchine: 1932). Except here they have a logical connection with the whole dramatic structure as do even the divertissements of *Aurora's Wedding* in their original context.

The famous "Blue Bird" *pas de deux* is an excellent applause number. It is perennially useful because even the most resistant members of an audience can understand that its steps are intended to be difficult and hence can applaud with clear conscience if their execution happens to be negligible. An evening's otherwise tiresome program can be edited towards success by the judicious arrangement of divertissements as a climax, but if there is necessity to resort to this hypodermic it is only an index of the ill health of the rest of the repertory.

E

ECHAPPE: From the French, to slip or escape. A slipping movement, in which the body in *fifth* position, bends both knees equally and jumps, regaining the floor in *second* position. Feet retouch the ground toes first, heels last.

EFFACE (see plate 4): From the French *effacer,* to shade or diminish in plane. This term is generally applied to head and shoulders when they are placed at angles to suggest greater plasticity. In dance lessons, *effacé* positions are used to elevate the chest and give a prouder carriage to the upper body. This raised position supports the expanded lungs, and hence aids breathing. Cyril Beaumont (1931) writes it is "A particular placing of the body, legs and head in which the dancer stands at an oblique angle to the audience so that a portion of the body is in shadow."

ELEVATION (see plate 3): Mastery of *la danse d'élévation* is a conquest of air. If one had to pick a single symbol with almost universal connotation for dancing in our century, it would be Vaslav Nijinsky's leap (active 1909-1917). How high that leap actually was is no longer of interest, although his Russian companions tell us that it was never seen at its peak in America, and to less advantage in Western Europe than in Russia. In legend it has become super-human. But since Nijinsky was human, and since other dancers have exceeded him (notably the Muscovite, Nicolas Petrovitch Damashov (ca. 1900), his is merely a kind of Olympic record for others to aim at.

There are at least two divisions of elevation: the *actual* defiance of gravity, and the rendering of an *appearance* of high-jumping. Exercises training dancers to leap are not in themselves particularly difficult. Indeed, if a dancer is naturally endowed for leaping, it is early shown, and may become a difficult fault to overcome. Exuberant natural jumpers sometimes ignore musical and dramatic expression for sheer height and easy applause. A dancer with little natural gift for jumps can often, by starting low and landing low, with a subtle recovery to full height, give the impression of considerable altitude conquered. The "secret" of Nijinsky's phenomenal leap has been frequently explained by his "double-preparation." With his lungs full of air to their capacity, he would leap. In mid-air he would still inhale breath to expend on his peak-effort, thereby giving the impression he remained momentarily suspended. The *danse d'élévation,* a preference for activity in the aerial province, is sometimes opposed to the *danse par terre,* or work on the floor. For a complete dancer, both are mastered, although some artists have fine legs which can be capitalized. A smooth spring, musically phrased, is frequently more satisfactory than a dancer's equivalent of a running high-jump or pole-vault.

ENCHAINEMENT: A combination of steps which may be a phrase in an extended theatrical dance pattern or simply a chain of harmonious movements strung on a fragment of music for use in the class-room. One can think of the contrivance of *enchainements* intended for stage use, as a melodic line. Some steps by their nature have a logic, or lack of it, when used in combination with others. A tactful juxtaposition of various constituent parts is like a smoothly forged chain, rather than a bumpy string of stones. A given *enchainement* may have its own individual climax which has been built up by steps calculated to frame an ultimate effect. A well-designed *enchainement* can have a gracious rhythmic and melodic sympathy, although by no means literally interpreting the largest melody in a musical accompaniment. Some *enchainements,* harmoniously conceived with a gracious curve of interest, may be accompanied by music which is little more than attenuated filler-in. An *enchainement* is only a choreographic phrase, the notes of which are *pas,* or steps. It can, however, be built up into a danced aria or *variation.*

ENTRECHAT: A step in which the feet braid back and forth in air.

The word has two traditional sources. The first (Compan: 1787) comes from *capriola intreciata* (Italian: a braiding jump). The second (Desrat: 1895) from *entrechas,* the French *châsse* (chassis), a piece of squared wood, framing metal work, combined with *entrelas,* twisted cords, interlacements or braiding,— hence *entrechat,* or interlacing of legs and feet as if they were restrained within the slots of a frame. This last ingenious if dubious etymology is traced to the Jesuit Menestrier's *Des Ballets Anciens et Modernes* (1682).

The shift of feet in mid-air, toes pointing straight down to earth, has a legible flash and twinkle which spells obvious brilliance to the public, since it requires some elevation to accomplish, for the higher the dancer jumps, the more beats can be flashed, and since the combination of transverse movements of the feet with a perpendicular motion of the rest of the body seems to denote control of two actions at once.

Desrat explains *entrechat* as an appellation coming from the changings of feet operating between (*entre*) each of the dancer's jumps. This is better understood when we realize that in *entrechat trois, quatre,* or *six,* the feet beat three, four or six times during or in between (*entre*) each jump. *Entrechats* are divided into two general divisions; the even: that is to say, *deux, quatre, six, huit*—and the odd: *trois, cinq, sept.* The first terminate in a dancer regaining the ground on two feet; the second, in holding one foot off the ground. An *entrechat deux* is a simple *changement de pied;* with *entrechats quatre, six, huit,* the feet change completely back and forth, twice, three or four times while the dancer is raised in air during the jump. The toe always touches before the heel. In the odd *entrechats* the feet change three or five times while the dancer lands on one foot with the other kept *croisé* in front or back. It is absolutely necessary to make a preparation for the *entrechat* with both knees deeply bent, *grand plié,* to get enough push for a good jump.

A fresco on a wall in Egyptian Thebes, shows a dancer apparently executing a rudimentary *changement* in mid-air.

The step was used traditionally in antique *contredanses* and the *gavotte,* during the eighteenth century,—obviously in a non-theatrical form, at least for women, for it would not have been visible in their long skirts. Camargo (1710-1770) is popularly accredited with "inventing" the step in 1730, but Rameau in his "Dancing Master" had already described it in 1725. Camargo perfected it, however, so it frequently is associated with her name, although in 1750 Mademoiselle Lany is supposed to have executed *entrechat six* and even *huit.* From 1760 to 1800, the steps became an accepted part of the theatrical dancer's vocabulary. Contemporary myth tells us that Vaslav Nijinsky (active: 1909-1919) could execute his *entrechat dix,* but it is difficult to discover anyone who has counted them, personally.

Nicolas Legat, in his "Story of the Russian School" (1932) tells of the phenomenal dancer, N. P. Damashov (ca. 1900). He was generally unknown even in Russia, outside of Moscow.

Legat saw him execute an *entrechat huit* on his ascent;—then pause for a split second in mid-air and slowly descend with motionless legs. Then he reversed the process, executing the eight beats descending. Legat, who knew both dancers well, considered Nijinsky's marvels child-play beside those of Damashov.

ENTREE: The arrival by individuals or groups of dancers, usually in a ballet *divertissement*. The *entrée* originated from the epoch when ballets were masked balls at feudal courts, and arrivals entered in order of social rank, according to protocol. The entries in a masked ball, linked together by a single idea for costume pretext, might be the Queen of Night and her attendant owls, Fire and his Sparks, or Water and her mermaids and tritons. In a ballet Entry, the soloists arrive attended by dancers arranged to frame them, serving as a small individual *corps de ballet* background for a particular variation. Formal *entrées* arrive to a march time, or to a similar measure, such as a polonaise. The various *entrées* maintain their characteristic identities, and if they lose them in the *ballabile* or big finale, one may be sure to find them grouped again in character at the final curtain.

Compan's Dictionary of Dancing (1787) describes the arrangement of the usual mid-eighteenth century five-act ballet. "Each act consists of three, six, nine, and sometimes twelve entries. The term *entrée* is given to one or more bands of dancers, who by means of their steps, gestures, and attitudes express that portion of the whole theme which has been assigned to them."

J. G. Noverre wrote in his first letter (1760) that "Symmetrical figures from right to left are, in my opinion, only supportable in the *corps d'entrées*, which have no means of expression, and which, conveying nothing, are employed simply to give the premiers danseurs time to take breath."

We are all familiar with the formal entries in *Aurora's Wedding* (Petipa: Sergeev: 1890-1921) of Little Red Riding Hood and her Wolf, The Three Chinese, The Three Ivans, all of whom join hands with the rest in the Farandole. This is an academic nineteenth century Russian adaptation of the French eighteenth century form. But in a contemporary ballet, like

PLATE 2

FIRST
ARABESQUE
DEMI-
PLIÉ

SECOND
ARABESQUE
SUR
LA
DEMI-
POINTE

Petrouchka (Fokine: 1912), there are still *entrées,* only here the actual entrances are masked by the impressionist nature of Stravinsky's score. For example: there are entries of Nurse-maids, Coachmen, Gypsies, and the tipsy barin. Only they all emerge from the carnival crowd and are reabsorbed into it without that final apotheosized pose which might call attention to the fact that their *entrée* is concluded.

F

FEET: To the uninformed, it is frequently assumed that a dancer's most important individual equipment is the feet. J. G. Noverre, in 1760, already attacked those who "dance for the sake of dancing, imagining that all consists in the action of the legs." It would be impossible to dance without them, but they are not any more important than any other member. However, since we stand on them, and they are our immediate connection with the floor, we may be more immediately conscious of them. Classic dancers are frequently inclined not necessarily to over-train them, but at least to desert the canonical positions of arms, hands and head, as if these half-forgotten aids could take care of themselves. We jump from the feet, and since jumps are immediately spectacular (see *Elevation*), hours are spent cultivating *entrechats* (vide passim) while arms like tired car-rots dangle as they may. In boxing and running, the crux of a foot's structure is also in the metatarsal arch. Special exer-cises (*relevés*) are continually provided to strengthen this essen-tial bridge. A clean, snappy spring for beats and jumps is particularly effective. The toe must always be kept as much as possible straightly pointed down to continue indefinitely the extended direction of the body's action. Feet must not flap loosely like slapped fish. Since the feet receive the greatest impact at all times, they must be guarded against casual injury or careless fatigue. They support the weight of the whole body, not by a steady pressure, but by irregular jolting shocks. Vaslav Nijinsky (active: 1909-1919) is supposed to have had disarticu-lated bones in his feet caused by congenital mutation. His toes, assuming this to be accurate information, were almost evolved at birth to be like a bird's talons. The disarticulation of the bones spread into a further cushion of expansion and received the extra shock of his phenomenal jump. He frequently burst his slippers from the swell of his powerful feet. Whether or not this is fact, it has a symbolic truth and happens to a lesser degree with all well-trained dancers.

FLOOR: Few except professional dancers realize how important is the surface on which they work. The floor can be considered almost as a dancer's violin. Bow and arm produce the vibration, but the wood reflects it, and renders it audible. As few theatres are designed specifically for dancing, floors are hardly ever tuned to the given need. Dancers accustom themselves to any floor; linoleum, hard-wood, canvas covered to hide dry-rot; or ideally, and if they are in luck, soft pine,—cheap yet unbeatable, unwaxed, unoiled and unvarnished. Elasticity, as well as a slight surface friction are desirable; a dancer is never, unfortunately, in a position to say they are essential. Soft pine with enough rosin powdered over it, gives a sense of security which can hearten a nervous dancer and exhilarate a phlegmatic one. Ballet dancers work in slippers or shoes, not in bare feet. Leather needs the slight lock of wood-fibre to create the minute frictional drag necessary to provide a spring-board balance. The good dancer imagines his feet as almost sucking the floor surface, pressing into it, as it were, for assurance and release when the pressure is removed.

On a fine stage which had been creosoted against dry-rot, in one of the newest and handsomest theatres in America, an experienced company of dancers was recently rendered almost impotent. Dancing upon such a surface was like hot roller-skating on ice. The audience instinctively felt the edge taken off the performance, but assumed it was the fault of the dancers. The management of many auditoriums prefer a handsome varnished expanse of hard maple, bright as a mirror, to the professional comfort of traveling artists. Unwaxed linoleum is not impossible and is excellent for bare-foot work, but even chipped pine and cracked joints are preferable to shiny varnish.

FOUETTE: From the French *fouet,* a whip. A step executed usually by girls on point, in which the free leg is whipped

323

smartly up and around from fourth to second position and then into the knee. This step, often used in combination with a double turn on point, if kept up long enough, is a sure-fire applause net. For some time it served as a kind of graduation degree for the technically proficient ballerina.

Pierina Legnani, an Italian ballerina, as guest artist in Russia, is generally supposed to have first executed thirty-two *fouettés* in Tchaikovsky's Swan-Lake (Ivanov-Petipa: 1877-1895), creating a sensation. Rayner Heppenstall, in "Apology for Dancing" (1936), says this was in Petipa's *Zolushka*, ostensibly on information from Nicolas Legat, who had been Legnani's partner and who learned her secret to teach it to his fellow Russians. The Russian ballerina, quick to meet the challenge of a southern invasion, soon exceeded her.

Dancers today can easily execute many more. The *fouetté* remains a show step, although certain contemporary choreographers have contrived to endow it with a logical dramatic significance. The Top, in Massine's *Jeux d'Enfants* (1932), spins convincingly. The Finale of Balanchine's *Cotillon* (1932) permits the ballerina to commence her *fouettés* and by a large spiral design for the entrance of the rest of the troupe, she seems to whip the stage into a frenzied finish. In Balanchine's *Serenade* (1934) sixteen girls executed thirty-two *fouettés* without difficulty.

G

GESTURE: Literally understood, gesture is all voluntary or involuntary movement of the human body, the aim of which is to signify something. Cicero (*De Oratore*) considered "action" as the *external* part of oratory, hence gesture is corporal eloquence, or the language of the body, just as spoken words are the language of the vocal cords. The dance is generally silent. It may use gestures which normally enhance verbal speech and thereby have come to bear an associative reference, but necessarily in a heightened theatrical manner, suitable to stage use. Gesture is by no means a question of arms alone. Cicero included facial expression, as well as *Chironomia* (Delivery) or improperly, Elocution. All through classical literature, we find works on gesture as compiled by rhetoricians and orators. These were restudied during the classic revival of the eighteenth century when an attempt was made to reduce everything to rigid canons based on antique precedent. Parliament, the Courts of Law, the pulpit itself, became places of entertainment due to the theatrical delivery of orators who aped Demosthenes.

Gesture can have literal associative reference or can be broadly suggestive. The narrative portion of dancing is composed of designed gesture. Gesture is the stuff, subdivision and working material of pantomime. If *enchainements* of dance steps comprise the *variation* or danced aria, then *enchainements* of gesture create pantomime or the danced recitative. But in ballet, gestures must not result in mere dumb-show but should be transferred into the more lyric terms of dancing.

As for academic gesture used by actors, orators and preachers, the Reverend Gilbert Austin, writing his great "Chironomia" in 1806, admitted that the English look to the French, the French to the Italians, and the Italians to the ancient Greeks as their masters. Each nation has a manual sign language accompanied by the rest of the body, which has erected over the centuries a corpus of associative reference. Stage-gesture cannot be wholly appropriated from oratory, because it is used in the accompaniment of speech not as complete explanation, but chiefly as attendant emphasis. It is necessary to have a particular style of gesture to construct a vocabulary of pantomime fitting not only the subject of a given ballet—but its music as well, which may be considered the words of the otherwise silent danced play.

Certain professional occupational gestures are familiar to all of us; the policeman directing traffic, the baseball pitcher winding up, the orchestral conductor building a climax. Of all the animals, said Buffon, man alone gesticulates, although some of the higher apes approximate it. This is due to the peculiar construction of the erect biped, who stands with dangling forearms. A man is not a four-foot. His arms give a direct significance to gestures supported by inclinations of the rest of the body. There is a different quality describing masculine and feminine gesture based on biological structure. Gesture is of the greatest human significance, not only in social intercourse, but as a stage instrument and more recently even as a political manifestation, with the mass arm-movements of Fascist and Communi't ualutes. The Italians are traditionally endowed with the expressive language of arms and hand, from the salute of Caesar's legions to the silent pacification of the Neapolitan mob by King Ferdinand in 1821.

The classic study of gesture is formulated in Charles Darwin's "Expressions of Emotions in Man and Animals" (1872). His three basic principles are:

1. The principle of serviceable *associated* habits; spontaneous natural activity under given stress which has become habitual, whose reference we understand by association from the history of our race. If these are consciously controlled the muscles check them. This check creates characteristic reflex movements, equally recognizable.

2. The principle of antithesis or *opposites:* motions arise from a reaction to habitual ones (Principle 1) which are of no definite use, but assert themselves with involuntary strength and have the significance of contrast.

3. The principle of actions due to the *constitution* of the human system, independent of conscious direction, and to some degree of habit. The direct action of the nervous system under excitement produces an excess of nervous energy which is transmitted into various definite channels. The release of this energy into gesture is recognizable as *expressive*.

Students of the dance often despair that gesture cannot be learned in an academy like the classic ballet. There is a considerable literature on the subject both ancient and modern, from Cicero and Quintillian to Sir Charles Bell, the anatomist, and Mantegazza, the criminologist. However, for those seriously interested in practical results rather than historical curiosities, almost everything of value may be limited to studies attributed to François Delsarte. This remarkable man, who published nothing while alive, left sufficient material to provide a fundamental background for a universal academy of gesture. Famous as a teacher during his life, he enjoyed an even more remarkable posthumous reputation, particularly in America, from 1880 to 1900. However, lacking his presence to activate his theories, his system as promulgated by his heirs, fell under the severe and just criticism of being purely mechanical and arbitrary. The apostolic fervor of his disciples may easily have been fanatic, but this does not excuse the disfavor and ridicule which has subsequently obscured his essentially important contribution. Almost the only reference to Delsarte in the repertory of the contemporary dance is a series of parodies worked out by the mime Angna Enters (ca. 1930), based on the naïve pictorial diagrams with which early editions of his system were illustrated.

To be sure, a few contemporary dramatic-teachers employ his underlying structure of expression, but its large system, which is in fact, an analysis and ordering of all effective gesture, is ignored or unknown by those very students of dancing, who, in search of a basic skeleton for pantomime, might need it most. Delsarte claimed no particular originality for his studies. They were practical results in research, not only through the classic rhetoricians but of comparative anatomy in clinics, morgues and hospitals. His reluctance to publish is perhaps significant. His contact was directly with his pupils. His generalizations were for their use, not as arbitrary formula for mechanical application, but as a kind of plastic geometry for universal correspondence. Delsarte did for gesture, and indirectly for dancing, what the other great formulators of the nineteenth century accomplished for their chosen fields. As Comte in exact science, Ruskin in aesthetics, Buckle, J. S. Mill, or even Marx, in historical analysis, and Carlo Blasis in the classic theatrical dance—so Delsarte provided an apparatus for the investigation and use of gesture. Unlike these others, Delsarte's theories received little subsequent amplification or challenge.

François Delsarte was born at Solesmes, November 11, 1811. His father, a doctor, abused his mother so that she fled to Paris with two small sons. Her early death was followed by that of Delsarte's brother, who expired of starvation in his arms. As a child of ten, he was kept by a rag-picker, and, developing a passion for music, invented his own system of musical notation to preserve songs of the beggars whom he daily encountered. At thirteen he was discovered in the gardens of the Tuilleries tracing his invented notes in the sand, by Bambini, a well-known music-teacher. Through his aid he entered the Conservatory.

Too original to receive official academic encouragement, he nevertheless finally received a contract to sing at the Opéra Comique. But the errors in his wretched conservatory training caused a complete failure of his voice in 1834, only four years after a successful debut. From that time he devoted himself to providing a more intelligent means of instructing students by methods of expression which would aid rather than destroy them. Combining a surgeon's science with an artist's passion, he became one of the most remarkable teachers of his day. Although among his pupils were Jenny Lind, Sontag, Macready, Rachel, and the great preachers: Père Hyacinthe and Lacordaire, he died comparatively unknown in 1871, under the shadow of the Franco-Prussian war. The American, Steele Mackaye, attended his pantomime classes and became an ardent disciple. Plans for bringing Delsarte to America for the establishment of a theatre and conservatory were prevented by his death.

Delsarte's system of expressive gesture is simple in essence, yet extremely complex in applied detail. It is founded on a *triune* division of the human organism, established by the triune conditioning of natural law. That is, the body restricted by space, time and motion, has correspondence in the physical, intellectual and emotional sources of its action. In every human, one of these three natures dominates, the degree of dominance causing the difference in personality. Delsarte separated the body into three grand divisions. The head represents the intellectual,—legs and arms the physical,—the trunk, the emotional nature. Each of these divisions is in turn subdivided and we have a trinity for each division. In the head, for example, he considered the eyes and forehead intellectual, the nose and cheeks emotional, the mouth and lips physical. In the torso, the region of the upper chest is intellectual, the central section (the heart) emotional, the lower abdomen, physical. As for arms and legs,—feet and hands are intellectual, forearms and lower legs are emotional, while upper arms and legs are physical. Still further subdivisions are made in the face, hands, legs, etc. But the application of the corresponding trinities is more significant than the formulation of further categories. In Delsarte's grand division, the arms and legs have the physical dominance. They disclose the most *apparent* strength and activity. In the zones of the leg, the thigh is designated as physically vital because the impulse of locomotion is first felt there. The lower leg as an emotional source is demonstrated by the use of knees in gestures of kneeling or subordination to another's will in supplication, request, reverence or obedience. The intellectuality of the foot is shown by the unconscious nervous tapping of impatience and the control by the feet as the sources of advance or retreat.

The mental zone is shown in the brain's effect on the shape and quality of head and its bony structure, the confirmation of visual expression. The emotional seat is in the diaphragm. As Lavatar, the author of a curious and influential work on Physiognomy (1772-83), has been quoted: "These three states of the Soul do not lodge in separate apartments of the body, but co-exist in every part, and form, by their combination, one whole; yet it is true that each of these principles has its particular place of residence in the body, where it is preference manifests and exerts itself."

With the sources of human movement thus consciously divided into a fabric of trinities, Delsarte proposes his nine laws of gesture.

1. The law of *Motion:* the center of his system. Motion is energy expending itself. Physical motion moves *outward* from a centered focus; intellectual motion moves *inward* towards this center; emotional motion appears in either concentric or eccentric forms, or by a poise or *balance* between the other two.

2. The law of *Velocity:* "The velocity of any agent is in proportion to the mass moved, and the energy moving. That is: serious ideas require deliberate gestures; lighter ones need shorter and more rapid ones."

3. The law of *Direction* and *Extension* (in ballet, the *Arabesque* and *Attitude*): All gestures have direction; physical gestures are projected forward or lengthwise; intellectual gestures above or below, emotional spread out laterally. The "extension" of gesture is in the intensity of its surrender to the dominant intellectual, physical or emotional source.

4. The law of *Reaction* (Darwin's Second Principle): "Every extreme of emotion tends to react to its opposite. Concentric

states tend to explosion; explosion to prostration (i.e., cessation)": The shift from physical activity to repose, from anger to tears, from tears to laughter, etc.

5. The law of *Form:* The exterior shape, or restraining figure by which matter is rendered visible. In gesture, all movements describe shapes or forms in air. Straight lines are said to be dominantly direct, hence physical; circular lines, emotional; while broken lines are considered the result of obstruction consciously conquered, and hence intellectual.

6. The law of *Personality:* Idiosyncratic characteristics conditioned by heredity, environment, and local culture.

7. The law of *Opposition* (see "Opposition"): "When two limbs follow the same direction, they cannot be simultaneous without injury to the law of opposition. Therefore, direct movements should be successive and opposite movements simultaneous." This law is based on the physical human mechanics of equilibrium and gravity.

8. The law of *Priority* or *Sequence:* The suite in which agents of expression act. "Impression always precedes expression; we must have before we can give, and give in the order of having." In general, Delsarte considered the physical nature asserts itself first, then the emotional, last the intellectual. But "The Will lends itself to which ever side of the being is in action." The eye reveals impressions first, the face responds, then follow the hands and other members. *Articulate speech is last.*

9. The law of *Rhythm:* "The vibration or swing of matter through equal spaces in equal times." The pulsation corresponding to the heart beat under given emotional tensions. In gesture, the consecutive inflections of the bodies' members from joint to joint.

With these nine laws presupposed, Delsarte proposed a series of "decomposing" exercises for freedom and relaxation, calculated to separate and analyze the sources of gesture in a conscious order for future *composition.* The decomposing exercises are intended as a complete, objective education of the many parts of the human body as an expressive agent, both in underlying detail and as a legible entity.

The above brief abstract has been compiled from a half-dozen available records of Delsarte which differ considerably in nomenclature, application, and even interpretation. However, the more one searches, the more one respects the critical wisdom, elastic logic and lack of arbitrary schematic thinking, of which Delsarte's superficial opponents have accused him. While not recommending either a particular book as an evangel, nor a particular series of exercises as fool-proof, any serious student can find more of value even in Delsarte's recorded shadow than in all the other "authorized" books on gesture and pantomime put together.

The reputation of Delsarte has suffered, not because the findings of his practical research have ever been seriously questioned, but largely because his literary remains were found to be full of a great mass of irrelevant, foggy philosophical drapery, parallels to Plotinus, the neo-platonists, the Hermetic doctrine, the Cabalists, the Christian mystics, and Oriental "secret" writings. He attempted to corroborate his essentially simple system with a testimony of universal and complete cosmic truth. No doubt the lasting part of his work partakes of that truth, but its particular revelation to its author took the form of an unending testimony of historic witnesses. Hence, posthumous critics have tended to spread their valid ridicule indiscriminately also over what was objectively sensible. Delsarte's misfortune lay in that he never superintended the publication of his own work, nor yet did Steele Mackaye, his most devoted pupil. In spite of a style which is no longer in vogue, the studies of Genevieve Stebbins are extremely well-arranged. It is she, who more emphatically than anyone else, stresses his greatest service,— the recreation for his own time (and for ours) of a system of correspondences. Delsarte did not exactly discover any original method. But by the *arrangement* of facts already known, he affected a structure of infinite correspondence. His great service was not so much to the small field of gesture, but to the broader science of *semantics*.

Semantics is the science of significance, or correspondence. "Correspondence is derived from three Latin words, *cor re spondeo;* it literally means to answer again, from the heart. We use the word in common speech to show that written communication has passed between two people. It is only complete when the one written to has replied; has spoken to the other again *from the heart."*

Delsarte's *semantics,* his science of signs, is hence the science of the forms of human gesture. He categorized human beings into the dominantly constitutional (congenital or hereditary), the emotional, and the habitual, who are not so much bred as created by habit. The emotional type explains the habitual, and the habitual the hereditary or congenital. This is his complete analysis of people all of whom have essentially but three kinds of expressive gesture; the habitual bearing of the expressive agent (dancer, actor) which is the most permanent. The emotional attitudes are less so, and the various accidental inflections affecting the agent are only temporary.

It almost goes without saying that Delsarte's ideas have a particular reference to lyric theatre in Western Europe and America. There are of course numerous *oriental* academies of gesture, of which perhaps the most familiar is the "Mirror of Gesture" (or Expression), first edited in the West by Dr. Ananda Coomeraswamy (Harvard University Press, 1917), with a suggestive introduction. It was later more fully presented by Manomohan Ghosh (Calcutta, 1934). The system of gesture, and particularly of manual expression, presented in "The Mirror" is extraordinarily complex, arbitrary and traditional. Its use to Western actors or dancers, in spite of Dr. Coomeraswamy's good wishes, seems remote. The oriental actor-dancer has suffered a gradual thousand-year decadence, and even religious mandates governing dance technique have not prevented such contemporaries as the Javanese, Raden Mas Jodjana, and the East Indian, Uday Shankar, from appropriating the methods of European stage-presentation to aid their own presentation or personal adaptation of oriental classic dancing. The basic metaphysical principles of Eastern and Western art may both ultimately coincide to praise the life force, whatever it may be called,—but the specific use of Western dancing is for spectacle, not for praise. In the East, the great emphasis is on the gesture or the dance; in the West on the particular actor or dancer. Separate hierarchies of movement are repositories of meaning and may be read like a book, presupposing the audience's familiarity with Hindu folk-lore. In the Western tradi-

PLATE 3

EXERCISE AT
BARRE ON POINT

ELEVATION

ATTITUDE

tional classic dance, the human unit, the dancer, by his designed behavior, has a purely emotional reference to his audience, based on little more than association and direct sensuous appeal. In the East, the various static positions are ends in themselves, denoting final meaning; in the West, the named steps or stations are merely means to an end, which is the *enchainement* of gestures towards kinetic dramatic action. To be sure, Eastern gesture has been used as a "style" by Western choreographers.—*Sacountala* (L. Petipa: 1858), *Le Dieu Bleu* (Fokine: 1913), *Padmavâti* (Staats: 1923); but the actual effect is no more profound than the use of the sari a few years ago by Paris dressmakers, as an evening wrap. In spite of their respective beauties, Eastern and Western conceptions of individual action are too dissimilar to permit any practical interchange of much theatrical interest.

GRACE: The single most widely used noun applying to the dance. "Graceful" or "ungraceful" is a synonym in the minds of most people for the quality which renders a dancer easy or difficult to watch. What constitutes this quality is more difficult to define. The overlying ease by which a sequence of physical movements are flowingly accomplished is often applied to a very narrow range of activity. Yet a dancer can be graceful in an ungraceful position or dance. Grace is the binding element in a dancer's style, a mercurial fluid spreading invisibly over the body in an imperceptible film. It is an elastic endless chain of connections which link and at the same time contain separate movements in a supple net, never allowing one portion or motion of the body to become inconsistent with another, however outrageous the separate individual movements may be. Girls are assumed by virtue of their softness to be more graceful, but there are as few essentially graceful girls as boys. A boy is said to be graceful *for a boy*, or else *too* graceful, hence effeminate. Gracefulness is a quality covering all danced action, not a category applying to a certain ·aspect of free motion. This confusion arises from the antique philosophical concept that grace and beauty were identical, that the opposite of grace was any restrained or "ugly" action.

Despréaux, in his letter to Després (Journal de Paris, May 7,

1820), wrote:—"There are three kinds of grace; grace of form, grace of pose, grace of movement." His typically eighteenth century reasonable or rather rationalized argument tells us grace of form is a gift of nature,—and rare. Grace of poise is the ability to select a position of the body consonant with "good taste." Grace of movement is not merely the facility to pass from one pose to another in accordance with the rhythm of the music. It demands expression according to the character portrayed, particularly in the dance *terre à terre* (on the floor), which demands quite a different type needed for *la danse d'élévation* (in the air).

The Scotch philosopher, Henry Home, in his "Elements of Criticism" (1762), proposed that the quality of grace could be identified with physical movements of the human race, especially with the expressive, necessarily with the dignified. Herbert Spencer's essay on "Gracefulness" (1865) established that grace is present in all movements accomplished *with ease*. Behind this easy accomplishment must be *an economy of effort*. Such ease and economy arouse a *sympathy* in the spectator. To further paraphrase Spencer,—grace is physical action achieved in a manner to conserve muscular energy. Grace is animation calculated to demonstrate this economy. Grace of pose may be found in postures which are sustained while conserving the energy.

A further development of the theories of Home and Spencer may be studied in two large volumes of Raymond Bayer's, *L'Esthetique de la Grace* (1933). Bayer finds also that the ultimate base of grace is in an economy of effort, but only if such effort is concealed. He claims to have discovered the principle in grace for a *demonstration* of power, and an element of surprise or the *unexpected*.

Bayer divides the means of grace into the "natural" and the "artificial." The natural comprises a given person's hereditary endowment, his muscular structure, weight, instinctive mobility and capacity to coördinate. The artificial is a general interior control, regulation or counter-balance, the independence of the various members of the body and a certain softness, or rather elasticity. All of these combine to corroborate Spencer's principle of the concealment of effort. Bayer carefully analyses the academic vocabulary of the classic dance, proposes definitions of equilibrium, static balance, and asymmetrical counterpoise as concomitants of grace.

J

JETE: From the French, *jeter*, to throw. A jump in which the body is thrown on to one foot, after the other has been raised, and is completed with the other foot at the side, or in front in third or fifth position. The term is also pronounced and even written *shtay* or even *stay*, a corruption of the phonetic French.

L

LESSON: The arrangement of exercises into daily periods to instruct a dancer in technique and to maintain technical proficiency during an active stage-career. The lesson consists of approximately the same movements from a pupil's first introduction to the *barre* down to the last year of his professional appearance. There is a natural difference bred by the ease of familiarity, but even the youngest student immediately tries to execute steps which will later be part of his accustomed vocabulary.

The class starts easily while progress is at first, by necessity, slow. Children without previous training, as well as accomplished dancers, commence with the *barre* and follow by work in the center of the floor, in a dry and rather invariable sequence. Soon, combinations of more complex movements are permitted at the *barre,* and then without its aid, in the center. The five fundamental positions, their variants in arms and legs as well as principle of *opposition* and *plasticity* are mastered. An easy *adagio* combination is ventured to prepare for instruction in *balance*. The *adagio* becomes increasingly complex and difficult to sustain. Later on, new combinations are continually substituted for others. The student cannot afford to make any short cut. Everything follows inexorably from the simple sources: self-control, aplomb, balance, stamina, and limberness become the normal properties of a body which will finally be prepared to assume the more difficult department, *allegro*.

The slower exercises (*adagio*) coming first, warm up the muscular mechanism for its peak load of exertion.

Allegro cannot be undertaken until the feet are so correctly trained that their behavior is almost instinctive. The *turn-out* of the legs must be broad and effortless. The instep must be firm and well muscled. The exercises begin with simple jumps in which both feet are used to spring: *temps levé* and *changement de pied*. These are first practiced with the hands on the *barre*, the dancer facing the wall. Then comes the more complex *assemblé*. The *assemblé* correctly performed is a base for the rest of the division of *allegro*. The legs must coördinate into the rise and fall, and *yet* be turned-out in landing. There is no possibility of muscular laxity. Afterwards follow the *glissade, jeté, echappé, pas de basque,* and *balancé*. The last step cannot be learned until the muscles have been properly developed by single jumps. Having mastered the primary *jetés*, the lesson passes to jumps in which only one foot is used for a spring (the other resting *sur le coup de pied,* after the jump) and to the *sisonne ouverte* in various directions. More difficult jumps, as the *saut de basque*, come later, with *cabrioles* and the rest of *batterie*. *Allegro* is the basis of the rapid *enchainements* which constitute most of classic stage dancing. In advanced classes every one of these named steps is varied in execution by being practiced *en tournant*.

This is a rough outline for most of our standard "Russian" ballet classes, and does not apply to character-dancing, which has its own *barre* system, or to supported *adagio,* or to lessons for *pointes*. Agripina Vaganova, the author of the best modern work on the subject and academician of the Soviet Technicum for ballet in Leningrad, gives almost the same order. She wisely insists on no absolutely rigid rule for planning her class, recognizing that dancers are artists, not soldiers, and that theatrical life is variable. Fatigue must be taken into consideration as well as the individual progress of pupils.

Vaganova's daily exercises (except for the first-year pupils) follow. For advanced professionals it is naturally greatly amplified and rendered more complex and difficult to accommodate and enlarge their capacities.

1. *Barre; Plié* in the five absolute positions of the feet. (This is a period for warming up the muscles.)

Battements tendus, to accustom the legs to *turn-out* in an automatically perfect *fifth* position.

Ronds de jambe par terre, battements fondu and *frappé, ronds de jambe en l'air, petits battements, developpés* and *grand battement jeté.* All of these steps may be recombined and complicated at the discretion of the teacher.

2. *Centre-practice:* simple *adagio* with correct *porte de bras.* Repetition of No. 1 without the aid of the *barre.*

Combinations of *allegro.* The lesson tapers off with *changements de pieds.*

LIBRETTO: In the classic French vocabulary, the plot of a ballet was referred to as the *prétexte* or *intrigue.* Ballets can be roughly classed in two groups, those with plots and those without. All ballets have a subject. *Les Sylphides* (Fokine: 1909), for example, has no plot, but its subject is the atmosphere of "romantic" theatrical dancing (ca. 1840). The plot of *Petrouchka* (Fokine: 1911), based on a folk-tale, is direct and narrative. The plot for *Choreartium* (Massine: 1934) is abstract and "epic." In *Petrouchka* the soloists possess human characteristics and act with conflict, climax and denouement. It is a dramatic scheme. In *Choreartium* the characters are symbols with generalized reference. They follow a logic dictated by the dramatic nature of the music (Brahms, Fourth Symphony). The libretto for *Choreartium* seems as if it were a rationalized description written to coincide with the dancing *after* it had been composed. Except in purely formal *divertissements,* the plot as an order of action, even in purely atmospherical work such as *Cotillon* (Balanchine: 1932) is important. It is the pretext which provides a possibility for an audience to suspend momentarily their natural expectation of logic, and accept the lyric super-logic of a ballet libretto. A good libretto, even an impressionist, double-exposed or portmanteaued one, follows most of the rules of simple dramaturgy. Balanchine once said the perfect type plot for a dramatic narrative ballet was the story of the Prodigal Son. Once there was a man who had everything, then he had nothing; finally he had everything again. Here we have in persuasive causal logic a maximum dra-matic contrast. Complex plots which have to be explained by program notes, since the drama in the dancing is not in itself sufficiently legible, have more or less disappeared except for Massine's symphonic ballets and the elephantine Russian fairy stories such as *Le Coq d'Or* (Fokine: 1914) and *Bogatyri* (Massine: 1938). In the eighteenth and nineteenth century, however, ballet libretti were written by such well known poets as Gautier and Heine, to be printed and widely sold, just as are opera libretti today. At that time, people were accustomed to prepare themselves with a specific narrative background for what they were going to see. Today, we are either lazier or more sophisticated.

Unless the choreographer is a librettist himself, the problem of a contemporary ballet librettist is mostly one of tact. It is he who has the original idea which will be nursed into a ballet. It is his conviction about atmosphere, decorative incident, style and even the quality of music, which may dominate the chore-ographer and mould an ultimate production. Boris Kochno, Diaghilev's last secretary, was skillful in understanding how much plot a ballet could stand, the temper of its picturesque-ness and its just needs as to scenic investiture. Kochno also was conscious of various fashionable artistic and literary trends at work among the painters of the School of Paris (1924-1934). The heirs of Dada, the literary virtuosity of Jean Cocteau, the sad grandeurs of neo-classicism and neo-romanticism, dance-hall, music-hall, and film provided topical pretexts for the late Diaghilev repertory.

M

MAITRE DE BALLET: The classic French term is literally cor-rect. The equivalent English "Choreographer" means a sten-ographer of dance steps, while a composer of dance steps, to which this appellation has come to refer, is in truth Master of the Ballet. A *maître de ballet* is the single most important element in the complex organism of theatrical dancing. It is for him, that the Impressario arranges an instrument for crea-tion, for him the commercial manager books tours, for him that dancers prove the results of their schooling. It goes without saying that a *maître de ballet* is himself something more than a dancer. Indeed J. G. Noverre, Carlo Blasis and Fokine urge him to be a scholar, poet, painter, sculptor, and, most important of all, geometer and musician. Primarily he must be a dancer and a good one. There have been no great choreographers who were not first-rate dancers as well. It is impossible for a dance-designer to imagine, devise or demonstrate steps which are not capable of arising from within his unique instrument, his own dancer's body. While it is metaphysically conceivable that a brain can envisage what a body cannot accomplish, it is nevertheless a working truth that unless a ballet-master is nearly all-capable, certain combinations of gestures will not occur to him, as he will have had no direct experience of them in practice.

MANNERISM: All dancers have mannerisms which are fragmentary unconscious expressions of their private characters. In personal life, these accumulated mannerisms are often endearing. If we love a person, we love their tricks of intonation, of turning their heads, or snapping their knuckles. On the stage, mannerisms can also be attractive. However, many merely spring from errors in training. An over-emphatic preparation for a *pirouette* by jogging madly on both points distinguishes a recently popular ballerina. Her actual turns were highly incorrect. Her body was never held rigid, nor her spine straight enough to prevent her from falling out of the spin. But by her preparatory attraction of notice to the difficulty of the evolution which she was about to perform, she knew that the audience's eye would be distracted from the execution of the step itself. Unfortunately, by the very authoritative ugliness of her mannerism, it was. She got away with it on a basis of blatant vanity. "This may look funny, but only because it is very difficult. It must look this way. You, the audience, are wrong. I am the criterion."

Mannerisms compensating for technical inadequacy can develop into almost pathological manifestations repeated like nervous *tics*. The best dancers consciously eliminate any mannerism to which their attention is drawn. The possession of a clean instrument, devoid of any left-overs from other rôles or styles is the prerequisite of an artist who is occupied with giving maximum expressiveness to every part.. Each dancer has a personal manner as forever individual as his proper face or finger-prints. The intrusion of affectation is like a smudged face or hang-nails. In young dancers, affectations are, unfortunately, sedulously cultivated by imitating the stage-manners of admired dancers. The young dancer is not sure enough of himself to allow his own personality to make its slow emergence. He jumps the gun to acquire a set of idosyncrasies which are vanitous, arbitrary, more often than not inapplicable to a given rôle. The late Anna Pavlova, through no fault of her own, was responsible for a great crop of youngsters appropriating her swan's down, waxen fading-away, although these were her unique property. The Pavlovettes arranged their hair, their arms, their skirts in a perpetual death vigil and took on themselves aspects of taxidermists. Manner is personal expression of a given theatrical style, which is frequently a traditional accumulation of collective manners. Pavlova's manner, of course, recalled that of Taglioni, but she was accidentally close in spirit to the original sylph from the beginning. Mannerism is the dancer's conceited comment on his own individual personality as human being, not as dancing artist. By imitating the manners of other better dancers, they think to excuse an essential inadequacy. One hardly ever notices the mannerisms of character dancers, of an Argentina or an Escudero. Their idiom is compact of national mannerism, elevated into a classic idiom, so rigid that it requires only an intense execution, not a personal comment, to be effective.

N

NOTATION (Stenochoregraphy or Dance-Script): Of all forms of art, dancing alone still has no generally legible means of saving its literature. Music for the last five hundred years, literature for the last five thousand, have their preservative scripts. Painting, sculpture and architecture fend for themselves. Dancing, which in essence is the most transitory and ephemeral of the arts, if by no means the least intense, must depend for its survival on fragmentary graphic rendering, usually so transposed as to be only atmospherically suggestive, and on verbal description. Neither the film nor the still camera have much helped except to preserve more or less static poses, portraits or fragments of danced action seized out of context or taken under unfavorable circumstances.

To be sure, there have been innumerable systems of dance notations, yet the Egyptian, Greek, and Roman methods are almost as illegible as our most recent inventions. From Arbeau's essay in 1588, through Beauchamps, Pécour and Feuillet (ca. 1700), Magny (1765), Malpied (1770), Théleur (1831), Zorn (1840), Saint-Léon (1852) and Stepanov (1892), down to recent proposals of Nijinsky (1917-unpublished), von Laban (ca. (1914), and Meunier (1923), the ingenuity of dancers has been unquenchable.

A desire to avoid oblivion is the natural possession of any artist. It is intensified in the dancer, who is far more under the threat of time than others. The inventions of systems to preserve dance-steps have, since the early eighteenth century, shared a startling similarity. All the books contain interesting prefatory remarks on the structure of dancing. The graphs presented vary in fullness from the mere birds-eye scratch-track of Feuillet, to the more musical and inclusive stenochoreography of Saint-Léon and Stepanov, but all are logically conceived and invitingly rendered, each equipped with provocative diagrams calculated to fascinate the speculative processes of a chess-champion. And from a practical point of view, for work in determining the essential nature of old dances with any objective authority, they are equally useless. The systems, each of which may hold some slight improvement over its predecessor, are so difficult to decipher even to initial mastery of their alphabets, that when a student approaches the problem of putting the letters together, or finally fitting the phrases to music, he feels triumphant if he can decipher even a single short solo enchainement. An analysis of style is not attempted, and the problem of combining solo variations with a corps de ballet to provide a chart or an entire ballet movement reduces the complexity of the problem to the apoplectic. Yet every year, a new mutation of an old theory, or an invention of a new one appears to perplex innocent students. The film is the only answer, not alone as record, seen head-on through the proscenium-arch but from all four sides, and from the flies as well. Who will pay for it is the historian's problem.

Assuming one could record dances by notation, except for the choreographer himself, it may not be a particularly valuable undertaking. The very essence of dance is evanescent. Arbitrary notation could be canonized into tyrannical rules by unimaginative dance theologians. A repertory, which is by nature changeable, might decline in an effort to maintain its "original" quality. Every style of dancing, as well as dress, has to be restudied for the special conditions of each epoch. Time passes; it does not stand still for scholars or aestheticians to delight in. The dance occurs primarily in time. An aesthetic historian may idly speculate on what Lully (ca. 1670) danced, as far as steps go, but he scarcely ever occupies himself with how Lully appeared dancing, since even he must recognize that a man's idiosyncratic manner dies with him. Always suspect a person occupied with dance notation as an unsuccessful choreographer, a disappointed dancer, or a person whose main relaxation is the kind of intellection which would be more profitably spent on symbolic logic or cross-word puzzles.

Before 1765, Giovanni Andrea Gallini wrote, in his "Critical Observations on the Art of Dancing," "Granted also that the enumeration of the motions and steps was possible which it unquestionably is not, considering the infinite variety of gestures and inflexion, concomitant to such motions as have received certain distinctive names; granted withal that such motions distinguished by names appropriated to them, may be specified by their respective characters, still there offers one invincible objection, and that is the nomenclature of those more complicated motions which mock all description, and which can only be comprehended by sight, so that like the most simple ones, they may have their peculiar character readily enough apprehensible by a master; they can be of no use in the world but to their master who does not need them. Nor even to him will that imaginary choreography preserve any dance, but some very plain ones. The written or engraved description by lines and characters, where there is anything complicated, offers such an untoward medley of motions and figures that it is scarcely possible to decipher them. The plan has more the air of puzzling mathematical problems, or of figures in a conjuring book—than that of happy regularity and cleanness of which the notes of music are susceptible."

In the thirteenth of his "Letters on Dancing and Ballets" (1760), J. G. Noverre asserts, "I have learned choreography, sir, and I have forgotten it; if I think it useful for my progress, I shall learn it anew. The best dancers and most celebrated *maîtres de ballet* disdain it because it is of no real help to them." But he goes on to suggest a feasible if incomplete choreography in criticizing Cahusac's superficial article on the subject in Diderot's·and d'Alembert's Encyclopedia (1751-1772). He proposes that choreographers provide the track or floor plan which they alone know; that what they could not explain, should be described by the ablest theatrical journalists, and finally an artist like Boucher coupled with an engraver like Cochin would make renderings of essential groupings. However unwieldy this method may be, it is at least possible and had it been followed we might have a far clearer idea of how past ballets actually appeared than by attempting to decipher the ingenious devices of academic stenochoregraphers. In 1735, Kellom Tomlinson, a well-known English dancing-master, issued his "Art of Dancing" in two splendid volumes, anticipating the method suggested by Noverre. The finest representations of the Minuet to be found are rendered the more complete by a series of careful portrait engravings of dancers moving on the floor-track of a choreographic short-hand.

O

OPERA-BALLET: Opera-Ballet, as we know it, continues a nineteenth century institution. The elaborate ballet-divertissements of Lully (1632-1687) and the opera-ballet of Rameau (1683-1764) had been absorbed into purely atmospheric aids in such a work as Mozart's *Don Giovanni* (1787), where the famous minuet serves as background for the drama played by principals. Thus Verdi arranged the opening ballet for *Rigoletto* (1851). However, after the restoration of the official

Opéra under the Empire of Napoleon, ballet again resumed its more or less preposterous place as a decoration of the lyric repertory. Opera houses were maintained more as a sign of cultural prestige by rulers of European capitals than as entertainment for the general populace, who, incidentally, bought tickets, but whose support equalled only a fragment of government subsidies. Ballets for European operas had their own schools and professional hierarchies. They were maintained as a kind of perennial bait for a certain section of the almost professional audience of permanent opera-subscribers.

The *corps de ballet* on stage fluttered in ball-rooms, throne-rooms, at country-weddings, joyful celebrations, or as sprites or devils. Pretexts were provided by librettists for divertissements exhibiting a favorite soloist for seldom longer than ten minutes. This gave an opportunity for the evolution of a *corps de ballet,* variations by the ballerina, a duet with her partner, and the finale. Meanwhile, singers could rest their voices from the demands of *bel canto* and astronomical *fiorotura.* Opera-ballets, to be sure, danced in their own independent productions, but this note has special reference to ballet in operas.

Why ballets are inserted in Opera in 1939 is something of a mystery. They serve no practical purpose except to employ a limited number of dancers on a precarious basis. There is as little attempt to study the place of ballet in opera, as there is to study the *mise en scène* of opera as a whole. The victory scene in *Aida* as produced by the Metropolitan Opera Association in New York City, or at any other American house for that matter, is a case in point. The Ethiopian captives may indeed be negro supers, but they are followed by girls in black-face representing small negro boys in the tradition of the *travestie* (girls as boys) of the Paris Opéra. The *corps de ballet* evolves around an Italian ballerina on toe-point who does *cooch* gestures with "Egyptian" plastique. To omit the "ballet," however, would be to risk a circus without elephants. Hence opera-ballet is scrubbily maintained in its haphazard limbo, out of habit. It is more important to keep a shadow of dancing than abandon it entirely, since this might be interpreted as loss of face. Except for an unfortunately small fragment attaching to musical interest, the entire persistence of opera is purely a deter-

345

mination to maintain a certain social or economic prestige. Ballets in the opera are like the gardens of the Tuilleries. Even in war-time, they are tended to prove the country is still healthy.

A choreographer for opera-ballet must have by nature a character in which talents for compromise amount to an almost total lack of self-respect. Assistant stage-managers, the faithful serfs of starred singers, eliminate rehearsals for dancing, and simultaneously decrease space given to dance in. The conspiracy is furthered by the bland disregard of the wardrobe department, and the surrealist caprice of wigmakers, shoemakers, and property-men. For those who have a developed taste for taxidermy, a trip to the Metropolitan is fun. For such connoisseurs, the Bacchanale of *Tannhaüser* is rare cheese. Originally written for its Paris première in 1861, it had even then violated a protocol that opera did not introduce a French ballet until the members of the Jockey Club had finished their liqueurs, which was certainly not before the middle of a second act.

Wagner's indications for the choreography he desired are almost pornographic. The fulfillment of them, from Bayreuth to Petersburg, has been sterilized. To be sure, Isadora Duncan (ca. 1905) momentarily managed to clear away some ballet-skirts, but in revenge after her departure, the Bacchanale appeared in costumes which were a frantic corseted parody of the American Maenad herself.

One recalls the first words sung by the tenor representing Tannhaüser. The Minstrel lolling on the couch of Venus, passes his hand woozily before his eyes, avowing, "Heavens! This is unsupportable." There is a superstition backstage that he is referring to the preceding ballet.

OPPOSITION: A term denoting the means used to break the rigid, static and symmetrical position of a dancer's body. For example: when a dancer moves right arm and right leg together, it is less effective plastically than if the right arm moves against the action of the left leg. This opposition (Italian: *controposto*) creates an asymmetrical balance. It increases plasticity by a physical, though symbolic vivification of both sides of the whole body. Actually, the whole body is not affected. Symbol-

PLATE 4

CROISÉ DEVANT

BATTEMENT À LA SECONDE

PORT DE BRAS

EFFACÉ

ically, however, the right arm represents the movement of the entire upper half, the left leg that of the entire lower. If only the right arm and right leg were used it would appear that half the body were dead. Half a body is too great a proportion to be supported as dead weight, even by a completely alive other half. The actual impression given is that a body so shown is awkward and hence ineffective for all dancing purposes. The opposed balance of arms and legs, the alternation of head to shoulders, the counterpoise of the torso, twisted, faced front or back and then twisted again, showing to the public different aspects of the same body at once, suggests if it does not actually display, the difference between the muscularity of the chest and of the back. A parallel contemporary example may be found in the late double-image heads of Pablo Picasso, in which the front face masks a profile. This enhanced plasticity makes legible to an audience the dancers' existence in their element of air. It minimizes flatness, a hard, unresilient silhouette, a cold, inactive outline. J. G. Noverre and Salvatore Vigano carefully observed Hellenistic and Italian Baroque sculpture. Michelangelo, Giovanni da Bologna, Bernini, and the Imperial Romans indicated in static terms of bronze or stone peak positions of plastic expression suitable for climaxes of various *enchainements* which choreographers may be able consecutively to develop.

Carlo Blasis explained in 1829 that "In the Bacchanalian groups which I have composed, I have successfully introduced various attitudes, arabesques and groupings, the original idea of which was suggested to me during my journey to Naples and through Magna Graecia, on viewing the paintings, bronzes and sculptures, rescued from the Ruins of Herculaneum."

As Anna Morgan paraphrases the ideas of Delsarte ("An Hour With Delsarte": 1895): "The law of opposition in gesture has for its mechanical or physical basis, the laws of equilibrium and gravity. A vertical line directly through the body standing erect and perfectly poised, will mark the center of gravity. Any departure of the body from this right line, in any direction, must be compensated for by an equal portion of the body in the opposite direction, else equilibrium cannot be maintained. Equilibrium is one of the elements of physical grace, and, while there may be equilibrium without grace, there can be no grace without equilibrium, so in gesturing this law of compensation or balance must be preserved in the interests of grace. A gesture by one member of the body demands a compensating gesture by another member in opposition."

P

PAS: Theoretically, the *pas* is not a single but a combination of steps or movements of the feet. In classic ballet it also refers to a dance executed by a soloist (*pas seul*), a duet (*pas de deux*), or familiarly: *pas de trois, pas de quatre,* etc.

According to the Encyclopedia of Diderot and d'Alembert (ca. 1772), in an article based heavily on Rameau (1725), Cahusac (1754), and Noverre (1760) there were five types of steps. Steps in a *straight* line; slow, *spread-open* steps made as in walking, when one foot after the other describes a semi-circle; *struck* or beaten steps, in which one foot strikes in back or in front of the other before placing it on the floor; *turned* steps, in which the legs make a complete circle in the air or on the floor, and *twisted* steps.

Certain ballet movements have no other meaning than to display or praise the dancing organism through the mechanics of the human body. The vocabulary of active steps is considerable, and is based on the five absolute static *positions* of the feet. On this basis, choreographers and individual dancers for five hundred years have contributed to build on one another's work until we have been given the dancing practice of our contemporary stage. The two prime categories of *pas* govern the twin provinces of earth and air. Steps predominantly the gift of the seventeenth century demonstrated the resources of the plane stage-surface with adaptations of ball-room walk or march. By the middle of the eighteenth, new steps began to predicate the conquest of air. As time went on, greater subtlety, variety and plasticity evolved themselves into a fluid idiom. The nineteenth century provided a language accentuated by heel and toe beats borrowed from the characteristic national dance sources (polka, mazurka, cachucha, etc.), which gave color to the corpus of steps which had tended to become theatrically sterile. If the twentieth century has provided new steps, these have been appropriated from popular entertainments, public ball-rooms and music-halls. The steps of traditional social or ball-room dancing have always been amplified by theatrical gesture, but as for their execution from the minuet down to our two-step, it is more a question of tempi than of complex physical activity.

By a "step" in theatrical dancing, we usually refer to a combination of movements which has become popular enough to enjoy written definition or inclusion in dance manuals. The step thus defined becomes canonical, part of the material of dancing, which can be taught. But there are innumerable steps created by choreographers for their own private and transient uses, which may never bear a name.

Chefs invent new dishes in honor of persons or events. Dancers and choreographers are as ingenious. Sometimes the name sticks, and we have Pêche Melba or Spaghetti Caruso. When the great Italian teacher and dancer, Enrico Cecchetti (1850-1928), opened a new school in London, his *glissade de Mami* honored a black kitten mascot with which he had been presented. This was a *pas de chat*, indeed. There are steps named with reference to birds and animals, passing personalities and events.

PIROUETTE: From the Burgundian, *pirouelle:* spinning top (Littré): or from the French, *pied-roue,* foot-wheel (Frisch).

Cyril Beaumont (1928), in his excellent introduction to Lambranzi's "New and Curious School of Theatrical Dancing" (1716), has a paragraph on the German word *pirole,* which also appears as *piroleten* and *birollets. Pirouette* is a term for turning, in French and German, *pirouettd* in Italian; *pirueta* in Spanish. *Pirole* is Italian for peg or pin.

A *pirouette* is the complete spinning turn or whirl of the dancer's body in one place, usually in sequence of from two to eight or more. The effect of the well-executed pirouettes is to present the dancer's body in its full plasticity, front and back superimposed on one another, almost as in a double-exposure.

An audience necessarily remains stationary in its seat. If the seats could be imagined to revolve rapidly to enable spectators to see back and front in a single frontal position, there might be no reason for pirouettes. In any case, it is one of the most brilliant steps in a classic dancer's vocabulary. A quick pirouette, performed high on the half toe, perfectly accompanies a run of notes in music. It can be accelerated in sequence, and a dancer cleanly stopping short after the swift spin produces a maximum contrast, complete immobility after intense mobility, in the same plane. *Pirouettes* on the floor are the basis for *tours en l'air*. Slow *pirouettes,* which few dancers execute well, can be as effective as fast ones. Instead of diminishing their already quiet pace, a good technician can perform slowly almost as many turns as he can quickly, producing thereby a remarkable display of controlled energy and reserve force. *Pirouettes* for girls are executed on toe point. They can be employed meaninglessly, or for their own sake as an irrelevant trick. Some unimaginative choreographers, when invention fails them, fill up gaps in design by a string of *pirouettes* which at least appear brilliant. The *pirouette à la seconde* is a turn with the leg extended and is a spectacular preparation for a final explosive twirl. (See plate 4.)

While the complete turn of the body must be among the oldest steps in the vocabulary of dancing, there is a tradition that the *pirouette* in its present theatrical form, arrived from Stuttgart in 1766. From that city came Mlle. Heinel and her young partner Ferville, to the Paris Opéra, where the subscribers were astonished by the multiplicity of the German debutante's *tours*. Both dancers supposedly executed the turn on *une seule pointe,* or as we would probably translate, on the high half-toe. The dancers Maximilien Gardel (1740-1787) and Gaetan Vestris (1729-1808) perfected the step until they were popularly thought to "shine like the sun" or "twinkle like a star." Serge Legat (ca. 1890) is said to have performed fourteen turns at a single time. Eight is still excellent for anyone. In our own day, Enrico Cecchetti (1850-1928) was known as *le roi des pirouettes,* or even sometimes *le diable des pirouettes,* but his typical Italian training limited him to turns in but a single direction. His pupil, Vaslav Nijinsky (active: 1909-1919), executed a series of renowned *pirouettes* at the end of his variation as Harlequin in *Carnival* (Fokine: 1909). Another Cecchetti pupil, Mascagno, who settled and taught in America, was partly responsible for the astonishing pirouettes of Lew Christensen, the brilliant young American dancer and choreographer. The slow pirouettes of André Eglevsky, with arms held arched over his head, are the despair of many of our best living dancers. In the summer of 1939, he is reported from Hollywood to have executed eighteen on a bet.

PLIE (see plate 2): "Dancing is no more than knowing how to bend (*plier*) the knees at the proper time." P. Rameau, *Le Maître à Danser* (1725).

The bending of the knees is perhaps the single most important foundation exercise in the classic academy. The index of a dancer's excellence can be recognized even at the barre by the depth, ease and steady rhythm of a *grand plié* from standing position, *demi plié*, deep down almost to the floor. The *plié* develops balance and muscularity, renders joints easy, and makes tendons strong and supple.

POINTES (see plate 3): The exact origin of dancing on toes is obscure. Throughout the eighteenth century, artists represented dancers supported on conventionalized bare toes to enhance an appearance of lightness, and long after toe-shoes were worn, draughtsmen still depicted dancers floating on bare pink feet. Sometime in the late eighteen-twenties or early thirties the heelless slipper with boxed toe made its entrance; the cardboard boxing of the toe, supported by stiff satin and thin sole-leather shank, added just sufficient extra support, while providing enough shock-absorption to enable girls to support their whole dancing weight on the tips of their toes. Drawings of Taglioni dated 1826 (Stuttgart) show her poised on point. The static position was soon abandoned for actual movement (such as the *pas de bourrée*) on the *pointes* themselves.

Toe-dancing requires considerable strengthening of the muscles involved, as so great a weight is not normally carried on that portion of the foot. Some Cossack tribesmen supposedly danced on their unsupported toes. But in western theatrical tradition men do not use points since it tends to suggest a finicking effeminacy. An exception was the Irish dancer, Anton

Dolin (Patrick Kay) in *Les Facheux* (Nijinska: 1925), where an approximation of seventeenth century atmosphere permitted it. Several contemporary American male-dancers are able to dance on toe, but do not in public.

Toe-dancing came into being, it is generally understood, as the logical outgrowth of the dancer's eagerness to quit the floor. A longing for the ethereal sphere (*élévation*) characterized the general idea behind these ballets based on French and German romantic literature as exemplified by Heine, Hoffman and Gautier, and as danced by Taglioni, Elssler, Cerrito and Grisi (1830-50). However, since this time, the use of points has been developed from a stylistic trick, into a useful, general attribute of classic dancing, far beyond the local expression of a limited literary and artistic tendency. It permits, by the use of a base smaller than the flat foot, more brilliance in turning (*pirouettes*). The extended toe-point when raised from the floor aids the continuous line of a dancing body, prolonging its direction, at least in the imaginations of the public, into infinity, rather than stopping it abruptly with the normal right angle of the walking foot. The sharp attack of the point on the floor can be accentually important. The arrow shape of the point gives the upper body an appearance of lightness and facile mobility. When the points sharply strike the floor it is called *la danse taqueté* (from *taquet:* peg). This staccato style was first so termed around 1834, to apply to Fanny Elssler's debut in *La Tempête* (Coralli). The effect of her feet was compared to golden arrows bouncing off a marble pavement, and contrasted with Taglioni's *danse ballonné*, one more example of the eternal duel between floor and air.

The artificiality of the convention of *pointes* removes the dragging banality of the association or identification of a stage-walk with a normal walk. Progress over the stage on points held more or less closely together is known as the *pas de bourrée*. It has little to do with the *Bourrée*, a quick eighteenth century dance-form, coming originally from the district of Auvergne. It was popularized for our time as the effortless locomotion of Anna Pavlova in *La Mort du Cygne* (Fokine: 1909), when she seemed to float over some impalpable yet polished surface. Movement on *pointes* effects an almost imperceptible advance or retreat. There is scarcely any shift of weight and the bodies seem borne on stage, supported more on air than on legs.

Slippers which sheathe dancers' toes have become almost a totem or fetich of the dancing tribe. A conclave of Muscovite balletomanes, relates Alexander Pleschayev, having paid two hundred roubles for the ballet shoes of Marie Taglioni on the occasion of her leaving Russia in 1842, solemnly had them cooked with a special sauce and ate them. Those who saw the French film *Ballerina* (Jean Benoît-Lévy: 1937) recall the little *rat de l'Opéra* made an altar on the mantelpiece for the *chausson* of her adored god-mother.

One may hear violent arguments as to the respective merits of the Italian versus the French toe-shoe. Some dancers need a considerable strength in the cardboard or stiff satin box, others want little. Some learn to crochet a knotty protection in heavy pink silk to protect the tip of their shoes; others feel this dulls the sensitive contact with the floor.

The entry of the Journal of the Brothers de Goncourt for July 23, 1868, tells us that Théophile Gautier came down to their country place and talked about dancers at the Opéra. "He described their white (*sic*) satin ballet-slippers, saying that each slipper is re-enforced by a bit of wadding at the point where the dancer feels that her weight is concentrated; and that an expert could tell you, from a glance at the wadding, the name of the dancer."

The wadding is still in use. It is usually made of lambs wool, to be bought at the drug-store. The ordinary slipper is traditionally pink, or flesh color, unless a costume designer orders otherwise.

POSE (see plates 2 and 3): A static position demonstrating the body in a fixed plastic design, such as *attitude* or *arabesque* in distinction to an active step (*pas*) or fundamental station (the *five positions*).

POSITIONS (see plate 1): The *positions* usually refer to five absolute positions of the feet which are the foundation of classic ballet exercises, and hence of western traditional theatrical dancing. Positions of the feet have their complements for head and arms, although these latter are frequently ignored, since in America, at least, our academic training is uncoördinated. The five positions of the feet permit no change, those of the head and arms have a less canonical rigidity based on less mechanical logic. Positions of the feet are founded on support of the spinal column, on the turn-out of pelvis, hips and thighs, and on locomotion. Text-book positions of head and arms have a secondary, decorative function which is frequently rendered more plastic and appealing by individual teachers. *Port de bras* (carriage of the arms) is largely a matter of taste, and positions of the head, framed by the arms, are determined by it.

The five absolute foot positions according to P. Rameau, "The Dancing Master" (1725) were established by the *maître de ballet*, Beauchamps, first director of the Académie Royale from 1671 to 1687. Rameau states that before his time the positions were "unknown." They were known, but not codified. In 1701 Feuillet, in his *Chorégraphie*, or "Art of Writing Dance Steps," stated that there were five types of steps (*pas*) to which the innumerable varieties could be reduced. They were the direct (straight ahead), open, round, twisted, and struck. Each is based on one of the five original positions of the two feet.

1. Heels together, toes turned completely out, so that the feet are in a straight line. In the time of Beauchamps (ca. 1670), when dancers wore high heeled shoes, the toes were turned out only to about 90°, but this gives far less mobility to the legs, stability after action, and support to the trunk than our contemporary extreme position.

2. Feet in parallel line, as in first position, weight evenly distributed on both, but separated by a distance of about twelve inches.

3. The heel of one foot locked against the instep of the other, weight equally distributed, with complete turn-out.

4. With weight divided equally, in complete turn-out, the fore foot is twelve inches in advance of the back.

5. In complete turn-out, the feet are locked, right heel to left toe, right toe to left heel.

Rameau gives many rules for "honours" (bows) and of particular positions of holding the arms in specific dances, of moving wrists, of doffing hats. Carlo Blasis (1820) established for the theatre (Rameau was occupied chiefly with social-dancing) various exercises for wrists and arms for stage-use. But his statement of absolute arm positions is vague. He tells us that in most cases a dancer should arrange them "as gracefully as possible."

Looking in a French text-book such as Meunier's *La Danse Classique* (1931), one finds considerable difference in the position of arms, head and of the body, from the Anglo-Italian method as demonstrated by *A Primer of Classical Ballet*, by Cyril Beaumont (1933). The Russian School, at least as instructed in the West, holds closer to the later (Cecchetti) method. In both French and Italian schools, there are more than a single station for many positions, since they can be executed high, low, or in front (*en haut, en bas,* or *en avant*). There are five canonical positions of arms and head. They complement the five positions of the feet. There are eight canonical positions of the body, but space is too limited to define each of them here.

The five positions of the feet bear a similar relation in the dance to the five staves of musical notation. Other systems of musical notation are possible, just as different systems of geometry besides the Euclidean may be invented. In dancing, also, particularly in forms invented by insurgent imitators, attempts to establish new positions are not unknown. However, they usually resolve themselves in arguments of nomenclature without establishing any new principle of mechanics.

E. A. Théleur, in his "Letter on Dancing" (1832), states reasons for dissenting with the accepted practice, insomuch as he claims to have found but *one* position, in the traditional sense, "the others, commonly known under that name, are nothing more than stations, their utility being to direct or determine us where we are to commence, change or finish our movements, while in the performance of an *enchainement,* the first and only position being that in which we should place the body, so as to be able to balance ourselves while performing any movements that may be required of us, as far as regards dancing." This is the *first* traditional position. Théleur's stations are divided into "ground," "half aerial," and "aerial" *stations,* and he analyzes the classic dance according to his categories, which are logical enough, but of no more use than the ordinary.

The more one considers the five positions, the more absolute their logic seems. Simplicity itself, the underlying principle is based on our human anatomy, reduced to its essential capacities. It permits a five-note scale from which an infinitude of visual chords in innumerable keys may be rationally arranged. The five positions are a kind of net or comb through which dance movement must accommodate itself in its ceaseless shift.

R

RELEVE: From the French *relever:* to lift again. However, in ballet terminology it means raising the body in any position, by lifting the flat foot to half-toe, or with girls, to full point.

ROMANTIC BALLET: The term "romantic" as applied to ballet is a misnomer. Familiarly, it is a style of dancing as exemplified by revivals of *Giselle* (Coralli: 1841) or *Les Sylphides* (Fokine: 1909). Yet both ballets are familiarly labeled *ballets classiques,* although Fokine's is subtitled "a romantic revery" and is indeed an atmospheric pastiche of Taglioni's *La Sylphide* (P. Taglioni: 1830). In each case romanticism becomes not an opposition to, but a stylistic department of, classicism.

By "romantic" we generally understand an attitude in reaction to neo-classic Greek revivals of the late-eighteenth century and the republican Roman frigidity of Directory and Empire. Under Napoleon, dancers in Paris and Milan wore "Greek" tunics, not far from what Isadora Duncan would have considered "natural." But neo-classicism exhausted itself as a merely decorative style without reference to the life of its time. It was replaced by what came to be known as the "Gothick," but which was no more Gothic, as we understand it, than was its predecessor essentially antique. In philosophy, it was a shift from the finite, rational, orderly and demonstrable based on arbitrary archaeological precedent to the vague, atmospheric, warm, remote and infinite. The novels of Walter Scott and Monk Lewis, with their wild and loosely constructed plots, the tortured compositions of the painters Delacroix and Gericault, the verses of Byron and Victor Hugo, the dancing of Taglioni and Elssler on their elevated toe-points, were the facts of this revolution in action.

Taglioni embraced the colder aspect of romantic dancing, the marble maiden, the virgin lover, the human angel, the pure evanescent, ephemeral longed-for-eternal-feminine. Elssler embodied the warmer rôle; the exotic gypsy-hearted dashing earth-force of vague Central Europe, mysterious Spain, forbidding Scotland. National dances were the decorative frames for her characterizations. Romantic ballet did not forswear reality, since the neo-classic theatre itself had had little pretensions to realism. It merely denied logic, reason or formal design. Its principle was without ethic,—emotional and decorative. It disappeared (ca. 1850) because it could not survive the departure of its original exponents, and since it had even less connection with the life of its epoch than its predecessor, and was as well completely lacking in moral ideas. It had become instead of a comment on life through art, merely an outworn theatrical parody or pastiche of literature, painting and itself.

Hence the so-called Romantic ballet is not a department of the dance, but merely a localized theatrical echo of a transient influential literary and artistic movement.

ROND DE JAMBES: A movement in which the pointed toes describe circles on the floor (*à terre*) or in the air (*en l'air*) in both directions, while the body is supported on the other foot. It is used as an elementary class-room exercise to turn out the hips, feet and legs.

T

TOUR-EN-L'AIR: A *pirouette* (turn) executed not on the ground, but *in the air*. Desrat (1895) curiously enough speaks of this now familiar step as new to the vocabulary of the academic theatrical dance, having more reference to acrobatics than to classic ballet. The step to be brilliant is usually a *double* turn and perhaps it is the multiple *tour* to which Desrat refers. Spectacular dancers who claim triple air turns, in fact usually accomplish at most two and a half, faking the complete frontal landing of the final *tour*.

Beauchamps, Louis XIV's choreographer, and first superintendent of his Académie Royale (ca. 1661-1675), was praised by La Bruyère, *"qu'il j'etait (jetait) les jambes en avant, et faisait un tour en l'air avant que de retomber a terre"* (for he leaped with his feet held in front, and made a turn before regaining the ground). *Un tour* must have referred to the single turn.

TURN-OUT: "In order to dance well, sir," wrote J. G. Noverre before 1760, "nothing is so important as the turning outwards of the thigh, and nothing is so natural to men as the contrary position." Turn-out of legs and thighs at a ninety degree angle, while always recognized as a fundamental for stage-dancing since the *first* and *fifth* positions were established (ca. 1700), received academic canonization somewhere between 1760 and 1780. Indeed, it was considered so important that a machine, the *tourne-hanche,* was invented to accomplish it all the quicker, and was in use as late as the middle of last century. In Albéric Second's *Les Petits Mystères de l'Opéra* (1844), so charmingly illustrated by Gavarni, a dancer complained, "Each morning the Master imprisoned my feet in a grooved box. There, heel to toe, and knees turned outward, my martyred feet became accustomed to remain in a parallel line. It is called 'turning oneself out' *(se tourner)."* Nearly a hundred years before, Noverre had warned that far from being efficacious "it cripples those who make use of it by forcing the waist to take on a much more disagreeable effect than the one it is desired to eliminate."

Carlo Blasis, in his "Code of Terpsichore" (1829), analyzed for our time, as well, this essential mechanical element in stage dance movement. "In the management of your legs, endeavor chiefly to acquire a facility of turning them (out) completely. To this end make yourself easy about your hips, that your thighs may move with freedom, and your knees turn well outwards. All the openings of your legs are thus rendered easy and graceful."

"Some young people are framed by nature with their limbs turning outwards; they possess, therefore, more facility, and succeed to greater advantage than those whose legs turn toward each other; a person of the latter kind indeed can cherish no hope of becoming a good dancer how diligent soever his labour and study be. Practice will do no more than turn his feet and bend his soles a little downwards, but his thighs and knees must remain always in their natural state. . . . The movement of the hip is a sort of guide to that of the knee and instep, as it is impossible for these last to move unless the hip acts first. In some steps the hips alone are set in motion, as in *entrechats, battements tendus,* etc."

TUTU: The familiar symbol of the ballet-girl is her many layered tarletan skirt. In comparison with the long history of theatrical dancing, it is a comparatively recent invention. All through the seventeenth and eighteenth centuries, dancers wore theatricalized versions of customary civil or court dress, no matter whether they portrayed a Greek god or a Roman emperor. Big skirts, wigs, and heeled shoes impeded free movement. Gradually, individual dancers protested by personal revolutions in their costume, which successively became accepted as academic practice. After the French Revolution, due to archaeological researches of the official painter, J. L. David (1748-1825), stage costume assumed a considerable historical accuracy. Neo-classicism attached itself to the name of the first Napoleon. When his dynasty fell, neo-classicism as a mode fell with it to be replaced by the "Romantic" revival,—an interest in Gothic architecture, dress and stories. Romanticism was at once reactionary and revolutionary. Antiquity was abandoned and Europe, however picturesque and unreal, was discovered as a more vital source of material. The court of Louis-Philippe undertook great balls, recalling the lost glories of Versailles and the *ancien regime.*

After the coronation of Charles the Tenth, the Duchesse de Berry became Madame; Le Pavillon de Marsan at the Louvre, her château; and its theatre Le Théatre de Madame. Her *Quadrille de Mary Stuart* was announced for the second of March, 1829. More than six weeks were spent planning this stupendous fête, the costume and decor of which were scrupulously designed after monuments of the sixteenth century. There was not one, but many costume designers, each noble participant choosing a particular painter: Lafitte, Lecomte, Isabey and even Fragonard. Eugène Lami recorded the ball *after* it took place, as well as designing dresses. The skirts were bell-shaped, full to the floor with square cut bodices, low across the bosom, and small puffed sleeves recalling subtly or else anticipating, the actual civil dress of the season of 1829-1830.

Taglioni appeared as *La Sylphide* at the Opéra on May 14, 1832, to become the lyric apotheosis of the Romantic Revolution. Her costumes were designed by Eugène Lami. Cyril Beaumont writes in his monumental "Complete Book of Ballets" (1937): "The dress consisted of a tight-fitting bodice, leaving the neck and shoulders bare, bell-shaped skirt reaching midway between the knee and the ankle, and pale pink tights and satin shoes; the only adornments were a pale blue ribbon about the waist, a pair of tiny wings between the shoulder-blades, a posy at the breast, a pearl necklace and bracelets, and a garland of convolvuli to frame the hair."

This costume was a transposition of the Stuart dress, adapted from ball-room to opera-house. Bodices, waist-line and skirt-shape were identical whether or not Lami consciously remembered his earlier fête. Taglioni's long arms were well-known to be the despair of her father. Some critics said the new skirt was intended to hide her long legs, but this was not true. In any event, the *Sylphide* costume was like a nun's uniform for ballet-dancers for almost thirty years, due to the persistent memory of the original sylph's prestige.

In 1887, the Italian ballerina Zucchi created a sensation in Petrograd by snipping her long tarletons to knee length in the already accepted Italian manner. In spite of Imperial interdict, Russian dancers followed suit, clipping theirs even shorter to give freer play to the feet. The short tutu skirt is now the badge of "classic" ballet, the long that of "romantic."

U

UNIONS: Dancers may consider themselves artists, but they are also workers, and need the mutual protection of other workers in their field against exploitation in wages, hours and against unemployment. Musicians, variety artists, and actors have been organized into unions for many years. Dancers in musical-comedy have fitted into a category under "actor" but now dancers are being unionized on an independent basis.

Before the musicians became welded into their present powerful units, it was possible for unscrupulous managers to hire foreign aggregations at low salaries for exploitation in the American concert market. This severely restricted the cultivation of native talent. The same situation now exists in the dance field and only strong dancers' unions can assure an artist that they will enjoy anything like even the precarious security of the permanent large white-Russian companies. Individual soloists and orchestral conductors are permitted to work here due to their unique artistic gifts, and the same could be arranged for dancers or choreographers. But for the rest, our own should have preference. If not, any attempt at maintaining an independent artistic ambition or standard will disappear at best into commercialism, at worst vanish completely.

V

VARIATION: A solo dance in a classic ballet, which, by association, has come to mean any portion of a ballet undertaken by individual dancers at which time the chief dramatic attention is focused upon them. The term undoubtedly is connected with the "variation" upon a given musical theme.

Y

YOUTH: The early years of a dancer's career are generally considered the most brilliant. Those who knew Nijinsky and Pavlova in Russia (ca. 1907) tell us they were never the same again. A brilliant debut can blot out the fame of subsequent seasons, and what might have been maturity turns into decadence. A dancer's instrument is his body, and, unlike a violin, it does not improve with age. The physical mechanism has an early prime, but it can be prolonged by strict attention for twenty years. The flash of agile energies, the exuberance of post-adolescent muscles are the most obvious attributes of a dancer, but it is important to remember that these are superficial beside intensity of expression or purity of line. These are not natural gifts, but come only with experience on and off stage. One recalls Nijinsky as a young dancer, yet he expected to dance until he was an old man, just as had his master, Cecchetti (1850-1928). Except, even as a young man, Nijinsky knew he would not perform the same rôles at fifty which he had created at twenty-five. The transition from a *jeune premier* into a mature *danseur noble* is as difficult to achieve in ballet as it is on the dramatic stage, where few juveniles become accomplished character actors. The juvenile remains young until he is old. The persistence of the rôle of youth disqualifies an artist from his final achievement. Exuberant dancers have at atmosphere of play, or sport, an ingenous exhibitionism which is touching because it is so transitory. The audiences know better than dancers how fast youth flies. A young dancer may look forward to a career of twenty or even thirty years, and afterwards to a score or more of teaching. Men tend to last longer than girls, but we recall Karsavina and Pavlova not as debutantes, but as distinguished women.

WHAT BALLET IS ABOUT

1959

WHAT BALLET IS ABOUT: An AMERICAN Glossary

by
Lincoln
Kirstein

CONTENTS

Dance 371

Ballet 372

THE Ballet 373

Classic Ballet 375

Character Dancing . . . 378

Choreography 383

Choreographer 383

Young Choreographer . . 383

Ballet Master 384

Dancing Master 385

Tradition 385

Style 388

Stars 389

Invention 393

The Dancer 395

The Audience 400

The General Public . . . 401

Special (or Balletomane)
  Public 402

The Critical Public . . . 402

Critics 403

Russian Ballet 406

French Ballet 409

English Ballet 411

American Ballet 413

Argentine, Australian,
  Danish, Dutch, Swedish
  and South African Ballet 417

Modern Dance 419

Ballet Music 422

Ballet Scenery 427

What Is Ballet About . . 433

Lincoln Kirstein

WHAT BALLET IS ABOUT:
An AMERICAN Glossary

for Wystan and Chester

Ballet dancing is a form of spectacle now popular to an extent which would have seemed improbable twenty-five years ago. Foreign companies make lucrative tours here. Our own, sponsored by plane-fares from the State Department, are dispatched all over the world as hopeful cultural ambassadors. Ballet at home commands a big and growing public. However, its art and craft are relatively new to the great audience, and ballet has now reached that point of historic development when it must have a popular audience to survive. There are those who, through vagueness or lack of curiosity, permit themselves prejudice against it which precise definition might alleviate. Much of the trouble is semantic. Many terms used to define elements of theatrical dancing overlap. Categories are superficially confusing. Hence, this short glossary for the American audience.

DANCE: Ordered bodily movement accompanied by a regulating percussive or rhythmic beat. A universal human act, it became theatrical or spectacular comparatively late in history. Originally, its designs sprang from rites; its end was social and religious. Its aim was to secure by mimetic action and gesture energy through the schedule of the seasons to gain Great Nature's bounty, conquer enemies, ward off evil, make babies, find food. On the most popular (dance-hall) level it is still communal or playful, done for fun rather than to be looked at, for pay.

BALLET: A codified language of exercise, movement and gesture designed for instruction, transmission and legibility; an ordering of formal patterns covering or filling a limited space. In the West, this is our opera-house stage floor, and for the efficiency of sight-lines, a triangular space, flat-surfaced under the scenery-grid and an area some ten feet above it. The ballet of India, South East Asia, China and Japan have even stricter vocabularies, older and more unchanging forms than Western dancing, calculated to be done in open air, temple or palace precincts rather than enclosed theaters with proscenium arches.

André Levinson says:

> The movement of the oriental dance is concentric. The knees almost instinctively come together and bend, the curved arms embrace the body. Everything is pulled together. Everything converges. The movement of the (western) classic dance, on the other hand, is excentric, the arms and the legs stretch out, freeing themselves from the torso, expanding the chest. The whole region of the dancer's being, body and soul, is dilated.

However, Western ballet, (our academic, traditional, classic theatrical dance), in the last fifty years has become an international language, comparable to that of the pianoforte keyboard, and is taught in approximately the same methodology everywhere. It derived from an analysis and codification of folk and social dances in North Italy during the early Renaissance. Steps were divided into fast and slow, high and low, to be done in the provinces of earth and air. Dominated at first by Milanese masters at the Medici court in the Louvre, it was subsequently developed, organized and amplified by French, Central European and Scandinavian dancers. Russians, Czarist and Soviet, have had hegemony for the last seventy-five years; before, ballet was Italian, French, Viennese and Danish. In our generation, in England and America, new crops of dancers testify annually to native independence. Our particular idiom of ballet in the West runs closely parallel to the development of Western music, from the sixteenth century dance-suite through the sonata, symphony and tone-poem, with powerful influences from folk-lore, and more recently from popular dance-music.

Our (Western) ballet is a clear if complex blending of human anatomy, solid geometry and acrobatics offered as a symbolic demonstration of manners—the morality of consideration for one human being moving *in time* with another. The visible projection of contact, support and release, of keeping step, shifting pace and weight is framed in styles of movement from the courtier's correctness to the athlete's competitive courtesy in obeying ground-rules. The formal bow (*révérence*), the curtsy (as in the minuet) are simple gestures from imperial protocol, based on mutual respect, expressed in legible physical terms.

The feudal ball-room turned itself into a theater by lifting a platform at one end. This stage, for so it became, was later raked towards footlights and structurally separated from the rest of the enclosure by a baroque picture-frame proscenium arch, locating the spectacle that it held as more elevated, different and apart from the social dancing that was conducted below on the flat parterre or orchestra-floor. A flashier extension of social dancing, ballet soon developed a rationale of readable movement, as well as dancers who were more than amateur performers. Its ultimate aim, building on each successive epoch, has been the most intense projection possible of the human silhouette in plastic action. Ballet has become a means for the extreme release of physical and mental capacity involving measure, melody, memory and money. Through the schooled elegance of skilled muscularity strictly ordered by music, there developed a drama of acrobatic excitement plus a melodrama of hazard dominated. The privy purse of king and courtier provided richness, and competitive ostentation had political employment.

The use of the trained body in field sports tends towards exhaustion in competition, mastering dangerous chances, breaking established records. The use of the dancer's body in ballet is an expression of spectacular skills, endlessly repeated for an unattainable perfection, non-competitive (except towards some metaphysical ideal) which must be coördinated with the behavior of all other performers, stars and soloists, on stage at the same time. It tends, however deviously, towards the state of ritual from which it remotely sprang.

THE BALLET: When people say that they love or they hate THE Ballet, they are usually speaking of a repertory of dance-compositions familiar to them over a five, or at most a twenty-five year period. This repertory is currently in performance of varying efficiency by touring companies, showing combinations of music, scenic decoration, costume and movement, invested with life by dancing personalities.

THE Ballet is administered by organizations presenting a repertory which may or may not have been created for it, performed by dancers who may or may not have originally created the rôles in which they now appear. THE Russian Ballet, specifically the Diaghilev company, appearing in Western Europe from 1909 to 1929 and in the United States in 1916-17, meant THE Ballet for the first forty years of this century in our hemisphere. Its shadow, or rather the faded pattern of its policy, is still active, but its proper repertory as well as the analytical method which caused it to be born, and the historical necessities which framed it, are no longer vivid. Diaghilev himself was prodigal of novelty. His means were frequently more interesting as paint, poetry, music or personality than as dancing itself. After his departure from Russia by 1913, he was separated from the academic source of a dancer-pool and Western Europe, at that time, provided almost no executants of first quality. Western Europe did, however, provide the Paris School of painters, poets, musicians, dress-makers and an audience which made the city of light the capital of the world. Diaghilev was far less impressed by the importance and lasting powers of his novelties than his heirs; he, unlike them, was always able to find new combinations. His immediate successors chiefly preserved what they could of his. Attempts are now made to endow later revivals of his early repertory with sacrosanct prestige; they are presented with all the authority of a kept canon.

The difference between the ballets of Diaghilev and the accumulated repertory of his epigones was a unique personal predeliction in good taste and in bad taste, and his conviction for serious caprice. His successors had interests in a repertory that could be merchandised. They appropriated his repertory in desuetude as anchor, launching-pad and gilt-edged security. Whole troupes as far flung as Australia and Argentina lived for decades on works which were fresh in quite other circumstances, which did not improve in revival, nor in dilution, nor in a variety of pastiche which was evoked to show something as close as possible to an original without transparent plagiarism. Indeed, close imitation was a sort of abject flattery while here was a workable selling formula in making publics think they'd seen it all before.

A great number of new works equipped with scenery, costumes

and music to some sort of dancing have received first performances since Diaghilev's death in 1929. Three quarters of them have been attempts in one style or another to cash in on the fame of his innovation, but rarely with the focused taste or elevation of collaborative talent which he, for personal and historic reasons, commanded, not as dilletante or impresario, but as a powerful analytical intelligence, operating in the world of lyric theater, as amateur, craftsman, patron and prince.

CLASSIC BALLET: The books say this means ballet opposite to Romantic Ballet, the opposite of Classic Ballet. Romantic ballet is a period designation referring usually to works in a climate established under the influence of the poets Heine, Gautier and E. T. A. Hoffmann in the middle of the last century. It is loosely used to signify ballets in which dramatic pantomime or character-dancing predominated over the school-exercise academic vocabulary. Romantic Ballet today is a category which does not, like the developed classic dance, renew itself. Oddly enough, the archtypical Romantic works (*Giselle, Swan Lake, Coppelia*) are now considered The Classics, and serve as chief tests for the status of international star-style, in spite of an insistent presence of theatricalized folk-dancing and quasi-operatic pantomime.

It is easier to speak of classic style or even of 'classicism' than of Classic Ballet. A classic style may be recognized sooner than it can be defined. It is by no means, like classical sculpture or plastercasts, frigid, chaste, pure, serene or hard. It can also be warm, bright, soft and sharp, even gay. A true classic dancer is one whose instrument includes the mastery of traditional academic lessons to the degree that a pianist of mettle imposes his own ideas on a keyboard or a fine voice plays with coloratura. In addition to mechanical mastery, the classic dancer embodies a controlled energy towards a perfect delivery of the dance vocabulary, so concentrated, balanced and directed that new dimensions in the realization of steps and combinations of movement are manifest. Presupposing the instrument, an educated body, the distilled energy of the dancer's temperament colors his or her quality as pure pigment stains clear water. Control, concentration and balance in the self, both physical and psychic (control of the ego), combine into that final element which serves both as definition of personality and signature of an epoch. Whether we have ever seen them or not, we know by analeptic analysis that Taglioni means one date, Pavlova another, Spessiva another. Embodied classicism or peak performance in this kind of equilibrium seems even to repeat itself, identifying main dancers with each other so that there is a dynasty of dancers in being, a sequence of bodies born decades apart who may never have seen each other. What was the classic climate of the Romantic era of 1840 hinted of human loss, decline, wasting-away in waltzes; ethereal persistence of frail soul over proud flesh; love over death.

Our criterion, our classicism (in the American Century) a hundred years after Heine and Hoffmann, is the mastery of the human body over the machine, or the persistence of the body's possibility to move freely despite general dehumanization. Today the dancer's innate metric and musical accompaniment is no longer the sadly or the strongly flowing waltz. Rather, it is measured by syncopated, interrupted, discontinuous rhythms and serial forms; assonant melody and dissonant song. The shapes are abrupt, asymmetrical; movement can even be spastic. Accents are hit with unsuspected or even apparently unrelated emphasis; the correspondence is in their relative placement. Anything can happen, all over the floor or lifted off it, but it happens to an order—anything, that is, (in the classic dance) except the vanity of improvisation. Surprise is our substitute for solemnity, playfulness for fated purpose. Toes have a trip-hammer beat; the whole body finds a piston's pulsation. Sharp, clean, reiterant, hinting at irony even when the atmosphere is lyric, it is the impermanence of mortal performance alongside its chances for ephemeral perfection which is its own subject rather than a narrative explication of fading flowers or distraught innocence. While contemporary classicism, like all dancing, is haunted by the evanescence of energy and the delicate counterpoise in all extremes or opposites of action, it magnifies the meaning of liberty in disciplined dancing, almost while mocking it. The human machine can do as well as an invented machine, or even better, because while it automatically remembers to perform, it thinks during performance. While bodies sweat, machines rust. Balanchine said his *Agon* (Stravinsky, 1957) was a machine that thought; John Martin added that it also smiled.

In *The Trembling of the Veil,* Yeats wrote:

. . . . . Samuel Butler was the first Englishman to make the discovery, that it is possible to write with great effect without music, without style, either good or bad, to eliminate from the mind all emotional implication and to prefer plain water to every vintage, so much metropolitan lead and solder to any tendril of the vine. Presently I had a nightmare that I was haunted by a sewing machine, that clicked and shone, but the incredible thing was that the machine smiled, smiled perpetually.

At Versailles, where the classic style as we recognize it in the West received its first framing, chiefly in ball-rooms that were pretheatrical displays for propaganda purposes, partners were princes in their proud youth. These dancers would one day be kings and queens. On the apex of a social pyramid, dancers moved through the weather of majestic dominance, a gracious and graceful deliberate consideration symbolic of the sovereign's obligation to his realm. Just as imitations or mutations of Versailles appeared in the independent masterpieces of Potsdam, Schönbrunn and Peterhof, the Grand Style of classic court manners took over European operatic dancing. After the French Revolution, when kings started losing their crowns and large urban play-houses replaced intimate court-theaters, princes became disguised as peasant-lads who betrayed real peasant-lasses. The folk-dances of Central Europe and the Mediterranean countries widened the dancer's vocabulary lending freshness and frankness to the fusty court-style.

For our time, the first statement of a 'modern' classicism was presented by Diaghilev for Nijinsky, through a rediscovery of classic Greece, both archaic and Hellenistic, and then through sport (*Jeux*: Debussy-Bakst, 1913). On the eve of the first World War, tango and tennis replaced minuet and waltz and gave us our sportive manner, which has, nevertheless, taken the next forty years to be recognized as our one own really suitable style. Retardative repertories which, ironically enough, have attempted to freeze taste and style in the borrowed plumes of the earliest Diaghilev (who would have hated this more than anyone), try to make the audience believe that THE Ballet and the *Classic* Ballet are one and the same.

The new classicism is classless in essence, although its first expression symbolized a vaguely aristocratic, or at least detached leisure-class, which raced sports-cars and spent week-ends in big country houses or summers in the south of France. The music that was first heard on Petrouchka's barrel-organ developed into the *musiquette* of

Satie's heirs, perforated rolls of the player-piano, mechanical rag-time, loud-speakers and recorded jazz. Machine-music and even the music of the Machine (*Le Pas d'Acier*: Prokoviev-Massine, 1927; *Iron Foundry*: Mossolov-Bolm, 1932) soon became domesticated as an accompaniment of the developed classic dance. As our century advanced, as elegance became more identified with the promise of leisure, sport and recreation through labor-saving machinery, rhythms from popular music took on a new lightness, heartlessness and nostalgia, a new classic irony and our proper classic chill. Just as IBM computers are housed in streamlined metal boxes, tastefully tailored with sharp stamping and a milky palette so the classic dance of today at its peak, (*Apollon-Agon*: 1926-1956, Stravinsky-Balanchine) takes its traditional feeling from necessities in history.

Dress-makers speak of classic clothes which persist or recur in a useful repertory of models, but the classic dresses of 1908, though quite reminiscent of the classic dresses of 1808 and 1958, are each recognizeable as representative of their own epoch.[1] So is our present high style in the academic dance. And nothing is less classical, or indeed less 'modern' than a lazy approximation of romantic classicism or the classic romanticism of a past epoch.

CHARACTER DANCING: This term was formerly used to designate the theatrical use of familiar folk-dances, heightened and intensified for performance in opera-houses. Long before there was a developed language of the academic classic ballet, the two chief provinces of Western dancing were High and Low, which meant that a rowdy peasantry jumped up off the ground when making merry in open air, while the gentry stuck to the floor when dancing in roofed ballrooms. The folk danced fast and high; the nobility grave and low. Later, folk-tunes were expropriated by courts and country-dances were adopted by palace people. When planned dances entered de-

1. "Those dance-critics who write as if dance criticism were penal servitude insist that the choreography of *Apollon* is pastiche, a parody of *Lac des Cygnes*, a transient echoing of 'Parisian smartness'. This last it certainly is, if one translates smartness not as smart-aleckness but as essential human elegance. *Apollon* has its chic; it partakes of the permanent international elegance characteristic of French thought, letters, painting, dress-making and cooking, upon which neither American industrialism nor military defeat has had the slightest effect. The dancers in *Apollon* were dressed by Mme. Chanel, who cinctured them with Charvet's striped cravats. They were Olympians of 1928; they remain Olympians in 1948. . . ." (L.K.: "Balanchine Musagète," *Theatre Arts Monthly*, November, 1947)

signed theaters, folk-dances from many remote provinces characterized the quality of racial or national geographical identity or difference. The nostalgia of distance made an international audience ac-
quainted with rhythms from Spain, Italy, the Slavonic realms and
Central Europe. What remained 'authentic' in these dances was their
basic thematic material—melody, tempo and certain characteristic
steps of jota, tarantella, mazurka, hopak, etc. Choreographers embroidered on the slight given groundwork and made solo-numbers
or divertissements for opera-repertory, which was often placed in
exotic national settings, and which also affected the independent
ballet-repertory, itself. Impressive native soloists, with their troupes
of fiery nationals started coming to Paris, capital of the world, fairly
early in the last century. These were to include not alone Spanish
and Russians, but also South East Asian and Japanese as well, frequently attracted by world-fairs. There was often an addition of
purely classic school-steps too, in order that the natural or characteristic limitations of authentic steps could be rendered more interesting, indeed more legible, when seen in the alien air and huge spaces
of opera-house plateaux. Waltz and cracoviak were performed on
toe-point. These impure numbers were called *demi-caractère*; soloists in big institutions like the Paris Grand Opera or the Petersburg
Marie Theater specialized in this genre.[2]

The chief use of character-dancing at the present is in divertissements traditionally required in nineteenth century opera-repertory,

2. In a lecture delivered under the auspices of the Dance Teachers Guild
of New York City, June 22, 1958, Igor Moiseyev, master of Russian character-
dancing said:

"If we analyze the movement of the dance of any nation we find that, in
its basis, each system of folk dance possesses only a limited number of different
movements. The movements upon which is based the entire system of the dance
we call root movements. If we know a number of fundamental movements, a
number of the roots of which the language of the dance is composed, and are
familiar with the laws of connecting movements, our own fantasy will make it
possible to add a number of new movements which would belong in the same
system.

This is exactly like knowing a number of basic words in some language and
wishing to express a certain thought or emotion. We could make ourselves understood in such an instance by combining the words we know even though we
had never come across a complete sentence appropriate to the occasion.

As a rule, root movements are extraordinarily simple. Complexity begins with
the combining and uniting of movements. It is important to recognize root movements and to realize how the people vary, embellish and complicate these movements, combining them with other movements." (As reported in *Dance News*,
September 1958)

or in revivals of romantic-classic ballets. There are still ex-dancers, chiefly of Russian or Slavic extraction, who teach these dances, but they no longer greatly interest the younger generation of North American performers. The sources, to say nothing of the actual statement, have all the vitality of habitat groups in the Museum of Natural History or photographs of Holland and Norway in the *National Geographic Magazine*.

Spanish dancing is, strictly speaking, hardly 'character-dancing' within the international theatrical vocabulary, since the Iberian peninsula still holds a very ancient and elaborate idiom of its own, just as the peoples of South East Asia and Japan have their own brands of an academic classic dance, remote from ours but scarcely less exact or complex. Spanish dancing has a large body of steps, song, music, costume, style and tradition in performance which demands as much authority in execution as any other expressive idiom. It is a coherent and classic school with overtones of oriental sensibility and mystery from contact with the Moors in Spain. Some foreigners learn to perform it fairly well, just as some strangers learn to fight bulls, but the fact that they are not native to the manner is more interesting than how well they manage it.

However, it can now be amply demonstrated that the United States, unlike any non-Mediterranean or Central European country, has a veritable character-dance style and language of its very own, born in the present century, based on popular musical materials of five decades, attending the development of social-dance band music from rag-time through jazz to rock'n roll. In describing the Newport Jazz Festival of 1958, fourth in a series devoted to the performance of live popular music, *The New Yorker*, July 19, 1958, reported:

> Marshall Stearns, a jazz historian, gave an informed and amusing rundown on jazz dancing, which was illustrated with two dozen interludes by two remarkable dancers, Leon James and Al Minns, who seemed in motion even while standing stock-still, and who did the Cakewalk, the Shake Dance, the Camel Walk, the Eagle Rock, the Shimmy, the Charleston (several variations), the Jig Walk, the Lindy Hop, Trucking, the Suzy-Q (the Arthur Murray version, as taught in 1936, and the legitimate version), the Shorty George, the Big Apple, and a good many more. During the Big Apple (1938), a dance with sixteen separate steps, Minns executed a section in exquisitely slow motion, moving his arms and legs in a series

of spare swoops and wide steps, which sustained, for perhaps a minute, a liquid tension that was extraordinarily poignant and graceful. This was balanced by a dance called the Shag (1938), which consists of extremely fast, short steps, delivered while the dancer—stiff as a ramrod, his arms at a forty-five degree angle over his head—moves directly up and down like a lightning pile driver, and by the Apple Jack (1945), a dance done to bebop—a music with peculiarly nervous, oblique rhythms and melodies. . . . . .

While these dances, in one form or another, have been utilized year after year in Broadway musicals, reflecting the season's fads in public dance-halls, and while the social dance-bands of the pre- and post World War I era have developed increasingly into an aural virtuoso phenomenon far more to be listened to than danced to, nevertheless a few choreographers have used our jazz vocabulary with arresting effect, most notably Jerome Robbins. His great gift in manipulating popular steps both in the commercial speculative theater and in ballet repertory derives from his classic academic training and innate gifts as a performing dancer. His jazz ballets remain in repertory because they possess a strong formal structure and show, over and above their employment of characteristic steps and combinations, a strong personal attitude. The nature of so much American popular music is its steady uninterrupted ground-base plugged with startling eruptions of improvised cadenzas. Robbins has made sinister games and drugged duets that contain the atmosphere of street-corners at night where teenagers are disguised as ballet dancers, and dancers are domesticated delinquents. He has proposed spasms approaching hypnotic or self-induced exhaustion with fierce bursts of fancy footwork, by no means always funny. Robbins' ballets were designed for particular bodies and qualities of dancers who moved to jazz from having been born into it, as a Balinese child hears the gamelan, and who have also benefitted by schooling in an academic dance. Robbins has made true character-ballets, defining much of the characteristics of his time (mid twentieth century) and place (urban society). It is no easier to make a good jazz ballet than any other kind; possibly it is more difficult, as few choreographers take the trouble to inform themselves in the chaotic vocabulary of steps which seem to wipe themselves out from year to year, where the very persistence of a dance form stamps it as worn-out. But the exuberance of invention piles up its own accumulated vocabulary for future cultivation.[3]

While the atmosphere of sport has enhanced a new definition of classicism in the projection of the academic tradition, borrowings from ball-games and field-sports don't much help character-dancing. The Moiseyev company of character dancers had a delicious energy, exuberance and physical freshness in all their dances from Russian provinces, fast or slow, and even in a number based on the city social-dances of the epoch of Tchekov. But when they performed in a number inspired by soccer, they had to resort to stiff doses of not very notable pantomime to hold it together.[4] Newspaper photographs of basket-ball players, traffic cops and tennis players are often captioned with some reference to 'ballet', but the resemblance makes sense only through purely accidental slices of action. Most ball games and competitive sports are designed for the efficiency of pushing human muscular capacity to physiological extremity; this is incidentally spectacular, but a designed legibility would hamper the economy of movement which is necessary to win games and break records. It may be interesting to watch games, however hidden the actual strain of muscle, but a dancer's aims are different. Legibility

3. "By the fall of 1913 America had gone absolutely dance-mad. The whole nation seemed to be divided into two equal forces, those who were for it and those who were against it, and even the champions of the cause had to compromise to stay in business. When 'ragtime' swept the country the one-step came right along with it, killing off the waltz and the two-step. A list of the popular dances of the time reads like a table of contents for a zoo, with the turkey-trot, the grizzly bear, the bunny hug, the camel walk and the lame duck." (*Castles in the Air*, by Irene Castle, as told to Bob and Wanda Duncan, Doubleday, 1958)

4. Moiseyev reported in the Soviet Embassy magazine *USSR* (No. 8: 23): "I consider *West Side Story* by Jerome Robbins really good theater, done with beauty and great skill."

Moskovsky Komsomolets, the organ of the Moscow Young Communist League was reported on August 27, 1958 to say that a taste for jazz is a step towards murder. In reporting a trial of four youths held for murdering a policeman, the New York *Herald Tribune* said:

"The Newspaper attempted to explain by saying that the good influence of school and factory where they work was wasted on the four youths who were *stilyagi*. The epithet comes from the Russian word for style and is applied to youths who favor extremely narrow trousers, rainbow-colored shirts and long jackets with padded shoulders.

The paper said their ultra-fashionable clothes caused ironic smiles at the factory and mockery from Y.C.L. members. The youths began to hang out with other *stilyagi* dancing rock'n roll with girls and drinking cocktails instead of vodka.

The Newspaper said the boys next lost all interest in work and Communist ideology and began listening to the Voice of America. They turned to crime to get money for foreign clothes and bootleg jazz records made out of old x-ray plates."

is as important to him as maximum audibility for a musician. If he is not seen in all his possibility, he does not exist. If he is only partly seen, he does not entirely exist. Classic ballet, within the limits of the proscenium frame, by restrictions of theater-vision and a seated audience, has its maximum legibility. Character dancing has a blunted legibility; its roughness helps it characterize a particular place or epoch; if generalized, or rendered Olympian, its special aura is lost.

CHOREOGRAPHY: Space- and time-patterns in several dimensions, historic, geometric, literary and spiritual of what dancers do, not alone traced as an itinerary on stage-floors, but throughout all the air of their cubed area. It is a fluid contrapuntal and polyphonic architecture of groups and individuals, each unit of which bears other separate but corresponding counterpoint and harmony to the various moveable parts—head, neck, arms, trunk, legs down through fingers and toes, to their several working anatomies. And all this musculated apparatus is organized on a floor of rhythmic sonorities, clothed and orchestrated in light and color.

CHOREOGRAPHER: A dance-designer; one who composes dance movement to music, in a variety of styles, all governed by his own vision or commentary on historic periods, including his own. He must ultimately be judged by his personal capacity for stylistic and formal analysis. This determines his gifts as an individual inventor, just as a solo dancer becomes known for certain idiosyncratic talents projected in performance, distinct from the passive anonymity, however correct, of the corps de ballet.

YOUNG CHOREOGRAPHER: A term used to signify anyone under forty-five who designs dances. Young, in this designation, is an honorary token. After a dance-designer reaches the age of thirty and is still known as 'young' there has been little evidence that he has much to show for himself except the repeated promise in delayed maturity. Careers of 'young choreographers' have often announced themselves by flashy bits of ballet; this is infrequently followed by a succession of works embodying a coherent vision, primarily about movement to music, although even secondarily about gesture or pantomime. Young choreographers rarely consider themselves as carpenters or cabinet-makers of the dance. They want to stay young forever, so they may be forgiven ineptness and praised for possibility. One is most grateful when a choreographer of any age, boy, middle-aged or older makes a serviceable suite of dances which can survive in repertory five years, that will serve as faithfully as a kitchen table. Carpenters of the dance are as scarce as genuine ballet-masters.

Young choreographers, or dancers who decide they should compose dances, tend to lapse into the limbo of disputable success at about the age of thirty plus. If they have not done it by then, they are unlikely ever to do it. There is not much surprise or cumulative development in this field. Just as first-dancers or ballerinas are born heirs-apparent, and never need in a nice democratic way to climb the ladder of slow if merited advancement, a ballet-master is heralded at the outset by the unmistakeable clarion of his own gifts. Certainly, with a young choreographer, signs of newness are confusing; smart tricks and sexy shocks may momentarily mask an absence of analytical instinct.

Lack of opportunity for any dancer of energy to compose dances in America does not obtain at this epoch. Choreographer's workshops, studio chums, or just a couple of other dancers of good will are always at hand to let their bodies be borrowed to be worked on by ambitious characters, generally feeble performers. These should be educating themselves in the rules of musical form, or looking at any pictures or sculpture (except Abstract Art) or reading science, poetry and mythology, but they are licensed to waste the time of their technically more gifted colleagues purely by the promise of novelty. New ballets of value are so rare; ones that actually work and persist, so valuable, that any hint of a chance for a win is blown up by the infectious blackmail in expectation. As between an inventor of pure blood and a craftsman of proven capacity, there is no choice: take both. But as for the Young Choreographer, you tell me how many of them over the last three decades are even capable dance-designers, however old or young they may be in wicked years.

BALLET MASTER: A choreographer who has assimilated the language of the traditional, academic, classic theatrical dance to about the same degree that a Liberal Arts college student with an M. A., or an interne with his M. D., have mastered their materials. A ballet-master is capable of dancing creditably himself, of giving instruction, of reading at least a piano-score, and of dominating a troupe of professional dancers so as not to waste their time nor that of the company-management's, which must always be budgeted on union scales per hour; time and a half, overtime. Ballet-masters are trained dancers with good memories who are sufficiently well organized to approximate the repertory in which they have been trained, and able to reproduce it for dancers unfamiliar with it. But they are not to be confused with the veritable and excessively rare,

DANCING MASTER (*Maître à danser*): A choreographer whose gifts or developed talents make him (seldom, if *ever*, her), capable of imposing upon the entire field of Western spectacular dancing an individual manner, so that the repertory he has been able to call into being defines a dominant taste for his time. He is an inventor, finder and amalgamator of dance-steps, gestures and movements, adopting and adapting what has been transmittable from past masters, so that his own combinations are transmogrified into apparent novelty either by reformation or deformation.[5] Often, with a brilliant youthful talent, deformation, a reversal or turning inside out of the expected leads to fresh syntheses of old and new. By the distillation of metrical action and musical mimicry he also enlarges the given language of the dance while elevating standards of capacity in actual performance. He heightens the receptivity of the combined eye-and-ear of the entire audience. Only a master of dancing creates masterpieces of the dance by which the repertory extends itself for survival and revival, constantly tickling a public always avid for the unfamiliar. On the average, through the last three centuries, there have been in all about two masters to a generation. And in each century there has been one master who made the period's durable output virtually his own.

TRADITION: Relative to ballet there are at least two meanings. There is a handing down of instruction, descending uninterruptedly for some three centuries, and a chain of performance of a more or less extant repertory applicable to the last twenty-five years. The tradition in instruction means that successive generations of aspirants learn a language of exercises, steps, movements and combined gesture in order that their stage-performance be accurate, legible and brilliant. The models for this teaching are five basic elementary positions, exer-

5. J.A.D. Ingres: "Le tâche n'est pas d'inventer, mais de continuer."

cises, fragments from past works, clad in a variety of styles, fitting many musics. Just as an inherited accumulation of gathered information swells the body of law, medicine, musical notation and poetic metric, so a descent of irreducible constants and accretions on these, form a method for transmitting lore. What is now danced in public is what has been found useful to teach in private, increasingly meaningful and exciting through the annual theater seasons of centuries. This uninterrupted and developed tradition, supported by the flowering of the symphonic band and the formal organization of musical composition is continuously amplified by shots in the arm from popular sources (for us, jazz), as it was for our great-grandfathers by theatricalized folk dancing (the later waltz, polka, mazurka, polonaise, etc.).

Tradition in performance is, unlike teaching, discontinuous, always interrupted, depending upon shifts in the social structure, manners, accidents of historic taste and revivals, tensions and treaties between nations, exiles of minorities, class wars and colonial settlement, reformations and revolutions. As understood today, particularly by Britain, bulwark of feudalism in decline, tradition means correctness in the restoration of an older repertory. The traumatic experience of the initial appearances of the Diaghilev company in Western Europe placed an almost insupportable weight on succeeding generations of producers and has precipitated them into a deep double dilemma. Any new ballet has its instant of dewy freshness and novel shock. This impact comes from a combination of the performances of those dancers who first appear in it, and from the fact that it has never, as a whole, been viewed before. If it enjoys success, it must be exploited. Then, eventually, soon or late, the moment arrives for retirement, having exhausted an immediate audience; finally, every audience has its limits. Hence the appeal of every new work, however triumphant, has limits too. If and when it is revived, as part of 'tradition' it often falls into the custody of a ballet-master whose only energy is memory. Assuming that memory is impeccable, complete and imaginative rather than partial and approximate, which is normal, the first flash of impact can never really be recaptured, re-created, nor a first cast re-assembled. As in recent revivals by the Royal Ballet of early Stravinsky works, the initial landmarks of the Diaghilev era (*Firebird, Petrouchka*) many still living collaborators associated with the original productions of pre-World War I were convened. But, first of all, Stravinsky's considered re-scoring and his revisions were ignored. His partition in its first performance had scaled theatrical heaven and was not to be tampered with, even by its own author. Portions disavowed both by Stravinsky and Diaghilev, who generally seem to have known what they were doing, were 're-stored' making the revived version even more original than the original. Surprise was registered that the resuscitation fell short of the recorded effect of the debut, since music was the same, decor and costume were more than the same, and the choreography, at least in the steps of the chief dancers, was 'exactly' the 'same'. Three things were not the same and never could be: the dancers themselves (origi-ginally Nijinsky, Karsavina, Bolm); the taste of the public already long modified by Diaghilev and Stravinsky; the historical moment with its new necessities, interests and answers. Tradition invoked was correctness documented. Vain hope. Here is no lively continuum but an invidious attempt to repeat the unrepeatable.

The liveliest tradition of our ballet was that which Diaghilev came to introduce through annual seasons of Parisian novelty, coin-ciding with the showing of new salons, of automobiles, dress-making, painting and sculpture. Through the agency of international music and the plastic arts based on Paris, through an important connection with great dress-making (Poiret, Paquin, Lanvin, Chanel) and originally the chamberlain's wand of Jean Cocteau, Diaghilev trans-lated the researches of painters and composers into a living tradition of focussed surprise. Cocteau's role in all this has been vastly under-estimated, except by himself. When in 1909, Diaghilev commanded the adolescent flâneur: *Amaze me*, it was an imperial ukase. Diaghi-lev knew well that astonishment was not merely amusement. *Etonne-moi*: and that parade started which has not yet entirely stopped.[6] Cocteau, for half a century, has been the metaphysician of novelty. More than any other poet, except Stravinsky, with whose career he has had important contact, Cocteau has affected our lyric theater in drama, dance and film. Starting as an amateur court jester dis-guised as an harlequin (whose social background was not unlike Diaghilev's), he has had himself canonized as a respectably disrepu-table academician with a career that is paradoxically consistent. Only

6. "Le célèbre mot: 'Etonne-moi', qu'il me dit. place de la Concorde, ré-sume sa soif marcopolesque d'inconnu." (Jean Cocteau: *Encyclopédie du Théâ-tre Contemporain, Paris,* 1957, Vol. I: 1850-1914.)

Cocteau could say: "The principle of novelty becomes very difficult to recognize when our age forces us to remove from it its usual attributes of strangeness." Cocteau, for example, has had a far more influential role in the practicing world theater than Gordon Craig, whose position through history books looms larger, year by year, more shadowy and out of scale than his own unrealized renderings. Cocteau's divinations through Diaghilev channels imposed much of the quality of ballet taste and style which has become our commonplace. He spelled out the policy simply and early: the rehabilitation of the everyday, the use of magic in the ordinary; circus, cinema, choreography, or wherever the usual could be tricked by retouching into the humanly touching. Cocteau substituted a lyric contemporaneity for historic revivalism, the actual for the decorative: *Parade* (Satie-Massine-Picasso, 1917) in place of, for example *Le Pavilion d'Armide* (Tcherepnin-Fokine-Benois, 1909). He took the ballet out of the realm of bureaucratic administration and gave it hectic life from the boulevards, that busy Bohemia of *la fourmillante cité* which has been Paris' gift to the rest of the world at all times, even today. When we watch our jazz ballets in dungerees it is only an extension of the deliberately 'poor' style which Cocteau first tapped forty years ago.

STYLE: The lively classic tradition in performance depends upon the style in the dancing which is, like stoicism or elegance, a moral virtue. Individuals as well as companies can be recognized by particular qualities which, when analyzed, define their particular manner. The style of companies reflect their sponsorship, social, economic, personal and political. The style of soloists is determined by private character and temperament. An artist tries to frame a performance as a self-portrait in action distilled from dross, cut and polished to flash from fiery footlights like fifty diamonds in the face of helpless adoration. The conquest of untidy egotism, the elimination of self-consciousness, the ragged preoccupation with personal inadequacy, the denial of unsureness which renders watchers doubly insecure, and a visible concern in his public self for others, audience as well as colleagues on stage, mark the start of style. Then, with all technical considerations conquered or presupposed, begins to appear that graciousness easing all risk, disability or ineptness which is the dancer's free-will offering of a simulacrum of perfection. Its height is the most simple pleasure in pleasing. Selflessly, the artist gives his all and it's not too much. Here is the ultimate gauge of elegance. It becomes the face or mask of individual style.

There are stylistic ornaments, some borrowed from history, others acquired in the present, affected or inherited, but none useless or merely decorative when great persons absorb them into their own rhetoric. The grand manner is elaborately transparent; it displays the purged personality like the insides of a glass anatomical model. The whole complex apparatus functions, but with self-illuminating light rather than vital juices. Grace seems to wipe out every trace of vulgar toil. In the reflection of this fierce inner glow the gratitude of audiences for revelations of super-human capacity dissolves in tears and cheers. The bravos of balletomanes mean: thanks for your elegance. You do what we hardly believe can happen. You are what we never can be. You redeem our meanness and weakness by hints of strength purified. Pardon our mortality by stillness in sound and unarrested action. In your balance is our chance.

Style is braided with manners, morals and morality. Manners indicate mutual concern, embracing a conservative tone determining the presentation of Self, its harnessing, pruning and cultivation. Ego is at the heart of style; the somatic energy in self must be granted its immediate and concrete expression. I must be seen and brightly; but how? As a master, with the manners of mastery. I am so marvelous, so capable, so full of potential that, in my performance, in all the betrayals of personal behavior bridging my purely acrobatic skills to fuse them as art, I must seem really kind, genuinely gracious, truly pleasing, relaxed, generous in an acme of attention to my partners and my public.

Distinction between the performance-manners of a ballet dancer, a bull fighter and a circus acrobat are matters of scale since all make motions determined by the limits of necessity. A circus-arena is circular and enormous; so is a bull ring. All eyes are riveted on defiance of gravity and death. The bodies in play are as vulnerable as they are essentially nude, but they find an impersonality from being at so great a distance from the watchers. The scale of presentation must be broad to be legible. In bull fighting, where some creature's death is always desired, manipulators are clad gloriously in raiment of heavy light; the sequins at once dehumanize and glorify the player. Concentration in the passes is terrific, but movement must be comparatively compact. The risk is so appalling that, to survive, fighters diminish the apparent weight of danger by neatness; this makes it tolerable. Diminishment or deprecation adds up to nobility, disdain of hazard.

Ballet has its risks, too. Snapped Achilles tendons are no jokes; sprains and strains are the gorings of the dance. There is exhaustion, too, but unlike in rings for lions, tigers or bulls, death is not a present partner. Hence the style of physical domination is lighter, more transparent, sweeter and less stern. But there is parallel striving to reach pinnacles of spectacular intensity. Discipline, hazard and display are always in triangular polarity as factors to be refined, combined, calibrated and kept wide open. Elegance is laconic; ostentation is channelled as modest championship. Skill keeps its own secrets. The peak of ballet style strives toward power in all star performances, but lacking the iron needs of the bull fighter, some ballet soloists, if they are not constrained, topple over into sweeping effects more appropriate to the circus. On tanbark, this broadness is a normal response to necessity; in the opera house it seems pure selfishness, a flaccid style, swollen scale, bad manners. The big-star style veers easily towards parody, self-impersonation, the negative sincerity of burlesque and party-camping.[7]

STARS: First dancers hold a peculiar place in ballet repertory. Their position is hard to equate with stars of stage, screen or opera. There are relatively few starring rôles for the male specialist; he must content himself with divertissement, support of just fine dancing. Lady stars have their *Giselle, Swan Lake, Sleeping Beauty, Coppelia* and the few others. There is a received idea that Giselle is the Hamlet rather than the Ophelia of ballet. It is a charming two act work with a delicious score and a strong libretto. Anyone familiar with

7. Jim Brent, a British acrobat, described a Soviet circus-school over the BBC (August 21, 1958):

"In Moscow the circus school had just started. To this center came young people with talent and the right physique to be taught in the basic skills of circus. Their teachers were veteran performers, people with a rich experience, eager to pass on their accumulated knowledge to those following them. A stipend was paid to each pupil and academic subjects were fitted into the course. Many people saw the graduates of this school when the Soviet State Circus visited this country [England] recently. Perhaps, like me, they were struck with the neatness and grace of these artists; there is a ballet *barre* and mirror in every circus building in the Soviet Union. The circuses there are all permanent buildings with programmes running all the year round. The Russians are great circus lovers."

the correspondence surrounding its original collaboration knows that the great poets responsible for its book had their tongues firmly in cheek while they worked it up. Notwithstanding their witty canonization of an epoch in European taste, the work has become, thanks to the keepers of the true flame of ballet tradition, sacrosanct. It is also commercially powerful as a star-vehicle. It is the hereditary property of whatever ballerina can claim legitimate descent from the first 'romantic' ballerinas. In our memory, the line is conceded to stem from Anna Pavlova, to have included Spessiva, whom few in the West saw but who seems to have been the best if poets and painters are to be believed. When you see *Giselle* today it is not easy to know whom you really see, since there is always a double or triple-exposure of shadowy precedents. It is the star rôle par excellence but it seldom glows with genuine individual incandescence. The currently starring star is fated to borrow an ancestral prestige from all those who have shone before her. As she adopts the romantic hair-do, she assumes the habit of an order. So it remains a real test for an intelligent dancer, because there is a lively tradition to buck, or accommodate. Of course it may be said that many in the audience know none of this; to them, Pavlova is as remote as Taglioni or Elssler, and Spessiva does not exist. This is true, but it is also true that the ikons of the great ones of the past are very much alive in the minds and imaginations of reigning stars, and in those of the critics who prepare their images; those images blackmail as much as they inspire. Often they even cloud individual identity and jealously prevent a good artist from knowing who she really is.

Sometimes audiences identify the special language of the classic dance in its many facets of formal, informal and deformed styles with the personal idiosyncrasies of individual performers. It is sometimes difficult not to confuse dances with dancers. Serge Lifar thought that he invented *Apollon Musagète*. Many among the public even have the notion that a strong solo performer designs his or her own variations. This is only true to the degree that a clever choreographer will try his best to show off certain qualities or specialities calculated to fit a given temperament and body, rather than to impose an arbitrary expression of his own which might be against the star dancer's idea of himself or herself. Balanchine invented *Apollon* on orders from Diaghilev to create a star out of a splendid body that had little training in the orthodox classic dance. That such a tour de force also embodied the greatest modern rôle for a male dancer indicates the capacity of this choreographer, then twenty-three years old.

The more overweening the personal stamp of a star, the less relation he or she has to the company in which he or she appears. All most stars want is a concentrated chance to display breath-taking excercises. Weak dance-designs are sometimes salvaged, if rarely distinguished, by personal insistence. Many ephemeral compositions are contrived not as patterns interesting or lasting in themselves, but as expedient space-suits for popular jumping-jacks. In most ballets, apart from frank divertissements, which content most stars, their very presence may flatten out other aspects of the choreography if it has much intrinsic interest. The ballerina exists, not to demonstrate ideas of art, but herself: instrument and personality. This is acknowledged in most ballet-programming at least once an evening. It is natural for stars to prefer flashy brief numbers, starting slow, building to fast, ending in a dazzle to reap their rousing reward. The chief use of a star in repertory is to set a standard of execution at which competitors and aspirants aim. A star-turn is important on the evening's bill of fare. It allows other members of the company to relax through one whole ballet. It sharpens the eyes of the audience in a heightened focus on a single body or pair of bodies. It instructs the eye of the public into a dissection of what actually goes on in the basic vocabulary of the classic academic dance. It presents in small units, those chords and clusters combined and employed through multiple moving bodies which is the stuff of dance design.

It is almost impossible, however, for stars once more or less securely set in ballet's firmament to accept repertory rôles. Somehow, no part of newness seems ever really to fit them. New rôles have no precedent and each one has its logistical presumption of failure. Stars are helped to think of themselves as souls apart, locked in their private specialties, only pleased to display those aspects of their personality which they have lazily selected. This does not make them easy or grateful in working for a choreographer, who may have different and even broader ideas of what they might well do. Since stars know in advance what they want to look like in addition to what they want to do, it doesn't leave much room for a dance-designer. The worst of it is that pretexts for dictated vehicles don't add up to much in repertory, except in those 'dramatic' or 'psychological' ballet-pantomimes where emoting replaces dancing. But it is too much to expect that stars should be modest or analytical; would we adore them as much if they were?

It would seem normal that dancers have realistic ideas about ballets in which they appear; this is often true if it refers to them, individually. Stars consider almost any choreography composed without them in mind, and indeed without them uniquely in mind, uninteresting. They cannot be bothered with standard repertory. When they can be persuaded to perform in it, which happens now and then mostly for emergency reasons, they are not very rewarding since they have performed the rôles too infrequently to realize the most that can be derived from them.

It has been said that stars are born, not made, and that audiences, not managements, make stars. Both are true. And stars are useful as long as they are good dancers. As one Broadway director replied when told to hire a Hollywood name: Look, I have nothing against stars, if they can act. Stars are splendid, particularly when they have pretty manners, do not give offensive personal interviews and make few demands which the management cannot fulfill. But, alas, there is a professional deformation or occupational hazard, not confined by any means to ballet alone, but present in baseball, bull fighting, opera and every performing art. A self-generating egotism based on the awareness of special skills mastered, often manifest in ballet by an excessive sweetness or 'modesty' which can be a heavier bludgeon than brass knuckles, takes over. The persona, the self-awarded mask becomes the real iron puss. Stars begin to believe their personal press-agents. The self is won away from the fragile concept of balance in perfection that keeps great artists both on their toes and on their track. The greatest talent of the Thirties, at an unpardonably early age, turned into an ex-dancer who impersonated herself; grotesque, wasteful and very sad.

INVENTION: A term often confused with Creation, Originality or Novelty. In the Age of Faith, the word Creation, and its parent Creator, was a theological appellation with strict limits. It referred to Lord God, Creator of Heaven and Earth, before Whom there was no thing; or else the range of great nature brought into being, balance and movement through His Will. Later, in the Renaissance, a new artistic device was *trovata,* a finding, not a creation. Vasari praised the gifts of eminent masters as *belli invenzioni,* fair findings or fresh handlings. Towards the end of the Age of Reason such terms as Creative, Creativeness and Creativity corrupted the idea of the irreversible fact of a Prime Mover, from which all other moving and ordering is organized. As creation was from God, to be creative was deemed god-like. Artists became god-like creators. Craftsmen disappeared into self-expressors who created their own autobiographical myths, although there is no evidence that many artists, and particularly young choreographers, are even masters of a craft let alone of an art. Artists are now expected to make newness by projecting their selves, instead of redistributing observable elements according to their gifts, their energy to develop these gifts, the taste of their time and the needs of the ballet-repertory at a given moment. Talent to whatever degree of ignorance or indiscipline, since it belonged to the same big family of energy shared by the god-like masters, has been assumed to possess some unique and absolutely qualifying authority.

Invention, meaning to come upon (among much phenomenon), or discover, or sometimes rediscover, not from nothing, but from what is given or available to find, has been confused as creation in our massive dragnet for novelty. In ballet-repertory, a new work is novel to the degree that its elements have not been seen before, or recently, by a given public, in this form. In ballet, in our time, novelty has been recognized as a healthy or tasty inversion, a systematic or even apparently haphazard reversal of the academic or expected: broken phrases, deliberate denial of suavity, silence for sound and rest where movement would ordinarily have been awaited. One of the advantages of the iron-maiden of classic academic instruction is the violent launching towards a new liberty impelled by breaking its rules. But too often, shock in surprise is an end. It's hard to be surprised twice running if the only virtue in astonishment is the unexpected. The hope of every novelty is to remain in repertory. When analyzing the creativeness of a contemporary creator, it is useful to tally up his total number of works currently in use and their respective longevity, rather than the whole roster of first performances for which he has been responsible.

It will astonish few familiar with the story of theatrical dancing to find that while originality is the sine qua non of a dancing-master, this newness consists finally of neither shock nor surprise. True originality is rarer than uranium, and like it generates enormous power for influence in both positive and negative directions. Invention, apart from its essential drive towards discovery, uncovering or recovering is also dependent on the gift for designing consistent and fluid movement in continuous sequence, equations of joined or disjunct physical phrasing. The true inventor has an over-all concept of an audio-visual totality in composition, based on his analysis of the governing music, and a power to move many bodies about a stage with as much ease and freshness as the separate parts of a single dancer's body move by themselves in balance with its whole. It is this wholeness of mortised parts inlaid in the stylistic cabinet, which by its transparent clarity of structure demands to be looked at with skinned eyes, that stamps the master craftsman long after its initial unfamiliarity has worn away.

An original work, as opposed to one in which there is a studding of novel morsels set in a commonplace bed, is a self-illuminated whole which maintains its equilibrium by a conviction or a revelation of a chosen palette or serial octave of human movement which is parallel (one of unnumbered parallels) to the basic musical impulse. True originality refocuses the attentive eye, not alone on a new ballet, but after this has become domesticated, extending the whole language of moving on stage. It subtly modifies the rest of the repertory as well which becomes lit with a new light, appears in a new perspective, and serves as a point of departure, as one of many origins for further useful and even original works.

THE DANCER: He or she is the unit of human capacity which makes ballet possible in performance. The dancer's professional training may be equated with that of the medical interne; army, navy or air-corps cadet; divinity or law-student, piano player or bronze founder. That is, dancers must submit their bodies (and minds) to a specialized, rigorous and competitive discipline for at least ten years. This discipline is partly acrobatic, musical (either conscious or instinctive) and to a degree greater than is commonly recognized by the great public, moral, since it involves hard choices about the usual pleasures of youth.

Young dancers have no time for anything much but dancing in order to emerge at an age very much earlier than most masters of a craft, capable of activity immeasurably beyond those not so trained, and of making their living by it. Apart from a dancer's innate gift of potential virtuosity, which he or she is granted at the outset and which alone justifies the servitude of preparation—aside from a fair appearance (straight legs, small head, small hips, facial features either interesting in themselves or capable of being made so), inborn musicality and some (not a lot) of analytical intelligence—there is that supreme extra, but indispensable gift of being able to know how to exploit the (ultimately) comparatively few talents that are ever grudgingly given to any one person. The tragedy in lack of fulfillment of many aspirants is their inability to push their few real assets into that unique extremity which tests their triumph. How few artists of any sort recognize their identity; how few can tell you when you ask them with final exasperation: who do you think you *are*? An artiste? A dancer? A worker in theater? A lover of the Dance? A plumber? Me: who, ME? Yes, you.

The failure to risk identity is finally the failure of energy, physical and moral. A girl of fourteen pleads with her parents to let her go to the big city for advanced training: Darling mummy, dearest daddy, all I want to be is a brainless ballerina. That she was far from brainless goes without saying, for early, but at an age crucial to the dancer, she had already made her well-informed, realistic choice.[8] No college-education to fit the home-maker; no proms; no dating (or not much); not much fun as ordinarily understood by teenagers; little togetherness. Virgil Thomson says dancers are autoerotic and have no conversation. That they possess a special temperament is true, and if they do not feel eminently suited to their life which is a secular retreat, they will be, however accidentally endowed, unhappy in it. Either they cannot stick out the training or they may take an easier route. With what they have managed to pick up in studios, combined with what ambition they have been able to husband, they can carry their little bundle of craft into the squalid routine of musical comedy, television or the deadly drudge of the Broadway hit-or-flop. In the one you die of boredom; in the other you don't eat. Dancers outside the classic, academic theatrical dance are in a separate category. Today you don't find many younger students de-

---

8. "Baseball is an endless chain of unconscious actions. A batter's swing is composed of reflexes. Once he started to think he'd be as lost as a ballet dancer starting to think. She'd wind up in the orchestra pit. Students of the sport claim that the only ballplayer who was master of his reflexes was Ty Cobb. He was thinking sixty seconds per minute." (Arthur Daley, The New York Times, September 23, 1958)

termined to make a career in the so-called 'modern' dance. Those who enter it take this vocation comparatively late. They are not unlike lay-analysts who for a variety of reasons, good and bad, cannot stand the long internship or long residency in institutions that tradition determines. Some dancers stand on the periphery of theater just as some therapists on the brink of medicine.

A ballet-dancer's training includes the assimilation, indeed the mastery of boredom in repetitious practice, excercise, rehearsal; practice, exercise, rehearsal; practice, exercise, rehearsal. They must abjure a 'fascinating' social and personal life or anything approaching that dissipation which would be useful education for poets, but which would prevent prompt attendance at early morning practice, exercise or rehearsal. In Colette's marvelous novel, Chéri taunts his icy wife, then busying herself as a volunteer hospital superintendant, when she won't cuddle snugly in bed. "It's as if I'd married a ballet-dancer. Nine o'clock sharp, the Class: it's sacrosanct. It has to come before everything else."

What keeps dancers going (and there is that point of no return when passed; like a ship launched, you can't stop it), is a one-tracked dedication to an increasingly less vague idea of perfection in performance. This standard must finally be set by the individual dancer alone; only he or she can know of what he or she is ultimately capable. Sometimes they will be surprised, not always agreeably. The higher the aim, the nearer approached (and every useful memoir of a famous dancer's career is filled with sincere and convincing admissions of various degrees of failure at each epoch of their careers), the more intense the self-competition. No records of speed, honors or dollars are inscribed on class-room or rehearsal-room walls to inspire their surpassing. There is no four minute mile to smash. One does not go on practicing year after year because Mount Everest is *there*. The dancer's energy, like that of other artists when possessed by the muse rather than the self, is somewhat akin to the talent for indignation in saints and martyrs, a longing towards super-service or super-performance, approaching divinity in execution. Why are supreme opera-singers hailed *diva*? Why is Maria Callas veritably *La Divina*? Why was Sarah Bernhardt recognized *divine*? And to make masochism more maddening, dancers must always be at the mercy of choreographers to whom they entrust themselves. They remain the creatures of the choreographer, but without them he is hamstrung.

The dancer's career is not viewed kindly by that American family who is depicted as the core of our country, backbone of TV, supermarkets, automobiles and eaters of mass-media, except those who have been sufficiently tenderized by television to bank on a chance for a quick Hollywood contract for home-grown starlets. Infants are mildly abused all over the nation by unscrupulous teachers who force toddlers up on toe-point about as fast as they can talk, and trick them out annually in pink and green recital tarletans (of nylon) for toe-tap or baton-twirling routines. Most of these kids, some of whom might have had promise, are wrecked for any practical purpose but cheer-leading by the time they are ten.

While professional dancers make a poor to fair living, they can teach long and quietly after they quit the stage, and their stage career is quite long. If you start from sixteen to eighteen, you can dance anyways for more than twenty years. It is a craft naturally determined by the physical ebullience of youth but the greatest performers are those well along in their thirties; ripeness is all. Very few dancers persist in their hard lives from any false hope of high pay. They dance because they are possessed by the gods or demons of dancing. They dance because they want to. Security is not a consideration. They throw their lives away and find them. Naturally, any cautious parent would worry, but dancers eat more regularly (and a great deal more) than other artists (painters, sculptors, poets, composers). They are healthier, support themselves sooner, are cleaner and live longer.

The problem of the young male dancer in the United States is awkward. In Soviet Russia today, as in other countries where the state assumes responsibility for the talents of those children who may be expected to bring them glory, irrespective of their parent's capacity to pay (artists, as well as scientists), boy dancers have long worn the same style of uniform as military or navel cadets. The only distinction is in the collar insignia; dancers wear lyres, sign of Great Apollo, Leader of the Muses, rather than crossed rifles or anchors, the badge of Mars or Neptune. In America, where skills at speculative ball-games are fixed at a premium past any other human capacity, dancing to good music on a stage has an effete smell. A talented youth, unless, he happens to come from a theatrical or musical family, or one so low in the social structure that even dancing is some sort of advancement, must kill his parents, symbolically at least, if he is finally to achieve his heart's desire. It would be better for most artists, except novelists, to be orphans. For the Dance there is the crucial moment in the ritual encounter: "Son, if you persist in this folly you will Kill Your Mother." Mother rarely allows the same for Dad, but it would,be more honest if she did. The worst of it is that by the time Son has had the sense to blast this blackmail, the guts to leave home and get a job operating an elevator to pay for his lessons, he will be too old to profit by them. The very few brilliant (i.e. well-trained) male dancers bred in the West have all had, by some fluke or another, ten or more years of hard training before they were twenty. To make matters worse, the army demands its pound of flesh, and while some boys get themselves deferred, it is the rule that the best young dancers must waste two years at the very instant when they could be serving their country far more usefully, appearing in State Department tours to impress our hoped-for allies with our spiritual superiority.[9]

The prejudice against male dancing (which never extends to high-paid performers in variety, TV, films or Broadway, or to visiting British or Russians) has its roots in the position of the Ballerina in the last century. By 1850 male soloists were reduced to almost no activity but supporting ladies; they were called porteurs and transported girls about the stage. The men became so uninteresting that they were replaced by other girls who were dressed in men's uniforms. Opera ballet had whole categories of performers *en travestie*. Girls look good in tights. Ballets, such as those enlivening the first famous extravaganzas that were shown in this country (*The Black Crook*, 1866; *The White Faun*, 1868) gave our great-grandfathers and their young sons a serious trauma. The women were painted hussies to be sure, but those boy-things were straight from Sodom. Girls they

9. In a brilliant article analyzing the national interest in watching sports, Edward L. Rousseau wrote in "The Great American Ritual" (*The Nation*, October 4, 1958):

"Unlike basketball or football, the so-called national game (baseball) does not have the nostalgic association with high school or college days glanced at above. Like any ritual which has not degenerated into a relic, it is a unifying factor in society, imitating real life and yet different from it. The comparison sometimes made with ballet is false. The center of interest both in sports and in American life is a compulsive concern with what the score is. You don't keep score at the Ballet Russe—one reason why the American male is not at home there, in spite of the appetizing scenery. The world of professional athletics is as remote from the everyday round of American life as any art form, but sport—while sufficiently exotic to serve as an escape—appeals to a motive that is immediately intelligible. . . ."

might be, but they were called "ballet-boys." "I'd rather see my daughter (son) *dead* than on the stage." These atavistic, murderous, half-voiced and half-remembered sentiments still obtain among a majority of families who could easily provide as good boys as they have, grudgingly indeed, good girls. They deprive that department of the dance of what is perhaps its greatest glory since the man's body is capable of athletic extension denied the (mechanically) weaker sex.

Only with the emergence of the Russian Ballet in Western Europe before the 1914 war, did our time catch the first breathless astonishment of dancing men, perhaps unequalled at any epoch before or since. And ironically enough, the appearance of the boy dancers of the Moiseyev folk-ballet on American TV in the winter of 1958 may have accomplished more than anything else in showing the mass-public how good youths can look if given the full chance to be well schooled. Ted Shawn in our Twenties and Thirties did pioneer work on an evangelical rather than an aesthetic level. His men were strong and athletic. But flexed deltoids are only a superficial apology for male dancing; elegance is the real criterion. Americans now understand elegance in small foreign cars, cravats, sports-clothes, TV cabinets and the typography of luxury-advertising.

Contemporary male Soviet ballet-dancers (as distinct from their character-dancers) are strong as weight-lifters; indeed this is the way they are mostly used. The whole climate of native Russian ballet is retardative, even in its vast efficiency; men are generally considered as carriers or mimes, just as in the mid nineteenth century. Nijinsky was exiled from the Imperial Theaters. He made his great reputation not in Russia, but in the West.

In the best dance-theater, there is a polarity of male and female on an equal see-saw of elegance and muscularity. The power of the male for leaps in the lateral conquest of space sets off the softness, fragility, speed and multiplicity of the ballerina's action on pointe and in the sustainment of held, breathless equilibrium. Male dancers make girls more feminine and vice versa.

THE AUDIENCE: Lacking the patronage of princes, a privy purse or state subsidy, audiences in the United States (but not in Europe) are what finally pay for the ballet. Ballet is now far too expensive to support for single patrons even with means, as was the rule for three centuries. And Diaghilev had a devilish time finding enough money even for his earliest seasons. Nor is this to say that a ballet-company costs more annually on the basis of its service than a symphony orchestra, opera company, library or museum. Actually, a first-class company playing forty weeks of work a year, maintaining a fairly progressive policy of commissioning new works, keeping the old ones spick and span (sweat rots clothes fast), paying the artists at least on the minimum union level, needs about $100,000.00 a year over and above an approximate $1,000,000.00 gross. In America, ballet is just on the brink of being institutionalized. Ballet, like Shakespeare, Verdi and Beethoven must be institutional, public-service theater. (The public in one way or another even has to pay for the housing of Raphael and Degas.) Ballet is not speculative theater, like Broadway, where people buy shares hoping for hits. Ballet can more than make its own way if it has a revolving fund for an intelligent management to play with. Ballet has partially supported itself, and also very handsomely those entrepreneurs who import foreign troupes. Native managers don't much like the native product. Native companies lack the selling prestige of the appellation Royal or even National. It's hard to sell the provinces without a massive commercial organization. The condition for the expansion of ballet into a future situation worthy of its great capacity, by the coherent and comprehensive training of a dancer-pool from all over our nation, like the training offered by the new Air Corps Academy, and a logical program for the commanding and production of new works, as well as the steady maintenance of a superior trained personnel, can never be assured. Most Americans don't care, and those who do can't pay. Yet there are signs that the fascinated audience (sometimes stated to be larger in number than the gross public for live ball-games) having at least tasted a promise of development, might mobilize itself into annual support for organizations with attractive programs and policies, who are capable of guaranteeing dancers a year-round job, and who know what history has taught them about repertory, its revival and renewal. There are at least three kinds of audiences: a general public, a special public and a critical one.

THE GENERAL PUBLIC includes those who like theatre in its multiformity, including music, drama, sport, films and Shakespeare. They are, by and large, unprejudiced, attentive, if not habitual customers, and promptly throb to broad or massive effects without demanding, or indeed noticing refinement in detail. Like those ignorant of chronology, to them the past is simultaneous. They neither know nor care which choreographer anticipated which, or if ballet is actually Russian, British, or American. They are satisfied with what appears to be technical prowess and they applaud obediently if a single movement, no matter how simple or tiresome, is repeated more than three times. To them, apparent physical fireworks are more satisfactory than energy robed in elegance. They like wide stages filled with scads of dancers moving more or less in unison to a strong beat and swinging tune, hoked up with costumes and scenery that cost money. Some of them develop into a more responsible

SPECIAL (or BALLETOMANE) PUBLIC which corresponds to opera lovers, boxing, baseball or bull fight enthusiasts. These have strong personal preference in dancers, companies and choreographers, and share a passion for the performance, if neither the art nor science of stage-dancing. They loyally attend first-nights of new seasons and new works, providing an electric social air of anticipation, although their initial reaction to a debut is frequently ambiguous and insecure. They have endless good-will and always expect a smash-hit which justifies or corroborates their interest in being in the theater just ahead of the great indiscriminate audience. They are by no means sure that they know what they like. If a season has been latterly distinguished by a 'new' score of Igor Stravinsky (his twenty-first in nineteen years) this serves as standard. Here is gilt-edged security. Correspondingly, they may be shocked (well, yes, *shocked*) by a new number to music by John Philip Sousa, previously tagged as a hack of military marches. This balletomane public is custodian of serious and significant ballet, conservative at core, constituting itself guardian of tradition, which means they identify excellence with past performances they may have seen or happen to remember. They have no knowledge of the idiom or vocabulary of the classic dance, even to the extent of some of them snapping photographs, painting abstracts or playing the piano. They should be made to pay, but it is too much to expect that they will pay well.

THE CRITICAL PUBLIC numbers among it poets, painters, musicians, journalists, diplomats, dentists and lovers of fine furniture, gardens, dogs, books and cooking, who bring to their observation of theatrical dancing some schooled sensual analysis from the parallel criteria of their own vocations or avocations. A working background in architectural logic and style, musical history and composition, poetic metric or landscape gardening enables a member of this specialist public to make responsible judgment past mere enthusiasm or accidental personal revelation, without in any way removing the 'pleasure' from a performance. There is a common American superstition that if you know too much about an art you will be deprived of that first fine rapture which absolves you from learning anything more about it. You cannot know too much. Few people who don't know anything about it *do* know what they like. They can't, because their eyes and ears are only open to a surface slice of spectacle. However, they need to be far less instructed in the particulars of the classic dance, the various names of steps or combinations, than about the existence of skill in other art or craft. If one has a qualitative opinion about a new office-building that pretends to be monument rather than shelter, if one recognizes the difference between two civic orchestras, and if one honestly cares about The Dance (many do not; why should they?), chances are that this unit of the critical public does actually know what he likes, that how he likes it is not small talk, and that if he likes a certain new work it will probably be continued in the repertory until it has a chance to be generally inspected. There are also

CRITICS, in the formal or professional sense, those who are paid for their opinions of performances; these also form a division of every audience—general and special. Critics are working journalists who earn their living by servicing each group, reporting for the daily, weekly and monthly press, and for less than half-a-dozen high-brow quarterlies, all of whom feel an urge to encourage dancing and dancers if they possibly can. Very often they are music critics on detached service. It would make more sense to let art-critics cover choreography, since in spite of a musical base it is essentially a visual matter; just as some painters are tone-deaf, so many musically trained writers are form and color blind. Professional critics are neither very discriminating nor very harmful; the weekly press takes its tone meekly or lazily from the daily press; the weekly recapitulations in the two most influential New York papers make the most sense and can be read as the record over the years, allowing for over-generosity in the encouragement of secondary activity, which is legitimate educationally and from charitable aspects. The audience—general, special and critical—over the last decade has come to by-pass the working critics who are read more for curiosity or corroboration than for advice. Individual poor notices of a new ballet cannot kill it to the same degree that a play is assassinated by the two major New York drama critics. Apathy in personal conviction is greater in the field of speculative theater. People don't want to be wrong about an investment, but they can exercise a modicum of personal preference when money is not involved; everyone knows new ballets are a dead financial loss, although some of them have their triumph through survival in repertory.

In our provinces, critics advise but are not able to fill a theater unless the program contains *Swan Lake*. Some provincial critics have a ferocious local reputation; this is a reflection of the area's vacuum: we love Teacher, she's so mean, particularly to all those phonies from foreign parts who are trying to put something over on us. The provinces do not suffer novelty with patience. Poets make the best critics and always have. Baudelaire, Gautier, Mallarmé, Claudel, Cocteau, Yeats, Marianne Moore, Carl Van Vechten, Edwin Denby have written words that transcend reportage and achieve a poetic permanence in fixing the ephemeral. It is the nature of poets to observe closely. Their pleasure in finding words which are equivalents of action, their precise sense of a verbal image related to visual pattern and musical form make their memoirs delightful, even illuminating. But poets do not often make very good journalists, and the more careful they are with their words and ideas, the less likely they are to fulfill the requirements of workaday journalism and the demands of the city-desk. Poets don't write about news in the dance, but the essential residue, if any, that stays in their minds, and in the echoing minds of parts of the public, after an event has ceased to be novelty and becomes history.

Historians of the dance are more archivists than critics; they record but rarely vitalize performance. Most of their researches are simple antiquarianism, useless to choreographers whose business is not archeological gossip but invention. A smug and obedient revivalism is no substitute for a search for new steps nor are documents proof of successful reinterpretation. Except for a few chronicles in the high-brow quarterlies, ballet has been spared that ratiocination which smothers famous literary figures, substituting free fantasy on themes from Kafka, Joyce, Proust, Melville, James, D. H. Lawrence, etc., for attention to the intention of the authors. Ballet won't stand still long enough to be mauled.

It is sometimes feared that the critical audience or its journalistic voice, issuing snap judgments from which there is no appeal, determines the span of a novelty at its debut. There is infrequent correspondence between what many journalists write at first and what the general public ends up by liking later, if the new work under observation has any genuine claims to invention, newness or originality, which few works ever have. The general amorphous and unconsidering audience ends up by liking, after a certain period of repeated exposure to the novel ballet, (it may take years; the dancers who first made it may have quit the scene), choreography of the greatest internal consistency, vitality and strength of structure. Durability does not depend upon a debut.

Time and *The New Yorker* are so committed to the wise-crack and their idiosyncratic rhetorical tone that their comment on dancing is only news-worthy. This is odd, since the reporting on horse-racing, popular music, architecture, science, even politics have high degrees of professional capacity. Both magazines are famous for the dim visibility of their art-coverage; *The New Yorker* is rather worse, since *Time* makes no bones about its mass-soothing Philistinism. Reports from great cities of the world in *The New Yorker* are written by observers of care and conscience; its critics of painting, sculpture, serious music and the dance are incompetent; that is, they are not equipped with the materials of the craft which they attempt to judge. Their air of smug domestication, the reduction of any unfamiliar sight or sound to patronizing intimacy, dismissal past damnation, is the exact reflection of the style of luxury-advertising copy for which the magazine now chiefly exists. A recent English critic called Stravinsky's last ballet, written at the age of seventy-five, 'experimental.' He was referring to the score; he had not then seen it performed. *Agon* is not an experiment; it is a masterpiece. But this is characteristic: Stravinsky innovated; he must have experimented. He still innovates, hence, he must still 'experiment.' How experimental can you get? Critics who serve the drain of audience apathy are recommended by their own looseness. If there was not this exact equation they would not hold their jobs, as the mass public can only swallow a drop at a time.[10]

For the last twenty-five years, from a variety of sources—musical comedy, films, television, ballet itself—the general public has been provided with a very eclectic repertory of permissive taste, all the way from revivals of nineteenth century full-evening, triple-length 'classic' monuments to free-form concert-recital 'modern' dances. The general public might not be able to answer a quiz-program based on ballet but one way or another they have seen a lot of it, and neither ice-skating nor modern-dance have won out as popular favorites. Theatrical dancing to most people means the academic classic dance. Ballet, beyond about five couples is quite lost on TV, but it must finally come to terms with popular theater or it can't afford to exist, as its apparatus is so costly to maintain. This was the prime fallacy of the Modern Dance. It thought it was too grand for the gross public. This public is blessed in its ignorance. It no longer expects any fulfillment of a preconceived formula. The special public can be more upset than any other since it feels it knows what is and what is not *the* ballet. The general audience just thinks good ballet is good dancing and is often right.

RUSSIAN BALLET: Formerly, dance-spectacle as organized at the Imperial Czarist courts in Petersburg and Moscow, ca. 1750-1910, founded on French, Italian, Scandinavian and Central European models, but with excellent native specialists starting from ca. 1865. Then, 1909-29, the dance and musical repertory called into being by Serge Diaghilev, the emigré aristocrat and ex-amateur bureaucrat of the Imperial Theater in Petersburg, with overwhelming influence on painting, music and theater in London, Paris and New York. Then, 1930-45, the exploitation in dilution of this repertory by his direct heirs in Europe and America, with notable additions invented

10. When *Agon* was presented by the Royal Ballet in London, compulsively but perfunctorily, with a cast augmented beyond the indications of its composer, *The Times* (August 28, 1958) continued the loyal service of the official press to this master, unaltered through fifty years: ". . . But there are limits to penury of invention if a choreographer is to make a satisfactory pattern of movement. *Agon* represents bankruptcy of melodic invention, which was anyhow never Stravinsky's strong point, disintegration of rhythm, which was once his forte, and collapse of texture, which is his principal interest in musical composition. Mr. MacMillan [the choreographer] has somehow made bricks without straw, a silk purse out of a sow's bristles. . . . It is true that it could have been better played . . . but it would need more rehearsal than the music is worth . . . for the ballet is a total loss."

by his final collaborators. Now, (1925 to the present), the establishment and repertory of the State Academies of the Classic Dance in Leningrad and Moscow, of massive splendor, prowess, efficiency and security but which bear absolutely no effect of the revolutions in music, painting and choreography exercised for our era by Stravinsky (left Russia, 1914); by Picasso (entered Russian collections, ca. 1909 but then unshown for forty years), or by Balanchine (left Russia, 1924). The institution of ballet in Russia presently enjoys the highest political and diplomatic prestige. Foreign statesmen make mandatory visits to the Bolshoi Theater to meet and greet the ballerinas and have their pictures taken, which does not happen at either the opera or drama. Contingents of dancers from the Bolshoi pool are sent east and west as prime examples of Soviet cultural achievement. But the Soviet ballet (and theater), after the fall of Lunacharsky, the first and only (from our standpoint) progressive minister of education, has been cut off from any international advance-guard movements since about 1930. Contemporary Russian taste in the plastic arts, music and architecture is a blank vulgarization of the retrograde official taste of 1890, which was then already provincial, except for small liberal circles in Petersburg, compared even to Rome or Berlin at the same period.

If unlimited government subsidy, social security, a great personnel pool to draw on, political necessity and selfless concentration in administration can accomplish high art, the Soviet ballet can be said to lead the world, nor need it heed the West's strictures that it is also the bald expression of gross style and brutal taste. For purposes of domestic policy, refinement has been of slight use. Character-dancing, as witness the Moiseyev company, is excellent. Long stretches of operatic pantomime are executed with a conviction and detail known nowhere else in the world, except Japan, where the tradition is older, more stylized and far more interesting. To Western eyes there is a heaviness in the women (except for those two stars Europe has been permitted to see) and a lack of imaginative approach which characterizes our own comparative material poverty with all its gentle elegance and intellectual piquancy. The Russians have the real sputnik-style; is it an index of our self-indulgent decadence and general decline?

However, there is evidence that the Russians themselves are not entirely happy with all they do. This has come to light as their companies make foreign tours and are forced to face up to international developments that have proliferated outside the Iron Curtain for the last quarter century, to say nothing of the still active effects of Diaghilev. Under Lunacharsky, who tried to persuade him to return and head the state theaters, the October Revolution stood for the international advance-guard in theater, dance and film. Meyerhold, Goleizovsky and Eisenstein had not yet been immolated. After all, it was not the United States that offered Isadora Duncan, the most famous dance-revolutionist of her era, a state-supported school; it was the Russia of Lenin, who had first hailed her in the days of the 1905 revolution.

We have seen in Russia, Czarist as well as Soviet, that intellectuals and artists were not only expendable but were a recognized danger to crown and state. Experiment was interpreted as obvious insecurity, and the novelty of choice as attack on the normal establishment. Russia had frozen, but long before the epoch of our own Big Freeze. Petrification set in as the taste of the Nineties, before Diaghilev launched his own reforms, when the Imperial theaters were ruled by ex-army officers and all the proprieties preserved for the sake of the puritanical governesses of a Germanophile court. Now, Russia feels the need of showing her dancers to the West, and we have been gladdened by their demonstrations of academic proficiency, political prestige and brio. We have been saddened by the sounds of their new music, and its consequent curse on choreography. However, Russian dancers have seen Western works. It is interesting to read the notices of Balanchine's *Symphony in C* (Bizet, 1947) recently performed in Moscow by the French Opera Ballet, in a version which did not benefit by the restorative powers of its inventor. M. Gabovitch, artistic director of the Bolshoi Theater, writing in *Sovietka Cultura* (June 6, 1958) said *"Le Palais de Cristal* of G. Balanchine had a very great success before the public. I think nevertheless that the development of such a genre is however limited, for finally this might lead to an end in itself, and there is the danger that the classic dance might transform itself purely as a demonstration of technique." This is the orthodox Marxist attack on 'formalism' (art for art's sake) ; any work must have elementary social-content (as if any work can avoid it, since before everything it must come from *some* society), every work must fulfill an ameliorative social function, like first-aid, or else it is useless or rather, dangerous. Oddly enough this attitude was attacked by an official Soviet voice. In an article dated July 10, 1958, only a month after the visit of the French company, B. J. Cutler of the New York *Herald Tribune* reported:

> Russia came out today with a real man-bites-dog story: a ballet dancer criticized the state of modern Soviet ballet.
>
> The surprise which this caused came from the position ballet holds in the Soviet Union. It is one artistic field in which Russia excels and its famed Bolshoi ballet has invariably been the Kremlin's most successful cultural ambassador abroad.
>
> The courage to tell proud Russians that all was not well with their ballet was found in Viktorina Kriger, sixty-two, who joined the Bolshoi in 1910, won a Stalin Prize in 1946 and is not in awe of prima ballerinas or producers.
>
> Her indictment was brief. In classic pre-revolutionary ballets such as *Giselle, Swan Lake* and *Don Quixote,* no one can touch the Russians, she said. But the bosses of new Soviet ballet have forgotten one ingredient: dancing.
>
> The outspoken woman took dead aim at *Spartacus,* perhaps the most successful new Soviet ballet. It came well recommended, with music by Aram Khatchaturian and choreography by Igor Moiseyev, whose folk-dance troupe was a sensation in the United States.
>
> Naturally, Mrs. Kriger found no fault in the ballet's ideological line. It tells of a slave uprising in ancient Rome. Spartacus, its gladiator hero was a favorite historical character of Karl Marx, and its theme is thoroughly approved by the Communist party.
>
> But, Mrs. Kriger said, it is a spectacle and not a ballet at all. Its hero does not dance once, and the role could be performed by any dramatic actor with a stately figure and the ability to pantomime.
>
> She said the country has many talented dancers, both male and female, whose active years are passing without the chance really to dance. She added that heavy acting, known here as 'suffering' has taken over ballet.
>
> "When will the ballet dancer dance?" She asked.

FRENCH BALLET: Dance spectacle as performed by the state troupe of the National Academy of Music and Drama at the Grand Opera in Paris, for the last twenty-five years usually under the direction of Serge Lifar, the last premier danseur of Diaghilev, a choreographer of vast compulsion and few gifts.[11] Visually luxurious in dress-making and scenic decoration, it corresponds to the demands of the Parisian public. A typical manifestation (outside the Opera, but in no way alien to it) was reported by Laura Sheelen in the June-July, 1958 *Dance Observer*:

In Paris, not all dance is doomed to failure. The French company of Janine Solane enjoyed undisputed success. The afore-mentioned Palais Chaillot [a theater about the size of the New York City Center] was swarming with people and the intended run was extended by popular demand. There was enthusiastic applause, with the adoring audience shouting "Bis, Bis" (Encore, Encore). One could only gasp in amazement as one sumptuous costume outdid another, in all about two hundred. The eyes were assaulted by the color and glitter, and the ears were ravished by some of the best Bach and Vivaldi. The heroine of the extravaganza fully justified the 'richesse' with which she had surrounded herself. Her ego quite eclipsed her company of forty and her passions were limitless. I am sure the more materialistic Americans in the audience were the only persons stunned into quick computations of the fortune invested; for it was impossible to believe the immorality of such an expenditure in the face of the present economic and political crisis which is crippling France. Perhaps only a few embittered foreign dancers, eating sour grapes, labeled this parading of flapping posteriors and amateurish skipping about with distended emotion an artistic treason. . . . . . .

Within the Grand Opera, the administration has suffered from the intrusion of a disorderly bureaucracy so that the normal scheduling of consecutive seasons is often rendered problematical by a series of crippling work-stoppages. This only reflects the lack of central authority endemic in France. It is not surprising that no new native ballet-masters have been developed for the Opera, no repertory has been invented which is representative to the degree that French letters, architecture or painting is exportable, while any dancers of promise always feel forced to leave the official house in an attempt to discover some open future. It might be demonstrated that the disorganization of French ballet and the petrifaction of Soviet is the result of state-sponsored bureaus which must always tend towards the

11. Mme. Misia Sert, who originally placed him in the Opera: "Serge, tu es le spectre d'un faune dans l'aprés-midi d'une rose."

mediocre, the weight of historic precedent, bureaucratic tenure and self-perpetuating incompetence. It is the echo of the political matrix rather than individual personnel that are finally to blame.

ENGLISH BALLET: Dance spectacle as performed by the Royal Ballet companies at Covent Garden, London, the leading administrators of which were developed under the Diaghilev aegis or immediate influence. British ballet reflects the present social climate of the Court of St. James; its Royal Patent is no token symbol. At our period in world history, there have been recent petulant attacks on the manipulation of the Crown Establishment, but there is no real general disloyalty to the idea of a need for the dynastic principle. The English predeliction for matriarchy is evident in its great queens from the first Elizabeth, Anne, Victoria, through the second Elizabeth, her able mother, grandmother and her beautiful great grandmother. This is reflected in the management of the Royal Ballet Company, with its Queen, Dame Margot Fonteyn, and its Winston Churchill, Dame Ninette de Valois. The male principle is recognized and admired when manifest, as everywhere else in the world, but is seldom encouraged into reckless independent thought or dashing action.

Correctness of execution, efficiency in administration, devotion to the tradition of the Diaghilev canon; a sweet, moderate graciousness and a heavy load of painted decoration have not encouraged much active competition towards choreographic exuberance or invention. Its most successful repertory has been revivals of the full-evening nineteenth century ballets, or imitations of them, with a strong interest in pantomime in which the English have shone for centuries. *The Sleeping Beauty* alone has had some three hundred performances at its lovely home theater. However, in contemporary British ballet there is slight trace of the fire or ferment present in today's English painting, sculpture, drama or fiction. Today, the richest vein of energy in Britain's plastic arts and literature is an activated protest of a still powerful people against blank political decline. The chief vein of British classic dancing is a discreet homage to feudal echoes clad in occasional borrowings from Parisian chic. Paris has always been a lovely place for a holiday. Good-taste is always a dire threat to progressive policy; this has been widely recognized ever since Diaghilev was enshrined in history, where it is shown how he was the enemy of accepted good-taste as soon as he had found Cocteau to astonish him. The British firmly believe that the only legitimate bad-taste is Parisian; Italian and U. S. bad-taste are just Bad Taste. The British confuse the Paris of dress-makers with the France of poets and painters. But the London audience naturally gets what it likes. An editorial in *Dance and Dancers* (London, August, 1958) puts it neatly:

> . . . . .by ballet what you really mean are vast companies performing well-worn classics whose music you can hum in your baths and whose stories are so familiar that you don't have to think. . . . . .
>
> There should be a place in every country for small mainly experimental groups. . . .for they have a vital part to play—a part, moreover, which is quite outside the limited terms of reference possessed by the large or State-owned companies. Workshop performances are fine, but there is also a mezzanine between them and the major companies—on this half-landing appear the professional performances of more off-beat works by choreographers tried and trying. . . . . .
>
> London has already done pretty well in discouraging foreign dance visits, with the result that New York City Ballet avoids the place like the plague, American Ballet Theater by-passes us and goes to Ireland, Maurice Bejart's company only appears in Devon, Roland Petit wriggles out of a London engagement to appear in America, the Danes are reluctant to come, etc. etc. . . . . . .

Custodial discretion, reinforced by the stupendous financial success of many American tours has placed the Royal Ballet at the pinnacle of local and world prestige, yet at the very instant of its grant of a Royal Charter ensuring its descent as an independent organization, it must find itself at its most problematical period, regarding both repertory and personnel. The resuscitation of the distant past is no longer a working policy; the nineteenth century has been sacked of works to revive. The perpetuation of part of the repertory of the first half of the twentieth century has not resulted in a sequence of invention which has added many works to the international repertory. What British ballet could do with is some untidiness, intrusions from underprivileged taste, a sense of legitimate outrage and some red-brick energy. This is not easy to manage in a court-theater by means of a royal company. But maybe there is a public in Britain that might welcome an Angry Young Man on his way to rouse the Sleeping Princess right out of Windsor Forest.

AMERICAN BALLET: Dance spectacle as performed by native dancers in New York City, through our provinces and the world entire in an international (melting-pot) manner, combining elements of the more suave and acrobatic Russian Imperial and Soviet Academies (the best of our teachers still derive from the Petersburg-Leningrad tradition), with notable additions from jazz, free-form or individual lyric developments, pushed into a sharp, percussive, hard, clean accent, athletic and metrical which seems when exported to South America, Europe or the Orient, heartless, anti-theatrical (i.e. anti-pantomimic), under-clad, ill-decorated and relentlessly ingenious in its insistence on the academic classic dance as a propulsive or compulsive basis. In France it is greeted as *le style Frigidaire,* dismissed as mechanical and dowdy. The British hate it on principle since the dominant American repertory is both against Tradition (except in vocabulary), and has no Establishment. The Russians admit our jazz ballet is all right but think we should leave *Giselle* to them; we should, too. In Japan, critics expressed pity for poor dancers who were forced to fly about the stage with such soulless rapidity in Balanchine's merciless flagellation for every spirit of time-less grace. The sense of time is the heart of the matter, our American sense of time. Mr. Sumio Kam'bayashi, Press and Program Manager of the Tokyo American Cultural Center, distilled the essence of the Japanese ideological conflict with the New York City Ballet's repertory, (April, 1958):

> For the Japanese who are aesthetic (that is, sense-ly) rather than intellectual or volitional, who appreciate more leisurely tempo and less bustling activity, who prefer contemplation to action, etc. (Japanese may be in favor of the first part of the pair of dualisms that follows: introvert-extrovert, aggressive-fatalistic, adagio-allegro). Too much speediness is vulgar. That's why Kabuki (the Japanese traditional classic drama) and even Japanese film move on in a slow tempo. Pauses in which an actor strikes an effective pose are the order of day with our theater. Often you find the slow-speed film technique in Kabuki as pointed out by Eisenstein. This love of stillness, void or *nirvana* is typically Buddhistic Japanese. For such nations as we are, the ballet that moves with

presto tempo is almost unbearable if you want to watch it emotionally. Many dancers said they wanted the *Swan Lake* [Balanchine version] danced more slowly so that it gives time and room for them to identify themselves emotionally with the dance.

In his conversations with Robert Craft, Stravinsky said:

I myself have no habit of anything oriental, and especially no measure of time in oriental music. In fact, my attitude resembles that of Henri Michaux: in the Orient I recognize myself as a Barbarian—that excellent word invented by Attic Greeks to designate a people who could not answer them in Attic Greek.

What most people complain of in the dominant American style of classic dancing is our sense of Time, which is often speedier than moderate. The best trained Americans move faster, fill in more steps in a minute to more elaborate and concentrated music than most other Western performers. Also, the dominant American repertory uses music impelling dancers to a density in sharp, silhouetted and plastic action demanding a more attentive eye and ear than previous gentler numbers. The American sense of Time is not static; time does not pass; we pass through it, but we impose on it an active analysis; we break it up for our fun and games, a sometimes insolent imposition on a fourth or fifth dimension. Stravinsky says that portions of *Agon* contain three times as much music for the same clock length as some of his earlier pieces. Hence Balanchine's choreography for it needed to contain an equivalent dosage of choreographic concentrate, requiring much more looking-at than less packed compositions. The sonorous analysis of time, due to possibilities not alone in electronic devices but in researches in serial forms from Schoenberg and Webern through the later Stravinsky, opens up a whole new world in the temporal structure of the classic dance. Balanchine's choreography to Hindemith, Charles Ives and Schoenberg, his interest in Varese and Webern indicates an extension of possibility never closed to the limitless perspectives in the academic dance. The reason that Balanchine has imposed his personal vision on the world of theatrical dancing in our time to the degree that he has stems from his technical interest in and technical mastery of musical form. An analytical study of a score at his piano, often culminating with a personal piano transcription for rehearsal purposes, starts his choreographic analysis; the oscillation of his interest in certain types of scores and certain clusters of composers tells us much about his method, for it is a logical procedure and corresponds to needs that he senses in the development of his company and his audience at a given period. In a recent season, anticipating export values necessary for an extensive Far Eastern tour, he composed four ballets for American dancers with scores by Vivaldi-Corelli, Gounod, Stravinsky (a commission) and Sousa (a discovery). The fast and sharp music gave the dancers no trouble, but the tender, transparent and gentle modulations of the Gounod symphony were not mastered by his own dancers whom he had over-instructed in a fast percussive beat. He did not have time enough to teach them to dance slowly. Balanchine handles time as some painters, color; for him, time is the plastic definition of movement in its sequence and separation; he requires unfamiliar music, music which has not been too much heard, music devoid of association, with a temporal urgency and strangeness, to be heard newly, at least in the season of its introduction.

The American response to new music is not a question of nationalism; *Billy the Kid* (Copland-Loring-French, 1938) had a charming score based on folk materials. The ballet had success since it was then a popular response to an historical need; but its choreographic value was slight, in few ways equal to Martha Graham's *American Document* from which its processional portions largely derived. It is not Americanism but the American dancer's capacity to utilize music which most nearly corresponds to his unprejudiced energy which makes American ballet as strong as it is, with the American ability to recognize changes in time, sensitive also to relentless mutations in history. Robert Craft writes of Pierre Boulez in the recent Columbia LP recording of *Le Marteau Sans Maître*:

> One of the most difficult items in *Le Marteau* is speed. Whether or not the world is moving more quickly than ever before, fast tempi today are faster than any past period. Boulez's characteristic fast tempo is 208 beats per minute whereas only a generation ago Webern's was 168. . . . . . . Beethoven begins the race by breaking through the conventional tempos designated by Italian words. He greatly extends the ranges and varies the kinds of tempos and, at the same time, adds new speed. But Beethoven's *allegro molto* is 144 (the "Eroica") and 144 is only *molto moderato* for Boulez.

> In *Le Marteau* speed as a whole, not only the speed of fast
> movement, is much greater than in any music of any earlier
> period. . . . Perhaps if the tendency continues we will be able
> in the future to learn to hear the motor of the hummingbird.

Perhaps one day also we will be able to mark the discrete motion of the hummingbird's wings. Certainly there is no physiological barrier to what American dancers can, properly schooled, manage. The capacity of a good dancer in our corps de ballets today would have amounted to star (technical) capacity thirty years ago. The requirements of the post-Russian Stravinsky repertory have precipitated the increase of automotive efficiency; what could be, or can be, done if there were an all-out effort towards a real crash-program in ballet might be amazing. Most American dancers have some chance at adequate training, but let us assume for a moment that the academic dance was considered a legitimate exercise in the (cultural) defense of our nation by the Congress. Even in a dream, one could not ask for $133,000,000.00 which the newly opened Air Corps Academy in Colorado cost so far. There, some eleven hundred picked young men would be given training which no expense of mind or money could improve. Ballet is not a necessity. If it were, the efficiency in the instruction of dancers, the quality of human material, and the prestige involved, would be, to put it modestly, superior. So much for a social and economic absolute; as far as the physiological absolute, which depends practically on the first two, there seem to be fewer limits here, too, than one might think. Roger Bannister, the young Oxford physician who smashed the four minute mile, said in *Sports Illustrated* for August 18, 1958:

> What is the ultimate in miling? Four minutes was only a
> milestone with the magical ring of round numbers on the path
> to a physiological absolute which axiomatically runners will
> never reach, though they will approach it more closely. Unless there is a process of eugenic selection of athletes—horrible
> thought—the limit depends on the athlete's ability to transport
> oxygen to his muscles. Over this distance without oxygen the
> muscles can no longer be driven by the mind. . . . . A mile
> in 3 minutes 30 seconds is impossible with the present human
> physique, but there remains a no man's land of 24.5 seconds.
> Gradual improvement is inexorable.

Even if it is not welcomed with open arms, even if our dancers on foreign tours do not always make the residual total impression so nervously hoped for by our State Department, there is no doubt but that from a progressive standpoint, American ballet, even lacking a state or national theater, dominates the epoch. Nor is envy entirely absent when foreign critics speak of the presence of Soul in the home team and its absence in honored guests. Since the dominant American repertory depends upon the most eclectic and advanced musical basis now available, since it has borrowed benefits from the researches and inventions of the greatest contemporary specialists in new rhythms, new harmonies, new balances of form in sound; and since we materially deprive ourselves in the departments of dress-making and decoration, our choreographers have had a wrenching of their imaginations to disassociate themselves from the expected, the easy or the merely decorative. We have a rich local vein of character-dancing in popular music and dance forms, which has contributed one master-mason in Jerome Robbins. The basic beat in jazz is perpetually liberating, not alone through syncopation, but from the ingenuity in the improvisational style of its reversible rhythm. Seemingly invented out of nothing, it embodies the exuberance of virtuoso playfullness. The style is hard to dry out because our popular music changes seasonally with a new hem-line or a waist-line. It keeps us, literally Up On Our Toes.

The American Style is disciplined but irreverent. Since we have no mythic national gallery to which we must always pay homage and no prototypes but the dubious heroes of Pioneer, Mechanic and Athlete, we are not bound by servitude to a sacred past, either personalities or sacred monstrous works. Everything we do is done to be done again and again, invented each time new, with new gags. This breeziness may seem brash to older communities, but mark how blue-jeans have conquered the world. What we dig is a new and fancy sharpness. We appear to the rest of the world exasperatingly capable of anything, good and bad. But there are not any paths of invention or range of performance that our home-grown dancers of energy and determination find shut to them. This now happens to be untrue anywhere else in the world.

ARGENTINE, AUSTRALIAN, DANISH, DUTCH, SWEDISH and SOUTH AFRICAN BALLET: The problem of the provinces is delicate. Possibly it should never be mentioned, but there is activity in the field in many remote parts of the world, each place bidding for its quota of prestige and getting it. The Danes have a moderately interesting history, but it is no absolute service to their modest excellences to over-exaggerate it. Dancing-masters in Scandinavia did influence the Imperial Russian schools in the last century, but Bournonville was no Petipa, no Ivanov. Canadian, South African and Australian dancers have become valuable members of the Royal Ballet and American companies, which proves the point: provinces are interesting for what they can contribute to capitals. Mr. Anatole Chujoy has written a valuable monograph on "Civic Ballet" which he has done much to foster:

> National Ballet Festivals were held in Canada every year for six years until 1955. They were discontinued for a very interesting reason: most of the talented dancers in the non-professional companies, which participated in the festivals were absorbed by the then newly established Canadian professional companies, the Royal Winnipeg Ballet and the National Ballet of Canada, and the television programs originating in Toronto and Montreal.

Provincial ballet-directors are always being betrayed in their selfless efforts to bring national or local companies into being, for their best dancers will always be picked off by bigger companies. The smaller troupe at its best, is usually in a state of hopeful evolution, interesting to those responsible, and to a very small, if passionate, portion of the local public, which is always dismayed that there is less energy for money in them than, for example, in the art-museum or symphony orchestra. The art-museum often has an endowment, and objects of known value; the orchestra plays a repertory of famous works; the ballet has neither. To persist, the managers of provincial companies must always ignore the true state of their place's history, geography and economy. When one is building a South African, a Canadian or an Atlanta, Georgia company, one can have no patience with the historian who tells you it can't be done, or that everything done here derives from centers far away, and everything good developed here will revert to those centers. It can, too, be done; we are doing it. More power to you. You are doing part of our work for the rest of us, and even if we are not very grateful you may find your names in the histories. But you are in the education business, not in the theater business, and if you doubt it, ask any of your dancers where they would rather perform: Vancouver or Covent Garden? There are local excellences, local strengths, in some cases gifts and resources, even superior to those sometimes enjoyed in the big gardens of culture. We can admire the devotion, envy the fun, smile at the smugness and forgive the innocence, hope and heart break. But, except for practical training of dancers and choreographers who will do their best work in some larger town, the prognosis is limited. Auden wrote of the Portuguese colony of Macao:

> A weed from Catholic Europe, it took root
> Between the yellow mountains and the sea,
> And bore these gay stone houses like a fruit,
> And grew on China imperceptibly . . . . .
>
> Religious clocks will strike; the childish vices
> Will safeguard the low virtues of the child;
> And nothing serious can happen here.

MODERN DANCE: A loose idiom of idiosyncratic, free-form movement, identified with careers and contributions of half a dozen individuals, all in their prime by 1935, when their loose connection (there was no formal association) represented an unorthodox attack on the academic classic ballet as it was then known (or unknown) in the United States and Central Europe. Its chief inspirer was the Californian, Isadora Duncan at the turn of the century and the following decade; while Jaques Dalcroze, a Swiss musical theorist, seemed to provide an anti-academic, as well as anti-theatrical body of instruction in measure and rhythm. His big point was that the Russian dancers of the Diaghilev company could not 'keep time' to their music. He was interested in theater if it was in the open air. Rudolf Laban, a Hungarian theorist, was even more puritanically anti-theatrical. Most modern dancers had strong ethical objections to the over-decoration of stage dancing, some of which was salutory, but much of which was a rationalization since they developed outside official theatrical institutions and had neither home base nor localized public.

Martha Graham, like her historic ancestors Loie Fuller, Isadora and Ruth St. Denis, is in a different category. Acclaimed over the world as America's leading 'modern' dancer, her method is hailed both as justification and salvation for the Modern Dance as a legitimate, legible and transmittable vocabulary. This is neither fair to a remarkable personality nor accurate as apologia for a movement. Graham is an exceptional artist, not comparable to Isadora, because Isadora had only the rudiments of training. She didn't need any for what she actually danced. She was an improviser of great personal magnetism who arrived at that moment in history when there was a corset around every woman in the West, aching to be thrown off. Isadora robed herself in the three-century old prestige of Hellenistic sculpture and the century old repertory of German symphonic band music. Swept in on a healthy breath of California poppies, her performance was a danced sermon with Whitman as gospel. Her influence was ethical and social rather than theatrical.

Graham is an accomplished and meticulous artist who served a long and arduous apprenticeship in eclectic presentations of the dances of Spain and the Orient, including enough classic ballet to have respect for it as a training aid. Graham's mistress was Ruth St. Denis, who as anybody who has read her fascinating autobiography knows, is a creature of enormous appetite and intelligence, an impressive historic figure. With nothing at hand to borrow from, she filled an epoch in the American theatre, bringing the idea of Dance, as well as American Dance, to more lands than Duncan ever knew. Her instinctive passion for the East, her later knowledge of it from first hand, made her evocations and her evocativeness in the minds of the young dancers like Graham, an experience far livelier for them than the Diaghilev Ballet. Ruth St. Denis knew theatre from vaudeville, variety and from what Ted Shawn called "A Thousand and One Night Stands."

Graham is also the professional, outside the descent of the academic tradition, but she has contributed to it in a variety of openings-up, even as Isadora did more ambiguously. What is more important, she has been exactly right for herself, possibly for herself alone. She has a consummate analytical gift for expressing her particular intensity. Her face and form are not what they are by any chance. She worked for them, and they show it. But just as there was little in precedent to promise her, there is not much that directly descends from her. One has only to see her own well trained young dancers in those rôles she first created for herself. Not that she lacks choreographic talent for pattern, gesture or oddity. Simply, she has analyzed her own assets and their place in our present; what she decided to do corresponded with what she felt she could do plus what needed to be done; her repertory was both self-assertion and oblique critique. There was only herself to do it; this was what she was born for, just as Isadora and St. Denis had their call and saw their light. You never had to ask Martha Graham who she thought *she* was. She was Martha, and she did dances for and around Martha, and they have been of lasting interest around the world.[12]

As an original, one of the rare ones, what is evident as her personal tone refers only to herself and its theatrical framing; this limitation she has embraced and used as strength. That she is the only contemporary figure outside the academic dance to be able to do this demonstrates her intensity as well as the wide uses of the academic traditions, beyond which she alone found a unique path. *Herodiade* is the name of one of her famous dances, based on Mallarmé's poem. Years before Graham, Yeats had written words which also apply to her:

> Yet I am certain that there was something in myself compelling me to attempt creation of an art as separate from everything heterogenous and casual, from all character and circumstance, as some Herodiade of our theatre, dancing seemingly alone in her narrow moving luminous circle.

But lacking other equally powerful personalities, the Modern Dance *soi-disant* produced no second generation of performers of intensity, little repertory disassociated from first-performances and no extensible code of movement. While there were flashes, or fragments of spiritual grandeur of some depth if extreme narrowness, the future of Modern Dance either as program or philosophy is obscure. What

12. Stark Young, perhaps the most sensitive and exact critic of theater-as-a whole who has ever written in America, said of Graham:
"There are times when the Graham programme or some number in it seems too long. If you have full faith in the dancer you get an unpleasant sense that, with so much given to it, more must be being said than you are taking in; a sense of inadequacy of perception is laid on you as it were. There are times, too, when the motif and the effect seems overpresented, and you are reminded of Talleyrand's remark that whatever is exaggerated is insignificant. And we may have found not too infrequently an evasion of the dramatic, a concentration on the stark pattern for the design-idea of the composition. The benefits of this—for a period of time, that is—are manifest in the fine cleanness and purity of her dancing. We have the sense that, no matter what has been left out, nothing has entered a composition that has not grown into it organically. . . ." (*Immortal Shadows: A Book of Dramatic Criticism*)

was most legible or negotiable of its thesis moved into the field of physical education in state-colleges, replacing gymnastics, or into musical-comedy dance-numbers where it instilled a little life of no greater importance than the vehicles it adorned. On Broadway it is dilute and serves as a base for an embroidery of jazz-character steps.

BALLET MUSIC: Skipping the long history of what past music has accompanied what lost dances, it is important to analyze what present music may serve us. Not everything available is suitable. Even the convinced preference of a certain choreographer for a chosen composer is no guarantee of sensibility. The most important thing to consider, if one works for a company with a musical conscience, is the size and quality of the available orchestra. How many men can you afford to pay to play those pieces you have chosen to use as your dancing-floor?

In the 1930s there was a vulgar tendency to seize large scores, the symphonies of Beethoven, Berlioz, Brahms, Tschaikovsky and Shostakovitch. The strength of the orchestras playing these pieces often bore little resemblance to the indications on the partition. The public, then a rather rudimentary audience without benefit of high fidelity radio stations or the LP record, was sufficiently familiar with the Pastoral, the Pathetic and the Fantastic, to bring them along half-memorized, to the theater. The attending choreography was naive, too. A first statement was proposed by a solo dancer; the corps chimed in at the tutti and pre-tenderized ears guided innocent eyes to fill up all the blank bars with partial correspondences in a musical visualization. It is not by accident that none of these works are any longer in repertory. Their interest was exhausted due to the over-familiarity of their music. And it is now far too expensive to employ on casual circuits the apparatus of the German state theaters where one hundred and ten men were the normal post-Wagnerian requirement. Approximation of Richard Strauss, and of Wagner himself, on a reduced scale, particularly if the pieces have acquired fame in the absolute symphonic repertory, were for a while acceptable; but today, in large part due to the greatly expanded service of the recording industry, the audience is better educated in their realistic demands for a scale of sonority fulfilling the original intentions of composers. A state-supported opera house is needed to maintain a great orchestra, which even reduced to fifty plus men, on the union scale must always cost more weekly than the total group of dancers.

Increasingly for us, the modesty of the orchestra's size determines a selection of music, but here economic necessity is not censorship. On the simplest restriction, there is a large catalogue of string-music, and in a variety of other combinations whose balance, scale and scope is suitable for dance. A clever choreographer gains piquancy by uncovering scores with unexpected provenance in divisions which can be incorporated within the body of an orchestra at his disposal. A ballet is launched by the choice of its music far more than any pretext of plot, libretto or literary idea. Music determines dances more than any single element. Naturally the choreographer must do things with it or to it. His analysis, his measurings, not in formal structure alone, but on the floor of its atmosphere, its charm or lack of charm, determines his range of gesture or motion and tells the most, at the same time about the nature of his own gifts.

The most able ballet masters are not those necessarily who are most prodigal of invention, or those who are compelled to attempt an approximate dancer's equivalent for every musical concept. Sometimes, even in the most propelling or suggestive music, too much goes on for its own accommodation. If some absolute consistency was forced equating entries and reëntries, restatements, variations and reversals, the visual part might collapse from the pressure of the aural. Synthesis of music and movement is what commands taste and ingenuity. When Balanchine was making *Jeux de Cartes* (1937), he found an ingenious device in which the pack unfolded itself in fan-like conformations, from the suite King, Queen, Jack, etc., held in a poker hand. He made the dancers vary the sequence three times, each totally different. Stravinsky, with the parsimony of experience, told him simply to repeat the first one unchanged three times: "They won't see it the first, nor applaud till the third."

Concepts of time in rhythmic divisions are the base of any truly contemporary dance-style. Pastiche is unsatisfactory, however nostalgic, because it only recalls and is neither superior to nor the equal of an original model. Stravinsky's method of revival is resuscitation through metamorphic transformation. It was the score of *Apollon Musagète* (1928) which made us listen anew to Delibes as a serious composer of dance-music. A general acceleration of incident and accident all over the world in the last sixty years has generally found its prophecy in Western music. Stravinsky marks the beginning of musical thinking which determined a new idea of dancing based neither on poetry nor painting but on analytical sonority and rhythmic play. He has led dancers since 1909; only those who follow him closely have been able to extend the repertory by amplifying the academic classic vocabulary. This is not to say that he has written the only dance scores of use or interest, but it is to insist that his initial contributions to the twenty Diaghilev seasons, and his masterpieces over the most recent thirty have affected every aspect of theatrical music as the seminal influence. What is remarkable still is that he can even presently, after half a century's history arouse consistently strong differences of opinion. His gifts are medicinal; his invention has the pungency of fresh iodine and the impersonal freshness of clean linen sheets. His atmosphere has the astringency and dis-comfort of certain therapies. His music has massaged the body of the dance; he offers super-sonic devices against arthritic choreographers, and an accumulation of calcium on passive hearing or snobbish seeing. On November 9, 1913, Claude Debussy wrote to Stravinsky to thank him for the score of *Le Sacre du Printemps*:

> For me, who descends the other slope of the hill but keep, however, an intense passion for music, for me it is a special satisfaction to tell you how much you have enlarged the boundaries of the permissable in the empire of sound.

The problem of musical taste, the choice of one piece of music rather than another upon which it is prudent to risk dancing forms the principal policy-decision of ballet management. Often accident seems the best policy. A choreographer, seldom a trained musician, is permitted to choose something he happens to have heard and liked and blandly proceeds. Or there are instances when vague outside pressures, overheard in conversations of critics and connoisseurs insist that some contemporary composer demands to be commissioned. When this happens on the basis of prestige rather than preference, the result has its compulsive nervousness in composition. Fulfillment is achieved only by conviction and collaboration. The streets of choreography's hell are paved with paid-for scores which though produced were unproducible.

People refused to take Balanchine seriously when he said of the music of John Philip Sousa: "I like to listen to it." Stravinsky makes a distinction between hearers of and listeners to music. Similarly, in the dance, a difference may be drawn between those who watch it and those who see it. Some choreographers have an instinctive awareness of sights and sounds, but their gifts, unclarified by analytical intelligence, are not sufficiently powerful to precipitate vague feeling into formal passion. This betrays basic lack of energy, for the schooling necessary is available if a mind is willing to be as rigorously exercised as a body. Listening to music systematically is in itself training; not just attending haphazard concerts, but the subjection of the ear to considerable sequences of many composers' products. In our times we have seen poets and musicians of the advance-guard swarm back to scores by Tschaikowsky and Puccini, two names proscribed in Paris at one time (although never by Diaghilev, who died singing *Butterfly*). Catholic taste and an eclectic policy are matters of discrimination rather than promiscuity. It is not by accident that Balanchine has done three works by Georges Bizet and two by Emmanuel Chabrier, although their music had not been previously considered promising for ballet.

It is not alone the choice of a score for its own unique quality that should be wholly determining, but also the choice of a piece in relation to all others against which it will be shown in combination in a given repertory. Choice is, or at least should be in order to serve and survive, something governed by necessity. We have the pieces we need to open an evening, and while it stretches analogy to think of every program as a menu, there are certainly soup as well as salad ballets. There are hors d'oeuvres, second courses and deserts. Some, like melon, can serve as a first-course, too, but at banquets we won't start with the beef. Surprise, re-freshness, re-creation are prime ingredients. It is not that our palate is jaded; it is seldom very profoundly stimulated. Our ears have heard some sounds so often that they are no more alive to them than our bodies to the chairs we sit in. An energetic choreographer must uncover new noises by old composers and even commission new noises by new composers. This last is tricky, expensive and comes off about one time in ten, but the attempt must never be abandoned, even though chances of even a semipermanent success are slim.

Part of the trouble lies with the commissioning choreographer. He chooses a composer, not for what this craftsman can finally make but for the purpose of getting a new piece formularized as much as possible like scores which have already been proven. New noises, new rhythms, new suggestions do not in themselves attract him. The choreographer naturally wants a hit; a hit is a ballet by Tschaikowsky. The trouble with Stravinsky's masterful suite of ballets is that they are all by him, including the one dedicated to Tschaikowsky. By trouble one means the trouble that must be taken by a ballet-master to find choreographic treatment worthy of scores of such savor, expertness and so much mystery. Cocteau, in the finale of his letter to Jacques Maritain, speaks of it best:

> In 1916, Satie was our schoolmaster. From the year 1923 we heard Stravinsky speaking our language better than we. The lack of appreciation he enjoyed in this new period proves to what point our language is disdained.
> *The Critics*: "Mr. Stravinsky discovers the classics."
> *Stravinsky*: "Exactly. I knew them; I knew them as you did; I had not discovered them."

Of course Cocteau meant discovered, uncovered from long neglect and recovered, through his own gifts of devination and composition.

It is difficult for musicians to know what is grateful for dancers to do. Few are interested in theater; their business is the orchestra. Whatever a choreographer does it can never be the complete answer to a musician's notion, since, even though he may be vague about movement, he knows what he would wish by way of dynamics and emphasis, while the choreographer, quite possibly will have wholly other feelings. It can't hurt a composer to know something about dancing, any more than it hurts a dancer to read music, and to know not alone counts, beat and tune, but what is actually being played in all its wholeness. It is more important that the choreographer know what he really wants in relation to what he can reasonably expect to get from a given talent. It is not always the composer's fault if the delivered score is useless. Maybe he did to the best of his ability what he thought he had been asked to do. When done, it did not correspond to what the choreographer had loosely imagined he had wanted. Neither Tschaikowsky nor Stravinsky had any failures in the great music they have showered on us, although their thoughtless choreographers have had many. To be sure, at the outset, *Swan Lake* was considered a Wagnerian disaster, *Nutcracker* a hodge-podge of opera-dances and *Le Sacre du Printemps* a madman's joke. You-can't-do-this-to-us is the accolade with which most great and many good new works are kissed, but debuts don't count. Scores survive, and if not for the stage, for which they may be too interesting, then like *Le Sacre,* for the concert-hall.

One way to have a final failure, although sometimes a quick hit, is to make parody music in which the composer conspires with the choreographer to flatter the public by making noises they already know, at the same time poking sly fun both at audience and at the original source of the material. The parody score, derived from the French *musiquette* of the 1920s has all the predigested sophistication of a book-club or record-library choice. You have seen or heard it all before.

BALLET SCENERY: The suggestion and adornment of space and atmosphere in which dancing happens. Ballet is a repertory operation; few theaters in the United States, even opera-houses, have much storage space. Most ballet scenery is soft, painted on large cloths, to be rolled and folded. Heavily built, solid practicable pieces are hard to move and stack. We dislike intermissions over fifteen minutes, for they break the flow of an evening. While the nineteenth century theater of illusion contained platforms, traps, aerial ballets on wire, simulations of fountains, oceans, fireworks, volcanic eruptions, forest fires and earthquakes, our minimal dance spectacle in the mid twentieth century is, comparatively, a tame affair, depending mainly on dancing, except in Russia. The Bolshoi still enjoys a maximum theatrical apparatus but their aesthetic is still that of a century ago. As possibilities for stage scenery in the West have shrunk due to the cost of union labor, real-estate, shifting taste and an accelerated sense of time altered by the scope of spectacle in wide-screen films, a consequent spareness has favored dancers. Our audience would rather watch dancers move than wait while scenery is shifted. Hence, ballet scenery has become the most naive mechanism for big scale spectacle, usually consisting of a back-drop with side wings.

In the seventeenth century when painted moveable scenery started to be hung in designed theaters rather than transformed ball-rooms, the aim was, by simulation of grand architectural or natural elements, to imitate an enclosed heroic space, gigantic, symmetrical and metamorphic. An enchantress's palace transformed itself before your eyes by having hauled up stretched, painted and cut canvas, into a subterranean dungeon which burned away into the splendor of glorious sunbursts. The dancing itself must have been far less amusing than the parade of such tableaux. The language of the dance was then comparatively undeveloped, but perspective illusionism was extremely sophisticated.

In the eighteenth century, frontal symmetry having been somewhat exhausted, there entered freer devices of forced and steeply precipitated vanishing points. Asymmetrical collonades replaced blocked twin corridors, and were pushed off-center to a deep apex. Columns were bent, enfiladed pillars warped and divided into a visual syncopation of modules, suggesting an increase of movement even in static paint. Vaguer spaces were suggested, triangular rather than cubed, and the stage-floor triangle, since it corresponded to the actual working area dancers used had more possibility for legibility and packed movement. Exotic archeology, Babylon and Peru, Ceylon and Muscovy, Martinique and Morocco, every sort of fantastic geography offered stupendous backgrounds against which regiments of dancers and figurants defiled.

Stage illumination was rudimentary. Oil lamps with reflectors gave way to gaslight. At the turn of the last century electricity began to be controlled. Paint was primarily illusionistic, like an architect's dead rendering. It strained to re-present literal imitations on plane canvas surfaces of the look of woodgrain, marble, tapestry, water, sky, with unchanging shadows from a single source of light, creating a papery plasticity, put in with a straight-edge, always illogical in some detail and under most light.

When Diaghilev became attached to the Imperial Theater, the tradition of scene-painting (designers not infrequently were the painters themselves) was inherited from the Franco-Italian opera houses. Foliage, cut leaf-borders on netted drops were broad in yardage but small in scale and photographic in detail. A painstaking literalistic naturalism was the rule. He brought with him to Paris two gifted designers, Bakst and Benois, and these took advantage of a revolution in rendering that had already been accomplished by the Post-Impressionist easel-painters. Broken color of Seurat and Signac, the daring chromatic contrasts and broad generalized vibrating areas of Bonnard and Vuillard and the forced night-illumination of Lautrec and Degas, who had instructed themselves in theaters and circuses, made the great cloths of the first seasons of the Ballets Russes an important revolution in visual taste.

The bravura brushwork in Delacroix, Courbet and Manet had not touched the stage-decoration of their epoch, but by 1905, later researches in palette intensity, poster-display and electricity had already triumphed. Essentially, Bakst and Benois were pasticheurs of taste, in love with an historic past, period by period, which they reconstructed on documents from the archeologists of their time with the broad effects of contemporary paint-handling. When Diaghilev became finally acclimatized to international Paris, which took him some five years, he was able to proclaim far more daring steps in the aims of stage-decoration for the non-realistic or lyric theater. At the start he was satisfied to use his professional theater designers, who had hoped to be, but who were certainly not, primarily easel-painters. While the early Cubists, Picasso, Matisse, Gleizes, the Post-Impressionists and Fauves were available to him by 1909, as well as independent lyricists like Modigliani, Dufy, and Pascin, he was then not thinking in these terms. It was still the epoch of exportable Russian nationalism: Golovin, Korovin and Roerich. It remained for Jean Cocteau to carry the painters of the School of Paris to the theater in the collaboration of *Parade* (Satie-Picasso-Cocteau, 1917). This was, so far, the single most influential manifestation of modernity in the century. It proposed, through splintered facets of Cubism, American rag-time and the journalism of megalopolis, aspects of that permanent 'modern life' of great cities which Baudelaire first found in Constantin Guys, but which the lyric theater had rarely ever employed with so frank and full an apparatus of painter's eyes and poet's vision.

In many cases, Diaghilev's late decor was accidental, insistent and had little to do with dancing. Scenery was often more striking than choreography and it needed have only the slightest relation to music. Stravinsky complains of Matisse's decor for *Le Rossignol* (Balanchine, 1926). "Diaghilev hoped Matisse would do something very Chinese and charming. All he did, however, was to copy the China of the shops in the Rue de la Boetie." Braque and Juan Gris were easel-painters too preoccupied with their personal plastic studies to take stage-decoration seriously, and Diaghilev himself leaned to a slapdash execution as a violent shift from the early over-meticulous detail and pinched scale of the official styles. Some of the painters used their stage-space as a kind of laboratory, but these were rarely decorators. At its period of greatest importance to him, Diaghilev thought of scenery as enormously enlarged sketches, never carried too far, more often than not seeming to be slight and unstudied but actually executed with fantastic virtuosity by Prince Schervachidze. Part of their piquancy came from the huge area of their playfullness, their apparent lack of serious intent. Picasso threw ingenious devices into the arena and his caprice was always the most monumental. These were tremendous one-man shows, or rather one-tableau (or two, or three) poster-like demonstrations which announced the next big exposition of a new period of the easel-pictures. André Derain, a painter of less depth than some of his colleagues, was, nevertheless, perhaps the most brilliant of the decorators, for he filled his space with a consistent painterly richness, the paint itself appetizing and luxurious, a glow of vast visual luxury on a human scale.

The Diaghilev repertory which enjoyed the most brilliant painting was not the strongest in terms of the dance. As an example, *Le Tricorne* (Falla-Massine-Picasso, 1919) has had numerous revivals due perhaps more to musician and decorator than choreography. Picasso and Matisse pinch hit for a large corps de ballet; the Diaghilev seasons launched the international success of many of the most expensive artists of our time.

Today, except in those companies which are still under the shade of Diaghilev's formula without enjoying the distinction of his collaborations, painted cloths are recognized to have many disadvantages. Contemporary conceptions of space are not entirely satisfied by boxing in a stage floor with static paint, however atmospheric, dashing or suggestive. The broadness of an easel-painter's sketch blown up to the scale of a proscenium opening must be coarse to be legible. Huge sketches were astonishing when they took the place of naturalistic drops, but the scale of the dancers was dwarfed by the very imitation of broad brush strokes. Today we desire, with our most progressive choreography, the form and light which enhance the three-dimensional plasticity of bodies in motion. To serve as foils to dancers we sometimes need objects as real as they are, unveiled in their own air, lit in their own light, not a simulated one. The decor that Gabo and Pevsner constructed in oilcloth and mica for *La Chatte* (Sauget-Balanchine, 1927) and the objects sculptured by Joan Miro for *Jeux d'Enfants* (Bizet-Massine, 1932) were among the first statements of detached forms which framed dancers by their architectural shape. The big shift in the scenery of our day has been the change of emphasis from paint and color to form and light.

Instead of providing a flat surface with indications upon it which could be read as three-dimensional, veritable three-dimensional objects were presented as light-traps, as facetted or curved surfaces upon which light was bounced or absorbed. Great changes came with the possibilities of the incandescent bulb, and our engineers have by no means finished with the enormous facilities offered by new kinds of light, its pre-setting, monitoring and the subtlety of an organ-like play in delicate balance of circuits in series. The American dancer, Loie Fuller had her own small experimental theater in the Paris Exposition of 1900 (which she shared with the first Japanese classical dancer to appear in the West). She took full advantage of the most recent inventions of Thomas A. Edison by strapping poles to her forearms upon which were hung huge wings of china-silk. These she waved and turned, and the light hitting them seemed like fire, water, petals or clouds under the shifting lamps. The movement of her veils in air, under light made more of a dance than her feet, but something of the Tiffany Glass incandescence of her act has been caught in Toulouse-Lautrec's lithograph.[13]

The painter Pavel Tchelitchev, in the ballet *Ode* (Nabokov-Massine, 1928) used a great range of visual devices for creating spacious air on stage with no pigment, only forms in light. He forced perspective by hanging rows of puppets, diminishing in size which merged with real dancers identically dressed; there was back-projection of cinema film, and a cat's cradle of ropes which made a variety of metamorphic vanishing points. Dancers became self-lit sculptural units; sometimes immobile when confused with the inanimate dolls, at others active, with their mobility enhanced by the mysterious opposition of live and dead; the principle unifying element was light. Later, Tchelitchev proposed a further step in increased plasticity: scenery was not to be any longer a lit surface but rather, in itself, the source of its own illumination. With the development of plastics

13. "A large American woman, rather ugly and bespectacled, standing on a transparent trap-door, uses rods to manoeuvre oceans of light veiling, and sober, active and invisible like a hornet in a flower, she stirs up the orchid of light and fabric which billows out, flares up, opens, roars, turns and floats, changing shape like clay in a potter's hands, twisted in the air under the sign of the torch and the hair. . . ." (Cocteau: *Paris Album: Portraits Souvenirs*)

which were weightless or nearly so and could be moulded into any shape, lamps could be placed on dimmers inside sculptured forms. The dancer's energy, action and dynamics illuminated his or her body; Tchelitchev wished his forms that framed them to be in a parallel self-illumination. Paint laid on, no matter how close the brush-strokes imitated the sketches of a painter, or however well lit the canvas might be, was finally static and hence dead. Light itself, vibrating in and on changing forms, had the fluency of motion. In subsequent productions, notably *Errante* (Schubert-Balanchine, 1933) and *Ondine* (Giraudoux-Jouvet, 1937) he pushed the principle of self-illumination further than it has ever been seen before or since. He made that influential part of the public which first recognizes innovation and remembers it longest impatient with the passivity of painted drops. The beautiful flow of the silk act-curtain for Noguchi's *Orpheus* (Stravinsky-Balanchine, 1947) was first seen in the finale of *Errante*.

Today, wherever the prime interest in ballet is dancing, choreography, its investment by performers, and neither pantomime, interior-decoration nor dress-making; the desideratum in decor is absolute plasticity. Bodies are robed in light to proclaim their three-dimensional properties. Paint on cloth can be lit and back-lit in a great range of color and atmosphere, but the plane basis is fixed. Luminescence, however, faced on an impalpable cyclorama plays back and around moving dancers and gilds their shifting silhouettes with the most legible accents and highlights.

Among the important inventions of Martha Graham are her stage-settings, which in spirit recall the mastery of scale, substance and plastic pruning of Japanese gardens, where shrubs, stones, moss and gravel make a mosaic of real objects, sometimes delimiting a landscape and at once enlarging it infinitely by the most subtle alterations of exact placement and diminutive scale. Her most notable designer has been Isamu Noguchi, a distinguished sculptor of Japanese tradition who has moulded and constructed separate objects of considerable size and complexity helping to order her space-forming doors, beds, frames, grills, trees, through and in which she weaves her movement and fixes her important gesture. The objects themselves are keys to her mysteries, opening up action. Painting, unless it is tapestry, has to be translated into other terms of form; sculpture is form itself.

Ballet is about dancing and scenery can help when it does not smother. There are not, however, many ballets of primary choreographic interest which could not get along quite well without much more decoration than is seen at a circus, where the great width of space is contained by tied lines, wires and nets of the trapeze, bars of the cages, the platforms and pedestals for man and beast. These linear divisions are real lines in continuous space. Everything is subordinate to the action of acrobats and animals, and dancers in their genre, have the same athletic physicality; they are the greatest race of big cats and are best viewed when naked.

Ballet-scenery requires far greater tact in design and discipline in the designer than opera or dramatic decoration. Songs are to be sung with a necessarily static delivery and can be launched before splendid surfaces. The movement in the control and release of breath and voice can be made the more thrilling from the depth and richness of the launching-site. Plays happen in a certain space and special time; period and locality must be proposed or suggested. Dancing happens in general space, in its own intense time, whatever the pretext of incident that can be imposed on movement. Space is passive, ready to be stamped and filled with the impress of bodies. A perfume of light and, even sometimes painting, is an aid but the best space is that in which the dancers move freest without being pinned on a grid of dead outlines, obtrusive shapes or insistent masses of unchanging color.

WHAT IS BALLET ABOUT: How does the audience feel about it? Is ballet about music? Must the steps danced be a literal transcription of music played? Is it indeed possible, even if it were desirable, to equate the filling of ears with sights or eyes with sounds?

Is ballet about scenery and costumes? When a performance is all but forgotten from its first impact, is it the scenic investiture that salvages the most vivid memory?

Is ballet about star-performance? When we recall a single dancer, fixed in light, approaching the super-normal through personal domination, grace or physical capacity, is this disassociated from every other theatrical element? If so, how often can we count on it to happen? How much has it to do with the temperament or soul of an artist, or with what the performer has been given by way of tradition, training or design?

Is ballet about choreography? Is the chief interest a maze of ordered movement which is woven for and by the dancers?

Ballet is, of course, about all these in varying degrees of importance at different periods of history, or at different moments in the same evening, but it is about one thing constantly, supremely to the despair of every scene-painter who attempted to compete with a choreographer, despite the music which is the base of the business, and at the expense of the choreography which is exhaustable after two seasons or five or twenty-five; for just as opera depends on song alone and its singing by a singer, as the spoken drama upon words embodied by players, so does ballet depend upon dance, the dancer, dancing whatever is calculated to raise public and performer to some transitory terrestrial paradise. Ballet is about dancing in time.

Index

Index

Numbers appearing in italic refer to illustrations.

Académie Royale de Danse, L', 293, 355, 359
Académie Royale de Musique, L', 293, 355
Academy of Saint Cecilia, Paris, 293
Accademia della Crusca, Florence, 293
Adams, Diana, 155
Adams, Henry, 169
Adrianova, Anna (Shirley Bridges), 239
Afternoon of a Faun (Nijinsky), 7, 11, 14, 29, 48, 170, 174, 226
Agee, James, 265
Agnini, Armando, 276
Agon (Balanchine), 32, 118, 125, 155, 376, 405, 414
Agon (MacMillan), 406n.
Air and Variations (Dollar), 60-62, 66, 268, 274
Akahito, Prince, 109

Albert, François, 299
Albertieri, Luigi, 174
Alembert, Jean Le Rond d', 306, 314, 344, 349; *Encyclopedia,* 306, 314, 349
Alexandre, Arsène, *Decorative Art of Leon Bakst* (1913), 11n.
Alma Mater (Balanchine), 184, 275
American Ballet, The, 31-32, 37-38, 77, 80, 82, 124, 184-92, 194-204, 216, 226, 239, 268-69, 275, 281
American Ballet Caravan, 77-95, 124
American Ballet Theatre, 69, 412
American dance and dancers, 44-46, 54-57, 64-67, 81, 114, 123, 130, 133, 154, 167-68, 180, 194, 200, 202-05, 221, 228-29, 236-39, 241-43, 245-46, 248, 250-58, 260-66, 413-17, 420; response to, abroad, 413
American Document (Graham), 69-71, 236, 415; conception of, 70; importance of, 70; influence of, on creation of *Billy the Kid,* 69
American Pattern (Page and Stone), 273

Americans in Paris (Page), 273
Angels With Dirty Faces (film), 66
Angiolini, Gasparo, 231, 294
Anna Ivanovna, Empress of Russia, 293
Antheil, George, 184, 216, 275
Apollinaire, Guillaume, 13, 260
Apollo (Balanchine), 5, 15, 20-22, 31-33, 35, 77-78, 82-83, 118, 195-97, 226, 248, 275, 282, 299, 378, 391, 423
Apollon Musagète (Bolm), 82, 193, 268
Apollon Musagète (C. Littlefield), 192, 268
Apparitions (Ashton), 184
Aragon, Louis, 16n.
Arbeau, Thoinot, 300, 342
Argentina, La, 22, 341
Armistead, Horace, 98
Armitage, Merle, *Martha Graham* (1937), 38, 47n, 63
Arnell, Richard, 97
Arnold, Matthew, 136, 224
art, movements in: Cubism, 253, 260, 262, 429; Dada, 339; Fauvism, 429; French Impressionism, 253; neo-Romanticism, 253; post-Impressionism, 253, 429; Surrealism, 253
Ashton, Frederick, 98, 111
Asplmayer, Franz, 300
Asquith, Ruby, 61, 65
Astaire, Fred, 45, 130, 201, 257
Astruc, Gabriel, 169, 222
Aubade (C. Littlefield), 192, 272
Auden, W.H., 265, 419; "Dance of Death," 265
Auric, Georges, 15, 17
Aurora's Wedding (Petipa), 80, 193, 199, 296, 310, 316, 320
Autumn Bacchanale (Fokine), 299
Avery Memorial, Hartford, Conn., 175

Babes in Arms, 234-35

"Bacchanal" from *Tannhäuser* (Balanchine), 186-87, 346
"Bacchanal" from *Tannhäuser* (Fokine), 174, 346
Bach, Johann Sebastian, 193, 244, 268, 272, 274, 276
Baiser de la Fée, Le (Balanchine), 31, 37, 195-97, 234-35, 268, 275
Baiser de la Fée, Le (Nijinska), 32, 35
Bakst, Léon, 6, 9n., 17, 43, 169-70, 259-60, 277-80, 428-29; *Miracle de St. Sebastien, Le,* 279
Bal, Le (Balanchine), 20, 22, 171
Balaban, Emanuel, 81, 83, 90
Balakirev, Mily Alexeievitch, 194
Balanchine, George, 3-4, 12, 19-22, 28, 31-35, 77-83, 86-87, 90, 93, 97, 100-01, 105, 111-19, 123-25, 130, 153-54, 174, 176-82, 184-92, 195-97, 201, 234-35, 275, 281-83, 299, 324, 338, 376, 378, 391, 407, 413-15, 423-25; and Stravinsky, 31-32; in musical comedy, 114, 124, 130
Ballerina (film), 354
ballet (terms): *adagio*, 10, 296-99, 336-38; *allegro*, 300, 337; *arabesque*, 301-02, 312, *321*, 329, 354; *assemblé*, 303, 337; *attitude, en attitude,* 303-04, 312, 329, *333,* 354; balance, 336; *balancé*, 304, 337; *ballabile*, 304, 320; ballerina, 45, 116-17, 121-22, 296, 304-05, 324, 391; *ballon,* 300, 307, 310; *barre,* 310, *333,* 336, 338; *battement*, 310, 338, *347; batterie,* 310; *brisé volé,* 310; *cabriole,* 311, 337; *changement de pieds,* 337-38; *corps de ballet,* 299, 307, 312-14, 316, 320, 342, 345; *croisé,* 314, *347; danse ballonée,* 353; *danse d'élévation,* 299-300, 317, 335; *danse par terre,* 317-18; *danse taqueté,* 353; *danse terre à terre,* 335; *developpé,* 315, 338; *divertissement,* 315-16, 320; *enchappé,* 316, 337;

effacé, 316-17, *347; elevation*, 10, 317-18, 333, 353; *enchaînement*, 301, 318, 337, 342, 348, 356; *entrechat*, 318-320, 322, 360; *entrée*, 320, 322; five positions, 129, 254-55, 289, *308-09*, 312, 316, 324, 338, 349, 354-57, 359; *fouetté*, 323-24; *frappé*, 338; *glissade*, 337; *glissade de Mami*, 350; *jeté*, 336-37; *pas*, 349-50, 354-55, 433; *pas d'action*, 230, 263; *pas de basque*, 337; *pas de bourrée*, 352-53; *pas de deux*, 10, 298; *pas de quatre*, 349; *pas de trois*, 349; *pas seul*, 349; *pirouette*, *303, 350-53, 358; pirouette à la seconde*, 351; *plié*, 301, 310, *321*, 338, 352; *pointe*, *321*, 337, 352-54, 358; *port de bras*, 302-03, 312, 338, *347*, 355-56; *premier danseur*, 45, 112, 297, 312, 363; *relevé*, 300, 322, 357; *ronds de jambe*, 338, 358; *saut de basque*, 337; *sissonne ouverte*, 337; *sur le coup de pied*, 337; *temps levé*, 337; *tendu*, 301, 338, 360; *tour en l'air*, 300, 351, 358-59; turn-out, 337-38, 359-60; *tutu*, 360-61; variation, 362
Ballet Caravan, 38, 53-57, 59-67, 69, 73, 77, 155, 198, 201, 216, 226, 268, 274
Ballet Comique de la Reine, Le (1581), 306
ballet d'action, 11, 230
Ballet du XXème Siècle (Béjart), 412
Ballet Imperial (Balanchine), 77, 81-82
ballet master, 339-40, 344, 355, 384-85, 423
Ballet Mécanique (Bolm), 193, 378
Ballet Russe de Monte Carlo, 37, 54, 57, 62, 80-81, 87, 123, 175, 181, 210-13, 217-18, 226, 231, 239, 241, 260-62, 264, 267-68
ballet shoes, 354
Ballet Society, 97

Ballet Theatre, 28
Ballets de Monte Carlo, Les (Blum), 28
Ballets Jooss, 210-11
Ballets 1933, Les, 176-77, 180-84
Ballets Suédois, Les, 182-83, 205, 294
Balon, Jean, 304
Baltasarini *see* Baltazarini
Baltazarini de Belgiojoso, 306
Bambini, 327-28
Bannister, Roger, 416
Barabau (Balanchine), 171, 226
Baranovitch II (dancer), 280
Barbour, Lyell, 93
Barn Dance (C. Littlefield), 271
Barnett, Robert, 98
Baronova, Irina, 176, 227
Barrymore, John, 193
Baryshnikov, Mikhail, 134
Barzel, Ann, 60, 221
baseball, 396n., 399n.
basse danse, 300
Bat, The (Balanchine), 31, 77, 187, 256, 275
Bate, Stanley, 97
Bauchant, André, 82
Baudelaire, Charles, 429
Bayer, Josef, 272
Bayer, Raymond, *L'Esthetique de la Grace* (1933), 335-36
Beach (Massine), 216, 260
Beau Danube, Le (Massine), 100, 176, 261
Beauchamps, Pierre, 293, 342, 355, 359
Beaumont, Comte Etienne de, 21, 44
Beaumont, Cyril W., 222, 315, 317, 350, 356, 361; *Complete Book of Ballets*, 361; *A Dictionary of Classical Ballet Terms*, 310; *A Miscellany for Dancers*, 315; *A Primer of Classical Ballet*, 356; *Taglioni*, 237
Beaton, Cecil, 226
Beaverbrook, Lord, 24
Beebe, Lucius, 54

Beer, Thomas, 202
Beerbohm, Max, 183
Beethoven, Ludwig van, 179, 181,
    244, 415; *Seventh Symphony,*
    244-45
Bekefi, Alfred, Julia, and Marie, 174
*Belle au Bois Dormant, La, see Sleeping
    Beauty, The*
Bennington School of the Dance,
    Vermont, 70-71, 128, 198, 247
Benois, Alexandre, 169, 388, 428-29
Bérain, Jean, 231
Bérard, Christian, 177, 181, 245,
    261-62, 275
Berlioz, Hector, 181
Berman, Eugene, 262
Bernini, Gianlorenzo, 255, 348
Bernstein, Aline, 97
Berry, Duchesse de, 360
Bert (photographer), 226, 279
Bianco, Errico, 90
Biches, Les (Nijinska), 15, 19, 48, 171,
    260
Billy the Kid (Loring), 53, 60-65, 69,
    73-76, 84, 86, 92, 202-03, 274,
    415
Biracree, Thelma, 203
Bizet, Georges, 425
Black Crook, The, 54
Blasis, Carlo, 231, 294, 296, 301-04,
    310, 327, 340, 348, 356, 359;
    Code of Terpsichore (1829), 359
Blitzstein, Marc, 180; *The Cradle Will
    Rock,* 81
Blok, Alexander, 124
Bluebird Pas de deux (Petipa), 241, 310,
    316
Blum, René, 176, 261
Boccaccio, Giovanni, 305
Bodenweiser, Gertrud, 22, 254
Boehm, Jerome, 221
Bogatyri (Massine), 261, 339
Bolender, Todd, 62, 97-98, 155
Bolero (C. Littlefield), 193, 268, 272
Bolger, Ray, 45, 201
Bolm, Adolph, 17, 62-63, 82, 169-70,
    174, 183, 193, 228, 268, 277,
    280, 387
Bologna, Giovanni da, 255, 303, 348;
    Mercury, 303
Bolshoi Ballet, Moscow, 199, 232,
    409, 427
Bolshoi Theatre, Moscow, 295, 406,
    408
Bonfanti, Marie, 174
Bonnard, Pierre, 428
Bonney, William (Billy the Kid), 74
Borodin, Alexandre, 6, 194, 261, 272
Boulanger, Nadia, 198
Boulez, Pierre, 415; *Le Marteau sans
    Maître,* 415-16
Bouquet, Louis, 231
Bourdelle, Emile Antoine, 50
Bourgeois Gentilhomme, Le (Balanchine),
    316
Bourman, Anatole, 174
Bournonville, Antoine, 294
Bournonville, Auguste, 294, 418
Boutique Fantasque, La (Massine), 9-10,
    14, 21, 87, 171, 261
Bowles, Paul, 86, 198, 216, 274
Bowman, Patricia, 45
Boys From Syracuse, The, 234
Brahms, Caryl, 224
Brahms, Johannes, 179, 181, 338;
    Fourth Symphony, 338
Brant, Henry, 216, 275
Braque, Georges, 17, 253, 429
Brecht, Berthold, 177, 180-81
Brent, Jim, 390n.
Briand, Aristide, 23
Brides on Strike (W. Christensen), 276
Bridge, Don, 240
British ballet, 14, 223-24, 227, 245,
    411-13
Brown, Ray, 221
Brugnoli, Amalia, 299
Bruyère, La, 359
Buck and Bubbles, 257
Bulnes, Esmé, 86
Bulrich de Saint, Julia, 87
Butler, Horacio, 86

Byron, George, Lord, 358
Bywaters, Jerry, 65

Caccialanza, Gisella, 60-61, 63, 66, 83, 86, 154
Cadmus, Paul, 56, 155, 201, 263, 274, 287, 289
Café Society (C. Littlefield), 203, 271
Caffery, T. Jefferson, 79
Cage, John, 97
Cagli, Corrado, 98
Cahusac, Louis de, 306, 344, 349
Calder, Alexander, 51
Calvocaressi, Michel Dimitri, 169, 222; *Memoirs of Opera and Ballet*, 222
Camargo, Marie, 319
Card Party, The (Balanchine), 31-35, 37, 196, 268, 275, 423
Carnaval, Le (Fokine), 11-12n., 14, 29, 170-71, 226-27, 351
Carpenter, John Alden, 193
Carter, Jr., Elliott, 97, 198-99, 202, 216, 274
Cassidy, Claudia, 221
Castle, Irene and Vernon, 257, 382n.
Cecchetti, Enrico, 5, 22, 86, 155, 350-52, 356, 363
Cendrillon (Fokine), 214, 216
Cent Baisers, Les (Nijinska), 181, 214, 216
Center Theatre, N.Y., 228, 232
Cerrito, Fanny, 299, 353
Cézanne, Paul, 253
Chabrier, Emmanuel, 274, 425
Chabukiani, Vachtang, 199
Champs, P.T., 271-72
Chanel, Gabrielle (Coco), 21, 214, 378n., 387
Chaplain, Charles, 260
character dancing, 378-83; choreographers' use of authentic folk dance in, 379
Chardin, Jean Baptiste Siméon, 258-59

Charles X, King of France, 360
Charvet, 21, 378n.
Chatte, La (Balanchine), 15, 20-21, 430
Chauve Souris (revue), 171
Chavez, Carlos, 89, 203; *Noble Dances of Victory, The*, 89
Chavez, Dominguito, 89
Cheney, Stewart, 275
Chetwood, Ron, 62
Chicago Ballet (Ruth Page Ballets), 198, 273
Chilean National Ballet School, 90
Chirico, Giorgio de, 17, 182
Chopin, Frédéric, 20, 178-79, 268, 272, 275-76
Chopinade (W. Christensen), 268, 276
Choreartium (Massine), 179, 181, 248, 338
Chotzinoff, Samuel, 221
Christensen, Harold, 61
Christensen, Lew, 60-64, 77, 80, 82-83, 86, 90, 97-98, 105, 188, 196, 198, 202, 263, 274, 276, 352
Christensen, Willam, 61, 193, 268, 276
Christensen Ballet, 268
Christie, John, 181
Chujoy, Anatole, 54, 221, 418; on civic ballet, 418
Cimarosa, Domenico, 17
Cimarosiana (Massine), 55-56, 171
classic dance (ballet), 5, 10, 12, 21-22, 54, 127-31, 167, 230, 232-33, 243, 246, 254-56, 258, 264, 293-96, 311-12, 334, 371, 375-78, 383, 408, 414; classicism of, 375-77, 382; social reverberations of, 23, 130; style of, 23-24, 117, 125, 131, 388-90; tradition in, 385-88; training for, 22, 127-29, 241, 243, 247, 255-56, 300, 322, 336, 397; training for, in U.S., 114, 124, 355; vocabulary of, 129, 232,

243, 289, 311, 349, 351, 359, 379; vs. modern dance, 128-29, 247-49, 397
Classical Suite (C. Littlefield), 272
Clayton, Jackson and Durante, 19n.
Cléopâtre (Fokine), 29, 48, 170
Clifford, John, 98
Cobb, Ty, 396n.
Cocteau, Jean, 7, 11n., 13, 19n., 48, 169, 222, 260, 265, 339, 387-88, 404, 411, 426, 429, 431n.; *Boeuf sur le Toit, Le,* 19n; *Cock and Harlequin,* 13n.; *Igor Stravinsky and the Russian Ballet,* 7; *Paris Album: Portraits Souvenirs,* 431n.; *Romeo et Juliette,* 181
Coeur de Glace (W. Christensen), 268, 276
Colbert, Jean-Baptiste, 293
Coleridge, Samuel Taylor, 224
Colette, 397
Colt, Alvin, 86
Columbia Broadcasting System, 205
Compan, Le Sieur, *Dictionnaire de Danse* (1787), 301, 318, 320
Concerto (Classic Ballet) (Dollar), 268, 275
Concerto Barocco (Balanchine), 77
Concierto de Mozart (Balanchine), 78
Concurrence (Balanchine), 176, 180
contrapposto, see opposition in dance
Coomeraswamy, Dr. Ananda, 280, 332; *Mirror of Gesture* (1917), 332
Cooper, Gary, 45, 64
Copland, Aaron, 69, 73, 75, 89, 92, 202-03, 216, 273-74
Coppélia (St. Léon), 315, 375, 390
Coq d'Or, Le (Bolm), 193
Coq d'Or, Le (Fokine), 29, 43, 170-71, 212, 233-34, 339
Corelli, Arcangelo, 415
Cornazano, Antonio, 300
Cornell, Katherine, 48-49
Corsa, Preston, 83-84
Costa do Ribiera, Sr., 83
Cotillon (Balanchine), 176, 179, 264, 324, 338

Coton, A.V., 224
Coudy, Douglas, 274
Courbet, Gustave, 429
court dances, 298, 344, 353, 377; *Bourrée,* 353; *Minuet,* 298, 344, 377
Coward, Noel, 259
Cowboy and the Lady, The (film), 64
Craft, Robert, 414-15
Craig, Gordon, 153, 277-81, 388; on "new theatricalism," 278
Crane, Hart, 173, 202
Crane, Stephen, 202
Cummings, E.E., 265; *Tom* (scenario), 265
Cunningham, Glenn, 240
Cunningham, Merce, 97, 111
Cutler, B.J., 409
Cutter, Murray, 271

Dalcroze, Emile Jaques-, 12, 20, 40, 252, 254, 278, 419
Dali, Salvador, 43, 177
Damashov, Nicolas Petrovitch, 317, 319-20
Damrosch, Walter, *Man Without a Country, The,* 187
dance, derivation of, 314-15
Dance Index, 155
Dance International, 1900-37, 228
Dance Perspectives, 155
dancing master, 385
Dandré, Victor, 28
Danieli, Fred, 61, 63, 88, 97-98
Danilova, Alexandra, 15, 87, 100, 177, 182, 227, 230, 242, 305
d'Annunzio, Gabriel, 262, 277-78, 280; *Mort Parfumée, La,* 280; *Pisanelle, La,* 280
Danse (Carpeaux), 24
Dante Alighieri, 305
da Parma, Nicola, 280
Daphnis and Chloe (Fokine), 29, 173
Daphnis and Chloe (C. Littlefield), 193, 272
David, Jacques Louis, 360

Davidson, Jo, 79
Deakin, Irving, 228
de Basil, Col. Wassily, 28, 43-44, 54, 176, 181-82, 214-15, 217-18, 237, 239, 261
Debussy, Claude, 17, 19, 260, 272, 377, 424; *Martyre de St. Sébastien, Le*, 262
de Falla, Manuel, 9, 17, 87-88; *Atalantida*, 87-88; *Retablo del Maese Pedro, El*, 194
Degas, Edgar, 428
Delacroix, Eugène, 358, 429
Delibes, Léo, 21, 196, 423
Delluc, Louis, 280
Delsarte, François, 326-32, 334, 348
de Maré, Rolf, 205, 210, 294
de Medici, Catherine, 305-06
de Meyer, Baron Gayne, 226
Denby, Edwin, 221
Denham, Serge, 217
Denishawn, 22, 51, 129
Denisova, Alexandra (Patricia Denise Meyers), 239
De Prado, Sr., President of Peru, 92
Derain, André, 9, 17, 171, 177, 181, 261, 275, 430
d'Erlanger, Baron, 181, 214, 216
Despréaux, Jean Etienne, 334
Després, 334-35
Desrat's Dictionary of Dancing (1895), 314-15, 318, 358
de Valois, Ninette, 222, 411
de Vinna, Maurice, 66
Diaghilev, Serge, 3-25, 28-29, 44, 48-49, 55-56, 63, 82, 98, 102, 114, 122-24, 130, 153-54, 167-72, 175-76, 181-82, 188, 193-95, 198, 205, 214-17, 227-28, 236, 250-51, 260, 268, 281, 313, 316, 339, 374, 377, 387-88, 391, 400, 408-09, 411, 419, 424-25, 428-29; character of, 16-18; death of, 3, 20, 167, 175, 183, 375; *Mir Iskusstva*, 4
Diaghilev's Ballets Russes, 3-25, 43, 46, 49, 81, 138, 168-72, 182, 193, 222, 239, 277-81, 313, 374, 386-87, 400, 420, 429; audiences of, 176; choreography for, 19-20; demise of, 20, 175; repertoire of: Golden Age, 19-20, 169-71, 174, 193, 216, 221, 226, 233, 235-36, 259; Silver Age, 15, 54-55, 171-72, 177, 183, 194-95, 253-54, 264, 305; tour of U.S. by, 172-73
Diamond, David, 265
Diderot, Denis, 306, 314, 344, 349; *Encyclopédie*, 306, 314, 349
Dietrich, Marlene, 45
Dieu Bleu, Le (Fokine), 29, 280, 334
Dieux Mendiants, Les (Lichine), 182
Dimina, Mira (Madeleine Parker), 239
Dimitriev, Vladimir, 176-77, 184, 195
Divertimento (Balanchine), 77
Divertimento from Le Baiser de la Fée (Balanchine), 32
Dobie, Dr. Frank, 65
Doboujinsky, Mstislav, 81
Dokoudovska, Tania, 212
Dokoudovsky, Vladimir, 212
Dolin, Anton, 5, 17, 239, 352-53
Dollar, William, 77, 82, 86, 90, 97, 184, 187, 198, 256, 268, 274
Don Juan (Fokine), 234, 261
Don Quixote (Petipa), 409
Donath, J., 271
Doré, Gustave, 244
Dorian, Dr. Frederick, 221
Downes, Edwin, 283
Doyle, James, 83
Draper, Muriel, *Music at Midnight*, 12n., 17, 216
Draper, Paul, 45, 79, 83, 201, 203, 257
Drew, Robert, 98
du Maine, Duchesse, 304
du Pont, Paul, 273
Duchin, Eddy, 79
Dufy, Raoul, 429
Duke, Vernon, 181, 216; *High-Low Concerts*, 216

Dukelsky, *See* Duke, Vernon
Duncan, Isadora, 11, 20, 23, 29,
    39-40, 50-51, 54, 69, 123,
    129-30, 186-87, 203, 213, 249,
    252, 277, 279, 281-82, 346, 357,
    408, 419-21; influence of, 420;
    repertoire of, 421
Duo Concertante (Balanchine), 32, 118
Duponchel, Henri, 190
Dying Swan, The (Fokine), 130, 199,
    353

Eakins, Thomas, 123
Eastman School of Music, Rochester,
    N.Y., 67, 203
Ebsen, Buddy, 45, 201, 257
eccentric dancing, 257
École des Femmes, see School for Wives
Edwards, Jonathan, 71
Eglevsky, André, 87, 352
Eichheim, Henry, 193
Eisenstein, Sergei, 124, 260, 408, 413
Eliot, T.S., 252
Ellis, Havelock, *Dance of Life, The,*
    299, 315
Elmhirst, Mrs. Dorothy Payne
    (Whitney), 255
Elssler, Fanny, 50, 54, 231, 299, 305,
    353, 358, 391
Emerson, Ralph Waldo, 129, 249
en tournant, 337
en travestie, 399
Encounter (L. Christensen), 268, 274
Enesco, Georges, 276
Enters, Angna, 327
Ephrussi, Mme. Maurice, 214
Episodes (Balanchine/Graham), 107
Epreuve d'Amour, L' (Fokine), 180, 261
Errante (Balanchine), 77, 84, 91, 177,
    179, 184, 235, 268, 275, 282,
    432
Escudero, Vicente, 38, 341
Eternal Road, The (play), 181
ethnic dance, *see* folk dance
Eunice (Fokine), 29

Euphrussy, Mme., *see* Ephrussi,
    Mme. Maurice
eurhythmic dancing, 12
Evening of American Theatrical
    Dancing (1937), 228
Fâcheux, Les (Nijinska), 316, 353
Fairy Doll, The (C. Littlefield), 272
Fales, Mary, 272
Fantasia (C. Littlefield), 272
Fantasia Brasiliera (Balanchine), 77, 83,
    90
Farrar, Geraldine, 23
Farrell, James, 202
Fastes (Balanchine), 177
fatigue, in dancers, 337, 390
Fauré, Gabriel, 23, 277; *Penelope,* 277
feet, in dance, 322-23
Ferdinand the Bull (Disney film), 64
Fernandez, José, 86
Festin, Le (Fokine), 29
Fête Champêtre (C. Littlefield), 272
Feuillet, Raoul-Anger, 342, 355;
    Chorégraphie (1701), 355
Ffolkes, David, 98
Fille Mal Gardée, La (Dauberval), 193
Filling Station (L. Christensen), 53, 56,
    61, 63, 66, 73, 80, 201-02,
    262-63, 274
Fine Arts Bill, 219
Firebird (Balanchine), 154
Firebird, The (Fokine), 4, 6, 29, 32,
    35, 170-71, 177, 195, 234, 386
Fisher (photographer), 226
floor, dancers' use of, 323
Fokina, Vera, 194, 277, 279
Fokine, Michel, 5, 10-13, 19-20,
    27-30, 114, 122, 124, 154-55,
    168-71, 173-75, 182, 193, 199,
    214, 226-27, 230-31, 233-34,
    236, 249, 259, 261, 265, 277,
    280, 298-99, 334, 338-40, 351,
    388; choreographic style of,
    29-30, 169
folk dance, 5-6, 29, 127, 256-58, 349,
    358, 372, 378-83, 386; and
    ballet, 256-58; in Argentina, 87

444

Folk Dance (Coudy), 274
Fontes, Mme. Lourival, 81
Fonteyn, Dame Margot, 100, 411
Ford Ballet, *see A Thousand Times Neigh*
Ford Foundation, 116, 133
Fragonard, Jean Honoré, 361
Françaix, Jean, 216
France, Anatole, 259
Francés, Esteban, 98
Francesca da Rimini (Lichine), 62, 182
Franck, César, 245, 272
Frankenstein, Alfred, 222
Frankie and Johnny (Page and Stone), 73, 203, 273
Fraser, Sir James, *Golden Bough, The,* 134, 185
Fratellinis, The Three (clowns), 19n.
Free, Karl, 274
French ballet, 167, 409-11
French Revolution, 377
French, Jared, 69, 75, 274
Fried, Alexander, 222
Frontier (Graham), 51
Fuller, Loie, 419, 430

Gabo, Naum, 21, 430
Gabovitch, Mikhail Markovich, 408
Gabowitz, M., 271
Gainsborough, Lee, 271-72
Gaîté Parisienne (Massine), 261
Galeotti, Vincenzo, 294
Galindo, Blas, 86
Gallini, Giovanni Andrea, *Critical Observations on the Art of Dancing* (1765), 343
Galpern, L., 272
Galster, Amélie, 299
Garbo, Greta, 45
Gardel, Maximilien, 231, 351
Garret, William, 90
Gastoldi, 305
Gauguin, Paul, 253
Gautier, Théophile, 50, 221-22, 265,
339, 353-54, 375
Gavrilov, Alexander, 173-74
Genée, Adeline, 183
Géricault, Théodore, 358
Gerschel (photographer), 226
Gershwin, George, 130, 216, 273; *An American in Paris,* 203
gesture, 324-32, 334, 348-49; and semantics, 331-32; Austin, Rev. Gilbert, *Chironomia,* 325; Bell, Sir Charles, 326; Buffon, Comte Georges Louis Leclerc de, 325; Cicero, *De Oratore,* 324, 326; Darwin, Charles, *Expressions of Emotions in Man and Animals* (1872), 326, 329-30; opposition in, 348-49; Quintillian, Marcus Fabius, 326
Get Together (revue, 1922), 193
Geva, Tamara, 177
Gifford, Walter, 274
Ginastera, Alberto, 86; *Panambi,* 86
Gioja, Gaetano, 231
Giotto, 262
Giselle (Coralli/Perrot), 35, 122, 193, 261, 357, 375, 390-91, 409, 413
Glazounov, Alexander, 170, 193
Gleizes, Albert, 429
Glinka, Mikhail, 17, 194
Gluck, Christoph Willibald von, 189, 231, 244, 261, 275
Glückliche Hand, Die (Schönberg), 194
Godard, Benjamin, 275
Godowsky, Leopold, 67
Gold Standard (Page), 273
Goldwyn, Sam, 124
Goldwyn Follies, The (film), 197
Goleizovsky, Kasyan Yaroslavovich, 408
Gollner, Nana, 63
Golovine, Alexander, 429
Goncharova, Nathalia, 261
Good-Humored Ladies, The (Massine), 15, 171
Gorky, Maxim, *Mother,* 180
Gorsky, Alexander, 174

Gottschalk, Louis Moreau, 271
Gounod, Charles, 415
Gounod Symphony (Balanchine), 415
grace, 334-36
Graham, June, 91
Graham, Martha, 37-41, 47-52,
    69-71, 107, 111, 128, 176,
    196-97, 226, 228, 230, 236,
    248-49, 419-21, 432; American
    quality of, 51-52; and decor, 432;
    method and technique of, 50-51
Grahn, Lucile, 294
Grand Jatte (Seurat), 24
Great Lady (musical), 82
Green, Helen, 276
Green, Ray, 70
Green Table, The (Jooss), 210-11, 255
Greffulhe, Comtesse de, 214
Grétry, André, 272
Grey, David, 86
Griffes, Charles, 193
Gris, Juan, 17, 171, 429
Grisi, Carlotta, 183, 299, 353
Grofé, Ferde, 203, 216, 271
Grondhal, Ilmar, 222
Group Theatre, 241
Guenard, John R., 91
Guerard, Roland, 241
Guglielmo Ebreo, 300
Guiablesse, La (Page), 273
Guion, David, 216, 271
Gunn, Glenn Dillard, 221
Guinzbourg, Baron, *see* Gunzburg,
    Baron Dimitri de
Gunzburg, Baron Dimitri de, 214
Guys, Constantin, 262, 429

H.P. (C. Littlefield), 203
Haakon, Paul, 45, 201, 230, 256
Hacker, Louise, 206
Hagemann, Werner, *Caponsacchi,* 187
Halicka, Alice, 275
Handel, George Frideric, 181, 244
Hansen, Paul, 226
Hanson, Dr. Howard, 67
Harding, Bertita, *Amazon Throne,* 83

Harlequin for President (Loring), 274
Harlow, Jean, 201
Harmon, Carter, 97
Harris, Jed, 262
Hart, Col. Liddel, 238
Haskell, Arnold L., 82, 169, 179,
    181-82, 217-18, 226-28, 238,
    245; *Ballet,* 227
haute danse, 300
Hawkins, Erick, 65, 71, 274
Hawkins, Frances, 38, 197
Hawthorne, Nathaniel, 52, 202
Hear Ye! Hear Ye! (Page), 203, 273
Heberlé, Mlle., 299
Heine, Heinrich, 190, 221, 265, 339,
    353, 375-76; *Der Doktor Faustus,
    Ein Tanzpoem,* 265
Heinel, Mlle., 351
Held, Jr., John, 184, 275
Hemingway, Ernest, *Death in the
    Afternoon,* 238
Heppenstall, Rayner, 223, 307, 324;
    Apology for Dancing (1936), 324
Herodiade (Graham), 421
High School of the Performing Arts,
    N.Y., 100
Hindemith, Paul, 89, 178, 216, 222,
    242, 261, 414
Hoffmann, E.T.A., 353, 375-76
Hoffmansthal, Hugo von, 43
Hollywood Bowl, 63, 193
Holm, Hanya, 228
Holmes, Berenice, 60
Home, Henry, *Elements of Criticism*
    (1762), 335
Home Life of the Gods (C. Littlefield),
    272
Homer, Winslow, 123
Hoogstraten, Willem van, 193
Horaces, Les (1708), 304
Horst, Louis, 244
Hosmer, Page, 222
House, Tom, 61
Houseman, John, 49
Howard, Ruth, 221
Hoyle, Sir Edmund, 196
Hoynigen-Huené, George, 226

Hugo, Jean, 181
Hugo, Victor, 358; *Hernani*, 6
Humphrey, Doris, 243
Huneker, 50
Huntington, Archer, 206
Hurok, Sol, 37, 154
Hurok Attractions, 217
Hylblom, Elizabeth, 222

I Married an Angel, 82, 234
Iberian Monotone (Page), 268, 273
Ibert, Jacques, 273
Icare (Lifar), 261
Imaginaires, Les (Lichine), 182
Immediate Tragedy (Graham), 52
Imperial Ballet School, St.
    Petersburg, 174-77
Indian (American) dance, 257
Inghelbrecht, Desiré Émile, 280
Inspiration of the Poet (Poussin), 24
Iron Foundry (Mossolov), *see Ballet
    Mécanique* (Bolm)
Isabey, Eugène-Gabriel, 361
Isamit, Don Carlos, 89
Isherwood, Christopher, 265
Islamey (Fokine), 234
Ivanov, Lev, 81, 126, 174, 196, 231,
    296, 298, 324, 418
Ives, Charles, 414

Jack-in-the-Box (Balanchine), 226
James, Henry, 202
James, Leon, 380
Japanese dance, 107-10, 407, 413
Jardin Publique (Massine), 181, 216
Jarin, A., 271-72
jazz (music and dance), 129-30, 171,
    257-58, 378, 380-82, 386, 413,
    417, 422; and ballet, 82, 258,
    381
Jenkins, George C., 271
Jeu de Cartes, see Card Party, The
Jeux (Nijinsky), 11, 19, 259-60, 377
Jeux d'Enfants (Massine), 176, 324,
    430

Jodjana, Raden Mas, 332
Johnson, A.E., *The Russian Ballet*
    (1913), 6
Johnson, Edward, 185, 188, 190, 283
Johnson, Joseph, 91
Johnson, Philip, 133
Johnson, Dr. Samuel, 305
Jones, Isabel Morse, 63, 221
Jones, Robert Edmond, 173; decor
    for *Tyl Eulenspiegel* and *Mephisto
    Waltz*, 173
Jooss, Kurt, 130, 210-11, 254-55
Josephslegende, see Legend of Joseph
Jouvet, Louis, 84
Juke Box (Dollar), 82, 84, 86
Julius Caesar, Mercury Theatre
    production of, 262
Junyer, Joan, 98

Kahn, Aga, 214
Kahn, Otto, 172, 184, 214
Kambayashi, Sumio, 413
Kameneff, Vladimir, *Russian Ballet
    Through Russian Eyes*, 237
Kamin, Mr. and Mrs. Martin, 154,
    222-23
Kandinsky, Wassily, 253
Karinska, Mme., 105
Karnovsky, Kari, 212
Karsavina, Tamara, 17, 46, 55, 122,
    168-70, 226-27, 277, 279-80,
    363, 387
Kennedy Center, Washington, D.C.,
    139
Kent, Allegra, 155
Kern, Jerome, 130
Kessler, Count Harry, 43
Khachaturian, Aram, 409
Kidd, Michael, 63, 155
Kingsley, Herbert, 203, 216, 271
Kinkeldey, Dr. Otto, 300
Kirstein, Lincoln, and Balanchine,
    111, 133; and Diaghilev's Ballets
    Russes, 183; and Fokine, 27; as
    librettist, 69; *Ballet Alphabet*
    (1939), 154-55, 285-363; *Blast at*

Ballet (1937), 63, 153, 159-284; on academies of dance, 293-96; on American dance, 53, 59, 73, 123-24, 184, 199, 203-04, 242-43, 250-58, 260-67, 405; on athletics and dance, 239-40, 382; on audiences for dance, 24, 40, 54-57, 67, 95, 118, 127, 130, 135, 138, 142-46, 168, 175-76, 194, 205, 213, 232, 250, 261, 266-70, 345, 348, 371, 391, 400-04, 410, 422, 427, 433; on Balanchine, 112-19, 178-80, 185; on Balanchine dancers, 112-13, 116-17, 125; on ballet, history of, 305-07, 372-73; on ballet, literalism in, 262; on ballet vs. "The Ballet," 373-75, 377; on balletomanes, 258, 389, 402; on ballets, ideas for, 258-62; on choreographers, 98-106, 339-40, 343, 346, 348, 350, 379, 383-84, 397, 404, 417, 423-27; on choreography, 10, 19, 29, 53-54,122-26, 130, 245, 255, 262, 307, 311, 346, 383, 393, 405, 420, 434; on creativity, 394-95; on criticism and critics, 25, 49-50, 117-18, 125, 220-24, 226-38, 245, 402-06, 417, 424; on dance in physical education, 127-28, 248; on dance, popularity of, 127; on dancers, ideal characteristics of, 255, 375, 395-402; on elitism, 145-46; on filming dance, 28, 289, 343; on imagination and invention, 134-37; 393-95, 412, 424; on male dancers, 398-400; on managers for dance, 205-23, 215, 217-18, 220, 229, 233, 242, 250, 266, 269-70, 393, 401, 424; on music for ballet, 267-69, 422-27; on patronage, 213-19, 232, 251, 269; on performing artists, characteristics of, 134-36, 138-39; on photographers of dance, 224-26; on pre-classic dance forms, 243-44; on promotion and publicity, 266; on repertory for dance companies, 373-74, 390, 394-95, 406, 417, 425, 427, 430; on scenarios for ballet, 264-66; on stardom, 45, 113, 117, 121, 390-93, 433; on subsidies for dance, 127, 133-34, 138-42, 144; on television, dance on, 134-35; on theatrical dancing, 38-39, 44-45, 48, 50, 69, 73, 127, 167, 228-36, 246, 250, 253-54, 266, 350, 380, 396, 414; on women in dance, 50; writing for and editing *Hound and Horn*, 3-4; *What Ballet is About* (1959), 365-434

Kleist, Heinrich von, 200
Kobelev, Constantin, 174
Kochno, Boris, 176, 264, 339
Koechlin, Charles, 177, 181, 268, 275
Kolodney, William, 267
Korovine, Konstantine, 429
Kosloff, Theodore, 170, 174
Krazy Kat (Bolm), 193
Kreutzberg, Harald, 22, 50, 130, 193, 197
Kriger, Viktorina, 409

Laban, Rudolf von, 22, 40, 254-55, 342, 419
Ladies' Better Dresses (C. Littlefield), 203, 271
Lafitte, Jean Paul, 361
Lambert, Constant, *Music Ho!*, 222
Lambranzi, Gregorio, *New and Curious School of Theatrical Dancing* (1716), 301, 350
Lami, Eugène, 307, 361
Lanvin, Mme. Jeanne, 387
Lardner, Ring, 238
Lasky, Jr., Jesse, 63
Laurencin, Marie, 17, 19n.
Lauterer, Arch, 71, 228
Lauterstein, Natalie, 61

Lavatar, 329
League of Composers, N.Y., 16, 193-94
Lecomte, Hippolyte, 361
Lee, Tom, 82
Legat, Nicolai, 22, 236, 319-20, 324; *Story of the Russian School* (1932), 319-20
Legat, Serge, 236, 351
Legend of Joseph (Fokine), 43
Legnani, Pierina, 324
Lerina, Lina (Jacqueline Leri), 239
LeRoy, Hal, 45
Let the Righteous Be Glad (C. Littlefield), 203, 271
Levinson, André, 10, 14, 82, 222, 227, 237, 307, 312, 315, 372; *Taglioni,* 222
Lewis, Monk, 357
Lewis, Wyndam, 23, 153; *Blast!* (1914), 153
Liadov, Anatol Constantinovich, 4
Library of Congress, Washington, D.C., 82
librettos, 338-39
Lichine, David, 182, 239, 241-42
Lieven, Prince Peter, 169, 222; *Birth of the Ballets Russes, The* (1936), 222
Lifar, Serge, 5, 12, 17, 21-22, 82, 174-76, 181, 192, 195-96, 211, 222-23, 226, 391, 409
Life and Times of William Bonney, The, 69
Lion Amoreux, Le (Lichine), 182, 216
Liszt, Franz, 178, 275
Littlefield, Catherine, 87, 192, 203, 216, 268, 271-72
Littlefield, Dorothie, 87
Littlefield Ballet, 91, 198, 267-68, 271-72
Lloyd, Margaret, 221
Lombard, Carole, 45, 201
London, Jack, 123
Lopokova, Lydia, 15-17
Lopoukov, Fyodor, 236
Lorenz, Pare, 265

Loring, Eugene, 64, 73, 77, 201, 274; creation of *Billy the Kid,* 74-75
Losch, Tilly, 177
Louis XIV, King of France, 121, 125, 144, 213, 293, 359
Louis-Philippe, King of France, 360
Louys, Pierre, 259
Love Song (Page), 268, 273
Lully, Jean-Baptiste, 231, 272, 293, 304, 343-44
Lumley, Benjamin, 265
Lunatcharsky, Anatoli, 407-08
Lurçat, Jean, 80, 275
Lynes, George Platt, 266

McBride, Robert, 198, 216, 274
Mackaye, Steele, 331
MacLeish, Archibald, 49, 182; *Panic,* 49
MacMillan, Kenneth, 406
Mad Genius, The (film), 193
Mad Tristan (Massine), 43
Magny (dancing master, 18th C.), 342
Mahoney, Arthur, 256
maître de ballet, see ballet master
Malaieff, 32
Mallarmé, Stéphane, 421
Malpied, N., 342
Manet, Édouard, 429
Mann, Joseph, 266
mannerism, in performance, 340-41, 391
Mannes, Leopold, 67
Mantegazza (criminologist), 326
Manzotti, Luigi, 230-31
Marie-Jeanne, 61-63, 81
Markevitch, Igor, 23
Markova, Alicia, 195, 224, 230, 239
Mârouf (opera), 78
Marsh, Lucile, 221
Martin, John, 40, 54, 82, 105, 184, 187-88, 197, 228-36, 243, 247, 376; *America Dancing,* 231; *Modern Dance, The,* 230; on theatrical vs. modern dance, 229-30
Martin, Keith, 187, 274-75

Martinez, José, 86
Marx, Harpo, 43
Marx, Karl, 409
Maryinsky Theatre, St. Petersburg,
29, 33, 81, 196, 232, 259, 400,
406, 428
Mascagno, Salvatore, 352
Massine, Leonide, 5, 12-13, 15-17,
19-20, 40, 43, 123, 130, 171,
174, 176, 178-80, 182, 184, 195,
197, 204, 208, 212, 215, 230,
236, 242, 244-45, 260-62, 299,
324, 338, 378, 388; symphonic
ballets of, 177, 179-82, 208, 222,
244-45
Masson, André, 181
Matelots, Les (Massine), 15, 21, 176,
260
Matisse, Henri, 9, 17, 130, 171,
429-30
Mayakovsky, Vladimir, 124
Melville, Herman, 123, 201-02, 405
Mendelssohn, Félix, 244, 276
Menestrier, Claude-François, Ballets
Anciens et Modernes, Des (1682),
306, 318
Mercure (Massine), 16n., 20, 171
Merejekovski, Dimitri, 218
Metropolitan Opera Association,
N.Y., 31, 153, 172, 185-92,
195-96, 282-84, 345
Metropolitan Opera Ballet, 28
Metropolitan Opera House, N.Y., 37,
82, 172, 185-86, 188, 193-94,
268, 281, 346
Meunier, Antonine, 342, 356; Danse
Classique, La (1931), 356
Meyerhold, Vsevolod, 277, 280, 408
Meyers, Harriette, 276
Michaud, Charlotte, 222
Michelangelo Buonarroti, 255, 348
Midnight Sun, The (Massine), 8
Midsummer Night's Dream, A
(Balanchine), 118-19
Mignone, Francisco, 77, 83, 90
Miguel, Pablo, 66-67

Milhaud, Darius, 17, 177, 181; Boeuf
sur le Toit, Le, 19n.; Christopher
Columbus, 181
Mills College, Berkeley, Calif., 247
Minkus, Ludwig, 122
Minns, Al, 380
Minotaur, The (Taras), 274
Minstrel, The (C. Littlefield), 272
Mirabeau, Octave, 23
Miranda, Antonia Garcia de, 82
Miranda, Nicanor, 82
Miro, Joan, 430
Mironowa, Dunia, 88
Mr. Deeds Goes to Town (film), 283
modern dance, 40, 127-31, 198,
228-35, 243, 246-48, 250, 254,
261, 406, 419-22; audience for,
40, 130, 198, 406; characteristics
of, 128, 131, 420; future of, 421;
training for, 128-29, 247, 254;
vs. ballet, 128-29, 247-49, 254,
397, 419
Modigliani, Amedeo, 429
Moiseyev, Igor, 379n., 382n., 400,
409
Moment Romantique (C. Littlefield),
268, 272
Mondrian, Piet, 253
Monte Carlo Ballet (Blum), 176,
260-61
Montgolfier, 300
Moody, Helen Wills, 60
Moore, Lillian, 100
Moore, Marianne, 155, 404
Moore, Marjorie, 60
Morand, Paul, 9n.
Mordkin, Mikhail, 17, 174, 182, 193,
212-13, 299
Mordkin Ballet, 212, 268
Morgan, Anna, "Hour with Delsarte,
An" (1895), 348
Morgan, Barbara, 226
Morgan, Helen, 201
Morley, Thomas, 305
Moross, Jerome, 203, 216, 273
Moscow Art Theatre, 241

Moscow State Academy, 295
Moscow State Choreographic
  Technicum, 295
Moss and Fontana, 257
Moussorgsky, Modest, 6
Movements for Piano and Orchestra
  (Balanchine), 32
Mozart, Wolfgang Amadeus, 178,
  180, 261, 268, 274-75; *Don
  Giovanni*, 344; *Petits Riens, Les,* 25
Mozartiana (Balanchine), 180, 184,
  235, 268, 275
Museum of Modern Art, N.Y., 80
music for ballet, 267-69, 422-27;
  commissioning of, 424-25
musical comedy, 23, 114, 124, 130,
  135, 178, 205, 257, 381, 396,
  422

Nabokov, Nicholas, 13, 182, 216,
  268, 431
Naginski, Charles,
Napoleon Bonaparte, Emperor of
  France, 360
Narcisse (Fokine), 29
National Ballet of Canada, 418
National Broadcasting Corporation,
  205
national dances, *see* folk dance
National Endowment for the Arts,
  133
Navarra, Reuben, 82
Neary, Patricia, 98
Neher, Caspar, 177, 181
Nemtchinova, Vera, 19n.
New York City Ballet, 32, 78, 97-98,
  104, 107, 111, 133-34, 154,
  412-13; artistic policy of, 121-26;
  as recipient of Ford Foundation
  grant, 133
New York Hippodrome, 194
New York State Council on the Arts,
  133
New York State Theatre, 77, 133
New York World's Fair (1939-40), 80,

82, 181
New Yorker, The (magazine), 405
New Yorker, The (Massine), 86
Newman, Ernest, 222, 243
Nicholas II, Tsar of Russia, 234
Nicolson, Harold, 227
Nietzsche, Frederick, 129, 249, 315
Nijinska, Bronislava, 19n., 35, 130,
  170-71, 176, 195, 214, 260, 353
Nijinsky, Romola, 86, 169
Nijinsky, Vaslav, 3, 5-8, 11, 12n., 13,
  17, 19-20, 23, 28, 40, 46, 55,
  114, 122-23, 130, 154, 168-71,
  174, 193, 225-26, 254, 259, 277,
  279-81, 300, 317, 319-20, 322,
  342, 351, 362-63, 377, 387, 400
Nikitina, Alice, 21
92nd Street YMHA, N.Y., 267
Noailles, Comtesse Matthieu (Anna)
  de, 214
Nobilissima Visione, see St. Francis
Noces, Les (Nijinska), 5, 32, 48,
  171-72, 195, 248
Nocturne (Lichine), 182
Noguchi, Isamu, 51, 97-98, 432
notation systems, for dance, 341-44
Noverre, Jean-Georges, 29, 168, 222,
  228, 230-31, 236, 294, 298, 314,
  320, 322, 340, 344, 348-49, 359;
  and *ballet d'action*, 230; *Lettres sur
  la Danse et sur les Ballets* (1760),
  320, 344
Novikoff, Laurent, 60, 174
Nutcracker, The (Ivanov), 127, 426

Oboukhov, Anatole, 154
Ocampo, Mme. Victoria, 85
Ode (Massine), 13, 171, 268, 431
Oklahoma!, 144
Oliver, Maria Rosa, 85-86;
  Geographia, 86
Olneva, Mme. Maria, 79
Olympia (Manet), 24
On Your Toes, 234
Ondine (opera), 84

Ondine (Giraudox/Jouvet), 432
opera-ballet, 344-46; ballet
    divertissements in, 344
opposition in dance, 346, 348-49
Orfeo (Monteverdi), 24
Orfeo (Gluck/Balanchine), 31, 153,
    179, 188-90, 196, 275, 281-83
Oriental dance, 129, 332, 334, 372;
    and ballet, 334; influence of, on
    modern dance, 129
Original Ballet Russe, *see* Ballet Russe
    de Monte Carlo
Orpheus (Stravinsky/Balanchine), 32,
    97, 432
Oukrainsky, Serge, 62, 174
Our Town (play), 262
Owens, Jesse, 240
Ozeray, Madeleine, 84

Padmavâti (Staats), 334
Paganini, Niccolò, 185
Page, Ruth, 60, 193, 198, 203, 216,
    268, 273
Papillons (Fokine), 170-71
Paquin, Mme., 387
Parable in Blue (C. Littlefield), 271
Parade (Massine), 4, 13-14, 48, 171,
    260, 388, 429
Paris Opera (L'Opéra de Paris), 22,
    144, 169, 176, 181, 190, 192,
    197, 232, 345, 351, 354, 379,
    409
Paris Opera Ballet, 81, 293, 295, 408
Parker, H.T., 50, 221
Parker, Theodore, 221
Pas d'Acier (Massine), 8, 260, 378
Pascal, J., 272
Pascin, Jules, 429
Pastorale (Massine), 14, 260
Pastorela (L. Christensen), 84, 86
Pater, Walter, 224
Pavillon, Le (Lichine), 182
Pavillon d'Armide, Le (Fokine), 29,
    226, 388
Pavley, Andreas, 174
Pavlova, Anna, 5, 17, 29, 46, 54, 79,

82, 88, 116, 138, 168, 182, 193,
    199, 213, 226, 299, 301, 304,
    341, 353, 362-63, 376, 391
Pécour, Louis, 342
Perrin (poet), 293
Perrot, Jules, 231, 299
Perugini, Mark, 28, 306; *Pageant of
    Dance and Ballet, A* (1935), 306
Pescht, Rudolph, 90
Petipa, Marius, 5, 20-22, 29, 81,
    112, 126, 174-75, 195-96, 231,
    296, 298, 315-16, 320, 324, 418
Petit, Roland, 412
Petrouchka (Fokine), 5, 11, 14, 28-29,
    32, 35, 55, 75, 169-71, 175-76,
    195, 212, 322, 338, 378-79, 386
Pevsner, Antoine, 21, 430
Philadelphia Ballet (Littlefield Ballet),
    91, 198, 267-68, 271-72
Philadelphia Opera Company, 192
Philadelphia Symphony Orchestra,
    198, 267
Picasso, Pablo, 4, 13, 17, 48, 130,
    171, 253, 260, 348, 388, 407,
    429-30
Pinto, A., 271-72
Pinto, Salvatore, 271-72
Pirovano, Ignacio, 85
Pischl, A.J., 155
Pitney, Robert, 217
Platoff, Marc (Marcel Leplat), 239
Platt Lynes, George, 226
Playford, John, *English Dancing Master
    . . . , The* (1728), 231
Pleschayev, Alexander, 354
Pocahontas (L. Christensen), 198, 202,
    274
Poème (C. Littlefield), 272
Poiret, Paul, 387
Polignac, Pierre de, Prince of
    Monaco, 214
Pollock, Benjamin, 14
Porter, Cole, 19n., 43
Portinari, Candido, 80
Poulenc, Francis, 17, 19n., 272
Powell, Eleanor, 45
Powell, John, 271

Powell, Leslie, 274
Présages, Les (Massine), 181
Prévost, Françoise, 304
Prince Igor (Fokine), 6, 9, 14, 29, 48, 62, 90, 170-71, 175-76, 212, 227, 234
Prodigal Son, The (Balanchine), 20, 22, 171, 282, 338
Prodigal Son, The (Jooss), 211
Prodigal Son, The (C. Littlefield), 272
Prokofiev, Serge, 8, 17, 130, 171, 178, 260, 378; Pas d'Acier, Le, 194
Promenade (Dollar), 65, 268, 274
Prometheus (Lifar), 22
Propert, W.A., Russian Ballet in Western Europe, The, 8-9, 11-12
Protée (Lichine), 182, 239
Proust, Marcel, 227, 405
Pruna, Pedro, 15
Prunières, Henri, 16, 82
Puccini, Giacomo, 425
Pudovkin, Vsevolod, 260
Pugni, César, 122
Pulcinella (Massine), 5, 35, 195
Pushkin, Alexander (poet), 234, 242,

Quadrille de Mary Stuart (1829), 360
Quintana de Concord, Mercedes, 87

Rackham, Arthur, 244
Radio City Music Hall, N.Y., 192
Radova, Nina (Vivian Smith), 239
Raffe, W.G., 295-96
ragtime, 260, 378, 382
Rain, Charles, 274
Rambert, Dame Marie, 131
Rameau, Jean Philippe, 231, 272, 319, 344, 349, 355-56; Maître à Danser, Le (1725), 319, 352
Ransom, John Crowe, 65
Raoux, Jean, 303-04
Rasch, Albertina, 22
Rathaus, Karol, 216
Ravel, Maurice, 17, 193, 268,

272-74; Bolero, 268; Valses Nobles et Sentimentales, 198, 268
Ray, Man, 226
Red Poppy, The (Glière), 256
Reed, Janet, 62
Reinhardt, Max, 181
Remington, Frederic, 69, 75
Reminiscence (Balanchine), 31, 275
Remisoff, Nicolai, 273
Respighi, Ottorino, 17, 276
Revil, Rudi, 97
Riabouchinska, Tatiana, 176
Ricci, Benedetto, 294
Richards, I.A., 224
Rieti, Vittorio, 97
Rimsky-Korsakov, Nicolai, 6, 17, 170, 181, 193-94, 276
Ripon, Gwladys, Marchioness, 214
Rite of Spring, The (Massine), 16, 40, 176
Rite of Spring, The (Nijinsky), 5-7, 11-12, 14, 21, 29, 35, 48, 177, 195, 253-54, 280, 424, 427
Rittman, Trude, 67
Rivera, Diego, 203
Robbins, Jerome, 98, 381-82n., 417; and use of jazz vocabulary in ballet, 381
Robinson, Joseph, 89
Rockefeller, Nelson, 77-78
Rockettes, 44
Rodgers and Hart, 114, 124, 130
Rodin, Auguste, 299
Roerich, Nicolas, 253, 277, 280, 429
Rogers, Ginger, 45, 130, 201, 257
Rogers, John Henry, 64-65
Rogge, Florence, 192
romantic ballet, 168, 357-58, 360-61, 375-76, 380
Romantic Variations (C. Littlefield), 272
Romeo and Juliet (W. Christensen), 62, 193, 268, 276
Romeo and Juliet (Nijinska/Balanchine), 14
Roosevelt, Franklin D., 145, 154
Roper, June, 239
Rosenfeld, Jr., John, 65, 221

Rosenthal, Jean, 105
Rossignol, Le (Balanchine), 9, 33, 195, 429
Rossini, Gioacchino, 9, 196
Rothermere, Harold, Lord, 214
Rouault, Georges, 17
Rouché, Jacques, 192, 197
Rousseau, Edward L., 399; "Great American Ritual, The," 399
Roxy Theatre, N.Y., 15-16, 176
Royal Ballet, London, 112, 386, 406n., 418
Royal Danish Ballet, 81, 176, 412, 418
Royal Opera House, Covent Garden, 212, 217, 411
Royal Winnipeg Ballet, 418
Rubinstein, Ida, 32, 35, 205, 213, 277, 279
Rukeyser, Muriel, 261; "Theory of Flight," 265; "U.S. 1," 265
Rumanian Wedding (W. Christensen), 193, 276
Russell, Francia, 98
Russian ballet, 5-6, 37-38, 44, 48, 53-56, 73-76, 81, 100, 122, 130, 154, 167-70, 172-74, 178, 181-82, 190, 194, 199, 204-05, 214-15, 217, 221, 223, 227, 232, 237-39, 242, 250-51, 256, 259-62, 267, 269, 295-96, 356, 362, 374, 400, 406-09, 413; American financial support for, 44, 46, 205, 211-15, 232; formalism in, 408-09; in U.S., 172-73, 194, 205, 211-13, 231, 238-39; Imperial academic tradition of, 173-77, 199-200, 282, 295-96, 407-09, 418; men in, 400; Russian folk dance, elements of, in, 6, 29; Soviet academic tradition of, 123-24, 199, 295-96, 400, 407-10

Sabinova, see Sobinova, Natasha

Sacountala (L. Petipa), 334
Sacre du Printemps, Le, see Rite of Spring, The
Sadko (Fokine), 9
Sadoff, Simon, 81, 90
St. Denis, Ruth, 50, 54, 69-70, 123, 128, 203, 419-21
St. Francis (Massine), 181, 222, 242, 261, 299
Saint-Léon, Arthur, 231, 299, 342
Saint-Saëns, Camille, 23, 272
Samingo, M., 299
San Francisco Ballet, 61, 268, 276
San Francisco Opera, 61
San Francisco Opera House, 62
Sanchez de Loria Errazuriz, Federico, 90-91
Santa Cruz, Domingo, 89
Santa Rosa (decorator), 83
São Paolo Municipal Opera, Brazil, 79
Sargent, John Singer, 123
Satie, Erik, 13, 20, 171, 198, 260, 272, 378, 388, 426
Sauguet, Henri, 21, 177; Chartreuse de Parme, La, 181
Sayre, J.W., 222
Scarlatti, Domenico, 181, 274
scenery for dance, 427-33; and lighting, 428, 430, 432; in 17th C., 427-28; in 18th C., 428; in 20th C., 429
Schéhérazade (Fokine), 6, 9, 29, 48, 170-71, 173, 212, 227, 234, 259
Schervachidze, Prince Alexander Constantinovitch, 430
Schönberg, Arnold, 20, 62, 414
School for Wives (Molière), 84
School of American Ballet, N.Y., 4, 38, 90, 101, 133, 176, 184, 197
Schoop, Trudi, 254
Schubert, Franz, 177, 179, 244, 268, 273, 276
Schultz, Mrs. Cecilia, 61
Schwezoff, Igor, 86

Scott, Sir Walter, 357
Second, Albéric, *Petits Mystères de l'Opéra, Les* (1844), 359
Segonzac, Dunoyer de, 50
Seligmann, Kurt, 97
Semenoff, Nicolai, 174
Serenade (Balanchine), 31, 37, 77, 80, 179-80, 185, 268, 275, 324
Sergeyev, Nicolas, 320
Serly, Tibor, 271
Sert, Misia, 214, 410
Seurat, Georges, 428
Seventh Symphony (Massine), 43, 181, 244-45, 261
Severn, Merlyn, *Ballet in Action*, 224-25
Seymour, Maurice, 226
Shabelevsky, Yurek, 182
Shaffer, Carl, 271
Shankar, Uday, 38, 50, 213, 332
Sharaff, Irene, 34, 275
Shaw, W.H., 16n.
Shawn, Ted, 400, 420; *One Thousand and One Night Stands,* 420
Sheelen, Laura, 410
Shollar, Ludmilla, 170, 174
Show Piece (Hawkins), 274
Signac, Paul, 428
Sitwell, Dame Edith, 14, 23
Sitwell, Sacheverell, 14, 223
Six, Les (composers), 198
Slavinsky, Taddeus, 15
Sleeping Beauty, The (C. Littlefield), 192, 268, 272
Sleeping Beauty, The (Petipa), 87, 122, 315-16, 390, 411
Sleeping Princess, The (1921), 223, 316
Smallens, Alexander, 193
Smith, Cecil, 221
Snow Queen, The (C. Littlefield), 271
Sobinova, Natasha (Rosemary Deveson), 239
social dance, 43, 64, 202, 246, 257-58, 356, 372-73, 380; Big Apple, 43, 202, 257, 263, 380; Black Bottom, 257; Bunny Hug, 257; Cakewalk, 257, 380; Charleston, 257, 380; Contredanse, 257; Lindy Hop, 257, 380; Shag, 257, 381; square dance, 64, 257; Suzy Q, 257, 380; tango, 43, 377; Turkey Trot, 257
Soirées de Paris du Comte de Beaumont, Les, 16n., 176
Sokolow, Anna, 228
Solane, Janine, 410
Songes, Les (Balanchine), 177, 184, 275
Soudeikine, Serge, 275
Soupault, Philippe, "Silent House, The," 7
Sousa, John Philip, 402, 415, 424
Spanish dancing, 380
Spartacus (Moiseyev), 409
Spectre de la Rose, Le (Fokine), 7n., 8n., 29, 54, 173, 225-26, 265, 279, 298
Spencer, Herbert, "Gracefulness" (1865), 335
Spessivtzeva, Olga, 230, 376, 391
Square Dance (Balanchine), 415
Stalin Prize, 409
Stanford, Leland, 206
Stanislavsky, Constantin, 240-41, 278
Starke, R., 271
Stars and Stripes (Balanchine), 415
Starzer, Joseph, 300
State Armory, Bennington, Vt., 70
Stearns, Marshall, 380
Stebbins, Genevieve, 331
Stepanov, Vladimir, 231, 342
Stetson, Mrs. Dorothy, 62
Stevens, Ashton, 221
Stevens, Jr., Housley, 71
Still, William Grant, 193, 216, 273
Stinson, Eugene, 221
Stokes, Adrian, 28, 223; *Russian Ballets,* 223; *Tonight the Ballet,* 223
Stokowski, Leopold, 176, 193, 194
Stowell, Kent, 98
Stowitts, Hubert, 62

Strakova, Kyra (Patty Thall), 239
Strauss, Jr., Johann, 272, 275-76
Strauss, Richard, 17, 43, 192, 422
Stravinsky, Igor, 4-5, 9, 17, 21, 23,
    28, 31-35, 48, 82-85, 97,
    109-110, 112, 118, 122, 125,
    130, 169, 171, 178, 195, 222,
    275, 322, 378, 386-87, 402, 405,
    406n., 407, 414-16, 423-26, 429;
    and Balanchine, 31-32, 97, 112,
    125, 178, 195-98; *Chroniques de
    ma Vie* (1935), 35, 222; effect
    upon dance of, 424; *Histoire du
    Soldat, L'*, 193-95, 268; *Noces,
    Les*, 194; *Oedipus Rex*, 5, 194;
    Persephone, 32, 85; *Renard, Le*, 5,
    195
Stravinsky, Theodore, 32
Stravinsky, Centennial Celebration
    (1982), 32
Stravinsky Festival (1937), 31, 195-97
Stravinsky, Festival (1972), 32, 118,
    134
Stroganova, Nina, 212
Stuart, Muriel, 38
Suarez, Olga, 90
Svetlov, Valerien, 20-21q., 22, 169,
    236
Swan Lake (Balanchine), 414
Swan Lake (Petipa/Ivanov), 21, 54,
    80, 122, 212, 296, 298, 324,
    375, 378n., 390, 404, 409, 426
Swift, Kay, 184, 216, 275
swing (music and dance), 257
Sylphide, La (P. Taglioni), 60, 264,
    299, 307, 310, 357, 361
Sylphides, Les (Fokine), 11, 14-15,
    20-21, 29, 54-55, 62, 170-71,
    175-76, 203, 212, 258-59, 261,
    268, 307, 338, 357
Symphonie Fantastique, La
    (Massine), 181, 184
Symphony in Three Movements
    (Balanchine), 32, 118, 408

Taglioni, Marie, 50, 183, 231, 299,

301, 304-06, 310, 341, 352-54,
    358, 361, 376, 391
Taglioni, Paul, 299
Taglioni, Philippe, 196, 231, 299,
    307, 310, 357; *Fille du Danube,
    La*, 196; *Laitière Suisse, La*, 196
Tallchief, Maria, 98, 100
Taras, John, 97-98
Tarasoff, Ivan, 174
Taylor, J.C., 276
Tchaikovsky, Peter Ilyich, 6, 20-21,
    35, 80-81, 112, 122, 178-79, 181,
    194-95, 268, 272, 275, 426;
    Mozartiana, 268
Tchelitchev, Pavel, 31, 78, 84, 177,
    181, 189, 242, 261, 275, 282,
    431-32; *Phenomena*, 181
Tcherepnin, Alexander, 170, 193, 388
Teatro alla Scala, Milan, 294
Teatro Cervantes, Buenos Aires, 87
Teatro Colon, Buenos Aires, 85-87,
    90
Teatro Municipal, Bogota, Columbia,
    94
Tempête, La (Coralli), 353
Temple, Shirley, 116
Terminal (C. Littlefield), 73, 203, 271
Terry, Emilio, 177
Terry, Walter, 105, 221
Thackeray, William Makepeace,
    186q.
Thamar (Fokine), 6, 29, 170-71, 234,
    259, 280
Théâtre de Madame, Le, 360
Théâtre des Champs-Élysées, Paris,
    176, 212
Théâtre du Châtelet, Paris, 176
Theatre Royal, Drury Lane, London,
    217
Théleur, E.A., 342, 356; "Letter on
    Dancing" (1832), 356
Thelma Biracree Dancers, 67
Thomason, Cptn. John W., 238
Thomson, Virgil, 56, 80, 151, 198,
    201, 216, 263, 274, 396; *Four
    Saints in Three Acts*, 198; on
    dancers, 396; *Plough That Broke*

the Plains, The, 198, 265; River, The, 198, 265
Thoreau, Henry David, 249
Thousand Times Neigh, A (Dollar), 82
Three-Cornered Hat, The (Massine), 4, 9, 15, 74, 87, 171, 177
"Thunder Bird, The" (Fokine), 194
Tiller Girls, The, 22
Time Magazine, 281-84, 405
Tomlinson, Kellom, Art of Dancing (1735), 344
Tompkins, Beatrice, 93
Toulouse-Lautrec, Henri de, 428
Toumanova, Tamara, 50, 176-77, 182, 199, 224, 227
tourne-hanche, 359
Train Bleu, Le (Nijinska), 260
Transcendence (Balanchine), 184-85, 275
Trefilova, Vera, 227, 312
Trend (Holm), 228, 230
Tricorne, Le, see Three-Cornered Hat, The
Tristan Fou, see Mad Tristan
Triumph of Neptune, The (Balanchine), 14
Tucker, Richard, 226
Tudor, Antony, 77, 98, 111
Tunis, John, 238
Turner, Godfrey, 276
Tuttle, Frank, 63
Twain, Mark, 123, 202
Tyl Eulenspiegel (Nijinsky), 173

Union Pacific (Massine), 73, 86, 182, 214, 216, 260-61, 268
unions, 361-62
United Nations, General Assembly, 109
United States, character dancing in, 257, 380-83, 417; civic ballet in, 418; dance companies in, 56-57, 73, 185, 212-13, 232, 267-70, 401; dance crazes in, 382n.; dance critics in, 223, 228, 237; origins of American ballet training in, 184, 197; patronage of ballet in, 60, 205, 213-19,

232, 267, 400-01, 407, 422; prejudice against dance career in, 398-400; responses to companies from, abroad, 413; Russian domination of early ballet training in, 173-75, 239, 248
United States of America v. Paramount Pictures, Inc., et. al., 207-08
Uthoff, Ernest, 90
Utrillo, Maurice, 17

Vacant Chair, The (C. Littlefield), 271
Vaganova, Agrippina, 221, 236, 337-38
Valery, Paul, Degas. Danse. Dessin, 237
van Vechten, Carl, 221; Music After the Great War, 6
Vanderbilt, Mrs. William K., 154
Varèse, Edgar, 414
Vargas, Getulio, President of Brazil, 79
Vasari, Giorgio, 393-94
Vaudoyer, Jean Louis, 265
Veloz and Yolanda, 257
Verchinina, Nina, 62
Verdi, Giuseppi, 344-45
Vernet, Horace, 274
Versailles, 377
Vestris, Gaetan, 351
Vic-Wells Ballet, 294
Viennese Waltz (C. Littlefield), 272
Viganò, Salvatore, 221, 230, 298, 348
Villa-Lobos, Heitor, 83
Vilzak, Anatole, 174
Vine, The (Fokine), 29
Violin Concerto (Balanchine), 32, 118
Vitak, Albertina, 221
Vivaldi, Antonio, 415
Vladimirov, Pierre, 154-55, 174
Voices of Spring (Mordkin), 212
Volyinsky, Akim, 236, 238
von Schadow, J.G., 274
Vosseller, Heidi, 79
Vuillard, Édouard, 428

Wagner, Richard, 43, 49, 137, 192, 249, 346, 422
Walery, Paris (photographer), 226
Wallman, Margarete, 87
Warburg, Edward M.M., 31, 32n., 184, 188, 196-97
Washington Irving High School, N.Y., 266-67
Watkins, Franklin, 184, 275
Weamer, Raymond, 60
Weaver, John, *Essay Towards a History of Dancing* (1721), 306, 314
Weber, Carl Maria von, 244, 298; *Invitation to the Dance*, 298
Webern, Anton von, 414
Weill, Kurt, 177, 181; *Johnny Johnson*, 181
Weiss, Robert, 98
Welchek, Constantin, 79
Well-Beloved, The (Nijinska), 184
Wells, Mary Ann, 61
Wescott, Glenway, 153, 265, 281-84; on American dance scene, 282-84; scenario on *Audubon*, 265
West, Buster, 257
West Side Story, 382n.
Whistler, James Abbott McNeill, 123
White Fawn, The (1868), 399
Whitman, Walt, 51-51, 123, 129, 202, 249, 420
Whitworth, Geoffrey, *Art of Nijinsky, The*, 281

Wigman, Mary, 22, 40, 49, 252, 254, 261
Wilde, Oscar, *Ballad of Reading Gaol*, 50; *Birthday of the Infanta, The*, 87
Wilde, Patricia, 98
Wilder, Alec, 82
Wiman, Dwight, 82
Winter, Marian Hannah, 54
Woizikowsky, Leon, 15
Wolcott, Leo F., 207
Wolkonsky, Prince Serge, 236
Wood, A.L.S., 221

Yankee Clipper (Loring), 53, 56, 60, 63, 201, 274
Yeats, W.B., 50, 199, 265, 376-77, 404, 421; *Trembling of the Veil, The*, 376-77
Young, Stark, *Immortal Shadows: A Book of Dramatic Criticism*, 421
Youskevitch, Igor, 100-01
youth, effect of, on dancers, 362-63

Zaharov, Sir Basil, 214
Zaroushka (Petipa), 324
Ziegler, Edward, 190
Zorn, Friedrich Albert, 342
Zucchi, Virginia, 361